Queen Christina

Other Books by Georgina Masson

THE COMPANION GUIDE TO ROME

ITALIAN VILLAS AND PALACES

ITALIAN GARDENS

FREDERICK II OF HOHENSTAUFEN

Queen Christina

GEORGINA MASSON

LONDON · SECKER & WARBURG

First published in England 1968 by
Martin Secker & Warburg Limited
14 Carlisle Street, London W1

SBN 436 27351 9

To Harry, who introduced me to David who
published my first book—and this one too

Printed in Great Britain by
The Camelot Press Ltd, London and Southampton

Contents

List of Illustrations

The old Castle of the Three Crowns in Stockholm, which was Christina's principal residence until her abdication; the suite of rooms on the extreme right, seen below the dome, was where Christina lived. (*National Museum, Stockholm*)

Between pages 192 *and* 193

The peace banquet given by Charles Gustavus at Nuremberg on 25th September 1649, engraved from a painting by W. Kilian. Charles Gustavus is seen seated at the head of the table on the left with his cousin Charles Lewis, the Elector Palatine, seated on his right. (*National Museum, Stockholm*)

The leader of the peasants in the Riksdag, by P. Olsson. (*National Museum, Stockholm*)

The great philosopher René Descartes, by D. Beck. He died in Stockholm in 1650. (*By kind permission of the Institut Tessin, Paris*)

Stockholm in 1650, by W. Hartman, showing the Castle of the Three Crowns in the centre, the De la Gardie palace of Makalös on the right and the Russian trading station, Rusche Bodar, on the left. (*National Museum, Stockholm*)

Count Raimondo Montecuccoli, Imperial Ambassador to Christina's court in Stockholm and Antwerp; he accompanied her to Rome. Portrait by E. Griessler painted in 1665. (*National Museum, Stockholm*)

Between pages 224 *and* 225

John Holm, who started life as a court servant and tailor and became Christina's confidential aide, entrusted with contacting the Jesuits Malines and Casati when they came to Stockholm. (*National Museum, Stockholm*)

Charles Gustavus, as Generalissimo of the Swedish army, painted by S. Bourdon about a year before he became King Charles X in 1654. (*National Museum, Stockholm*)

Christina by S. Bourbon, painted about a year before her abdication. (*National Museum, Stockholm*)

Christina's abdication at Uppsala Castle on 6th June 1654, drawn by W. Swidde. The Queen is seen divested of the regalia, which lies on a table on the right of the throne, with her successor bowing to her. (*National Museum, Stockholm*)

Christina at the age of thirty-five, painted by A. Wauchters in Norrköping in 1661, where the Queen stayed shortly after the death of Charles X. (*National Museum, Stockholm*)

Christina at the age of forty-one in the dress she wore for travelling and probably often in the privacy of her own home, attributed to W. Heimbach. (*National Museum, Stockholm*)

Christina lying in state on 23rd April 1689, in the Church of S. Maria in Vallicella in Rome, from an engraving by N. Dorigny. (*National Museum, Stockholm*)

Introduction: Christina's Heritage

In Berlin in the year 1615, a Brandenburger named Hieronymous von Birkholtz might have been observed assiduously courting the friendship of Dr. Saffius, the family physician of the Elector John Sigismund von Hohenzollern. It is unlikely that at first anyone but the good Doctor displayed much interest in his new-found friend, for von Birkholtz would have observed the caution natural to his profession. He was a counter-espionage agent of the Swedish government actively engaged in work against Poland.

In fact at this time von Birkholtz's employer, young King Gustavus Adolphus, needed all the weapons he could command if he was to preserve his own and his country's independence. On his succession four years earlier, when he was not yet seventeen, he had found himself with two wars on his hands. One was against Denmark, from whose suzerainty his grandfather, Gustavus Wasa, had wrested Swedish independence only sixty-seven years before, the other against Russia where an uneasy truce with Poland was enabling both her and Sweden to profit from Muscovite anarchy. But Gustavus Adolphus was even then well aware that sooner or later his Catholic cousin, King Sigismund Wasa of Poland, would attempt to enforce his claims on the Swedish throne.

It was a situation which might well have daunted a seasoned soldier and diplomat, nor was this all. By the terms of his father Charles IX's will, he was not to succeed unless another cousin, Duke John of Östergötland, renounced his claims to the Swedish throne, and Gustavus Adolphus's own accession was endorsed by the four Estates of the Riksdag. It says much for the outstanding qualities of the young prince that the Estates agreed to his recognition, disregarding the fact that he was not legally of age until he was eighteen, "seeing that God . . . has made up in understanding what is lacking in years." Needless to say there was a quid pro quo. At the Diet of Nyköping Gustavus Adolphus signed a charter in which he guaranteed Lutheranism as the state religion and promised to observe the rights and privileges of all four Estates.

Possibly its most important clauses, however, were those which placed great power in the hands of the nobility. These stipulated that the five great officers of state—the High Steward, Grand Marshal, Grand Admiral, Chancellor and Treasurer—must be Swedish nobles, also all the members of the Råd who had to be consulted before new levies of men or money could be imposed, or the Riksdag summoned. With time the functions of the great officers of state came to resemble those of a cabinet, while the Råd evolved from the traditional mediaeval council of the realm into an advisory body on the lines of the Privy Council of Elizabethan England.* Between them these two groups carried on the administration of the country during the King's increasingly frequent absences on campaign.

The man who had drafted this charter was Axel Oxenstierna, the twenty-nine-year-old son of one of Sweden's most famous families, whom the King now nominated Chancellor. Oxenstierna's commission of appointment was couched in the following terms: "It being impossible precisely to prescribe what he is to order and do in such an office and calling, We leave it to his discretion and understanding, as he may deem best, and as he shall be answerable to God and to Us, and to every honourable Swedish man." These words marked the beginning of a lifelong friendship and one of the most remarkable partnerships in history; one moreover which survived the King's death twenty-one years later. For Oxenstierna continued faithfully to interpret his master's policy to the best of his ability until his own death in 1654.

This bond of trust between the Monarch and a member of the

* Foreign ambassadors usually employed the term Senate for this typically Swedish institution, calling its members senators. In her autobiography, Queen Christina did the same.

aristocracy was something new in Swedish history. In the past the noble members of the Råd had used their influence as a brake upon the power of the country's elected kings. Many of them had been bitterly hostile to the establishment of the hereditary principle, vested in Gustavus Wasa and his descendants by the Riksdag of 1544. This opposition increased during the chaotic reigns of Gustavus Wasa's immediate successors—his sons Eric XIV and John III and his Catholic grandson Sigismund, who was also King of Poland. Under Charles IX it was only subdued by the blood-bath of Linköping, where in 1600 Eric Sparre, Sten and Gustavus Banér, Ture Bielke and Bengt Falk, all but one members of Sweden's greatest families, were beheaded in the market place. Five years later Hogenskild Bielke paid the same price, and at the time of Gustavus Adolphus's accession his head still mouldered on the South Gate of Stockholm. These men had tried to uphold the power of the Råd in face of that of the King, and their leader Eric Sparre was in favour of returning to an elective monarchy—possibly even its substitution by an oligarchy. It was in the hands of the relations and peers of these men that Gustavus Adolphus left the government of Sweden when on 4th January 1612, in a sleigh draped in black in mourning for his father Charles IX, he left Nyköping to go and fight the Danes. Characteristically he put his trust "in God" and in "every honourable Swedish man."

The "War of Kalmar," as it came to be called, was a brief and inglorious campaign that ended a year later in the negotiated Peace of Knäred, but it had some notable results. The most immediate was an alliance with Holland, instigated by Dutch fears of Denmark, a diplomatic triumph which freed Gustavus Adolphus's hands to deal with the war in Russia. Of less obvious consequence at the time, though its effects were to be more lasting, was an incident which occurred during the fighting. The King narrowly escaped death by drowning while retreating across a frozen lake. The man who saved his life was Per Banér, a son of Gustavus Banér who had perished in the blood-bath of Linköping; it was the first sign that age-old rivalries could vanish before the magic of Gustavus Adolphus's courage and personality. But the incident was to have a more specific result in focusing attention on the fact that Sweden's internal peace and outward security now rested upon the shoulders of one young man—a daring and gallant soldier—whose marriage became a matter of national concern.

Although in her autobiography, written many years after Gustavus Adolphus's death, his daughter Christina said that he had been "too fond of women," this judgment is not borne out by historical records. In his youth Gustavus Adolphus had been in love with the beautiful Ebba Brahe, but his mother had scotched the romance on the grounds of dynastic unsuitability; instead Ebba married the King's able general Jacob De la Gardie. The only other evidence of the King's youthful indiscretions was the birth, in 1616, of his illegitimate son Gustav Gustavsson of Wasaborg; but by this time Gustavus Adolphus had become fully convinced that his duty to his country required a political marriage.

It was in these circumstances that Hieronymous von Birkholtz's mission was destined to play a decisive role. His friendship with Dr. Saffius brought him, as he had no doubt intended, into personal contact with John Sigismund, Elector of Brandenburg. In pursuance of his instructions von Birkholtz urged upon the Elector the importance of friendly relations with Sweden. Von Birkholtz's advocacy proved so successful that within a few days a member of the Electoral entourage let drop the suggestion that his master's daughter, Maria Eleonora, would make a very suitable wife for Gustavus Adolphus. From the Swedish political point of view there was little doubt that she would; and in the seventeenth century neither of the contracting parties gave a thought to the fact that Maria Eleonora's maternal grandfather had been insane, as also were two of Gustavus Adolphus's Wasa uncles, and that the offspring of a marriage between two such families might, to say the least of it, be extremely unstable.

The Calvinist Elector John Sigismund had also been quick to perceive the force of von Birkholtz's arguments and to realize that the rivalry between the Swedish and Polish members of the Wasa family was ideological as well as dynastic. As a result of personal inclination, a Jesuit education and marriage to an Austrian Archduchess, Sigismund of Poland was identified with militant Catholic reaction, and a very uncomfortable neighbour for the Protestant states of Brandenburg and Prussia governed by the

Elector. Gustavus Adolphus, on the other hand, as the representative of the cadet branch of the Wasa who owed their crown solely to their profession of the Reformed faith, was a natural champion of the Protestant cause.

To the Elector, as well as the Swedes, who were anxious to strengthen their position vis-à-vis Poland and also to weld together a league of Protestant states, the projected marriage offered many advantages. However both the Electress and John Sigismund's heir, George William, opposed the match (the latter because he feared it would provoke Poland and the Emperor) and Gustavus Adolphus's proffered visit to Berlin in 1618 was politely refused as inopportune. John Sigismund's death in the next year seemed to have quashed the project, though possibly the Swedes knew that he had already extracted from his daughter a promise to marry Gustavus Adolphus.

Thus it was not in the mood of a "young Lochinvar," but as a seasoned politician and soldier, that in the spring of 1620 Gustavus Adolphus set out on an incognito visit to Berlin, to see what personal intervention would achieve. The moment was well-chosen, as George William was absent, and ostensibly the occasion was a private family visit by the Count Palatine John Casimir of Zweibrücken, who was a relative by marriage of the Elector. As he was also the husband of the King of Sweden's sister Catherine, the presence in John Casimir's entourage of "Captain Gars," a strapping young Swedish officer, at first passed without comment. Not, however, without making an indelible impression on Maria Eleonora, who fell passionately in love with the handsome blue-eyed Swede.

It is difficult to say at what stage she realized that in reality Gars stood for Gustavus Adolphus Rex Sueciae, for intelligence was never Maria Eleonora's strong suit. But she was a pretty young girl and Gustavus Adolphus, who must have been relieved to find that the path of political duty was not lacking in attractions, apparently reciprocated her feeling. Their united efforts finally overcame the Electress Dowager's opposition: an important point as, in accordance with Hohenzollern family custom, it was she and not her son who had the final word in bestowing her daughter's hand in marriage. In the end George William gave his grudging consent; in September Axel Oxenstierna came to negotiate the formal agreement and accompanied the bride to Sweden for her marriage in November.

One cannot but wonder what this austere Swedish statesman, whose favourite author was Tacitus, made of his future Queen during their long journey to the North. If he knew of it, he would certainly have disapproved of the fact that, in order to surround her daughter with sufficient splendour, the Electress Dowager had not hesitated to lay her hands on the treasury plate. Indeed in the character of Maria Eleonora herself there were certain extravagant traits which could scarcely have escaped an eye as shrewd as that of the Swedish Chancellor. Her petite, fluffy prettiness was matched by feminine emotionalism and a preoccupation with what must have seemed to him trifles—her dress and appearance, a liking for entertainment and sweetmeats. But much could be forgiven a young girl on her marriage journey, and of her attachment to Gustavus Adolphus there could be no doubt.

What Maria Eleonora made of Sweden when she arrived there on a bleak November day is another matter. Almost exactly thirty-three years later, although the country had progressed greatly in the interval, Cromwell's puritanical Ambassador Whitelocke painted a gloomy picture of what he was able to observe in the light of the brief four-hour winter days—the appalling roads, the sombre forests and primitive cultivation, log houses caulked with moss, the unappetizing meals of "boiled, roast or fried cow" and prevalent drunkenness. But as a scrupulous observer he also noted the people's honesty and the grave ceremonious demeanour of nobles and statesmen—admirable qualities but ones scarcely calculated to appeal to a pleasure-loving girl.

At first, however, all other considerations must have been swept aside by the fact that Gustavus Adolphus had come to Kalmar to greet her and the splendour of Kalmar Castle itself would have delighted her. Even today, surrounded by its moats and buttresses, Kalmar is one of the most impressive Swedish Renaissance castles, and in 1620 it was perhaps the finest building in the country. It was here that Gustavus Adolphus's uncle Eric XIV, the first Renaissance King of Sweden, who loved the arts and sciences and classical learning, had held court. But the rooms which he had caused to be so beautifully decorated with Renaissance stuccos and precious inlaid woods had also been the scene of his wild orgies, and in the end, a frenzied murderer, he was himself probably poisoned by order of his brother John, with the agreement of the Råd.

Of this dark and shadowy side of his extraordinary family's inheritance the young bridegroom bore no apparent trace. The broad sweep of his forehead, the dominant aquiline nose and the shrewd glance of his slightly protuberant grey-blue eyes bespoke the statesman and the man of action. His massive frame told of the tough soldier who, though he was frugal and sober in private life, loved battle and hunting, horses and outdoor life no less than dancing, music and gaiety. Gustavus Adolphus's furious temper was as famous as his personal charm and intrepid bravery, and these were combined with an irresistible wish to know and to see for himself and an extraordinary mental curiosity. An excellent orator and linguist, quick and keen in debate, he admired and participated in the graces of life as a musician and even as a writer. His taste for learning was exemplified by his reverence for Grotius—whose books he carried in his knapsack—while one of his last actions, on the eve of his departure for Germany in 1630, was to appoint Bureus as Sweden's first Antiquarian Royal.

That there was another side to the picture was known only to Axel Oxenstierna and a few intimates. The King, who in public could appear proud and sometimes vain and might be unable to resist using his presence and position to astonish and terrify people, could also in private be a prey to doubts and vacillation, to the morbidity and suspicion which were the curse of his family. No wonder that in the tranquillity and calm of Oxenstierna—the man who said that in all his long career he had passed only two sleepless nights and that he unburdened himself of his cares as he took off his clothes to go to bed—Gustavus Adolphus found the perfect partner of his working life.

His working life! When it came to marriage that was the rub. Maria Eleonora was, alas, not made to be the wife of a national hero who in a little over twenty years raised his country from an obscure northern kingdom to the status of a great power. Although she loved her husband the Queen hated and despised his country, and both during her lifetime and after the Swedes returned her feelings with interest, none having ever a good word to say for her. But foreign ambassadors, including the sophisticated French representative, found her a gracious and even a strikingly beautiful woman. A portrait of Maria Eleonora in Gripsholm Castle, painted when she was a young widow, does indeed show her as a comely woman, with a white skin, beautifully shaped shoulders and face and fine eyes; though with too prominent a nose and a sensual mouth. Here her face does not look like that of a woman who has endured violent sorrow. In fact it does not look like that of one capable of any really deep emotion but, with her elegant widow's weeds, as if she was absorbed by superficialities; and as far as we can discover, this is what Maria Eleonora was really like. She took good care of her looks, loved beautiful things—music, fine palaces and architecture—and was wildly extravagant in gratifying her tastes. But although she spoke French, the court language of the age, she never bothered to learn to write German or Swedish correctly. It was typical of her that, in common with her contemporaries of the princely houses of Europe, she succumbed to the current fashionable craze for buffoons and dwarfs—like Vincenzo Gonzaga who in 1621 spent much of the proceeds of the sale of the famous Gonzaga pictures to Charles I of England on such monstrosities.

Although the Berlin of 1620, which Maria Eleonora had left behind, was scarcely a metropolis, geographically it lies more or less in the same latitude as London, whereas Stockholm's position corresponds roughly with the Shetland Islands. To the contemporary mind, uncontaminated by nineteenth-century romanticism, Berlin's snug brick houses set in a flat plain would have appealed infinitely more than the northern city of the waters, whose picturesque site enchants us today. Moreover when Maria Eleonora arrived, Stockholm consisted mainly of clusters of one-storied wooden houses, roofed with turf, huddled round the castle on its island. It neither looked like nor was in fact a capital, though the great fire of 1625 and Gustavus Adolphus's policy of centralizing the government administration were soon to make a great change.

However if the town itself was barely worthy of the name, the castle was at least imposing. In spite of John III's efforts to make it a fitting royal residence, outwardly at least it was a fortress. As

Maria Eleonora first saw its massive castellated walls rising out of the mud and slush, it must have looked grim indeed, with its copper-roofed turrets and great circular donjon tower wreathed in northern mists. Only the national emblem of the three golden crowns, gleaming in the torchlight above, showed unmistakably that this was the King's palace.

If the exterior of the castle was forbidding, it is unlikely that the interior would have pleased the Queen much more. Even with huge logs blazing up the great chimneys, she would have missed the cosy, constant warmth of German stoves; while with her taste for fine furniture and bibelots she would have found the bare plank floors and sober Swedish furnishings of massive settles, chests and tables, simple in the extreme. Even if wall panelling and doors were now in Sweden beginning to be ornamented with marquetry, and the ceilings were painted with gay floral designs, there would have been hardly any pictures other than a few mediocre portraits. However, there was at least magnificent plate—huge platters and tankards of silver and vermeil, and splendid Flemish tapestries. Of these last Eric XIV and John III had bought lavishly, and so, rather surprisingly, had Maria Eleonora's sober-minded husband, adding to the accumulated wealth of storied sets of Scipio Africanus, Antony and Cleopatra and Julius Caesar, woven with gold and silver thread, purchases of his own, the latest specially made to celebrate their marriage.

With Gustavus Adolphus as a constant companion, Maria Eleonora might well in time have settled down in what must have seemed to her a barbaric setting. In spite of her limitations, they had tastes in common—the King shared her interest in architecture and love of music. Although he was not a composer like Eric XIV, Gustavus Adolphus performed well on the lute and, probably at his wife's instigation, he invited German musicians to the court where orchestral music and dancing now became the rage. But whereas these amusements were the young Queen's dominant interest, in the life of her husband they could play only a very small part. It was only by indefatigable energy and devotion to duty that, with all his genius, he succeeded in twenty-two years in transforming his country into a power in the forefront of European politics. The primary means by which this was achieved was, of course, war—and to the wars, to command the siege of Riga, he went within six months of their marriage, leaving Maria Eleonora in the early stages of her first pregnancy.

Now was the moment, with the arrival of a longed-for heir in sight, for the new Queen to identify herself with the country of her adoption. But instead, Maria Eleonora lived exclusively in the company of her German ladies-in-waiting and the foreign retinue which she had brought with her. Probably her health was not good, certainly she pined for her husband. A year after their wedding, she had a miscarriage and was seriously ill, and later, in 1623, a daughter, Christina Augusta, was born, but died in under a year. By the autumn of 1624 the Queen was again pregnant and, with her husband at home, in such good spirits that at the end of May she insisted on accompanying him on the royal yacht to review the fleet. Although her pregnancy was advanced there seemed to be no danger, as the warships were moored off the Island of Skeppsholmen just opposite the castle. But a sudden storm nearly capsized the little ship. The Queen was hurried back to the castle, but when she got there she was heard to exclaim: "Jesus, I cannot feel my child!" Shortly afterwards the longed-for son was born dead.

The same year brought the renewal of the war with Poland, and again Gustavus Adolphus had to leave his wife. There was nothing of the stoic Roman matron—so admired by classically minded Swedes like Axel Oxenstierna—about Maria Eleonora, and it is probable that at this point, as we know she did in 1627, she gave way to hysterical grief because of her husband's absence. She had some excuse. After five years of marriage she was childless and the only surviving male Wasa heir, since the death in battle of Gustavus Adolphus's brother in 1622, was Sigismund of Poland. It was probably for this reason that Gustavus Adolphus agreed to the Queen's joining him in Livonia at Reval (the modern Talinn), after the Poles had been defeated at Wallhof in January 1626. By April when the royal couple reached Åbo in Finland Maria Eleonora found she was again pregnant. No risks were taken this time, and in Stockholm on 8th December 1626 she gave birth to a daughter—Christina.

As might have been expected, the birth was a difficult one, but when at last the midwives heard the lusty roar of the child, buoyed up by the predictions of astrologers and their own wishful thinking, they believed her to be a boy; and so the King was told. They could be forgiven for their mistake, since Christina was born with a caul which enveloped her from her head to her knees, leaving only her face, arms and lower part of her legs free; moreover she was covered with hair. When the mistake was discovered no one had the courage to tell the King, until his sister Catherine took Christina in her arms, and, as Christina herself delicately phrased it in her own autobiography: "This great Princess carried me in her arms to the King in a condition for him to see and to know and realize for himself what she dared not tell him."

Gustavus Adolphus's reaction was characteristic. In her autobiography Christina described how he took her in his arms and said: "Let us thank God, my sister. I hope that this girl will be worth a son to me. I pray God that he will preserve her, since he has given her to me." His sister tried to reassure him, saying that he and the Queen were both young and that they would surely have an heir. But Gustavus Adolphus replied: "Sister, I am content, I pray God that he will preserve her," and later on with typically wry humour he said: "She should be clever, since she has deceived us all."

Although Christina's appearance at birth is not, gynaecologically speaking, a rare phenomenon, the circumstances which surrounded the event, that of a long-awaited royal heir in a superstitious age, caused it to be specially remarked. But it is unlikely that it would have been regarded as of such importance by anyone, including Christina herself, if her life had followed the normally accepted pattern of marriage and motherhood. However, of one thing there can be no doubt: the birth of a girl was the last thing anyone wanted. The Queen was in no condition to be told the truth and they waited several days before breaking the news to her. Evidently among the Swedes at court there were already some who heartily disliked Maria Eleonora, for they afterwards told Christina that her mother could not bear the sight of her because she was "a girl and ugly." Christina related this in her autobiography and, with something of her father's humour, remarked that "she wasn't far wrong because I was as dark as a little Moor." Nor was this all. In later life Christina believed that various "accidents" which had happened to her during infancy were contrived, and her informants had evidently hinted that her mother was aware of this.

Gustavus Adolphus gave orders for a Te Deum to be sung in thanksgiving for Christina's birth, and for it to be announced with all the solemnity usually accorded to the arrival of a male heir. Apart from his thankfulness in at last having a child, this seems to indicate that the King entertained little hope of having others. As he was only thirty-three at the time and Maria Eleonora a good deal younger, her state of health seems to be the most likely explanation for this, and in fact six years later Gustavus Adolphus described her as being a very sick woman. In spite of this Maria Eleonora lived until 1655, and from portraits painted during her widowhood and from her way of life—in 1640 she was capable of making a hazardous escape from Sweden to Denmark—it does not seem that she was really physically fragile; her trouble was probably psychological. Maria Eleonora seems to have enjoyed *une petite santé*, as the French say, the privilege of a thoroughly neurotic woman.

That she was neurotic there can be no doubt. In the year after Christina's birth the King's old tutor described her as being in a state of hysteria owing to her husband's absence, and later in life she displayed a capacity for weeping for hours and even days on end. There was some excuse for her; Gustavus Adolphus's life was constantly in danger when he was on campaign—in 1627 he was both ill and wounded and two years later he had a hairbreadth escape at Stuhm. She felt herself, too, to be an isolated foreigner in a hostile land, even more so after 1627 when for a while her brother threw in his lot with Sweden's enemies. It was a difficult situation even for a wise woman, but with her extravagant exhibitions of grief the Queen alienated even further the stoically patriotic Swedes, who came to regard her as yet one more trial inflicted upon a King whom they loved and revered.

Secretly, Gustavus Adolphus himself can hardly have avoided comparing his wife with Swedish women such as his old love Ebba Brahe, whose husband was a soldier too, but who was now father of a family of handsome children. A portrait in Skokloster Castle shows her as an old woman, with a rosy wrinkled face but sparkling eye. Did she still recall the "thousand nights of gladness" which the King had wished her in his farewell letter when she married? She kept the letter and she transmitted her good looks and charm to one at least of her fourteen children, Magnus De la Gardie.

There is no doubt that his troubles with his wife weighed heavily on Gustavus Adolphus, both as a man and a king. He could not banish them from his mind even when he was making the last preparations for the most decisive step in his life, his landing at Usedom, at the mouth of the Peene, on 26th June 1630. By this action he committed his country to carrying the Thirty Years War into the Imperial camp and to bearing the brunt of it for another eighteen years. Although he could not foresee all this, the King well knew what burdens had been shouldered by his people, who then numbered scarcely a million and a half and who had been heavily taxed in men and money by intermittent war during more than twenty years. He also seems to have had definite premonitions of his own death. But he believed that Hapsburg designs for Baltic supremacy threatened Sweden's very existence—let alone the religious freedom of the Protestant states.

It was in these dramatic circumstances, while discussing a possible regency with members of the government before he left for Germany, that Gustavus Adolphus was forced to admit his wife's weakness. With tears in his eyes he referred to her as "a miserable woman"; only the contrast between her behaviour and that of his countrymen in a moment of crisis could have wrung such a bitter admission from him in public. Even so, Gustavus Adolphus evidently could not bring himself to nominate a regency council in which her name did not appear. Nor did he then exclude her from the responsibility for their daughter's education, as Christina afterwards averred; these steps were only taken by the government after his death.

In private with Axel Oxenstierna, however, Gustavus Adolphus went much further. It was not only of guardians for his four-year-old daughter that he was thinking, but of a guardian for the Queen herself. Before embarking for Germany, for a whole hour he begged his friend to agree on oath to accept this responsibility. For all his devotion, the Chancellor would not agree; in the end the King only succeeded in extracting from him a promise to do his best. Anxiety drove Gustavus Adolphus to make yet another appeal to Oxenstierna in a letter written from Germany on 4th December 1630. It is a very revealing and human one, showing the affection mixed with pity that Gustavus Adolphus still felt for his wife, his simple piety and his implicit trust in Axel Oxenstierna. He wrote: "If anything should happen to me, my family are worthy of compassion for my sake and for other reasons. They are but women—the mother without judgment, and the daughter a young lady of tender age: unfortunate if they govern themselves and in danger if they are governed by others. Natural affection and tenderness dictate these lines of my pen addressed to you, you I say, who are the instrument that God has given me, not only to aid and support me in many great undertakings, but also that they should be well prepared to withstand all that may happen, and in all that is closest to my heart in this world. Nevertheless I submit all to the will of God, my life and all that he has given me, confident of the best in this world and hoping after this life to find rest, joy and eternal salvation."

Gustavus Adolphus seems to have had a premonition that he would never see Sweden or his child again when he wrote those lines. During the next two years he marched and countermarched across the length and breadth of Germany from Danzig to Munich. He conquered Pomerania and Mecklenburg, and twice defeated the Imperial commander Tilly, first at Breitenfeld and finally on the River Lech, but in the autumn of 1632 he was forced by Wallenstein to withdraw north. On 24th October at Nuremberg he saw Axel Oxenstierna and confirmed his appointment as his plenipotentiary in Southern Germany. Knowing that a great trial of strength between himself and Wallenstein could not be long delayed, Gustavus Adolphus also gave the Chancellor instructions for the government and education of his daughter, should he die while she was a minor. Then, early in November he went to Erfurt to say goodbye to his wife, who had been in Germany since the previous winter, before joining his army for the attack. The great leader of the Protestant cause was a very different man from the dashing "Captain Gars" Maria Eleonora had first seen twelve years before. It was a middle-aged man, corpulent and somewhat weary and dispirited, who now came to take what he seems to have known might be his last farewell. He was filled with forebodings; even his personal popularity with the crowds seems to have preyed on his mind, for he told his chaplain Fabricius that he "feared a jealous God."

In the dark of a bitter November morning the battle of Lützen began. The King set out at five a.m. to take command and at first the fighting went in his favour, then a heavy mist descended on the field. Contemporary accounts differ as to what followed, but it seems that in the confusion caused by the mist Gustavus Adolphus was practically isolated among the enemy cavalry and both he and his horse were wounded. In the *mêlée* he was shot in the back; he fell and was dragged for some distance by his horse. He managed to free himself from the stirrup, then when lying on the ground he was killed by another shot through his head.

For a while, no one knew what had happened, but the rumour spread rapidly that the King was dead, and defeat seemed inevitable. It was only averted in the end by Bernard of Saxe-Weimar's refusal to retreat and the gallantry of the Swedes. By nightfall both armies were exhausted, but Wallenstein had quit the field and Bernard of Saxe-Weimar and the Swedes had captured all the Imperial artillery and were in possession of the key position, the hill of the windmills. Both sides claimed a victory, but, although they were unable to follow up the Imperial retreat, Gustavus Adolphus's army remained in possession of the blood-soaked field of Lützen. More than 5,000 Swedes lay dead, and among them the body of their king was found, lying face downwards in the mud, plundered of everything but his shirt. He was only thirty-nine. But Gustavus Adolphus's epitaph was written in the hearts of the soldiers he had led; one of his Scots companions-in-arms called him "the Captaine of Kings and the King of Captains"; another said that he was "the best and most valorouse commander that ever any soldiers hade."

The news of the King's death was received with stunned astonishment on the Protestant side. Some would not believe it—for days afterwards London merchants were betting that the rumour was false—others attributed it to treachery, refusing to credit that so great a soldier could have been killed in the field. Although the story that even Pope Urban VIII mourned his passing is apocryphal, it is indicative of what people thought.

But the man to whom the King's death meant more than any other was Axel Oxenstierna; when the news reached him at

Frankfurt even his iron self-control gave way. Afterwards he recalled how for the first time in his life he spent a night of sleepless anguish. Personal grief apart, Oxenstierna had good reason; for many years to come his shoulders alone would have to bear the burden that before then had been shared. He had given his word to the King, and now it was his first duty to preserve intact the heritage of his new sovereign—the five-year-old child who had become Christina, by the Grace of God Queen of the Swedes, Goths and Vandals, Great Princess of Finland, Duchess of Esthonia and Carelia and Lady of Ingria.

CHAPTER 1

Childhood: 1626–1636

Christina's description of how she received, on the eve of her sixth birthday, the news that she was Queen, recorded many years afterwards in her autobiography,* bears the unmistakable imprint of a personal experience vividly and honestly recorded. "I was such a child," she wrote, "that I knew neither my misfortune nor my fortune. I remember, however, that I was enchanted to see all these people at my feet, kissing my hand." The phrase rings true in the midst of all the hyperbole with which the Queen surrounded her description of the death of her father and her own accession. "It was Victory that first pronounced my name upon the fatal field of battle," is a fair sample, interspersed with apostrophes to

* Among those of the Queen's papers which survived her and Cardinal Azzolino's deaths, there were several drafts and fragments of autobiographies and biographical material. The most comprehensive were:

1. An autobiography entitled '*Histoire de la Reine Christine faite par elle-même Rome 11 juin 1681.*' In this book, referring to it as the Queen's autobiography, I have used the text published by Arckenholtz in '*Mémoires concernant Christine, reine de Suède,*' Amsterdam, 1759, Vol. III, p. 1–69. Several other MSS versions and fragments exist in the Riksarkivet in Stockholm.

2. Synopsis for a biography of the Queen's reign entitled '*Mémoire de ce qui s'est passé durant le regne de la reine, avec notes ajoutées par elle-même.*' Also published by Arckenholtz, Vol. III, pp. 182–224, and referred to in this book as the Memoir or as the synopsis for the Queen's biography. MSS versions of this also exist in the Riksarkivet.

3. Of lesser importance was an outline of Christina's character, referred to as such in this book, entitled '*Esquisse de l'Histoire de la Reine Christine Auguste*' published by Arckenholtz, Vol. IV, pp. 287–90.

the Deity, to whom her work was dedicated. The baroque literary conventions of the period were not alone responsible for this high-flown style: the Queen quite evidently saw her own life as a suitable subject for epic treatment, and the fact that from the age of six she had seen the grandees of a proud and independent country on their knees before her, had not a little to do with it.

Among the first to "do his duty in this respect," the Queen recalled, was her uncle by marriage, the Count Palatine John Casimir. She also recorded that this scion of the ancient house of Wittelsbach (whose antecedents included four Holy Roman Emperors and, significantly, a King of Sweden) was a "sage and prudent prince" because he relinquished his post as Treasurer before the Regency Council could deprive him of it on the grounds that he was a foreigner. Chauvinism was not the only reason for the Council's point of view. John Casimir's wife Catherine was now the only adult Wasa in Sweden, and they already had flourishing sons, notably Charles Gustavus who was four years older than the child Queen, and in his parents' eyes possibly a more suitable candidate for the throne. Even if this were not so it was plainly evident that by marrying Christina, Charles Gustavus would ultimately become King in fact if not in name. So with the family fortunes wrecked by the Thirty Years War, prudence and sagacity indicated that the Palatine family's devotion should early be impressed upon the young Queen.

That the sight of her uncle John Casimir kneeling before her made an indelible impression upon the child is understandable, because during her parents' absence she had been left in the charge of his wife. Christina now continued to live with the Palatines, enjoying what seems to have been a happy family circle, for on her own admission she soon forgot the death of the father she had hardly seen. She had the company of children of her own age to console her, particularly her cousin Maria Euphrosyne who later became her intimate friend.

But there were other distractions, of a type calculated to appeal to Christina even at an early age. Although her autobiographical description of some of them is quite plainly based on hearsay of a kind more flattering than the simple truth, it is perfectly possible that she did remember the first diet of the Riksdag at which she was ever present, which was summoned early in 1633. It was indeed a momentous occasion, for the situation confronting the Råd was grave in the extreme. The Polish Wasas had good grounds for claiming the Swedish crown by right of birth, as vested in their family by the Riksdag of 1544, and a girl of six was a frail representative of the cadet branch which had ruled the country since Charles IX had seized power, especially as many Swedes still preferred an elective monarchy. Some, indeed, even suggested a Republic. But, as at the time of Gustavus Adolphus's accession, the sober Råd clearly saw that the country's unity and security in the midst of a desperate war called for the recognition of a representative of the Protestant Wasas. If Christina was only a child she was also the child of a beloved King who had given his life for his country. Thus the Riksdag was called to give its assent and due legal form to proceedings.

Judged against this background, the Queen's description of events, written some half a century later, makes amusing reading. She wished the world to believe (for the autobiography was evidently meant for publication) that her recognition was due to her own childish majesty when she was seated on the throne "with an air so great that it inspired respect and fear [*sic*] in everyone." As a matter of sober fact, the Marshal of the diet was actually interrupted by a member of the fourth Estate, when making the proposition that Christina should be proclaimed Queen. With the sturdy independence of his kind, this peasant, Lars Larsson, said: "Who is this daughter of Gustavus? We do not know her and we have never seen her," and he was supported by growing murmurs from his companions.

The Marshal's reply was to go and fetch Christina and bring her right up to the peasants for them to see. Larsson looked at her closely and then exclaimed: "It's her all right, look, there are Gustavus Adolphus's nose, eyes and forehead; let her be our Queen." By universal consent Christina was then acclaimed "Elected Queen and Hereditary Princess of Sweden," with the customary reservation that she should confirm the rights and liberties of the nation. The word "elected" was aimed at the hereditary pretensions of the Polish Wasas. At the same time a Regency Council was formed of the five great officers of state, all of them members of the Råd, which was authorized to govern in the Queen's name; Axel Oxenstierna's powers as legate in Germany were also confirmed.

The excitement of Christina's first appearance in the Riksdag was followed by the arrival of a Russian embassy. This the Queen was bound to receive in person, since it was at one and the same time an embassy of condolence for the death of her father and one of congratulation upon her own accession. It was also charged with a request for her ratification of the peace with Russia made by Gustavus Adolphus in 1617. It is in her autobiographical description of this, her first great state occasion, that something of Christina's own inimitable character emerges for the first time.

Understandably enough, her entourage were somewhat doubtful of their young sovereign's capacity to receive an embassy in due style, more particularly a Russian one, which to western eyes might look very odd indeed. She says: "They therefore coached me carefully on the subject, instructing me in all the details of the ceremonial and exhorted me not to be afraid," and continues: " 'And why should I be afraid?' They replied that the Muscovites were great big men dressed quite differently from us, that they had huge beards, and were terrible, and that there would be a great many of them; but that I must not be afraid. It so happened that my comforters on this occasion were the Grand Constable and the Grand Admiral, both of whom had large beards, whereupon I began to laugh and said 'But what do I care about their beards? Haven't you two got big beards, and I'm not afraid of you. Why should I be afraid of them? Instruct me well and leave it to me.' And in fact I kept my word."

With excusable satisfaction and some exaggeration, the Queen goes on to relate how she sat on her throne with all dignity and "with such an assured and dignified mien, that instead of being afraid, as has happened to other children on similar occasions, I made the ambassadors feel that which all men feel when they approach something that is greater." The memory of this childish triumph evidently remained very green in Christina's mind, as she recalled with unusual freshness and simplicity the pleasure which it gave her entourage "who, as everyone is over children's trifles, were so proud and delighted."

The summer of 1633 had, however, brought a sad awakening for the young Queen. In June Maria Eleonora arrived from

Germany bringing with her the embalmed body of her husband. Christina had already been at Nyköping for some time awaiting her, and with all the members of the Råd and the nobility of the court she went in solemn procession to the ship to receive her mother. "Our tears and lamentations were renewed by the sad spectacle. I embraced the Queen my mother, she drowned me with her tears and practically smothered me in her arms," such was Christina's somewhat unfeeling description of the occasion.

The fifty years that had passed between this encounter and the Queen's recording of it had evidently done nothing to soften Christina's memories of her mother. One is tempted to suspect that this dislike she recorded in her autobiography was not a matter of hindsight, but was already there at the time. Probably it was caused in part by the hostility of the Swedish entourage and the prospect of renewed parental control; but the precocious sharpness of Christina herself cannot be ignored. She had not seen her mother for months and, from all accounts, in the past the Queen Mother had shown little affection for the daughter whom she now regarded with hysterical and lachrymose adoration.

Children are quick to perceive and resent insincerity, particularly children of Christina's sharp-witted and independent character, and she now evidently saw clearly that she was destined to become part of the theatrical trappings of woe with which her mother surrounded herself. In her description of this period of her life, Christina was remarkably frank in her autobiography, especially for a century when her attitude might well be considered shocking, even though she was recording the feelings of a child. She honestly admitted that she had long since got over any sorrow she had felt for her father's death, adding shrewdly "because children who await the succession to a crown are easily consoled for the loss of a father." This bald statement, verging on the cynical, was at variance with the pious custom of the period and indeed contrasts strangely with the grandiloquence and, on occasion, falsehood of much of Christina's autobiography; but such contradictions were typical of her character as a grown woman.

Other interesting indications of what this future Christina was to be like emerge even at this early age. The child who had evidently thoroughly enjoyed her first taste of the complicated etiquette surrounding the reception of the Russian Ambassadors, was bored beyond endurance by the long, sad ceremonies and endless sermons and harangues that accompanied her father's obsequies. She admitted that "they were more insupportable to me than the death of the King my father, from which I had recovered long before." Christina had some justification, for the solemnities were protracted over many months and like her father she was impatient by nature. But there was another significant factor: during the ceremonies the dead hero occupied the centre of the stage—a place that even at the age of seven Christina had already come to regard as her own.

The Jesuit maxim on education—take a child till he is seven and he is yours for life—also works in reverse. The never-ending sermons and discourses to which a lively child such as Christina was forced to listen in mourning for her father, from the time she was six until she was nearly eight, aroused in her a loathing for this very prominent aspect of Lutheran worship. She also acquired a life-long dislike for the extravagance, in all senses of the word, of Swedish funeral customs. This last was one aspect of Swedish life to which Maria Eleonora at least took no exception. "She carried out her role of mourning to perfection.... She triumphed over all that our afflicted women do on these occasions" was her daughter's description of the Queen Mother's deportment, when in the summer of 1634 the interminable funeral procession finally wound its way from Nyköping to Stockholm.

Christina had, however, the honesty to admit that her mother's sorrow was genuine; her own protestations of the affection and respect she felt for her ring a little less true. Nor could she be blamed: for more than a year Maria Eleonora had condemned an active, spirited child—Christina was very much her father's child in her love of outdoor life—to an appalling mourning seclusion. In rooms draped with black and lit by candles day and night, from which every breath of air and ray of light was excluded, the Queen Mother sat incessantly weeping. She would scarcely let Christina out of her sight because she so resembled her dead husband, whose coffin stood nearby in the great hall of Nyköping Castle where they were living.

Even at night the unfortunate child could not escape her

mother's ceaseless weeping. Maria Eleonora made her sleep with her in a bed over which her father's heart was hung in a golden casket. Christina's last contact with a sane, normal world was removed when her mother insisted that her aunt Catherine should be sent away. Catherine shared her dead brother's robust common sense and probably had had something to say about this treatment of his daughter, who had previously been in her charge. She kept in touch with Christina as best she could by writing to her, and some of her niece's rather stilted childish letters of thanks, written from Nyköping in the spring of 1634, still survive. In vain did the tutors, appointed by Gustavus Adolphus himself, protest; so did the Regency Council; no one had the courage to intervene directly, partly out of pity, because the Queen Mother had been allowed no part in the Regency itself.

There was another horror for Christina in this nightmare world, which probably none of her contemporaries could have understood; the darkened rooms were filled with dwarfs, hunchbacks and other human oddities. In this her mother's taste was the normal one of the period; such beings existed at every court, were cherished and caressed by their royal masters and mistresses, and even by highly cultivated people such as Isabella d'Este and Charles I of England, their antics were considered a sovereign means of banishing care. Thus no one could have been surprised that Maria Eleonora kept her buffoons with her in the midst of her mourning; it was, on the contrary, Christina who was strange in not appreciating what most children of her time would have enjoyed. Christina admits: "I had naturally a mortal aversion for this scum." Was this a manifestation of the "natural delicacy" that she attributed to herself? She was not so refined in her person or her language. Or was it something that went far deeper? Christina was herself deformed, not by birth, but from being dropped when she was a baby. One of her shoulders was misshapen and higher than the other. Christina believed that the fall had not been an accident and all her life she was at pains to conceal her deformity. She referred to it as "a slight irregularity in my figure," but it was more than that: in spite of concealing clothes it was noted by all observers, and when she was grown up court artists generally avoided portraying her full-face.

Consciousness of this malformation may have been at the root of her strange antipathy for her mother's buffoons, inducing a feeling, particularly as she got older, of "there but for the Grace of God go I." It would also explain some of Christina's later curious traits—her passion for insisting on her hardiness and physical strength and her complete disregard for dress. Whatever caused her aversion for the buffoons it was no transitory thing; long afterwards in a synopsis for a full-scale biography of the Queen, copied out by her secretary in Rome, it is again mentioned. Christina even devoted two of her famous maxims to the subject: in one she says that these unfortunates are "birds of ill-omen to honourable people if they have easy access to princes," and that "although they sometimes tell truths that others dare not mention, one can also make them say what one wants."

Another custom of the time which contributed to Christina's misery was that she was not allowed to drink water: probably with very good hygienic reasons, beer and wine were considered to be safer. Extraordinary as it may seem, it was only later in the sixteen-thirties that the Swedes began to drink milk. The national diet of the time was copious, heavy and, given the impossibility of feeding stock during the winter, even for the rich largely composed of salted meat and fish. In these circumstances the unfortunate child who, unlike her compatriots could not bear either wine or beer, drank of them only when she was forced to by extreme thirst, until one day she discovered a stock of rose-water which her mother used for washing her face. This was stored in a closet in the Queen Mother's apartment, and after carefully spying out the land, Christina went secretly every day after dinner and drank her fill. After a time her mother noticed that her stock of what in Sweden at that time must have been a considerable luxury, was disappearing rapidly. She berated her maids, who denied their guilt, and a watch was set on Christina (possibly, one wonders, by the hated buffoons). She was caught red-handed by her mother, who personally administered a sound beating. In vain did the poor child protest that she could not bear drinking wine or beer; from now on she passed whole days without drinking a drop of liquid. In the circumstances it is not surprising that Christina became seriously ill, an ulcer appeared on her left breast, causing her terrible pain and a high fever until it burst. At last, however, she was allowed to drink the despised small beer of the poor—

of lower alcoholic content, but not renowned for its health-giving qualities. Twenty years later the abstemious English Ambassador Whitelocke was to complain of its bad quality.

Gustavus Adolphus's burial in the Riddarholm Church in Stockholm did finally bring some respite to Christina. She and her mother now went to live in Stockholm Castle and, as she says, "Once the interment was over, people didn't think any more of death but of their own business and amusements—the court would have been very fine if it hadn't been for my Mother's mourning." But she goes on to admit that even with Maria Eleonora time was having its healing effect.

In Stockholm, which was now the seat of government, with the chancery housed in a special wing of the Royal Castle, it was no longer possible for the Queen Mother to isolate her daughter from outside influences, as she had done at Nyköping. For one thing Christina had her own apartment and, although she was not allowed to live in it, she went there for her lessons. "I was delighted when my studies called me to my own apartment. I did not wait to be summoned, I went there with an inconceivable joy, even earlier than was necessary," she wrote many years later. Study was a means of escape from the stuffy gloom of her mother's surroundings and the hateful buffoons; indeed afterwards Christina blessed her mother's failings because she felt that it was to them that she owed her discovery of the marvellous world of learning.

Although Christina was not yet eight when she returned to Stockholm, she says that already she studied twelve hours a day. No doubt this was an exaggeration, but to modern minds even half this time would seem an intolerable burden for a young child. In the end its effects were to make themselves felt. But it must be borne in mind that Christina herself was more than willing, and that in the seventeenth century such precocity was not uncommon in children of her condition or in her own family. Her father learnt seven languages, studied rhetoric, optics, mechanics and mathematics, and when he was twelve heard plaints, received ambassadors and even addressed the Riksdag when Charles IX was ill; he held his first independent military command in time of war at the age of sixteen.

In spite of Christina's long hours of study, it is evident that neither the nobility nor the clergy were at all happy about the manner in which the young Queen was being brought up. This was due to their fear of the Queen Mother's influence and that of her foreign entourage. The Regency Council had indeed tried to separate Christina from her mother but because, understandably enough, Maria Eleonora wept and protested so bitterly nothing was done. It was probably this stalemate that induced the Riksdag, led by the nobility and clergy, to take up the matter of Christina's education, drawing up in March 1635 a directive on the subject. Suspicions of the Queen Mother's influence, and her well-known denigration of all things Swedish, obviously dictated its preamble. This states that Christina's education is of the greatest importance to her subjects because "In future they will have to give her obedience and maintain her royal power, sacrificing their goods and if need be their lives on her behalf. That in return she should hold them in esteem and affection, learn to speak well of them and of the present state of the country and the regency, also to respect her tutors, the senators of the Realm, and behave graciously to her subjects and uphold them all in the possession of their liberties, in conformation with the laws."

Even when referring to the lessons of deportment and etiquette which must form part of the education of a Queen, and while admitting that she must "learn foreign manners and customs as becomes her station," the Riksdag was careful to reiterate that Christina "should practise and observe Swedish ones and be taught them carefully." This is all the more remarkable when one considers that it is their great national hero's daughter who is under discussion—Gustavus Adolphus's mother had also been German, but nobody thought to question his essential Swedishness. After some rather touchingly naïve references to the young Queen's being taught good table manners and correct deportment in assemblies, the worthy members of the Riksdag arrive at what was obviously for them the other main object of her education. They stated that "the art of government should come first, but as this comes more with age and experience rather than by youthful studies, the most important thing is that she should have a real knowledge of God, His cult and word."

Christina's religious orthodoxy was to be ensured by the fact "that she should not be imbued with the errors of the Pope or

Calvinism." Furthermore she was to be allowed no frivolous books—savants were to draw up a list of suitable reading matter —and the morals and manners of even her serving maids were to be carefully supervised. In their peroration the members of the Riksdag again returned to the charge that Christina "should be given no false ideas of government or the affairs of the Realm" or ones "prejudicial to the liberty and the conditions of the Estates and subjects of the Realm, but that she should be imbued with affection for them."

It is a formidable document when one considers that it concerns a child of eight, who was already studying long hours every day in order to fit herself for her future responsibilities. There was, however, another side to Christina's education that, in its early stages at least, must have done something to counterbalance the hours spent poring over books. A year before his death Gustavus Adolphus had appointed two governors and a preceptor for his daughter. The first was Axel Banér, brother of the great Field Marshal and the King's own most intimate friend. Christina said of Banér that he shared all her father's personal secrets and, in accordance with the custom of the time, the King's bed before he was married or when he was separated from his wife. Banér had long been Gentleman of the Bedchamber, he was later made a member of the Råd and Grand Master of the Household; according to Christina he was "as able a courtier as could be found in Sweden at that time." Banér was evidently a Swedish noble of the old school—expert in the use of arms, a fine horseman, quick to anger, fond of wine and women (according to Christina, too fond, even in his old age), and an honest upright man. He died when she was only thirteen, but already Christina judged him very ignorant because he spoke no language other than his native Swedish. She did, however, regard him as a trusted friend because she was quick to see that he was absolutely honest with her, giving her a straight answer to a straight question and never putting her off with childish tales.

Wisely Gustavus Adolphus had chosen a totally different type as vice-governor in the person of Gustavus Horn, nephew of Sweden's other great Marshal. He too died when Christina was only thirteen, but not before she had come to appreciate the culture and poise he had acquired by foreign travel. In spite of the

Riksdag's efforts to the contrary, it is clear that Christina felt early in life the lure and fascination of foreign countries, especially the sunlit ones of the south. In fact the only criticism Christina made of her father's instructions for her education was that he had excluded all foreigners from taking a part in it. Horn's great attraction for her was that he was a good linguist, had been on a mission to France and had travelled there and in Spain and Italy; above all he had "some tincture of the politeness of foreign countries." He was also a member of the Råd, obviously a polished courtier, but equally expert in arms and sport. Christina had one fault to find with him—"the vice of the country": like most Swedes of the time he drank too much.

Evidently these two gentlemen were charged with that aspect of Christina's upbringing which, although it was carried out according to her father's specific orders, was in time to bring more discredit upon her, especially abroad, than anything else. Gustavus Adolphus had definitely stated that his daughter was to be brought up as a prince, that she was to be given a boy's education and to be able to do everything that a young prince should. No one was to inculcate into her feminine ideas or pursuits, except those of virtue and modesty. It was an extraordinary idea for a man of his time, especially as the memory of one of the most remarkable queens in history was still green in everyone's mind. Elizabeth I of England was well known in Sweden; Eric XIV had long courted her assiduously and his sister Cecily made a pilgrimage of admiration to her court. Elizabeth had received an excellent education, but a normal feminine one: she had not needed to learn manly exercises in order to have "the heart and stomach of a King," and all Europe knew it.

The recent precedent of a successful woman ruler, therefore, existed. Nor had Gustavus Adolphus any reason to fear that his daughter lacked spirit. At the age of two, to his delight, she had clapped her hands and laughed with joy when the great cannons of Kalmar Castle had boomed out the royal salute. Even the Governor had been doubtful of firing them, knowing that the baby Princess was present in her mother's carriage. But the King had ordered him to "Fire, she is a soldier's daughter, she must get accustomed to it"; and afterwards he always took Christina with him to military reviews. The explanation for this extraordinary wish to have his daughter brought up like a boy must be sought elsewhere—and the reason which immediately leaps to mind is Maria Eleonora's character and physique.

Everything indicates that Gustavus Adolphus, who must have suffered from her more than anyone else, made all the provisions he could to ensure that his wife's influence upon his daughter and his country should be reduced to a minimum if he died while Christina was still a child. She was only four when he embarked on what he knew to be a desperate venture in Germany and, although she promised well, how could the King be sure that she might not later take after her mother and develop into a sickly fearful woman, given over to feminine trifles?

If this were the case, what would be her ultimate fate and that of her country? It was not so long since the King's two uncles had suffered state imprisonment and one of them had been secretly murdered. Viewed in this context, the passage in his letter to Oxenstierna from Germany, "unfortunate if they govern themselves and in danger if they are governed," takes on its full sinister meaning. Gustavus Adolphus had implicit faith in Oxenstierna and evidently felt that as long as he was alive Christina and Sweden were in safe hands, but he could not know that the Chancellor would live to what was then the remarkable age of seventy-one. The best that the King could hope for his child and country was that she should resemble her mother as little as possible, and the most certain means of ensuring this, especially with regard to her physique and health, was for her to be brought up to the out-of-doors life he loved, with plenty of exercise, which no girl of her station enjoyed at that period.

What the King could not have foreseen was, as Christina herself phrased it, "my inclinations agreed wonderfully with his designs." In other words, instead of a naturally feminine little girl being trained to ride well, to hunt and even to shoot, a neurotic, lonely, overdriven child, who despised her fluttery feminine mother and all she stood for, took refuge in this only too welcome means of escape.

That in following her father's wishes to the letter, they might be turning the child into a freak, evidently never occurred to her entourage, or at least not until it was too late. In ordinary circumstances, especially if Christina had developed into a physically attractive girl, this tomboy attitude would have died a natural death. As it was she grew up to be slovenly in dress, to loathe and despise any sort of feminine avocation and to swear like a stable boy, taking her pleasure in extreme hardiness, riding, racing and hunting superbly, walking for hours on end. With unaccustomed modesty Christina said she could "handle any arms passably well," she was in fact a crack shot—a French ambassador once said she could hit a running hare quicker than any man. Some of these were admirable qualities if practised in moderation, but the only person who might have instilled some moderation in his wilful daughter was Gustavus Adolphus. Christina herself admitted that "People did all that they could to stop me, but they had to give up and let me do what I wanted."

There was, however, one man who did succeed in obtaining a considerable influence over Christina in childhood, and her affection for him remained with her always. This was John Mathiae, the Doctor of Theology whom her father had appointed to be her preceptor and to give her religious instruction. Mathiae had been Court Chaplain and had accompanied the King to Germany in 1630. Evidently he was very close to Gustavus Adolphus and had been chosen by him because Mathiae's liberal and unbigoted religious outlook resembled his own. Unlike many Swedish Lutheran pastors of the time, Mathiae, who came of an old family, was a travelled and cultivated man, wise and learned but not pedantic; he was kind, gentle and good and must have possessed considerable personal charm.

Christina was not yet seven when Mathiae first came to teach her—a proud, self-willed, suspicious unhappy child—but something in her instantly responded to her preceptor's goodness and gentleness. Soon he became her confidant, the repository of all her childish secrets and sorrows. Christina says herself that she was "secretive beyond belief" but that together they discussed everything; Mathiae told her what was going on among the members of the government and she in her turn told him what she thought about them. "Some of my reflexions astonished him . . . and sometimes I explained things to him that he did not understand, or that he pretended not to understand." It is a fascinating picture and presents a totally different aspect of Christina's character from any we have known hitherto—making one wonder how differently she might have developed if only her father had lived. For she called Mathiae "Papa" and evidently loved him more than anyone else at this period of her life.

Writing many years afterwards, Christina described her feelings towards those around her and one very illuminating incident of her life at that time. This passage was evidently not intended for publication, as it was not included in her autobiography. She said the events occurred when she was "six or seven," but as she mentions that her Aunt Catherine, for whom she admitted she felt "some consideration and even some love," was her gouvernante at the time, she must have been nearer six, as she was removed from her aunt in the summer of 1633 and was not returned to her care until 1636. Christina said, however, that already she could not bear to be scolded or corrected by anyone, especially women, and even with difficulty by her aunt; and that the only people for whom she felt genuine respect were Mathiae and her Governor, Axel Banér. "They were both very fine men and because of the friendship and respect that I felt for them I would do anything for them, though I wanted to know the why and wherefore of everything . . . thus, although I was unbelieving and suspicious, these two, who were friends, had complete authority over me. They knew so well how to deal with me that they gained my friendship and my entire confidence. I studied with pleasure and was unbelievably curious, I wanted to learn and know everything. But no matter how much authority they had over me or how much I was convinced of their integrity, I still questioned their answers and reasoned things out for myself."

It would be hard to believe in the independent mind and extraordinary intellectual curiosity of a child of six, if it were not for the fact that this had been one of Gustavus Adolphus's outstanding traits and was to remain Christina's dominant characteristic throughout her life. She really did want to know all and did question everything, and the incident she goes on to describe seems to have remained so vividly in her mind because it was the first time that this devouring curiosity was applied to something that really mattered. For the first time in her life Christina was taken to hear the sermon on the Last Judgment which was preached annually on the Sunday before Advent, with all the graphic realism of hell-fire characteristic of the Protestant Church at that time. The preacher had evidently been more than usually eloquent and the impression made upon the child was tremendous. She was terrified and believed that she might at any moment be swallowed up in this last cataclysm of heaven and earth. Coming out of church crying, she called to Mathiae and asked him: "What is this, Father? Why have you never told me about this terrible day? What will become of me then? Will it happen in the night?" Laughing at her naïveté, Mathiae tried to comfort her, saying: "You will go to heaven, but in order to do so you must be obedient to your preceptor, you must pray to God and you must study."

Christina said that this very natural reply to a frightened child aroused thoughts and reactions in her that she never forgot, very far in advance of her age and understanding. The following year she again heard the usual sermon on the Last Judgment, and although it made an impression on her, it was much less. "I didn't cry this time," she wrote, "but on coming out of church I again asked my preceptor 'When will this Judgment come that they talk so much about?' He said to me: 'It will come, it will come, but don't get upset, God alone knows when it will come, but we must prepare ourselves for it.' I was not altogether satisfied with this reply, and I began to wonder to myself and almost to doubt even my preceptor, although I loved and esteemed him so much."

She goes on to recount how when a year later she heard the same sermon for the third time, she "didn't take it seriously and didn't believe any more, and I began to have doubts about all the rest. One day when I was studying with my preceptor I said to him: 'Will you tell me the truth? Isn't all that they tell us about religion just fables like the Last Judgment?' He gave me a most terrible reprimand, telling me that it was a dreadful sin and impious even to think such a thing, and that if he ever heard me say anything like that again, he would have me beaten by my gouvernante. This threat made me angry and I said to him: 'I promise you never again to say anything like it, and I do not want to be beaten because you would have call to regret it very much if such a thing happened.' I said this with such an imperious air that I made him tremble."

This account was written probably at least thirty years after the event, and although the last line can of course be taken with a grain of salt, an English ambassador was amused to observe that Christina believed that she could produce the same effect at the age of twenty-eight. He said that people pandered to her in this because it flattered her; no doubt she had been told that this capacity to overawe was a trait of her father's that she had inherited.

However, not long afterwards, in July 1636, Christina came in contact with a man whom it is doubtful that even she ever believed she could overawe; this was Axel Oxenstierna, who in that year returned from Germany. Although Christina had not seen Oxenstierna since 1631, she must have been increasingly aware that it was in his hands that the reins of power were firmly held, and that even during his five years absence it was the Chancellor who really ruled Sweden. He it was who had drawn up the famous Form of Government, which became law at the diet of the Riksdag in 1634; it is a measure of the trust that Gustavus Adolphus was known to have reposed in him that after the King's death Oxenstierna could draft such a constitution, prefacing it with words which were accepted as being Gustavus Adolphus's own, as its content was acknowledged to be in accordance with the King's desires. In fact this remarkable document, which was subsequently used as a model by other countries, regularized and gave legal form to the machinery of government that had grown up during Gustavus Adolphus's reign. It was largely responsible for the transformation of Sweden from a mediaeval country into a modern state. The reign had in fact been one of the great transition periods of Swedish history, although many of these processes had begun before it, and were later completed during Christina's minority. It is also worthy of note that between 1611 and 1644 Axel Oxenstierna's influence was continuous and for a time paramount in guiding the ship of state.

The events leading up to this period began with Gustav Wasa's action, contrary to the tradition that the Råd were the King's advisers, in obtaining the Riksdag's sanction for the hereditary monarchy. This resulted in the beginnings of the Riksdag's development, which during his own and his sons' reigns was carried out at the expense of the powers of the Råd. The aristocracy's hostility to the Crown was one of the causes; but there remained the undeniable fact that the old "hunting, shooting and fishing" type of noble was ill-prepared to take part in the administration of a country emerging from a mediaeval way of life based on the manorial system. Gustav Wasa had to look elsewhere for the clerks and officers he now needed for his administration, and his sons continued the practice. This gave added fire to the rivalry between the King and the nobles, which was more or less latent throughout Swedish history. It came to a head in Charles IX's time, when a new generation had grown up among the aristocracy of young men who had travelled and been educated at foreign universities, and justifiably considered themselves as capable of taking part in the government as the King's bourgeois administrators. This was the situation that brought about the collision between Charles IX and their leader Eric Sparre, and the bloodbath of Linköping.

With the succession still dogged by the claims of the Polish Wasas, Gustavus Adolphus's accession to the throne as little more than a boy gave the nobles the chance to redress the balance of power in their own favour. The clauses of the charter which the King then signed, giving the Swedish-born nobility the monopoly of the Råd and the five great offices of state, achieved most of what Eric Sparre had striven for. Moreover the fact that the holders of these offices could only be removed by a judicial sentence (not at the Sovereign's pleasure) made them the servants of the state rather than the King. It is significant that it was in this charter that the hand of Axel Oxenstierna appeared for the first time, and that although he had served Charles IX, he was a member of one of the greatest aristocratic families and, on his mother's side, related to Ture Bielke who perished at Linköping.

The subsequent partnership between Gustavus Adolphus and Axel Oxenstierna symbolized the truce between the King and the nobility that distinguished his reign. Begun in a moment of national peril, it continued owing to intermittent wars in which the King's patriotism, courage and genius for statesmanship had full play, and resulted in an unprecedented relationship of affection between the Sovereign and the Råd and nobility, which also extended to the Riksdag. This situation and the King and Oxenstierna's capacity for organization were the circumstances which brought about the transformation of the system of government, and paved the way for further evolution during Christina's minority.

From its early beginnings in the fourteenth century as a body which elected and deposed kings, the Riksdag had come to consist of about 500 representatives of the four Estates—the nobility, clergy, burghers and peasants. These Estates remained constant throughout Swedish history, though at different periods others were temporarily added. Originally in Sweden any man was noble who could put a fully equipped cavalryman at the King's disposal in time of war (it was on these grounds that the nobles claimed exemption from taxation), though for long their status had been subject to royal patent as in other countries. The nobility was divided into three classes; the highest, bearing the titles of count or baron, was in 1626 limited to twelve families. The second class, represented by twenty-two families in 1626, consisted of descendants of former members of the Råd. Members of the third class, numbering ninety-two families in 1626, might be of very ancient lineage though economically their condition could be little better than that of peasants. Although primogeniture did not exist in Sweden, only the head of each family could take part in the diets of the Riksdag, but as all three classes had a vote each, their voting power equalled that of all the other three Estates.

The last six years of Gustavus Adolphus's reign saw a great expansion in the nobility, whose numbers rose from 126 families to 187. This process had already begun in 1617 when the King created several new nobles, including his old tutor, John Schroderius, who in accordance with the Swedish custom then changed his name to Skytte; he was also made a member of the Råd. Later, foreigners, including several Scots, were also ennobled, as the De la Gardies (who were of French origin) had been in a previous generation. This was an indication that those who had served the country, no matter what their origin, could now aspire to a place in the nobility and if they were Swedish-born, to membership of the Råd, which previously had been the prerogative of a few hereditary nobles.

Gradually, as the character of the nobility changed, so did its functions and way of life. To get on one must serve the government, and indeed the virtue of this service was recognized as early as 1617, when the nobility petitioned the King for some sign of honour to be given to senior civil servants who were not members of the Råd—to distinguish "those who serve the country and those who sit at home and do nothing." Thus the old country squire type of noble was fast disappearing and being replaced by the efficient civil servant brought to Stockholm by the centralization of the government offices. This in its turn transformed Stockholm from a series of huddled villages into a city filled with the fine brick and stone-built town houses of the nobles.

The processes which were transforming the Råd and the nobility also affected the Riksdag as a whole. After a few years' setback owing to the recovered power of the Råd, the crucial moment in the development of the Riksdag's position came in 1614. Then, after a passage of arms with the clergy over their proposal for a bigoted and narrow Church ordinance, Gustavus Adolphus forced his own judicial ordinance through the Riksdag, thereby establishing the precedent that together the King and the Riksdag made law.

In 1617 the whole organization of the Riksdag was reformed, diets could no longer take place in the open air and a permanent system of seating and procedure was instituted, as well as security measures. These last forbade the presence of any strangers, except the sons of the nobility; no copies of the King's proposals, which were submitted in writing, were allowed to be taken out of the building, and all answers, also given in writing, had to be presented in the Hall of State. Again for security reasons, in 1627 Gustavus Adolphus first called a secret committee of selected members of all four Estates, this later becoming a fairly general practice.

The Riksdag chiefly differed from the English Parliament in that its members could not initiate legislation. The King proposed legislation, giving his requests in writing; the Estates then separated to debate on their own, returning with a written reply. There was no open debate in the English sense, though Gustavus Adolphus tried to alter this, as he had instituted discussion when presiding over the meetings of the Råd; understandably so, because he was the best orator and one of the keenest debaters in the country. The Estates were free to accept or reject the King's proposal, but if no agreement was reached the King could act on his own initiative. In fact he possessed the right to issue ordinances and proclamations and grant privileges which had the effect of law, and he maintained the royal prerogative intact, handing it on to his daughter.

Nevertheless the King's powers were limited by his coronation oath and the charter agreed at his accession. This last included the stipulation that no new burden in the way of levies and tolls or taxes could be imposed without the consent of the Råd and those concerned, which in effect meant the various Estates, though the King could get round this by negotiating direct with the provinces. From being irregular meetings, organized in a somewhat haphazard manner, by the end of Gustavus Adolphus's reign the diets of the Riksdag had become a regular part of the machinery of government. While by the end of Christina's minority the principle was established that taxation could only be increased with the Riksdag's consent, and the limits of the royal authority were defined by law.

Gustavus Adolphus's constant absences on campaign, which had made the old peripatetic system of government impossible, later led to the evolution of the five great offices of state into something resembling a cabinet while the Råd performed the functions of a Privy Council. During the last eleven years of his reign, the King was away from Sweden for nearly half the time, and it became the custom, at first, for seven or nine members of the Råd to be nominated to carry on the administration.

After 1625 all members of the Råd not serving abroad were expected to assemble in Stockholm for this purpose, but ten were specifically nominated to continue the government. Their functions were administrative, they could not form policy but, with their continuity of service, in time the King's prolonged absences had something of the same effect as George I's lack of English had upon the formation of the cabinet system in Britain. Thus even before Gustavus Adolphus's death, the scene was set for effective government by something that amounted to a Regency Council. The holders of these great offices of state during Christina's minority were as follows: the High Steward, Baron Gabriel Gustafsson Oxenstierna (Axel Oxenstierna's younger brother) who died in 1641 and was replaced by Count Per Brahe; the Grand Marshal, Count Jacob De la Gardie; the Grand

Admiral, Baron Carl Carlsson Gyllenhielm (Gustavus Adolphus's illegitimate brother); the Grand Chancellor, Axel Oxenstierna; and the Grand Treasurer, Gabriel Oxenstierna (Axel Oxenstierna's cousin).

This then was the framework of the state when Christina and Axel Oxenstierna met for the first time as Queen and Chancellor, Sovereign and subject, in Stockholm in 1636. Neither has left us an account of that meeting, but at least we have a fair idea of what they both were like. Oxenstierna was fifty-three at the time and in a pencil portrait made by an acute French artist three years earlier he looks remarkably young for a man of his age, especially for the period. He had a broad, high forehead with hair slightly receding at the temples, curiously quizzical eyebrows surmounted an extremely shrewd pair of eyes. The firmness of the Roman nose was matched by a mouth severely drawn, but not lacking in generosity; for a Swede of his time his greying beard was of modest proportions. But in studying the portrait, our glance irresistibly returns to those eyes, and when looking at them we can easily believe, what Christina afterwards said, that Oxenstierna "knew the strength and weakness of every European state." The forehead also agrees with her statement that "he still read even in the midst of great affairs" and the mouth with her admission that "he had a great heart." They knew each other well those two, perhaps none better.

From a portrait of Christina, still hanging in Gripsholm Castle, we also have a shrewd idea of the young Queen as Axel Oxenstierna then saw her. The portrait was evidently posed in the Royal Castle of Stockholm, possibly in the room in Christina's apartment where they actually met, as with its chair of state and royal canopy it was probably the one in which she gave formal audiences. The window affords a view of the Island of Skeppsholmen, of units of the Swedish fleet and a purely imaginary range of mountains. We may be sure that her mother or entourage were responsible for Christina's elaborate puffed-out form of hairdressing, surmounted by a miniature crown; also for the sumptuous green and gold brocade dress, worn over a gold-laced red kirtle, the gold-fringed gloves, the ropes of pearls and the emeralds ornamenting her hair, earrings and even the fashionable feather fan. All the trappings of a Queen Regnant are there, even in a ten-year old, but so is a very sharp young face and a watchful glance from eyes that seem to be deep blue. The pronounced nose and chin leave one in no doubt as to the domineering character, but the mouth is curiously at variance with itself—the upper lip thinly pursed, the lower one red, full and pouting. They are features well worth studying, for they did not change much, no matter what artist interpreted them, during the next fifty-three years; and they remained still impressed upon the silver death-mask which was found in the Queen's tomb in St Peter's in Rome in 1966.

In her autobiography Christina says that although her father charged her guardians—the five great ministers of state who also formed the Regency Council—with the supervison of her education, he himself chose her governors, preceptor and even her masters, and "Above all he charged the Grand Chancellor Oxenstierna with the particular supervision of my person and to make this his special care." She said that Gustavus Adolphus had "also declared that he wished me to be separated from the Queen my mother as soon as I had reached the age of reason."

Presumably this was one of the secret instructions which her father had imparted to Oxenstierna before his death. In any event, whether it was as a result of this, or of representations made by the Regency Council and Råd, or of the impressions he himself received of the bad influence of Maria Eleonora and her entourage, one of Oxenstierna's first actions on his return was to insist that the Queen Mother retired to live in one of the castles of her appanage at Gripsholm. It was not a very encouraging choice, as Gripsholm Castle had more than once been used as a state prison for Swedish Royalty, and its lonely site on an isolated shore of Lake Mälaren was scarcely to the Queen Mother's taste. While admitting the justice of Oxenstierna's action, Christina said that her mother's sorrow aroused her pity on this occasion and that she thought that "It was a bit hard to separate her so completely from myself, as I will show in what follows."

With these words the surviving fragment of the Queen's autobiography comes to an abrupt end. It is unlikely that she ever completed it, and some other odd pages which exist are written in another style. Although this ending was evidently unintentional, Christina's separation from her mother did in fact bring her childhood to a premature conclusion. For the next three years she was placed in the charge of her Aunt Catherine, whom she evidently admired and who was certainly a much more sensible guardian, but her Aunt died in 1639 and in general Christina's feminine companions are usually referred to as "my women," members of a sex that with rare exceptions only aroused her contempt.

CHAPTER 2

Adolescence: 1636–1644

At the time of her separation from her mother, Christina described her days as being "occupied by affairs, study, sport and exercise" and that "no diversion or pleasure ever made me waste a moment from either my studies or my duty." This is not only totally untrue of her life when she was older, but it is more than a little exaggerated even when referring to it at the age of ten. Though she makes no mention of it beyond the words "I was taught to dance a little," in fact Christina had a passion for dancing and later she piqued herself not a little on her capacity in this direction and considered that to be able to dance well was a sign of good breeding. From 1636, she and the younger generation at court had the benefit of expert tuition by a French ballet master, Antoine de Beaulieu who, surprisingly, was summoned to Stockholm by the austere Axel Oxenstierna himself. It is possible, however, that on this aspect of her daughter's education even Oxenstierna had accepted some prompting from the Queen Mother, who the year before had been ravished by the Baron D'Avagour's accounts of ballets at the French court.

Afterwards, describing his time in Sweden, Antoine de Beaulieu said that he had "*poli toute la cour*"; he did it to such good effect that on 28th January 1638 he was able to produce the first ballet ever staged in Sweden. This was performed in Stockholm Castle for Christina's entertainment. With the title *Le Ballet des Plaisirs de la Vie des Enfants sans soucy*, it was in fact almost a pantomime in the French style, with serious and comic characters miming their parts and Beaulieu playing the lead as "Le Joueur," and a grand finale danced in honour of the Queen. All the other performers were Beaulieu's pupils—the young members of the court—and it is not difficult to imagine the excitement which this occasion must have aroused among them. History does not relate who they all were, but two of the "huntsmen" were destined to play more than a dancing role in Christina's life—they were young Magnus De la Gardie and Charles Gustavus Palatine. Two of the Palatine sisters, Maria Euphrosyne and Eleonora, probably also took part in the ballet and possibly even the younger brother Adolphus John, who was later to become as much a balletomane as Christina herself.

This ballet marks a period which was probably the happiest of Christina's young life. Since Axel Oxenstierna's return in 1636, her aunt and cousins had been living with her in the Royal Castle in Stockholm, the girls even sharing some of her lessons, though Maria Euphrosyne seems to have been lazy and could not hope to keep up with Christina's standards. Charles Gustavus was already studying at Uppsala University, but they evidently saw a good deal of each other and shared a youthful enthusiasm for horses and dogs—Christina took affectionate care of his gun-dogs while he was away. Obviously, as in any such family circle, the big brother was looked up to and admired by the younger children. As was only natural, Christina's affection for him began to be tinged with something more as she approached her teens. Charles Gustavus was then a good-looking young man with dark hair and a sensitive face. Her feeling for him may well have been increased by separation after Charles, as she called him, set off on the Grand Tour in 1638, for we find her following his travels with interest in her letters to his father, probably with envy too, for she notes the smallest details, even that he had spent a single night in Spain.

This particular letter was written in the summer of 1639 when, after her aunt's death, Christina had again been separated from the Palatine family. We are told that her ladies had been instructed to teach the young Queen not to put too much confidence in anyone; evidently Oxenstierna and the majority of the Regency Council, who were always very wary of him, felt that she might have been putting too much confidence in her uncle, John Casimir. Today, it seems to us extraordinary how so able a body of men as the Regency seem to have left all normal human affections and relationships out of their calculations in trying to have Christina brought up as a model Queen. Even in an age when royal children were often victims of protocol and affairs of state, one would have thought that the Council would have understood, if not a girl of thirteen's need of affection, at least that their separating her from the people of whom she was fond might have the opposite effect from what they wished, especially with a girl as headstrong as Christina.

In the event this is exactly what happened. The tone of her letters to John Casimir during and after 1639 is that of affectionate conspirators, a role which, from what we know of Christina in later life, she must have thoroughly enjoyed, and this period may well have been a formative one in developing her capacity for intrigue. Many of these letters end with the characteristically exaggerated salutation "the Niece faithful to the grave, Christina"; there are also cautious references to personal or "secret affairs that you have communicated to me" for which she was "wholeheartedly grateful." Already some remarkably shrewd and witty comments on international affairs appear, together with fun poked at members of the Regency Council and their families. On one occasion she wrote: "The Grande Maîtresse of the Court, Madame Beate Oxenstierna, and her daughter may arrive at any moment; the more they come the worse it is!" Evidently the Palatines were much more fun, and to those whom she liked and who amused her, Christina was already giving presents; she apologizes to John Casimir for the ermine skins that she had sent him not being as fine as she would have liked.

Probably a good deal of this reached Axel Oxenstierna's ears, and it would have confirmed him in his belief that the Palatines' affection for Christina was not altogether disinterested or for the ultimate good of Sweden. He was surely right about John Casimir. For it was in the family interest to ingratiate himself with the future ruler; her marriage to Charles Gustavus would assure them all a brilliant future, a future far removed from the poverty which he and his family had known when they had arrived as poor but noble refugees. But as to the good of Sweden, in view of subsequent events which Oxenstierna could not have foreseen, we may now well have reason to wonder. Firstly because it is possible that Christina might have grown up into a very different person if during the most formative years, between thirteen and eighteen, she had lived with people for whom she felt a genuine affection, and her girlish romance might have ripened into an early marriage with Charles Gustavus. Secondly because this separation seems to have increased, rather than otherwise, the doubts which had already been implanted in a naturally suspicious mind and were seriously to influence the Queen's actions after her majority.

Christina could scarcely have been ignorant of the constant rivalry between the crown and the aristocracy throughout Swedish history until her father's reign. To this general background was now added the insistent, though erroneous, belief of the Palatine family and, possibly more important still, of her father's illegitimate brother Carl Carlsson Gyllenhielm, that the aristocracy would gladly rid themselves of the monarchy. This was all the more telling in Gyllenhielm's case, because he was Grand Admiral and a member of the Regency Council, on which, in fact, he and Jacob De la Gardie were the only non-Oxenstierna representatives. From her autobiography we know that Christina had been told of various "accidents" or attempts upon her life that occurred during her infancy. She believed that her deformed shoulder was the result of one of these. If this were true, it was surely the result of the activities of agents of the Polish Wasas, but it is not at all certain that Christina's informants would have been convinced of this. Christina herself actually seems to have suspected her own mother as instigator. Later she made one very cryptic reference, in a letter to John Casimir, about people "who would like to give Charles Gustavus a *bouillon italien* in order to get rid of him quickly."

These plotters surely only existed in Christina's and possibly the Palatines' minds; but the important point is that she apparently believed in them. During most of her life, with the exception of the period between 1647 and 1652, Christina recognized Axel Oxenstierna for what he was, a great and consummate statesman of absolute integrity. Yet in 1644 she told the English Ambassador Whitelocke that during her minority Oxenstierna would have liked to "attain similar office in Sweden" to Cromwell's assumption of the office of Lord Protector, "but was not able to do so." That there was absolutely no truth in this Whitelocke was probably very well aware, but his great admiration for the Chancellor did not prevent the Ambassador from conceiving a hearty dislike for other members of the Oxenstierna clan, a dislike that Christina had also nourished for many years.

This antipathy had already been made evident in Christina's caustic comment on Beate Oxenstierna, who was now the dominant feminine figure at her court, and from her slighting references to her other ladies it does not seem that the young Queen cared for them much more. In this case, to her general impatience with and scorn of women, was probably added Christina's doubts about them all as nominees of the Oxenstierna clan. She was therefore deprived of any possible feminine confidante, such as Maria Euphrosyne later became for a while. Also in this crucial year of 1639 both her Governors died—her father's and her own old friends Axel Banér and Gustavus Horn—as well as her foster-mother, Anna von der Linden. Thus it was against a background of doubt and suspicion, surrounded by an entourage from which all familiar friends but one had disappeared, that Christina's adolescence really began.

The one old friend who remained was John Mathiae and it was now, probably much more than in 1634, that Christina turned to him and to her studies as a means of escape. Some of Mathiae's carefully kept records of Christina's progress between the years 1638 and 1643 have come down to us, showing clearly that classical history formed the basis of her education. It was during these impressionable years that Christina developed an admiration for figures cast in an heroic mould, who acted according to authoritarian and stoic principles—Alexander, Cyrus, Caesar and Scipio were to remain her heroes throughout her life and there is little doubt that Christina identified herself with them. Comparing Mathiae's careful notes (surely a much more reliable source of information) with Christina's own accounts, it is amusing to observe how this taste for grandiloquence was applied also to herself, also that her syllabus, in the early stages at least, was not so formidable as the Queen would lead us to believe. In 1638 (when she was twelve) Christina's religious and general studies included the Books of Moses, the Psalms of David, the Lutheran catechism, Swedish historical documents, "four kinds of arithmetic" and John Holywell's popular paraphrase of Ptolomy's *Almagest* and *Geography*. She was still studying Latin grammar and reading

Aesop's *Fables*, progressing later to Justinus's *History* and the first books of Quintus Curtius and Livy. Sallust and Cicero followed.

In 1639, Christina and her cousin Eleonora (who evidently shared her studies throughout this year, even after her family's departure) were kept busy learning passages from Sallust and reciting them by heart. In July the Queen was introduced to the art of rhetoric by reading Vossius's *Elements* and in December both girls were declaiming speeches from Quintus Curtius; characteristically Christina's choice was Alexander's speech to the ambassadors of Darius.

In this same year Mathiae noted that he began to teach Christina French (the books he mentions are obviously phrase and conversation manuals), providing an interesting comment upon Christina's own statement in her autobiography that "at the age of fourteen I knew all the languages, all the sciences and exercises that they wished to teach me." It seems, however, that her later reputation as a linguist may well have been based on a remarkable facility for picking up languages by ear, a gift which she inherited from her father.

In a synopsis for one of her several projected biographies, which closely resembles her own autobiography and was certainly drafted or inspired by Christina herself, there is a note stating that although she never liked speaking Latin, she knew it well and had learnt it before she could read. Apparently this curious facility caused her preceptor to despair, until Gustavus Adolphus's old tutor told him that the King also possessed this gift. In the same way when the Queen arrived in Italy in 1655 she could speak Italian, but still had difficulty in writing it years later. Christina had known German from infancy, probably thanks to her mother, at the age of six she was already writing letters in it to her father. There were childish mistakes, but right from the start Christina was encouraged to compose her letters herself. This sensible practice was continued as she grew older, so that the recipients could judge her progress.

In 1636, the Queen was writing both in German and Latin to John Casimir, and three years later she had sufficient command of Latin to write a witty and amusing letter. It was absolutely essential that this should be so, for, apart from being the basis of all European education, Latin was still the diplomatic language of the day, though to the disgust of the Francophobe Axel Oxenstierna French was beginning to make headway. Indeed French was to become Christina's preferred language, in which she wrote even to her most intimate Swedish and Italian friends. Her capacity as a linguist is perhaps best illustrated by the fact that in 1643 she was still composing simple letters of condolence in French and writing rather schoolgirlish maxims on patience, constancy and courage. Sixteen years later, however, the Duc de Guise said no one would have believed that she had not been born in Paris.

In 1641 Christina was evidently studying by herself, as there is no further mention of Eleonora in Mathiae's notes. By now she had graduated to Caesar's *Commentaries* and the plays of Terence. Later she was to tackle the advanced poets—Martial, Catullus and Lucan (significantly there is no mention of the Epicurean Horace or the sophisticated Ovid) and Tacitus, Axel Oxenstierna's favourite author. It is worthy of note that in this same year Christina was also reading Camden's *Annals of the Reign of Queen Elizabeth* as well as Justus Lipsius's *Politica*. It was natural that the young Queen should study the reign of another recent, and highly successful, Queen Regnant. It is particularly remarkable because no other near-contemporary work of foreign history is mentioned in Christina's curriculum. It is tempting to wonder if the career of the "Virgin Queen" may not have started a train of thought in Christina's mind, to which later as a good Catholic she did not care to admit, preferring to attribute her own celibacy to more orthodox inspiration rather than to the example of a Protestant Queen. Christina may well also have been secretly jealous of Elizabeth, whose name she sedulously avoids mentioning in her diatribes against the incapacity of women rulers in her own autobiography.

Given the admiration for stoic principles of Axel Oxenstierna and the Swedish intellectuals of the day, Lipsius was another obvious choice for her to read. His editions of Tacitus and Seneca were famous, and so were his own works which reconciled classical stoicism with Christian principles. Lipsius' writings evidently had considerable influence upon Christina. He was a great admirer of Epictetus who also became one of her favourites, together with Marcus Aurelius. It is a measure of the contradictions which were inherent in her character that she managed to combine this taste for the lonely musings of the gentle philosopher-emperor and the spirit of renunciation of the ex-slave, with a heartfelt admiration for such paragons of action as Alexander, Caesar, Cyrus and Scipio Africanus. Christina considered that they were even greater than her father. She later identified herself with her hero in an essay on Alexander, and in dwelling constantly on the glories of her own reign, it seems probable that she hoped she outshone her father just as Alexander had outshone his father, Philip of Macedon.

The Queen's education during these formative years was by no means limited to history and languages living and dead. She was also kept well abreast of current affairs by her governors and Axel Oxenstierna. There are discrepancies between the statements in her autobiography and the notes she added to a memoir on the events of her reign; thus it is uncertain when she first began to be briefed on current affairs. In fact we do not know whether Oxenstierna was keeping her personally informed as early as 1636. According to the autobiography he began to do so in 1636. According to the memoir, from 1639 he was seeing Christina every day for several hours. In her autobiography Christina said: "It was from he himself that I learnt part of all I know of the art of ruling," and with the knowledge of after years she admits "it was one of the greatest men in the world who gave me my first lessons." She continued: "I took great pleasure in hearing him speak, there was no study, game or diversion that I would not quit in order to listen to him. He on his side took great pleasure in teaching me . . . and if I may say so without offending modesty, this great man was forced more than once to admire . . . above all my desire for instruction and my capacity to learn, which he admired without understanding because it is so rare at the age I then was."

Axel Oxenstierna was certainly satisfied with Christina's progress in her studies, but that he did not understand her seems unlikely in view of a statement which he made to the Råd in 1641. Oxenstierna said: "I observe with satisfaction, as God is my witness, that Her Majesty is not like other members of her sex. She is full of heart and good sense, to such an extent that, if she does not allow herself to be corrupted, she raises the highest hopes."

To the worthy members of the Råd the news that their future Queen lacked the frailties usually associated with her sex, must have made reassuring hearing; though there was to come a day when they might well wonder at their former complacency. But already, if they had ears to hear it, the Chancellor had sounded a warning note. What was it that made him "who knew the strength and weakness of every European country," and of men and women as well, use the words "if she does not allow herself to be corrupted"? From the preceding sentence it is evident that it was not mere feminine frivolity he was talking about; could it be that he had already sensed a certain duplicity in Christina, a capacity for intrigue and dissimulation so acute that she could outwit even him in pursuing her own ends?

One of Christina's letters written to John Casimir about this time shows very clearly that not only was she learning how to get her own way with Axel Oxenstierna, but also that she possessed considerably more political finesse than the wily John Casimir himself. It is dated from Stockholm on 3rd April 1641, and was written at the time when the Råd was debating who should take the place on the Regency Council of the High Steward, Gabriel Gustafsson Oxenstierna who had recently died.

Charles Gustavus had summoned John Mathiae to his house in Stockholm to tell him what was afoot, which was that the Råd were debating whether Christina—who was now fifteen—should be asked to select her own candidate, and that in this case she might nominate Charles Gustavus. Christina goes on to explain in her letter that on hearing this she had decided on her reply. She would explain that she appreciated the Råd's affectionate attitude in wanting to give her an opportunity to choose a close relation as one of her guardians, but she did not want to run the risk of doing so because she was sure that John Casimir would not approve. Also she had resolved either to reply that it did not become her to designate her own guardian, or to refer the matter to the Chancellor in the Council; which would please the latter as they would gain Oxenstierna's favour. Or, alternatively, if several names were submitted to her, she would say they were all men of merit and suggest that the candidate should be chosen by lots. This was in fact what happened, and the Council were well pleased with the young Queen's sagacity. But she was worried in case John Casimir, who evidently wanted his son to be nominated, did not appreciate her finesse. So that there should be no mistake about this she wrote: "I hope you will agree with my attitude over Charles Gustav, because if I had nominated him, they (the members of the Regency) would have believed that I had done so in order to know all that happened among them."

The concluding paragraph of her letter makes the situation doubly clear and bears witness to the astuteness of this teenage girl who was able to see further than her uncle: "Your intention [of getting Charles Gustavus elected] is of the best in the world, but you have not reflected enough about it." Then, as a sop to John Casimir, "I hope you will write and tell me your feeling about what I have said above," and she signs herself once again, "the Niece, faithful to the grave, Christina."

By her clever manœuvring Christina gained all round. The new Grand Steward, chosen by lots, was not yet another Oxenstierna but Count Per Brahe; while, in recognition of her political sagacity (one wonders if he knew the whole inside story?) Axel Oxenstierna in the following year obtained the Råd's consent to the Queen's being present at their debates. Some forty years later in an outline of Christina's character (see Note on page 27) there is a note in the Queen's own hand in which, with remarkable candour she states that "her profound dissimulation, which even in her early youth deceived the most astute people, hastened her majority." This, however, did not prevent her from remarking on the following page upon her own "love of truth and aversion to lies." It seems to be true anyway that her remarkable political shrewdness was recognized at an early age, and that the Riksdag even considered recognizing Christina's majority before she was eighteen; but that she refused on the grounds that it was too heavy a burden for her to undertake at the time.

Indeed, although basically Christina's constitution must have been extraordinarily robust to have stood up to the strain which she imposed upon it during the physically and mentally critical period of her adolescence, from time to time it already showed signs of rebellion. When she had pleurisy early in 1637 she was seriously ill. At the end of 1638 even so slight a malady as chicken pox affected her badly, the marks of it being still visible eighteen years later; in 1645 she was again seriously ill, had a relapse and a bad attack of measles. As we have seen, Christina's descriptions of her own way of life must be accepted with a certain amount of caution. Yet Bourdelot's detailed diagnosis of her condition in 1651 (see page 167) endorses the fact that she had been suffering from overstrain for years and confirms her extraordinary personal habits. Christina slept for only three or four hours a night. Food she cared nothing about and would eat anything which was put in front of her, except pork. She had no objection to going without food if necessary and drank very little. When she was older, hours of study and discussion of state affairs filled most of her days, and alternated with violent exercise. She was indifferent to heat and cold, and habitually started her studies in the arctic Swedish winter at four in the morning, taking only a quarter of an hour for her scanty toilet and dressing.

To these self-imposed burdens a serious anxiety was added in the summer of 1640. For some time the Queen Mother's behaviour had been giving both the Regency Council and Christina grave cause for concern. Continual letters of complaint reached them both, and in vain during the summer and autumn of 1639 did they reply, inviting Maria Eleonora to Stockholm to discuss matters. Worse still, a letter of the Queen Mother's to Sweden's arch-enemy the King of Denmark had been intercepted, from which it appeared that Her Majesty wished to leave Sweden and return to her native land. Finally, early in the summer of 1640, after a peremptory summons, the culprit appeared at her daughter's court in floods of tears. Christina reasoned with her mother and in the end dissuaded her from her pressing desire again to take up residence at Nyköping, which was far too convenient for further correspondence with Denmark. With a somewhat suspicious alacrity Maria Eleonora returned to Gripsholm, but all concerned were reassured when they heard that she was to undertake one of her periodic fasts, for which she retired to the seclusion of her own apartment accompanied by only one of her ladies.

By this means Maria Eleonora succeeded in hoodwinking even the head of her household, Marshal Ivar Nilsson, and in putting the rest of her court off their guard. It had evidently never occurred to any of them that so frivolous and ostensibly fragile a woman could get out of the great fortress-like castle. But the Queen Mother's rooms overlooked the garden and the lake, and at dead of night she and her lady-in-waiting, Mlle. von Bülau, let themselves down from the window and were rowed in a boat to the other side of Lake Mälaren. It was a cleverly planned escape, involving a carriage waiting for them on the opposite shore, in which they drove post-haste to Nyköping, nearly fifty miles away. Here they boarded a Danish skiff which took them to the Island of Gotland where they were met by two Danish warships.

On the morning of 30th July all that anyone knew was that the Queen Mother, together with Mlle. von Bülau and two of her gentlemen, had disappeared. Next day Christina wrote urgently to John Casimir telling him that no one had the slightest idea of where her mother had vanished, and would he please come and discuss the situation. In the circumstances probably even Axel Oxenstierna was glad to see him, for the Queen Mother's flight had made Sweden a laughing-stock. So juicy a scandal was sure to go the rounds of Europe then as it would today, and with his family connections in many foreign courts John Casimir might help to put the matter in its true light. For, in addition to all their other troubles, Maria Eleonora was still a good-looking woman—Axel Oxenstierna's admonition to her to learn to grow old gracefully had apparently been the final spark that spurred her to fury and this adventurous escape. This undoubtedly added piquancy to the situation. Few things could have raised more anger and dismay in the Regency Council, and indeed in all Sweden, than the malicious rumours spreading round Europe that Maria Eleonora had fled to Denmark because she was in love with the King, who was sixty-three. The widow of Gustavus Adolphus marry the national enemy! But even if there was no question of marriage, this was precisely where the Queen Mother had taken refuge.

Her continued residence in Denmark gave rise to other rumours, equally ridiculous—that she was planning to marry Christina to the King's son or to one of the De la Gardies in order to avoid her being married off to Axel Oxenstierna's son, and finally that Maria Eleonora intended to give Pomerania back to the Elector of Brandenburg. She can scarcely have been a comfortable guest, and Christian IV of Denmark was probably as relieved as the Swedes when finally she took herself off to Brandenburg. Even here Maria Eleonora was not a welcome guest; with Hohenzollern caution, probably based on his father's tales of her extravagance, the new Elector Frederick William insisted on Sweden providing for his aunt's upkeep. Possibly her disgust at a pension of 30,000 écus a year was the deciding factor which induced the Queen Mother finally to return to Sweden in 1648.

In the meantime, as we have seen, Charles Gustavus was already back in Stockholm in 1641, and from Christina's intrigues it is evident that she and the Palatines were on very close terms indeed. By now the person who undoubtedly interested her most in the family was Charles Gustavus. How could it be otherwise? In childhood her aunt had lost no opportunity of trying to convince Christina that Charles Gustavus would be her ideal husband, and to memories of childhood affection was now added the appearance of a pleasant young man of nineteen, returned to Sweden surrounded by the glamour of foreign travel and, flatteringly, even more attached to herself than before. Naturally their meetings could no longer take place in the free and friendly atmosphere of childhood, but there were willing intermediaries—John Mathiae for one, and when he left the court to become Bishop of Strängnäs in 1643, Maria Euphrosyne acted as postman.

Charles Gustavus was, however, in a difficult position. His family were far from rich and to many, especially the Oxenstiernas, they were foreigners and objects of suspicion. Years before, when John Casimir had asked the Regency Council whether he should bring his children up to be Swedes or Germans, he had received the curt reply to "do as you please." Certainly ever since Christina's accession, even while accepting *faute de mieux* that her Aunt Catherine should become her gouvernante, the Regency had always kept watch on the Palatine family, and now that both Charles Gustavus and Christina were approaching marriageable age their suspicions would have been redoubled. To all this was added the fact that Charles Gustavus held no position in the country and that the government sedulously avoided giving him one.

To Christina the government's hostility and suspicion probably only added to her cousin's attractions, especially as it meant that they had to communicate by devious means. Although afterwards she absolutely denied it, there is no doubt that before she was eighteen Christina was, or believed herself to be, in love with Charles Gustavus. But what were his feelings for her? The fact that their marriage would have been so greatly to his advantage has led many people then and now to conclude that her cousin's show of devotion was purely interested. Due to his ambiguous position, it is probable that Charles Gustavus early learnt to present an impenetrable front of reserve and discretion to the world. But in following his actions, step by step, throughout their entire relationship, it does seem that Charles Gustavus really did love Christina. Even when he finally realized that there was no hope of marriage, he always behaved towards her with affection and gallantry, keeping his word to her in the face of violent provocation.

Right from the beginning of their relationship, Christina's attitude was very different. In spite of her protestations of devotion when she was sixteen and seventeen, her love was of the kind that could face with equanimity two years of separation from the young man whom she then considered to be her fiancé. It is true that, given the hostility of the Regency, there could be no question of marriage until she reached her majority at eighteen. It is also true that Christina personally intervened to get Charles Gustavus a good appointment in the army in Germany with 2,000 écus a year pay. But most girls of sixteen in the throes of their first love-affair would have exerted every effort to keep the object of their affections close at hand, rather than to help him take up a career in a faraway country.

Still, after Charles Gustavus had left for Germany, Christina resolutely refused a politically advantageous offer of marriage from her father's old candidate, her cousin Frederick William who was now Elector of Brandenburg. In view of subsequent events, it is interesting to note that when it was suggested that the young Elector might be persuaded to forsake Calvinism in order to become a good Lutheran and marry her, Christina replied: "The man who forsakes his God cannot inspire confidence in anyone." Frederick William was given a more diplomatic answer by the Regency Council, and apparently still entertained hopes of this highly suitable match. Christina had no doubts on the subject, and the reason for her confidence was Charles Gustavus. In the spring of the following year she was writing to reassure him yet again that "neither the Elector of Brandenburg nor anyone else" could separate them.

Several of Christina's letters to Charles Gustavus written during the spring and summer of 1644 are typically a young girl's love letters, filled with excitement at this secret romance. In them she suggests that either they should correspond in cypher or that he should send his letters to Maria Euphrosyne, putting the initials C.R. both inside and out. She reiterates her absolute confidence in both their feelings, promises eternal love—until death—and says more mundanely that she is prepared to wait for him. None the less these letters show how different were her feelings from those of her fiancé. Whereas Charles Gustavus shows a lover's natural impatience, Christina serenely counsels him that it is never too long to wait for something good. He must gain more experience as a soldier, she must wait till she is Queen in fact, as well as in name.

It did not, however, look as though they would really have so long to wait. Christina would attain her majority on the 8th of December 1644 and Charles Gustavus's natural genius as a soldier soon procured him Marshal Torstensson's approval and the command of a dashing cavalry regiment. Still the young man cannot have been easy in his mind, even if he did not know that the purposeful Frederick William, probably egged on by Maria Eleonora, was thinking of copying Gustavus Adolphus and paying an incognito visit to Sweden. If he had done this, would Frederick William have been equally successful? He was now a handsome young man of twenty-two, and the ability that later earned him the title of the "Great Elector" might have enabled him to carry the day with a girl of seventeen, or so it might be imagined. But the circumstances that ended Christina's and Charles Gustavus's romance were not to be so straightforward as that.

Meanwhile Sweden's political situation had been further complicated by another war, although this was almost a diversion when compared with the one which she had been waging in Germany since 1632. In December 1643, Swedish forces under Torstensson invaded Denmark from the south and by January all Holstein and Jutland had been overrun. One of the reasons for this attack, which was given in the Swedish manifesto issued in that month, was the affront to the memory of Gustavus Adolphus afforded by the part which King Christian IV of Denmark had played in Maria Eleonora's escape, also the insult to Queen Christina by taking her mother away from her. But the real causes for the war lay in Denmark's dangerous political isolation at that time and in Axel Oxenstierna's conviction that "Denmark is not less inimical to us than Austria, and the worse enemy because she is nearer."

In February Marshal Horn invaded the southern provinces of the Scandinavian peninsula which still belonged to Denmark. Traversing Skania he reached the shores of the Sound, but was unable to take the key city of Malmö. A decisive Swedish victory was frustrated by the unusual clemency of the season. There was no bridge of ice to the Danish islands which would have enabled Torstensson and Horn to join forces for an attack on Copenhagen, and Denmark still had superiority at sea. Here the sixty-seven-year-old King Christian recovered something of the daring of his youth, forcing a Dutch fleet to retreat and nearly succeeding in cutting off a Swedish one in the fjord of Kiel; however, on 1st August, Wrangel succeeded in extricating what was left of the Swedish ships.

Sweden's surprise attack on Denmark had failed to carry all before it as had been hoped, while her commitments in Germany prevented her from throwing a decisive force into the field. Stagnation began to set in after an imperial army, dispatched to attack Torstensson in the rear, failed in its objective owing to the incompetence of its commander. Even the victory of the combined Dutch and Swedish fleets over the Danish one in October 1644 failed to alter the situation, as King Christian still disposed of sufficient ships to prevent Copenhagen being attacked from the sea. In this state of deadlock the partisans of peace in Sweden were able increasingly to make their pressure felt. Such was the state of the Danish war in the months immediately preceding 8th December 1644, the date when Christina would attain her majority.

The twelve years which had passed since the death of Gustavus Adolphus had witnessed the nadir of the Protestant hopes in the débâcle of the battle of Nördlingen in September 1634, but since then there had been a gradual revival of the Swedish position in

Germany. Axel Oxenstierna admitted to the second sleepless night of a lifetime when the news of Nördlingen reached him at Frankfurt on the Main. During the next few weeks he was forced to watch helplessly while his German allies flocked to Richelieu for aid, while what was left of the Swedish armies withdrew 250 miles north to Magdeburg and Halberstadt. But Oxenstierna's political judgment did not fail him even now, when in November, acting in Queen Christina's name, he refused to ratify the penal terms of the Treaty of Paris which Richelieu had extracted from the rest of the allies.

Years afterwards Christina wrote that one of the political maxims she had learnt from Oxenstierna was to "try and gain time, which affords us better counsel." In the winter of 1634–35, Axel Oxenstierna had indeed played for time, time which would bring home to Richelieu the fact that the Swedish defeat meant not only the fall of an hitherto embarrassingly successful ally, but also a threat to French security. Six months later the Cardinal had realized that the Spanish victors of Nördlingen, now garrisoning the Netherlands, had brought a new aggressive spirit right up to the northern borders of France; while the same spirit of Hapsburg resurgence seemed likely to lead to a Spanish invasion of Provence.

In April 1635 Richelieu and Axel Oxenstierna met in Paris. It was diamond cut diamond. Oxenstierna afterwards said: "The French manner of negotiating is very strange and depends much on finesse." Richelieu described him as "*un peu Gothique et beaucoup finoise*." But Gothic or not, by the Treaty of Compiègne signed on 30th April, Oxenstierna got far better terms than he would have done six months earlier. In exchange for control of the Rhine from Breisach to Strasbourg, France agreed to accept Sweden as an equal ally, to make no peace or truce without her, and to declare war on Spain.

It was a turning point in the war which had now been raging since 1618; although another thirteen years were to pass before the Peace of Westphalia finally rang the curtain down upon the tragic scene in Germany, with the Treaty of Compiègne the last act had begun. France's declaration of war on Spain and her renewed alliance with Sweden altered the whole situation, though inevitably with her superior resources France became the paymaster and the dominant partner. This new alignment also brought about a change in the opposite camp, transforming the Emperor Ferdinand II's projected Peace of Prague into a new coalition for war. The announcement of its terms followed shortly upon France's declaration of war on Spain in May 1636, and finally resulted in the Emperor's obtaining the support of all Germany except the Calvinist states of Hesse-Cassel, Brunswick-Luneburg and the dispossessed Elector Palatine.

The grouping of the combatants had, however, by now ceased to have any relation to religious aims, the struggle had become a fight for supremacy between the House of Hapsburg and the House of Bourbon. It was waged almost exclusively by vast armies of mercenaries drawn from every country in Europe—from Ireland to Turkey. With their hordes of camp followers these motley multitudes had almost become powers in themselves—Banér referred to his own army as "this widespread state." But they were states liable to mutiny, only relatively subservient to their paymasters and, like Richelieu's famous dictum on Spain, they resembled "a cancer which gnaws and eats all the body to which it is attached." Such were the forces that for the next twelve years vied with one another to obtain supremacy in Germany.

For year after weary year, the fortunes of battle swayed irregularly from one side to the other, the only real vanquished being the miserable inhabitants of the country over which the armies fought. It is not surprising that for centuries afterwards the Thirty Years War lived on in German minds as the epitome of destruction, and that it was believed that three-quarters of the population had perished in the holocaust. Modern historians are more conservative in their estimates, but even they calculate that whereas the population of the German Empire (including Alsace but not the Netherlands or Bohemia) probably numbered twenty-one millions in 1618, by 1648 it was reduced to thirteen and a half millions.

Though these figures speak for themselves, they cannot conjure up the picture of horror and human degradation afforded by contemporary eye-witness accounts. One of the most striking of these was written by a member of the English Ambassador's suite who went to the Electoral meeting at Regensburg in the autumn of 1636. He describes how every town, village, and castle along the Rhine from Cologne to Frankfurt was "battered, pillaged and burnt," and how in the villages which were not actually deserted, people fled at the Embassy's approach, believing them to be yet another band of marauding soldiers. They saw starved children sitting among the ruins and heard that the people were reduced to eating grass—corpses were often found with it in their mouths. Even when the Ambassador tried to alleviate what misery he could, he found that "divers poor people lying on the dunghills . . . [were] scarce able to crawl for to receive His Excellency's alms." This is but one man's view of scenes which were repeated the length and breadth of Germany, where plague and pestilence had taken their deadly toll and cannibalism was widespread. Cases were reported from Alsace, Fulda, Coburg, Worms and Zweibrücken. In the latter town a woman admitted to having cooked and eaten her own child.

It must have seemed to the wretched inhabitants of Germany that the war would never end, but the spring of 1643 brought a decisive battle at last. On 19th May the French defeated the Spaniards at Rocroy, wiping out the veteran Spanish infantry which was the backbone of the army that had won the day at Nördlingen. The Emperor Ferdinand III saw the writing on the wall, and on 23rd June 1643 he authorized the opening of peace negotiations with France and Sweden; the epilogue to the drama of the Thirty Years War had begun.

Sometimes, a particular incident—a battle, a trial or a *cause célèbre*—lights up for a short space of time a whole period of history, revealing a way of life and its manners and modes, its follies and its cruelties, but more rarely its greatness or its strength. The four years of negotiations which were to produce the Peace of Westphalia and the end of the Thirty Years War was one of these catalytic episodes, in which we see the seventeenth-century attitude to life—the life of the privileged few as opposed to the voiceless starving multitudes—presented on the stage of history for our observation. As in some elegant drawing-room comedy the players go through all the complicated motions of contemporary etiquette, protocol and intrigue; we, not they, are conscious of the sinister noises off, of the galloping hooves of the horsemen of the Apocalypse. But war, pestilence and death did not hurry the deliberations of the delegates. They reached their rendezvous of

Münster and Osnabrück in March 1644; the Congress only opened officially on 4th December and serious negotiations did not begin until eleven months later.

On their arrival, the French representatives Claude de Mesmes, Marquis d'Avaux and Abel Servien, Marquis de Sablé, were horrified to find not only the Imperial but also the Spanish delegate waiting for them. France's peace plans did not include a settlement with Spain, so the French refused to treat with the Spanish delegate on the grounds that his credentials were wrongly drawn up—they referred to the King of Spain as sovereign of Navarre and Portugal and as Duke of Catalonia. Yet all the world knew that their own King Louis XIV (aged six) ruled over the Navarre and Catalonia, and in his eyes John of Braganza was the legitimate King of Portugal. Even if these weighty considerations could be tactfully smoothed out, the French delegates had another diplomatic card up their sleeves—the knotty question of who took precedence—the chief representative of the Most Christian King of France, the Duc de Longueville, or that of the Most Catholic King of Spain, the Count Guzman de Penaranda? This problem was so skilfully manœuvred that throughout the entire four years of the Westphalian negotiations these gentlemen never met; most conveniently, no form of protocol could be agreed upon because Richelieu's successor, Cardinal Mazarin, had no desire for peace with Spain.

Not very surprisingly in these circumstances, six months passed before the order of precedence for seating the 135 delegates round the tables at Münster and Osnabrück could be arranged. They could not meet at the same place because the papal Mediator, Cardinal Flavio Chigi (afterwards Pope Alexander VII), refused to countenance the presence of heretics. So the Swedish delegation, together with those of the German Protestant states, assembled at Osnabrück, while Sweden's ally, France, sat down with the Imperial delegation and the delegations of the German Catholics at Münster, where peace plans between France and Spain and Spain and the United Provinces were also discussed. In fact Spain and France had an interest in both camps, Spain as an Imperial ally in the negotiations between the Empire, France and Sweden, and France as the ally of the Dutch United Provinces in theirs with Spain.

Since she had the resounding victory of Rocroy to her credit, France at first held the advantage, hence her Fabian tactics. Leaving the preliminary protocolaire skirmishings to his official subordinates, the Duc de Longueville nonchalantly proceeded to lay out a garden at Münster and summoned his wife to join him. Even after the official opening of the Congress in December 1644, further pretexts for delay were found in the characters of the Imperial delegates—one was a playboy, the other (though an able lawyer) was not sufficiently noble to be accepted as representing His Imperial Majesty's intentions. By these means the French avoided committing themselves to serious negotiations until November 1645.

But evasive tactics between contending powers were not alone causing delay; to them were added jealousy and suspicion between allies (particularly bitter in the case of the French and Swedes and the French and Dutch) and even the personal hatreds of fellow delegates. Among the French d'Avaux and Servien were rarely on speaking terms, and a more veiled but no less bitter hostility existed between the Swedes—John Oxenstierna and Adler Salvius.

As might be expected, both Swedish delegates were Oxenstierna nominees, but during the winter of 1644–45 the acute Salvius must rapidly have sensed that another power was rising in Sweden; one moreover whose aims were to coincide with his own for obtaining peace as soon as possible. Cautiously at first, because they ran counter to those of Axel Oxenstierna, these aims were revealed by the young Queen who now enjoyed the full powers of sovereignty, having reached her majority on 8th December 1644. Few moments in European history have been less propitious for the debut of an eighteen-year-old girl as a Queen Regnant than the last years of the Thirty Years War, which has been summed up by one of its greatest historians, C. V. Wedgwood, as "morally subversive, economically destructive, socially degrading, confused in its causes, devious in its course, futile in its result . . . the outstanding example in European history of meaningless conflict." The war had cost her father his life and her country untold suffering but, with a mind unshackled by the claims of the past, Christina saw that Sweden's greatest need was peace and, inexperienced as she was, she had the will to pursue it through the labyrinth of devious diplomacy and shifting interests. However posterity may judge Christina's subsequent actions, and even her own motives at this moment, by her decision to opt for peace the young Queen earned the gratitude of the voiceless suffering millions in Europe and in her own country.

CHAPTER 3

Queen Regnant: The First Years 1644–1648

On 22nd November 1644, the members of the Regency Council and the Råd were received in solemn audience by Queen Christina in order to give an account of their twelve years' stewardship. To these men, grown old and grizzled in the service of their country, it probably seemed that this was a pure formality, that they were paying courteous tribute to the daughter of Gustavus Adolphus and the young girl who in a few days would be their sovereign in law as well as name, but that for several years to come, or at least until she married, the reality of power would remain in their own hands. A diet of the Riksdag had been in session in Stockholm since October, and on 7th December Christina made her first speech from the throne and took the sovereign's oath upon reaching her majority. She promised to maintain the Lutheran religion and its rites, uphold the Råd, conserve all privileges and to observe the form of government approved by the Estates.

This must have been the first time that many members of the Riksdag had actually seen their Queen. What they saw was a slight, rather pale young girl, with fair hair hanging to her shoulders, and a nervous, serious face. However, they would have been reassured to see that her broad forehead and prominent nose bore a marked resemblance to her father's, though the small decided chin and the firm line of the upper lip were all her own. Of all those present, probably only Axel Oxenstierna and the

Queen's uncle, the Grand Admiral Carl Carlsson Gyllenhielm, knew that these betokened a much stronger and more complex character than might be expected in a young girl. True, for a year and more Christina had been present at the meetings of the Råd, but she had been content to fill an observer's role and it is doubtful if the worthy senators had an inkling of what lay behind the youthful gravity of her demeanour.

During the first few months after her majority, Christina felt her way with caution. The matter of most urgent political importance was the opening of peace negotiations with Denmark; they began on 25th February 1645, at the little town of Brömsebro, on the borders of the provinces of Småland and Blekinge, which was then the Danish frontier. This was not simply a matter of interest to the two powers concerned. Cardinal Mazarin himself had intervened, sending M. de la Thuillerie as Ambassador to Sweden during the summer of 1644. M. de la Thuillerie's mission was to act as a mediator between the two belligerents and to bring to an end as soon as possible this, from the French point of view, minor campaign which threatened to affect Sweden's efficacy as an ally in the main struggle in Germany. It was not altogether an easy mission, as the Swedish attack against Denmark had originally been launched in the hope of wresting from the Danes the three southern provinces of the Scandinavian peninsula which still remained in their power and prevented Sweden from having direct access to the all-important Sound.

In the event the provinces were finally liberated in 1658, but meanwhile, after the high hopes of two years ago and months of fruitless struggle, it was a bitter pill for Swedish pride to have to abandon the attempt at their conquest. We do not know how soon the French Ambassador discovered that he had an ally in the young Queen; but that with remarkable diplomacy and tact, she was pursuing the same ends as himself is evident from the letters which Christina wrote to Axel Oxenstierna in the spring and summer of 1645, when the Chancellor was engaged in the negotiations at Brömsebro.

The first of these letters is dated from Stockholm on 12th April 1645, and although it begins: "Monsieur the much-honoured Chancellor of the Realm" and ends: "your very affectionate Christina," it also includes the significant phrase: "I can judge by your procedure that you have completely understood my will." However, having clearly underlined that their relationship was no longer that of a regent and ward, but now that of sovereign and minister, Christina went on to stress how well she understood the difficulties with which Oxenstierna was faced. The crux of the question was that while it was evident that the Danes wanted peace and were prepared to make sacrifices to obtain it, how much could Sweden expect to get in the way of reparations and guarantees? Even while saying that "an open war is preferable to a badly assured peace" Christina urged Oxenstierna to seize the present opportunity, as otherwise they might be blamed by posterity for not having made peace as soon as possible.

When the second letter was written on 20th June, the pressure of the peace party in Sweden had evidently become much stronger, which provided the Queen with an excellent reason for urging Oxenstierna to conclude the peace. Although she protested that she was entirely in accordance with his views and that "unless we have real surety it is better not to think of peace," most of the letter was devoted to explaining that the majority of the Råd "have feelings quite different from yours and mine . . . there are some who would give their hands to end the war." Further, she continued, failure to conclude the peace would be blamed upon her youth and inexperience, and worse still her ambition and "desire to dominate" that prevented her from taking wise counsel. Writing four days later from Uppsala, Christina returned to the charge, adding that not only she, but Oxenstierna as well, would be accused by Swedes and foreigners alike of "unbounded ambition founded on injustice and the desire to dominate" if they did not accept the terms offered by Denmark. The situation was further complicated by the Dutch having sent a fleet of forty ships into the Sound without declaring their intentions, and there were fears of Polish reactions.

Although Sweden was not able to enforce all her original claims, the Treaty of Brömsebro, which was finally signed in August, was a Swedish diplomatic victory which diminished Danish pre-eminence in Scandinavia. The blow to Danish prestige was such that the King is said to have thrown the treaty documents in the face of his minister, Corfitz Ulfeld, who had negotiated it. By its terms Sweden had acquired outright the Baltic Islands of Gotland

and Ösel and the provinces of Jämtland and Härjedalen (on what is now the Norwegian border), while for a period of thirty years she was to hold the province of Halland on the Sound, as a guarantee of her traditional freedom from paying dues in the Sound and Belts.

Christina and Oxenstierna had every right to be satisfied with the success of the negotiations of the last six months, and the Queen signalized this by creating him Count of Södermöre and making an oration in his honour. M. de la Thuillerie must also have been satisfied with the peace and the progress he was making in gaining the confidence of the young Queen; not always a very easy or grateful task. That he had succeeded, however, may be guessed by reading between the lines of Christina's letter to Oxenstierna in which she mentions the bad impression it would make abroad if peace were delayed. This is confirmed by the fact that the Queen even suggested that a day's holiday should be held in order not only to celebrate the peace of Brömsebro but also the victory of the French army at Allerheim. Christina's suggestion was all the more remarkable because at that time Sweden was profoundly mistrustful of French secret peace-negotiations with Bavaria; there had been stormy scenes in the Råd over French disloyalty to Sweden on this very matter.

Both this suggestion of Christina's and an episode in her relations with M. de la Thuillerie, show that the prim young ward of the Regency Council was beginning to develop in a totally unexpected way now that she was Queen. The Råd must have been more than a little annoyed by her suggestion of celebrating the victory of those perfidious French, but the idea could at least be put down to a young girl's political inexperience. Not so poor M. de la Thuillerie's embarrassing audience with Her Majesty when she suggested that some of her ladies should sing for him in French. Sing they did, without batting an eyelid, the most appalling bawdy soldier's ditty, of which they obviously did not understand a word. From Christina's subsequent history we can be certain that the latter incident was deliberately provocative (she probably coached the girls herself). M. de la Thuillerie, however, must have been very much of a diplomat and have extricated himself from this highly embarrassing situation with credit, for he got his reward.

The Queen now began to urge her unwilling Government to appoint a new minister in Paris, where the post had been vacant since March. This was the first indication of Christina's interest in France, leading to her subsequent pro-French policy that brought her into collision with Oxenstierna and had such a profound influence upon her own development. Some indication of what that development was going to be also emerges from the Queen's protection of the scapegrace but attractive Scots adventurer, Mark Duncan, who had adopted the high-sounding name of de Cerisantes; he was appointed Swedish Chargé d'Affaires in France in 1645. Duncan de Cerisantes not only involved himself in brawls and disreputable love affairs, but later actually deserted his diplomatic post in Paris. One would have expected the pupil of Axel Oxenstierna and John Mathiae to have dismissed the rogue with ignominy. Not so Christina, who actually offered him a post in the Swedish army. The explanation lies in the fact that the culprit was an exceedingly attractive and plausible rascal—a born bohemian, a poet of sorts and incorrigibly quarrelsome, but endowed with all the panache of a man of his type. Possibly because it was a type with which Christina had never come in contact during her severe upbringing, it seems to have held an irresistible appeal for the bohemian and the rebel which until now had lain hidden in the Queen's own character. In any case the fact remains that she, whose powers of dissimulation could outwit an Oxenstierna, was herself completely taken in by such adventurers. Duncan de Cerisantes was an insignificant incident in Christina's early life—he soon queered his own pitch—but the Queen's patronage of him, together with her outrageous behaviour to de la Thuillerie, are the first indications of the emergence of that other Christina who would in time shock the whole of Europe.

There is evidence, however, that although she was enjoying her first taste of power, Christina also suffered from the strain of the excitement and responsibility. Evidently she had not forgotten the tension of this period when many years later in Rome she annotated the synopsis for her biography. After a reference to the Treaty of Brömsebro she added in her own hand: "The Queen was so ill as to be in danger of her life from the great exhaustion and application of dealing with affairs, and after she had recovered she had a relapse and fell for the second time seriously ill with measles." It was not only the strain of political affairs that was telling on Christina's health, already in 1645 she was beginning to feel the effects of that emotional crisis which was to make it and the following year the turning point in her private life and to alter her whole existence.

When Charles Gustavus returned from Germany in 1645 he found a great change in Christina; the loving cousin had disappeared and been replaced by a rather aloof young woman who was very conscious of her duties as Queen Regnant. Charles Gustavus had himself inevitably developed a good deal during the months in Germany, but curiously the dashing young cavalry commander—whose life on campaign had not been exactly celibate—showed a marked diffidence when it came to courting the cousin who had secretly declared herself his devoted fiancée little more than a year before. In view of Charles Gustavus's impenetrable character, it is difficult to decide whether this attitude was dictated by political caution and an eye to the main chance, or a lover's fear of provoking a definite rebuff. But in any case the situation which he found upon his return would have given a much more impetuous young man cause to think.

The court was buzzing with gossip about the marked favour which the Queen was showing her new Colonel of the Guard, who was none other than the old friend of Charles Gustavus's childhood and university days—Magnus De la Gardie, recently returned from the Grand Tour and the Danish War. As the son of the Grand Marshal Jacob De la Gardie, Magnus would naturally have expected to receive some appointment at court, but not, in his early twenties and so swiftly after his sojourn abroad, one of such importance and which brought him continually into personal contact with the Queen. However, as the gossips were well aware, on both sides Magnus was descended from families whose members had held an extraordinary fascination for the Wasas. His grandfather Pontus had been a mere soldier of fortune taken prisoner by the Swedes in the Danish war of the last century, who entered the service of Eric XIV in 1556 and made such good use of his native Languedoc charm as to become a friend and favourite both of this king and his successor John III. The services he rendered to the latter as a soldier and a diplomat were in the end rewarded by his marrying John's illegitimate daughter Sigrid. In the next generation Jacob, who was one of the most distinguished generals of the day, was entrusted by Charles IX with Gustavus Adolphus's military education; he ended by marrying his young pupil and cousin's great love, Ebba Brahe, the most beautiful woman and richest heiress in Sweden.

To those with long memories and a romantic turn of mind, therefore, Magnus's very evident fascination for the nineteen-year-old Christina did not seem so surprising. All the more so because he was a handsome young man with long fair hair, a moustache clipped in the latest fashion, and endowed with a cosmopolitan polish and social poise rare in Sweden at that time, which had recently won him signal favour at the French court from Mazarin and the Queen Mother herself.

However as the months passed and Christina's preoccupation with Magnus became increasingly obvious, so that few people doubted that she was in love with him, a small family group including Charles Gustavus and Christina herself knew that Magnus did not return her feeling and was really in love with her cousin Maria Euphrosyne, to whom he had become engaged not long after his return. This would have been a blow to any young woman, but to Christina whose natural pride had been fostered since infancy, and who had inevitably been surrounded by the sycophancy with which the seventeenth century surrounded royalty let alone a Queen Regnant, the realization that this was so must have been a bitter shock. It was no longer a question of sentimental attachment between adolescents, but of the first man to whom Christina had been attracted as a woman, and although she was the Queen she had failed to make any impression on him. Though vain in other respects, Christina was far too intelligent to have any illusions about her own appearance. She took the line of scorning such things, but now for the first time realized that no woman can do so.

In her emotional crisis Christina's almost unbounded pride came to her aid—was she not later to say that she could have taken her pick among the kings and princes of Europe? She took a step which set the gossips talking even more furiously, but which removed Magnus from her side for seven months. In the spring of 1646 she announced his appointment as her Ambassador

Extraordinary to France. For a young man in his twenties it looked like yet another sign of extravagant royal favour, but in opposition to Axel Oxenstierna (with whom she was no longer on good terms) Christina wanted to cement the French alliance and of all the nobility Magnus was the man most calculated to appeal to the French court. To a naturally chauvinist race the mere fact that Magnus was descended from a distinguished French family counted for much—his grandfather Pontus had been born an Escoperier of Caunes and his *nom-de-guerre* of De la Gardie was derived from an ancestral fief. Pontus himself had served on diplomatic missions to France and the Swedish branch of the family had never lost touch with their relatives in Languedoc, so much so that today in the province a rich and powerful man is dubbed a "Pontus." When to these flatteringly successful French expatriate origins were added Magnus's own good looks and charm, his transparent admiration for all things French and his favour with the Queen, there was little doubt that he would be *persona gratissima* at the French court. From this purely superficial point of view Christina's choice was therefore an excellent one. But the shrewd French diplomatists were quick to spot something that Christina in her emotional state failed to see, which was that Magnus was no political genius and even lacked a decisive character—deficiencies which probably made him even more welcome to so subtle a negotiator as Mazarin.

Magnus's absence probably did much to lighten the tension of the situation, though it is evident from Christina's letters that she took great pains to ensure that his mission was a personal success. This can, however, be partly accounted for by the fact that it was her own first personal essay in foreign politics on a grand scale and that in sending an ambassador to Paris, let alone Magnus, she was running counter to the views of Axel Oxenstierna and his very powerful following. These same reasons can be adduced for the warmth of her welcome on Magnus's return, but there is little doubt that her emotional stress must have been heightened by the knowledge that Magnus's and Maria Euphrosyne's marriage was to take place shortly, and was indeed celebrated with great pomp at the end of March 1647.

Christina's attitude to Magnus was in her own time and has ever since been regarded as a mystery. In the circumstances it is not surprising that both then and afterwards there have been many who believed that they were lovers. If they had been, or rather if Magnus had reciprocated Christina's feelings, then history might have been different. As it was, Magnus became the first of a series of favourites, and owing to his position and because he shared the Queen's tastes and political views he lasted longer than most. For he had many successors—those flamboyant young adventurers with an eye to the main chance who gathered round Christina both in Sweden and in Italy—who are also supposed to have been her lovers. Though we know from her own letters that in the latter country, at any rate, she was passionately in love with someone else. Apart from one note, difficult of interpretation, there is no direct evidence of this kind of attachment having existed between her and any of her favourites, though her blind indulgence of their escapades gave a totally different impression. Towards the end of her reign the libertine atmosphere of her court, combined with the Queen's delight in shocking people, also gave European gossip plenty to work upon. Christina's partiality for Duncan de Cerisantes revealed this tendency early and his fall from grace, occasioned by his furious protestations to the Queen against Magnus's appointment as Ambassador to France, was the first example of a pattern which was to be repeated in the future.

Maria Euphrosyne's engagement to Magnus deprived Christina of the one person of her own sex and age with whom she had been on intimate terms. It was about this time that she found a substitute whose influence on her endured through the years. Some time in 1644 or early 1645, a beautiful young girl appeared at court for the first time; her name was Ebba Sparre. She was the daughter of Lars Erikson Sparre, a member of the Råd who died in 1644, leaving his daughter in the Queen's charge. Ebba became a lady-in-waiting but, unlike the rest of that race of beings for whom up to now Christina had shown nothing but scorn, the gentleness of this melancholy beauty evidently appealed to the Queen. At this crucial period in her life Christina had been at one stroke deprived of the man who fascinated her and of her old confidante with whom she had had an intimate friendship dating from childhood. In the circumstances, the normal reaction of a pretty young woman, conscious of her own physical attraction, would have been to turn to some other man and on the rebound to have replaced Magnus by some more willing admirer. But Christina seems to have been innately conscious of her own lack of sexual appeal* so now, with all the added intensity engendered by unreciprocated love, she found consolation in the companionship of the gentle and affectionate Ebba—or Belle as she soon came to call her.

Such a situation is familiar to modern psychologists as one of the initial stages in the appearance of lesbian tendencies, to which girls with a neurotic family background such as Christina's are particularly prone. Her tomboyishness and aggressiveness in childhood and adolescence constitute another indication of her propensity in this direction, which all-unwittingly her governors had encouraged by fulfilling Gustavus Adolphus's instructions for her education. The adolescent romance with Charles Gustavus and the separation before it could develop further and Christina could reach full sexual consciousness, also form part of this pattern. As we have seen, at this stage of her life she welcomed the idea of marrying Charles Gustavus when they were older; but she had no objection to being separated from him and did not wish for an early marriage.

With Charles Gustavus Christina was content to wait. Her feelings for Magnus were very different, and although Magnus continued to be showered with honours and to be the favourite *en titre* at court, by giving her consent to his marriage to Maria Euphrosyne Christina had put him beyond her own reach. This curious situation (of which something of a parallel is to be found in the life of Elizabeth of England who, when scandal made her own marriage to Robert Dudley impossible, offered him to her cousin Mary Queen of Scots) gave rise to much contemporary gossip and subsequent hypothesis, including the romantic fable that Axel Oxenstierna had revealed to Christina that Magnus was

* In fact in the outline of Christina's character she had said she "hated mirrors because they had nothing agreeable to show her," but further on insisted upon her "good taste in dress." Evidently she was not devoid of feminine coquetry—later at the French court her addiction to bows and ribbons and liberal use of face powder were noticed—but even in that age of fulsome compliments to royalty there is no record at this time of any man, except the unfortunate Charles, being attracted to her as a woman.

really her father's bastard. Although this is to be discounted absolutely, in the circumstances it is understandable that such a tale should have arisen. Even after Magnus's marriage, Christina continued to show an extreme partiality for him and remained on friendly terms with Maria Euphrosyne. Much of this attitude can be explained by the fact that Magnus was politically useful to Christina, and in private life his good looks, manners and cosmopolitan tastes appealed to her, while in both spheres, politically and privately, they shared an enthusiasm for all things French. Even so, the complete absence of "the woman scorned" seems to indicate that Christina's affections, after the initial shock of Magnus's defection, were increasingly engaged elsewhere.

In December 1646 the Queen was twenty, an age when most women of the period, let alone royalty, had been married for some time, and Swedes naturally supposed that Christina would do the same. In her intimate circle, however, there was at least one person who evidently knew that the Queen already entertained an aversion for marriage; this was Carl Carlsson Gyllenhielm, Christina's uncle and closest living relative apart from her mother, who had now been absent for five years. Earlier in the year Gyllenhielm had written to Christina urging her to marry Charles Gustavus. This was a natural step on the part of a man who had always been friendly with the Palatines and who shared their suspicions of the Swedish nobility's hostility to the monarchy. But a clear indication that her uncle knew something of Christina's dilemma, at a time when her duty alike to her country and her dynasty indicated that she should marry as soon as possible in order to produce an heir, is that he had already advised her that if she married and had no children, or did not marry at all, she should take timely action to designate a certain family (he meant the Palatines) as her successors.

Such advice given to a girl of twenty by her closest male relative, and one moreover who was a proud if illegitimate member of the house of Wasa, is a startling revelation of her uncle's awareness of Christina's mental and physical problems. For the crucial year of 1645 had also brought with it a physical crisis. The illness mentioned by the Queen herself as occurring in that year was no passing indisposition; this is clear from her physician Bourdelot's report written seven years later. In it he describes the physiological symptoms from which Christina then began to suffer each month. In the contemporary state of medical knowledge these symptoms might well have been regarded as being prejudicial to childbearing, especially in view of her mother's medical history in this respect. They included appalling pains in the left hypochondriac area (part of the abdomen beneath the ribs), sickness, severe headaches, fever, fainting and even convulsions. Seventeenth-century diagnosis attributed them to the heat and dryness of her "humours," and it is interesting to note that "heat and dryness" were considered to be masculine attributes as opposed to the "cold and wetness" of women. Today Christina's symptoms would be associated with spastic colitis, and it is true that the appalling contemporary diet of highly spiced and salted foods together with the lack of liquids, the irregular hours of meals and sleep, and the strain of long hours of study to which she had subjected herself since childhood would have rendered her prone to it. But the incidence of this complaint is practically limited to highly-strung, nervous people, particularly intellectuals, and it is also far from uncommon among homosexuals. Thus its appearance in Christina's case at a moment of great emotional strain is not to be wondered at.

The monthly reappearance of these alarming symptoms may well have been one of the causes of Christina's evident horror of childbearing. She showed a strong repulsion for the sight of pregnant women and on one occasion she said she could as easily "bear a Nero as an Augustus"—though her fear of giving birth to a monster might also have stemmed from superstition, awareness of her own curious appearance at birth and her deformity. There is all the same only one occasion upon which Christina is known to have shown affection for a child, and that when she was an old woman. These are mental attitudes which any doctor or psychiatrist today would expect to find in a woman of lesbian tendencies. It is illuminating to note that the medicine of Christina's own day, with its theory of humours based on classical medicine, also diagnosed her as a masculine type.

It is unlikely that Christina's relationship with Belle aroused much attention for some time—though it looks as if it was not lost upon her uncle Carl Gyllenhielm—owing to the much more spectacular favours shown to Magnus. But as the years passed and Belle remained, even after she had married, almost as the Queen's shadow, while the men favourites came and went, in the end the relationship caused covert comment among the more sophisticated in Sweden and scandal abroad. Christina's increasing delight in shocking people did much to foster this, especially towards the end of her reign. At this time she actually introduced Belle to the puritan English Ambassador as her "bed fellow," adding that her mind was as beautiful as her body. Given the customs of the time there was nothing odd in the Queen's sharing her bed with another woman, as her father had done this with Axel Banér both before and after his marriage—no one would have ever suspected either of them of homosexuality. But with the much more sophisticated Imperial Ambassador, Montecuccoli, Christina even said that she was in love with Belle, though this was done in a joking manner during a conversation in which she mocked at serious subjects like religion.

Whether Christina's being "in love" with Belle was a passionate friendship of the type that was fashionable among contemporary blue-stockings, or whether it was a lesbian relationship in the full sense of the term, is something which we will never know for certain. But in the eighteenth century, when homosexuality was much more common, the latter interpretation was put upon their relationship. A collection of letters entitled *Lettres Secrètes de Christine aux personnages illustres de son siècle* was published in Geneva in 1761; it included several faked letters of unmistakably lesbian content. However, one genuine letter that Christina wrote to Belle in her own hand still exists. Written from Rome in 1656, it begins: "Oh, how happy I would be if it was permitted for me to see you, Belle, but I am condemned to the fate of loving you always, esteeming you always and never seeing you." Further on appear the words: "Did I deceive myself when I believed that I was the person whom you loved best?" The whole letter is on this theme, no news or comment on other events appears and, even allowing for the extravagant style of writing of the day, it is difficult not to believe that this is a love-letter in the ordinary sense.

The letter, with an apocryphal addition, and two others believed to have been written by Christina to Belle, together with many genuine official letters and documents, were published by Arckenholtz in 1751. The earliest of these letters was dated from Brussels in 1655, about a year after Christina had last seen Belle. Apart from a rather dubious postscript, its style is so similar to that of the Rome letter that there can be little doubt that it is genuine. The same applies to the third letter, dated from Pesaro on 27th March 1657. This includes two particularly significant passages: "A friendship which has been tried by three years' absence should not be suspect to you, if you have not forgotten the rights that you have over me, and if you remember that it is already twelve years that I have been in possession of your love." Further on, when reminding Belle that she could always count on her, Christina wrote the words "remember the power that you have over me." These are guarded phrases, but it is difficult to doubt that for the writer and the recipient they had a very special personal meaning, more particularly because in expressing her love for Belle in these letters, Christina uses almost exactly the same turns of phrase as she was later to employ to the one man with whom she is known to have been passionately in love.

It is worthy of note that all three letters were written at times when, in spite of protests of present happiness, Christina had reason to feel lonely and depressed. For all we know there may have been, and probably were, other letters written on happier occasions. It is doubtful, however, that they would have been more revealing, as Christina well knew that letters can be intercepted, let alone read by the bearer (the Pesaro letter was delivered by a friend or acquaintance). These three letters do, however, indicate that the relationship begun in 1645—coinciding with the beginnings of Christina's emotional and physical crisis—persisted. Still ten to twelve years later it was to Belle that she turned in moments of anxiety and depression, with repeated assurances of love and a yearning for confirmation that she was still "the person whom you loved best." This last phrase is even more striking when it is borne in mind that Belle had been married since 1653 (the year before Christina abdicated and left Sweden) and had given birth to three children who died in infancy. Poor Belle's life was marked by tragedy: her husband was killed in battle in 1658 and she herself died four years later when she was only in her thirties. No wonder a contemporary recorded "she had long been ailing. Everyone pitied her and grieved for her."

This relationship with Belle could well be dismissed as an obscure passage in Christina's private life, were it not for the fact that it began in the vital year that intervened between the period when the Queen readily welcomed the idea of marriage with Charles Gustavus, and 1646 when she was twenty and her uncle realized that Christina was beginning to show an aversion for marriage. Thus it must be regarded as a factor in Swedish and even in European history: although Christina's decision not to marry was admittedly only one of several causes leading to her abdication, it was probably the principal reason and, according to herself, the only one.

The last day of the eventful year 1645 brought yet another influential figure into Christina's orbit, who remained her close friend throughout his life. This was Pierre-Hector Chanut, at first Minister, then Ambassador, accredited as the ten-year-old Louis XIV's representative at the Swedish court. The retiring Ambassador, M. de la Thuillerie, came to Stockholm to present Chanut* and, if de la Thuillerie told him anything of his past experiences with the Queen, the new Minister must have felt some misgivings about the future. But Christina, whose perceptions where her favourites were not concerned could be exceedingly acute, evidently realized at once that this was a totally different type of man from the probably rather pompous de la Thuillerie.

At the age of forty it was Chanut's first diplomatic mission. As a Conseiller d'Etat he had previously held the post of Treasurer General in Auvergne, but far from being an unimaginative administrator, he and his wife were highly cultivated and accustomed to move in intellectual circles—her brother was an intimate friend of Descartes. Unlike many French intellectuals of the day they were both devout Catholics and people of absolute integrity, while Chanut himself combined an endearing modesty with an acute political perception. His was a character well calculated to bring out the best in Christina, which accounts for the mutual appreciation and esteem that soon grew up between them, causing Chanut to view the Queen through rose-tinted spectacles.

* In the seventeenth century ambassadors were usually only accredited to the northern powers for a specific mission. Only ministers and residents remained actually *en poste* as today.

From the French point of view Chanut's appointment was a very important one. During the later years of the Thirty Years War the relations between the two countries, as we have seen, had become far from cordial. France paid the piper and felt she ought to call the tune. Sweden was inclined to view French participation in the war as being confined to a willingness to fight to the last Swede or, more precisely, to the last mercenary commanded by Swedish generals. Axel Oxenstierna's profound mistrust of all things French was symptomatic; it was shared by the Råd, and even the Grand Marshal Jacob De la Gardie viewed the land of his ancestors with misgiving. Although the peace negotiations of Westphalia had been officially under way since December 1644, France had only begun to treat seriously about the time when Chanut set out for Stockholm. The decision to send a permanent minister of his calibre to Sweden must be viewed in the light of France's increasing desire to extricate herself from Germany, which she regarded as a secondary field of action, so that she could deal decisively with Spain. In this situation an understanding of the character and intentions of the young Swedish Queen, who seemed destined to become a rising power in Northern Europe, was of great political importance.

Just how much Franco-Swedish relations had degenerated may be judged from the fact that a few days before Chanut arrived in Stockholm, the Swedish representatives at Osnabrück had discussed Swedish peace terms with the Imperial envoy Count Trautmansdorf at a meeting from which the resident of their French ally had been rigorously excluded. Even Mazarin was alarmed, but the meeting was really only a bluff by Trautmansdorf intended to make the French rescind their claims to Alsace, out of fear that Sweden might make a separate peace. The French need not have worried; the only thing that could have brought this about was the Emperor's agreement that Sweden should keep Pomerania, which was not his to give. However, when the news leaked out that Sweden was still standing by her original, enormous territorial claims of Pomerania, Silesia, Wismar, the Island of Rügen, and the Bishoprics of Bremen and Verden as well as other ecclesiastical lands and financial indemnities for her armies, French dismay was almost greater. Far from making a separate peace, it looked as if Sweden never intended to make peace at all, and would continue to expect French subsidies as long as she remained in the field. These enormous demands would obviously be subject to diplomatic bargaining, but in setting her sights so high Sweden must also be intending to hold out for a very stiff bargain indeed. Just what this bargain might be, it was Chanut's job to find out, and if possible cause it to be modified. A major factor in this situation was, of course, the character and intentions of Christina herself—an unknown quantity when compared with Axel Oxenstierna and his colleagues and supporters, whose grim determination to exact Sweden's pound of flesh was well known.

During the summer and autumn of 1645, however, the claims and counter-claims revolving round the three main territorial bones of contention—Pomerania, Alsace and the Palatinate—were approaching solution. The Elector of Brandenburg finally gave in to the Emperor's pressure, and let it be understood that he would be prepared to waive his dynastic claims to Western Pomerania if he kept the eastern half of the Duchy and was compensated by lands further west. He eventually got the Bishoprics of Halberstadt, Minden and Magdeburg. Sweden's claim to Silesia had never been very serious: Pomerania was the crux of the question. Even if Sweden had to disgorge half of this Duchy (which she had already occupied *in toto*) to Christina's cousin the Elector Frederick William of Brandenburg, the remaining portion still gave her a right to a seat at the Imperial Diet and a hand in German affairs. In the end Sweden also got Wismar and the Bishoprics of Bremen and Verden as well as financial compensation for her troops. The Emperor long resisted France's claim to Alsace, made on the grounds that it was a Hapsburg dynastic possession (this was only true of the upper half) and that France was fighting the dynasty and not the Empire. In the end, he had to give in and cede the Imperial rights, and Breisach on the east bank of the Rhine as well. Eventually, however, he managed to circumnavigate France's desire to hold Alsace as a fief of the Empire (and thus have a seat at the Imperial Diet) by agreeing to demilitarize the east bank of the Rhine from Basle to Philippsburg.

Meanwhile Maximilian of Bavaria's continual threats that he would make a separate peace with France brought him French protection against Swedish claims on behalf of Charles Lewis, the legitimate Elector Palatine, whose lands Maximilian had seized. Maximilian thus managed to keep the Bavarian Palatinate but was forced to give up Heidelberg and the Rhenish one to Charles Lewis, for whom a new Electorate was created. Deserted by all, Charles Lewis vented his feelings by striking a medal inscribed with the words "*Cedendo non Cedo*," but his gesture was as useless as the protestations made by the poor Pomeranians and Alsatians who were also allowed no say in their own destiny. In fact the phrase coined by a later historian, that the fate of Alsace had sown "the eternal seed of wars," could also have been applied to any other of these settlements, though towards the end of 1646 it looked as if they might speed the conclusion of the Thirty Years' War. There remained, however, the questions of religious rights and the financial "satisfaction" of the mercenary armies; these took two years to negotiate and, as fighting continued throughout the whole of that time, there was always a chance that the intended territorial settlements might return to the melting pot.

By the winter of 1646, however, Chanut knew that in the proposed Pomeranian arrangement Sweden had been offered the basis of a reasonable settlement, if only she could be brought to accept it. Ever since his arrival in Stockholm nearly a year before, Chanut had been preparing the ground to win the Queen over. His dispatches to Paris at this time provide an illuminating commentary upon the situation at the Swedish court. Naturally, as Axel Oxenstierna was known to be hostile to France, Chanut watched avidly for all signs of disagreement between him and the Queen, of which there seem to have been plenty. The French Minister found that in order to try and ingratiate himself with the Chancellor he had to pretend that he expected to carry on all serious negotiations with him, concealing his already friendly relations with Christina. She, on the other hand, required the most diplomatic reassurances that Chanut "appreciated her intelligence, full authority and power of decision in affairs." At this period Chanut was sure that Christina was extremely jealous of Axel Oxenstierna's power and great reputation, and was trying to build up for herself a position to equal it. Given the circumstances of a strong-willed young woman who had emerged only two years before from the Chancellor's tutelage, there was nothing surprising in this situation; in fact it could probably have been avoided only if Christina had possessed a totally different character. Nevertheless it gave Chanut his chance to encourage the Queen in her pro-French policy as part of her opposition to Oxenstierna.

He soon discovered further grounds for collaboration, in Christina's desire for peace. Already in the spring of 1646 Chanut reported that she wanted it more ardently than anyone, because she wished to re-populate the provinces, as one day Sweden might have to stand up to a combined attack from Poland, the Empire and Denmark: war casualties and long separations of husband and wife had inevitably reduced her population. Chanut may have felt at this stage that Christina was exaggerating this point slightly for his benefit. As he remarked, it was very difficult to know what was really going on as Christina kept her own secrets and, in spite of his great influence in the Råd, Oxenstierna did likewise because he was jealous of the Queen's other favourites. The chief of these was, of course, Magnus De la Gardie, and Oxenstierna was so furious at Christina's announced intention of sending him as Ambassador to Paris that when, on 23rd March, the Queen returned from a journey to the copper mines, the Chancellor did not ask for an audience for five days and even started to talk of retirement.

Christina continued using Magnus as her stalking horse in her battle with Oxenstierna, telling Chanut to treat with him directly on French affairs as Ambassador designate—a deadly affront to the Chancellor—and when Chanut cautiously tried to deal with Oxenstierna, and got short shrift, he not unnaturally turned to the Queen herself. However, Chanut's appreciation of the situation is best illustrated by the fact that he wrote to Paris to say that a splendid reception for Magnus, when he arrived there, would please Christina more than anything else; it would be the Queen's consolation for depriving herself of her favourite's presence, which he thought she was now regretting. But when Magnus actually left, Chanut warned Cardinal Mazarin that beneath the good looks and brilliant exterior there lay a curiously indecisive character.

Very different was the impression made by Charles Gustavus, who accompanied John Casimir to court in June to arrange Eleonora Palatine's betrothal to the Landgrave Frederick of

Hesse. Although the family were poor—the lady's dowry was said to be only 10,000 Riksdaler—and her brother showed little enthusiasm for France, Chanut admitted Charles Gustavus's "keen intelligence" and that he was much esteemed by everyone. Probably in honour of the betrothal, the court was entertained to a ballet on 28th June. The theme was a caprice on the effects of love, in which Christina was compared with the sun.

But the great social events of the summer of 1646 were the magnificent farewell banquet (lasting five hours) and ballet given by Magnus before he left for France in July, and the arrival of a Russian embassy. This embassy, like the one of thirteen years before, came to renew the peace treaty made by Gustavus Adolphus in 1617; though Chanut remarked that none of those present could have gathered as much from the speech delivered by the interpreter, who muddled all the words into complete nonsense. Possibly because she retained mischievous memories of the last occasion of this kind, Christina received the Russians in great splendour, with a cloth of gold laid out on the floor before her throne which was lined on either side by ninety lackeys. Chanut was fascinated by the Russians' clothes, which were heavily trimmed with sables, and their odd behaviour. The head of the mission carried the Grand Duke's letters of credence swathed in black crepe and, refusing to give them to the Chancellor, insisted on placing them directly in the Queen's own hands.

These were barbaric splendours indeed when compared with the reception with which Magnus De la Gardie was greeted on his arrival in Paris at the end of August. In accordance with the custom of the day, not only did the King send his own carriage to meet the Ambassador, but the Queen Mother, the Diplomatic Corps and the French nobility as well. Thus, preceded by heralds, trumpeters and pages, it was in the red and gold carriage of the King of France that Magnus made his entry into Paris at the head of a grand procession of gilded, velvet-covered carriages. The next day he proceeded to Fontainebleau, where a magnificent house was placed at his disposal, and on 3rd September he was received in state by the young King Louis XIV and his mother. Mazarin had evidently taken very much to heart Chanut's warning note about Christina's susceptibilities concerning Magnus's reception. There followed a bewildering series of entertainments, banquets, balls, receptions, hunts and spectacles of all kinds—rarely had an ambassador been so splendidly fêted. But when it came down to brass tacks and the exchange of ceremonial calls, as prescribed by etiquette, before negotiations could get under way, the differences in protocol as practised by Catholic and Protestant powers raised its ugly head, even between allies. In normal circumstances, as the King's Minister, Mazarin should have called first on Magnus as representing the person of his Queen, but as a cardinal in a Catholic country Mazarin was accorded the honours due to a prince of the Church and even an Ambassador was expected to make the first call on him. Oxenstierna—and Christina—obviously foresaw this quandary. Before leaving, Magnus must have received strict instructions on how he was to act. He did indeed make the first visit, but as a private person. That Mazarin swallowed the affront and returned the call in state, was an indication of how vital Swedish relations were to France at that moment.

The magnificent welcome and the difficulties of protocol resolved, Magnus had to apply himself to the serious matter of negotiations. Here again he had obviously been carefully briefed, and although Chanut evidently had no very high opinion of his capacities, he had warned Mazarin that Magnus was nevertheless endowed with native Swedish caution and "becomes very circumspect in his replies and very undecided about transactions, unless he clearly understands their aim." Apart from asking for French reinforcements to be sent to Germany in order to support the Swedes, the main point of Magnus's negotiations was to make certain that France did not make a separate peace with the wily Maximilian of Bavaria, who must be forced to hand the Palatinate back to its rightful owner, the Elector Charles Lewis. There were also the questions of the German Bishoprics—claimed by Sweden—and recompense for her allies, such as the Landgrave of Hesse-Cassel. Magnus was promised satisfaction on all these points. But the final settlement at Westphalia was to reveal how shallow those promises were.

His task accomplished, the young Ambassador now set out to enjoy himself in the city which he admired so much. With carefree abandon he spent money like water—on dresses for Maria Euphrosyne (including a magnificent one of white taffeta sewn with brilliants and pearls), lingerie, linen, household luxuries, a carriage, portraits. The flattery with which he was surrounded, the luxury and royal favour, combined with the apparent success of his mission, went to Magnus's head. It was not long before he had run through the fabulous sum of 200,000 écus, double the generous amount which he had been allowed to defray his expenses, and was forced to make up the difference by loans. Even in a century in which prodigality was equated with grandeur, and in a capital as luxurious as Paris, Magnus's spendthrift behaviour aroused comment; so did the warmth of his references to his own sovereign. That so young and handsome an ambassador should comport himself thus, could mean only one thing to the Parisian gossips—he must be the Queen of Sweden's lover. Certainly the expedients to which Christina resorted in secrecy to pay his bills and even to put more money in Magnus's pockets, would seem to confirm this. But shortly after his return home Magnus fulfilled his pledge and married Maria Euphrosyne and they seem to have "lived happily ever after."

This episode of Magnus was not the first, but it was the most conspicuous example hitherto of Christina's complacent acceptance of a favourite's extravagant behaviour. It must, however, be viewed in the light of similar incidents later in her life—such as partiality for the brawling Klas Tott, for the ne'er-do-well Francesco Maria Santinelli and, above all, for the tortuous Monaldeschi, almost to his very bitter end. Christina herself admired prodigality; it was for her a sign of greatness, as is made plainly evident in her famous *Maxims*. In one of them she wrote: "Generosity, liberality and magnificence are virtues which charm all the world. Any man who possesses them can hardly fail to find fortune sooner or later." Or again: "There are some expenditures which appear to be thriftless, but are in fact a true economy . . . one must never complain, one must provide gaily, this is the only economy of princes."

Although the report of Magnus's magnificent reception in Paris had been read out to a gratified Råd, their apathetic reactions to his account of his mission, on his return to Stockholm early in 1647, were probably influenced by the rumours of his extravagance which had preceded him, and the recent crisis in the Queen's relations with the Chancellor. Christina, however, probably for both reasons, received him with enthusiasm, made him a member of the Råd and dismissed criticism of his actions as "the calumnies of his enemies." How far she was prepared to go to protect her favourite, and of course by so doing to vindicate her choice of him as ambassador, is revealed in her private correspondence with Adler Salvius at Osnabrück. These same letters also show the Queen's earnest desire and increasing impatience for the conclusion of the peace treaties, in which her now very bitter rivalry with the Oxenstiernas undoubtedly played a part.

Although Axel Oxenstierna's eldest son John was the official head of the Swedish mission at Osnabrück, his was a personality ill-calculated to further goodwill for his country. Later the English Ambassador Whitelocke described him as pompous and discourteous. The brains of the delegation was Adler Salvius, who now had ten years' experience of affairs in Germany. As we have seen, where her personal feelings were not engaged, Christina could be a shrewd judge, and it is evident that she quickly spotted Salvius's remarkable capacity and made increasing use of him. She became accustomed to writing Salvius highly confidential letters giving her personal views and instructions, over and above the official ones which were naturally addressed to John Oxenstierna as well. In a letter written to Salvius from Stockholm on 12th December 1646, the Queen wrote: "I put my entire confidence in you, that you will not allow yourself to be turned aside by anything, and by this I recommend to you very expressly the advancement of the peace." By this time Magnus's extravagance in Paris had evidently become current European gossip, for Christina added: "For what concerns the 100,000 écus borrowed by M. De la Gardie in Paris, this was not done without my wishing it and without my express orders. Therefore I ask you not to let his enemies calumny him, because he is quite innocent."

Magnus's "innocent" extravagance was, however, to cause both his Queen and Salvius very considerable embarrassment and worry. In an undated letter written later, Christina addressed her "faithful servitor" in what she admitted to be her "extremity." She asked Salvius to negotiate on his personal credit a loan of 100,000 écus to pay the army in Germany, promising to refund it to him, either from the money she would receive for the sale of ships to France, or by making over to him quantities of copper of equal value. The reason for this dramatic appeal was that indignation at Magnus's extravagance had now apparently reached the proportions of a public scandal. Christina herself admitted to Salvius that "there are those who would like to make out that this money would have been sufficient to prevent and stop the advance of the enemy, and that Field Marshal Wrangel (the Swedish Commander-in-Chief in Germany) could have hoped to have done this, had he received this money." She continued: "I have no need to explain to you how this could be seized upon to cause me embarrassment if anything went wrong, which God forbid!" and reiterates that Magnus borrowed the money upon her express orders. Christina concluded by saying that Salvius would never regret having done this service for her. In this she was as good as her word, and later created him a member of the Råd in the teeth of fierce opposition.

But this was not to be the last, or the least, favour that Christina was to ask from Salvius on Magnus's behalf. In her letter to him of 13th February 1647, after urging him even more strongly to push for the conclusion of the peace treaty, she advanced a truly astonishing proposal. Would Salvius advise her if she could "without prejudice gratify the Count Magnus with the seigniory of Benefeld, especially if I have to cede it under the treaty? I am more sure of his fidelity to me than of anything else in the world. He knows nothing of this and I do not want him to know until I have your opinion as to whether this can be done, for many reasons. Tell no one but M. d'Avaux, on his promise of silence. Don't discover it to Gustavsson."

Benefeld was a small town in Alsace. At that time it was occupied by the Swedes. It was, however, plainly evident that this Swedish enclave could scarcely survive in the midst of a province which would surely go to France in the final peace settlement. Still, Sweden had a claim to it and, incredibly, the otherwise astute Christina thought she might be able to keep it for her favourite, whose interests be it noted (as in the case of the 100,000 écus) came before those of her country. Viewed in the light of contemporary morality this is not so surprising. John Oxenstierna and Salvius himself were to receive some remarkably valuable "presents" from Mazarin before the peace was signed. The audacity of the idea, and the fact that it was to be discussed in

Christina's father, King Gustavus Adolphus, by an unknown artist, showing the King in later life.

Christina's mother, Queen Maria Eleonora.

Count Axel Oxenstierna, Chancellor of the Realm, drawn by Daniel Dumoustier on 4th May, 1633.

Christina about the age of eight, a portrait from the studio of J. H. Elbfas.

Charles Gustavus Palatine (later Charles X) as a young man.

secret with one of the French representatives, but concealed from Christina's step-brother and confidential secretary—Gustav Gustavsson, already show what curious schemes the Queen could nourish for the advancement of a favourite. In any event, Christina clung to her plan with a zeal worthy of a better cause, and only by Mazarin's dexterity was the question finally settled—France presented the cannons of Benefeld to Count Magnus, who sold them back to France!

Confronted with this manœuvre, who could doubt the infatuation of a Queen in her twenties for a handsome young man a few years older than herself? But the situation was not so simple or clear-cut as that. The first months of 1647 had brought another crisis in Christina's life, and yet another and more serious bone of contention between herself and Axel Oxenstierna and the overwhelming majority of the Råd and the country. In these circumstances, if she was to maintain her authority, the Queen must build up a party of her own. In this instance Magnus, loaded with honours and therefore of guaranteed "fidelity" to her, would be Christina's pawn.

The situation which, in January and February of 1647, had brought about the first overt collision between the Queen and Axel Oxenstierna, was grave indeed. It concerned the Lutheran religious orthodoxy of Sweden, of which the Chancellor was a jealous guardian.

To modern eyes, the stand which the twenty-year-old Christina then made for a more liberal and less embittered and narrow approach to the Protestant religion in all its forms is wholly admirable. It places beyond all doubt the strength of her religious feeling at this period, which is also vouched for by the sincerely devout Chanut. Oxenstierna apparently precipitated the crisis by attacking in the Råd a book written by John Mathiae, now Bishop of Strängnäs. It is possible that by this action the Chancellor hoped to warn Christina against supporting the book in public. For no one knew better than he that Gustavus Adolphus had personally chosen Mathiae as Christina's preceptor, and he could scarcely have ignored the fact that this choice had been due to the dead King's liberal attitude to religion, which coincided with that of Mathiae.

If this was indeed Oxenstierna's intention, he could not have made a greater error in judgment. Christina, like her father, refused to accept the narrow and bigoted religious attitudes of the majority of her compatriots. Her loathing for the interminable, gloomy "hell-fire" sermons had become evident when she was a child. She never ceased to reiterate this and her hatred of pedantry. It was an understandable reaction in a young woman as intelligent and as well-educated as Christina, who must have counted many hours of her twenty years as having been wasted by being forced to listen, under the guise of religion, to the endless perorations of half-educated or pedantic ministers. It is not surprising, therefore, that she sprang to the defence of Mathiae, whose goodness and gentleness she knew and who had taught her the original, pure, evangelical Lutheranism, very different from the intolerant form, later upheld by so many of his cloth.

Mathiae's book, the *Idea boni ordinis in Ecclesia Christi* which aroused the storm, suggested a possible basis for uniting all Protestant forms of faith. This unification represented the syncretism abhorred by the vast majority of Swedish Lutherans. Mathiae was forced, and Axel Oxenstierna was instrumental in bringing this about, to make an apologia for his work before the entire Riksdag, then in session in Stockholm.

Christina's fury, compounded of outraged religious sentiment, personal affection and sheer injured pride, can well be imagined. It gave her the courage, and it required very considerable courage for a girl of barely twenty, to oppose the proposal of the Råd and all four Estates of the Riksdag for adopting the "*Liber Concordiae*" or "Form of Concord" of 1580. In this, however, Christina was following in the footsteps of her father, for he too in 1611 had refused for political reasons to countenance the acceptance of the "Form of Concord" which contravened all possibility of a syncretical movement.

At the same time the Riksdag made another attack on religious freedom in Sweden, the Estates protesting against the Mass being celebrated in Chanut's house. Apparently the Catholics who gathered there were not limited to his own household but included other foreigners brought back by Magnus from Paris. Chanut protested against this violation of diplomatic usage (Magnus and his embassy had practised Lutheran rites while in France); Christina told him to be careful while the Riksdag was in session, but gave him to understand that afterwards he could do as he liked. This was a pin-prick when compared with the greater issues, but here too the Queen may have suspected the fine Italian hand of the Francophobe and strictly orthodox Axel Oxenstierna. Her victory over the "*Liber Concordiae*" did not make her forget that he had been largely responsible for Mathiae's apologia. She had some bitter exchanges with the Chancellor over this and was not slow to take her revenge.

The long-term results of these events were, however, to be incalculably greater. From this moment the Queen seems to have decided on two things—to build up her own political power so that she would never again be subjected to so undignified a check, and to escape mentally (for the present at any rate) from what she must have felt to be the suffocating intellectual atmosphere of Sweden. It seems that Christina only had a vague idea of what this decision would lead to. But there were already straws in the wind. The same diet of the Riksdag in the first months of 1647 had raised the question of the Queen's marriage. She gave a temporizing reply that she must have time to think it over. But it is probable that her close friends and advisers (notably her uncle Gyllenhielm) had instigated this in order first to promote the idea in the public mind of her marrying Charles Gustavus, and secondly by this means to pave the way to get him declared her successor if necessary. Chanut got wind of rumours of the possibility of Christina's marriage to her cousin being debated in the Råd, and at the same time of her wishing to delay her coronation. Mystified, he questioned her about this and received the sibylline reply that "time would enlighten" him. It would explain the Queen's reasons for putting off her coronation as long as possible. Seven years later she told him that she had been thinking of abdicating ever since 1646.

Still, in the early months of 1647 abdication must have been but a vague dream, to be caressed by Christina only in secret while carefully preparing the way for the designation of a successor, ostensibly as a safeguard against her own untimely death without heirs. All this would take a long time to manœuvre and, although Christina could play a waiting game, her contradictory nature also craved action. But action was to hand. Little could really be done until peace was certain, and to the conclusion of this the Queen now turned all her energies with even greater zest, because it gave her a chance of scoring off the Oxenstiernas.

The diet of the Riksdag ended in March. On 10th April the Queen sent an official dispatch to her representatives at Osnabrück in which she blistered them for the delay in concluding the peace. She said that "without trifling any more you are to conduct negotiations to a desirable end . . . you are no longer to allow affairs to drag on at length as has happened up to now. If this is not done it will be your business to see how you will be answerable to God, to the Estates of the Realm and to me. Do not allow yourselves to be turned from this end by the ideas of ambitious people, at least if you do not wish to incur my deepest displeasure and indignation . . . you may be sure that then neither authority nor the support of great families will prevent me from showing the whole world the displeasure that I feel for such proceedings which are destitute of judgment."

There is no mistaking that this dispatch was the product of long pent-up fury which was at last finding an outlet. But was the fury entirely due to the delay in the peace negotiations? Christina knew too much about the political labyrinth in Westphalia to believe that the Oxenstiernas, father and son—for that is whom she was aiming at—were the only Fabians. But the delays gave her the excuse she needed to attack them. This much is transparently clear from her letter of the same date which was secretly dispatched to Salvius. The Queen wrote: "From your letters I know of your efforts to terminate a long, dangerous and bloody war. I also know from many circumstances how a certain party who, not being able entirely to upset the treaties, is trying to delay them. . . . I will conduct myself in such a way with this contrary party that the whole earth will know that the fault was not on my side. I will also make the whole universe see that R.C. [the Chancellor Axel Oxenstierna] is not able, alone with his little finger, to make the world turn round." Christina went on to say that the official dispatch was intended for John Oxenstierna alone, but that Salvius must see that its contents were also known to M. d'Avaux, so that the French did not think badly of her. She promised that if Salvius returned "bringing peace" she would make him a senator. To reassure him about her dislike of the old-established aristocracy (like the Oxenstiernas), she quoted

Sallust's account of Marius's words: "They despise me because I am a new man, and I despise them for the slothful lives they lead." Still, even in so serious a context, Christina did not forget to urge Magnus's claim to Benefeld; but her postscript provided the key to the whole letter. It ran: "I beg you to tell me what sort of grimaces G.J.O. [John Oxenstierna] makes when he reads my letter and my orders addressed to you both."

Christina made full play of her position as the injured sovereign let down by her servants: Mazarin's dispatches to Westphalia said that the exhorbitant Swedish demands caused the Queen great pain. She told the same story to Chanut, but had the honesty to admit that she was not averse to letting John Oxenstierna reap the unpopularity that his delaying tactics had brought him. Christina seems to have reserved her masculine traits for her private life. Her diplomacy was thoroughly feminine. Inevitably the virulent language which the Queen had employed became known in the corridors and whispering galleries of Westphalia. John Oxenstierna took the matter as a personal affront and in May wrote to the Queen to say that he was prepared to "submit his person to her"; but with characteristic tactlessness (for Christina was trying to assert her power and prove she was a Queen in fact as well as name) he said he would like to know who had prompted her to write such a letter. In June John Oxenstierna named his suspects —Salvius and the French—whom he in his turn accused of delaying the peace. Christina retaliated by sending this letter to Salvius and telling him to show it to Servien.

The Queen was now on the way to achieving one of her aims, that of building up her own party. Salvius and Magnus were now allies, corresponding with each other on the tactics to be employed in this whole imbroglio. Salvius even advised Magnus to absent himself from Court for a while, which he did for two months in the summer to see the estate which Christina had given his wife; though possibly this was because by June Christina had been forced to appear more conciliatory towards the Oxenstiernas. The Chancellor had tackled her personally about her attitude to his son John, forcing the Queen to excuse herself on the grounds that she "had not written to my son with any bad intention or as a man in disgrace, but from the fear that the plenipotentiaries were insisting too much on their claims and that the negotiations could be broken off." Axel Oxenstierna thus described his interview with the Queen in a letter to Eric, another of his sons, who was Governor of Livonia. The Chancellor added that "at the end Her Majesty explained herself sufficiently to me as to what had caused some alteration in her lately, and since then she has shown herself very gracious towards me and my family." Axel Oxenstierna attributed the differences of opinion between himself and his sovereign, which he admitted had given rise to "some words and discussion between Her Majesty and me" to French intrigues in Westphalia and Sweden, and "those who wish to create trouble between sovereigns and their servitors." But his recognition of how dangerous such people could be is implicit in the advice he gave his son to get married. The reason for this was that in 1646 Field Marshal Torstensson had suggested Eric as a possible husband for Christina—"a thing," as his father said, "only to be laughed at." But Axel Oxenstierna evidently did not think that such gossip being repeated to the Queen was any laughing matter, and counselled Eric to make up his mind to marry Elizabeth Brahe, as he subsequently did.

In her determination to create a Queen's party, Christina was succeeding in dividing the court into two camps, with the De la Gardie family, the Palatines, Field Marshal Torstensson and of course Carl Carlsson Gyllenhielm, on her side, and the Oxenstiernas, Field Marshal Horn, General Wrangel and the Råd on the other.

But Mazarin had put his finger on the spot, already in 1646. When it was evident that Christina was trying to escape from Axel Oxenstierna's influence, the Cardinal wrote to the French representatives at Münster saying: "The Chancellor Oxenstierna is so consummate a minister that although he seems to have lost credit, he will still continue to have a large part in the administration of the Realm, and the Queen who desires to instruct herself in great affairs could not find a source (of knowledge) more lively and reliable than he." This was indeed a cheer from "the ranks of Tuscany" for the French were only too well aware that the opposition to Christina's pro-French policy was led by Axel Oxenstierna on patriotic grounds. But his position was such that even the privileged Chanut dared not attack him openly. The Minister's feelings, however, got the better of him in his Paris dispatches. Here he could not resist some wicked digs at the disgruntled Chancellor's constant harping on his ill health, his desire for retirement and the probable imminence of his death; Chanut remarked tartly that Oxenstierna still seemed to be very much of this world and that from the French point of view it was a pity that this was so. In 1647 Axel Oxenstierna was sixty-five, a respectable age for those days, but he was still so active that he could spend a whole day in the saddle, keeping up with the young Queen who was a noted horsewoman. Thus to the years of experience of this consummate statesman was added a remarkable physical endurance. It was with this formidable adversary that the young Christina had now to join battle if she was to succeed in her secret plans.

To further these plans, the Queen allowed it to be generally believed during 1647 that she was going to marry Charles Gustavus. She also reverted to her previous tactics of sending him abroad. She now planned to make her cousin her Commander-in-Chief in Germany so as to increase his stature in the public eye—a safe bet now that he was known to be an excellent soldier. But here she met with Oxenstierna's opposition. He warned the Queen that it would be unsafe to give Charles Gustavus, whom he persisted in regarding as a slightly suspicious foreigner, such a post if she did not intend to marry him. Christina tried to avoid committing herself by promising to marry no one else, but in the end she had to give in and promise to marry her cousin. This must have been something of a bombshell to Charles Gustavus. For he had been idling in Sweden for two years watching honours being piled upon Magnus, and now suddenly came the news of what amounted to his public engagement to Christina. However she did not leave him in doubt as to her intentions. Privately she told her cousin that she would only marry him if it was absolutely necessary for reasons of state, but that to say she was going to do so was the only way to get him nominated Generalissimo. With more spirit than he had shown up to now, Charles Gustavus refused to leave Sweden until he learnt from Christina herself what their future really was to be. Here circumstances helped him, for the national finances were in such a bad way that not enough money could be scraped together to enable the new Generalissimo to cut a dash in Germany. Though she might not love him, Christina was determined that, like Magnus, her cousin should appear as a splendid figure abroad.

Charles Gustavus's appointment was announced in January 1648; Chanut wrote to his government that the news was well received by the army in Germany, where the young commander was loved and esteemed for his bravery and other good qualities. With his customary perspicacity, though he knew that Charles Gustavus was no particular friend of France, Chanut added that he was "liberal but without profusion, firm of spirit but moderate and very capable in council."

In May Chanut reported that although the Generalissimo's preparations for his departure were nearly completed, he was ill and suffered from headaches and fainting fits. Was the strain of his position telling on Charles Gustavus, or had he already started the heavy drinking that changed his appearance from a pleasant-featured young man to gross and premature middle-age? If he had, he could be forgiven for it, since rumours were floating around that Christina would make a more definite statement about her marriage to him before he left the country. Whatever the reason for his illness, Charles Gustavus now made a desperate and determined effort and insisted upon seeing Christina to discuss their marriage. She agreed, but stipulated that both Mathiae and Magnus should be present at their meeting.

At this strange interview Charles Gustavus learnt his unwelcome fate, but it is a measure of the trust which Christina reposed in him that she also told him a good deal about her secret plans. For one so devious, she was on this occasion unusually straightforward and honest. Evidently if she did not love her cousin any more, she respected him. The Queen began by saying—and Charles Gustavus's own account of the interview was recorded in his diary—that she refused to be bound by anything which she had said when she was a girl, as she was then too young to make any serious promises. Moreover even now she did not want to take away all hope of marriage nor to promise anything; but she assured her cousin again that she would only marry him if this were absolutely necessary. However Christina did say that if she could not overcome her unwillingness to marry, she would try to get Charles Gustavus nominated as her successor, though if the Estates would not agree to this she would marry him. In any case he would have her final decision before she was twenty-five and the time for her coronation had come.

Christina evidently felt that she had been generous and that the debt of affection had been paid, for either way Gustavus's future was assured. He would not accept this, and here surely his love for her rings out. In the embarrassing presence of two witnesses, Charles Gustavus declared that if Christina would not accept him as her husband he would not accept her offers, but would go away and never return to Sweden. By this one step the young man was threatening to throw away his future in the country where he had been born and lived all his life; moreover he had no estates or fortune elsewhere upon which to fall back. Even the head of his house, the Elector Palatine Charles Lewis, was a penniless refugee in Holland. Christina tried to stop her cousin's passionate refusal by ridicule, she accused him of nourishing "romantic fantasies." But when she found that he would not give way, she too mounted her high horse and said that Charles could count himself honoured, even if he died before her final decision was made. People would believe that he had received a signal honour: that a Queen like Christina had considered marrying him. However, she then seems to have relented a little; they had after all grown up together and what happiness she had known in childhood had been in her cousin's family. She agreed that Charles could write to plead his cause—not to her—but to his father and John Mathiae who would talk matters over with her.

One of the conditions Christina imposed on her cousin was that he must leave immediately to take up his command in Germany. The other, much harder condition imposed was that Charles Gustavus must behave as if he really was engaged to Christina. This was necessary as a matter of policy, as if anything happened to the Queen, even if the question of her cousin being declared her successor had not yet been raised, as her fiancé his succession to the throne would be much easier. In the same month of June 1648 Charles Gustavus took his oath of allegiance to the Queen as her Commander-in-Chief. According to Chanut it was after Morning Prayer on the third Sunday after Whitsun that the ceremony took place in the presence of all the great officers of the realm, with Christina seated under a canopy of state in front of the

Church. The young General knelt and, holding up his hand, repeated the oath as it was read out to him by the Chancellor; he then received his commission from the Queen and, after kissing her hand, stepped back and made a short speech of thanks which Chanut said "was well delivered in a soldierly manner and was praised by all."

Although Christina was four years younger than Charles Gustavus, and not exposed to the risks of war as he would be in Germany, two incidents had recently occurred which confirmed her uncle Gyllenhielm's insistence that it was necessary to provide for the succession. In July 1647 there had been an attempt on the Queen's life; the assailant, a ne'er-do-well called Presbeckius, was afterwards believed to be mad, but he had chosen his moment well.

On Sunday 27th, in the royal chapel in Stockholm Castle, when after the sermon the congregation was engaged in silent prayer and many of the men present had covered their faces with their hats, Presbeckius slipped through the crowd and advanced to the small raised dais where Christina was kneeling. Fortunately the High Steward, Per Brahe, saw him and shouted to the guards who crossed their halberds, blocking his way. But Presbeckius pushed them aside with such force that one of the halberds was broken, and he jumped over the other. The Queen had by now risen, she did not move but gave her spellbound Captain of the Guards a shove and he threw himself upon the man seizing him by the hair. Presbeckius was found to have two naked knives concealed in his clothes, but on being questioned he said that he wanted to kill a priest and gave such wandering replies that in the end he was shut up as a madman.

The other incident, which although less alarming could have proved more dangerous, occurred early in 1648 when the Queen herself discovered a fire on the stairs leading to the maids' rooms in her private appartment in the castle. Fire was a constant hazard in old Swedish buildings and Stockholm Castle was finally destroyed by one later in the century. This outbreak seems to have been serious. It burned for six hours and was only finally quenched when the wind veered to another quarter; the Queen, however, refused to leave the building until midnight, when she knew that the chancery papers were safe.

It is unlikely that Charles Gustavus saw Christina again privately after the stormy interview about their marriage. But he wrote pathetic and almost despairing letters from Germany to his father and Mathiae, in his efforts to try and get her to change her mind. He was now nearing thirty and his life had not been blameless. Stories of sordid affairs with barmaids had reached Sweden during his last period at the wars in Germany and he had a bastard—a whore's child, it was said. The bastard was presumably a boy, for he was entrusted to the care of Charles Gustavus's old teacher at Uppsala University. But these were incidents that might be expected in the life of any young soldier on campaign. What is much more revealing about his private life is that his name was never linked with that of a young woman of his own class. There seems to have been no Ebba Brahe or even a Karin Månsdotter in Charles Gustavus's life. In his late twenties, he clung to his hope of marrying Christina as he had six years earlier, and was apparently still to cling to this hope in the face of every obstacle almost until the Queen's abdication; though in the end this tenacity was probably not devoid of political consideration.

There is even a story that after he had been crowned King, and Christina was on the point of leaving Sweden, Charles Gustavus instructed one of his gentlemen to make her a last offer of marriage; though possibly apocryphal, this gallant gesture was in keeping with his behaviour to his cousin throughout his life. Even in the face of many provocations, of her conversion to Catholicism, and in the straits of desperate wars, contrary even to Christina's own fears that he would fail to do so, Charles Gustavus did his best to see that his cousin's appanage was paid to her, though he was now married and had a son.

This does not look like the behaviour of a man whose eye had been fixed only on the main chance, and the letters that came pouring in from Germany during 1648 and 1649 confirm this impression. In his appalling handwriting Charles Gustavus returned again and again to the theme that if Christina would not marry him he would not come back, she must find him some other employment abroad, or that he would retire and live privately somewhere in the Baltic provinces. Sometimes his pride evidently rebelled: after all his father was a Wittelsbach, a member of one of the oldest reigning houses in Europe compared with which the

Wasas were mere parvenus; for in some letters he said that he would not come back to Sweden with honour if Christina would not marry him. Even the ineffectual Maria Eleonora's aid was invoked; Charles Gustavus was delighted when he heard that she had opposed his nomination as her daughter's successor and hoped that she would push his suit instead.

That was his tragedy. Charles Gustavus was always trying to get others to push his suit—his father, Mathiae, Chanut perhaps and even Magnus. He was to prove to be a brilliant and audacious soldier and an able ruler, but he singularly lacked the panache of the type of young adventurer who appealed so strongly to Christina. Even Magnus told his brother-in-law: "You must hazard everything . . . *Audaces fortuna juvat.*" The advice was good and, as Chanut clearly saw, it would have been greatly to Magnus's advantage in the long run to have his brother-in-law married to the Queen. But it was easy enough for others to advise Charles Gustavus . . . they did not love Christina.

Meanwhile during the last two years, the powers had continued their haggling in Westphalia over the religious and financial settlements in Germany, while the war dragged wearily on. The news of Charles Gustavus's appointment as Generalissimo, however, now stirred Wrangel's jealousy, and he determined to seek a decision before he could be superseded. In May 1648, at Zusmarshausen near Augsburg, he and Turenne defeated the Emperor's army, under Melander, who was killed. The imperial command now fell to Grönberg and the Italian general Montecuccoli, who withdrew into Bavaria and were saved from further attack by the spring floods of the Inn. Meanwhile another Swedish army under Königsmarck invaded Bohemia and summoned Prague to surrender. Though the rest of the city held out, on 26th July the Swedes captured the Kleinseite and with it the royal palace of the Hradschin, filled with the Emperor Rudolf II's fabulous art collections. These were seized as loot.

In spite of these disasters, the Hapsburg resistance continued, then came the blow which finally broke the Emperor's spirit. At Lens in August, his beloved brother, the Archduke Leopold, Governor of the Netherlands, was utterly defeated by Condé. Ferdinand III capitulated and instructed his representatives at

Münster to accept the religious and financial settlements offered by France, Sweden and their allies.

The peace conference of Westphalia was doomed to end as it had begun—in an atmosphere of tragi-comedy. When the Emperor's dispatch accepting the allied terms arrived in Münster, it was naturally in cypher and some underling had mislaid the key. Thus the document which was to end the sufferings of the last thirty years' carnage lay unread, while secretaries searched frantically. The plenipotentiaries were, in any event, determined to stand on their dignity to the end; three weeks passed in earnest discussion before it could be decided in which order the treaties should actually be signed. Finally at 2 p.m. on 24th October the ceremony began and was completed to the firing of salvoes from the cannon ranged on the walls of Münster. The courier bearing the news reached Stockholm on 31st October, and early in November the event was celebrated by a solemn Te Deum. Dissatisfaction with the terms was widespread in Sweden (as in Catholic countries), and someone actually dared to say to Christina that the peace would not last long. She retorted with feeling, that although she knew that there was no eternal peace in this world, "providence, which has re-established the liberty of Germany by the arms of the neighbouring states, will help again to preserve it." The Queen also gave a trouncing to a Minister who was said to be an Oxenstierna supporter, and had preached against the peace terms in Stockholm at the very moment when the Te Deum of thanksgiving for the peace was being sung. Though some of her subjects might not appreciate the blessings of this hard-won peace, there is no doubt that as a Queen and personally, it meant much to Christina. Years afterwards in Rome, at the end of the chapter for 1648 of the synopsis for her biography, she added with her own hand the words: "This year the peace was concluded at Osnabrug [*sic*] on 2nd October, after it had been treated since 1st July of the year 1643."

CHAPTER 4

Spiritual Crisis and Plans for Abdication: 1648–1651

In after years Queen Christina said that the year 1648 had been the turning point in her life. The Peace of Westphalia and her interview with Charles Gustavus, where she first revealed her plan that he should become her successor, might alone have justified this declaration, but other seemingly unimportant interludes were probably also on her mind.

The first interlude began with the return of the Queen Mother to Sweden after an absence of seven years, though characteristically this was not mentioned in the synopsis for Christina's biography. Chanut, however, reported that the Queen went to meet her mother's ship and, because it was delayed by a storm, she slept in the open for two nights and contracted a fever which kept her in bed for some days. It seems possible that this may have been malaria, as from now on Christina suffered from recurrent bouts of this fever. On this occasion Chanut evidently did not take it very seriously. Not so Christina, or at least as she remembered events in after years, though it is possible that here, as on other occasions, the Queen or her secretary were not very exact in their chronology. At any rate, at the end of the chapter dealing with the year 1648 in the synopsis for her biography, the secretary noted that Christina is said to have remarked at the time: "The Queen fell dangerously ill with a prolonged, double tertiary fever. And it was during this illness that she made a vow to God to quit all and become a Catholic if God spared her life." On another occasion

Christina was at fault in dating an event in her reign by two years, and it seems as if something of the kind occurred here, as for many reasons it is unlikely that her decision to become a Catholic was made so early in her life. In any event a dangerous illness seems an impossibility in view of the fact that a month after it began the Queen was well enough to make the long journey to Kopparberg, a return trip of 500 kilometres by road today, and be back in Stockholm in time to receive the news of the Peace of Westphalia on 31st October.

This journey to Kopparberg, however, though seemingly a casual incident, did in reality have a considerable effect upon Christina's life. Chanut, who accompanied her, noticed that the Queen spent most of her time reading during the long and wearisome days in her carriage. He offered to read aloud to her some passages from Descartes's *Principes de la Philosophie*, and Christina was so fascinated that she took the book from him and started dipping into it herself. For days afterwards she was very pensive and, realizing what was on her mind, Chanut said to her that he thought that she must be torn between the desire to study this philosophy and the difficulty of doing so. The Queen admitted that he was right, and knowing how little time affairs of state left her for the study of so monumental a work, it was agreed that Chanut and the Royal Librarian, Freinsheim, should read it and expound the results of their studies to Christina. Chanut reported all this in a letter to Descartes, adding at the end: "Her Majesty is so much interested in your condition and in the attention which you receive in France, that I do not know whether, when she has taken a taste for your philosophy, she will not tempt you to come to Sweden." Thus Descartes's fateful journey to Stockholm also had its origins in 1648.

The discussion of Descartes and his work was no new topic to Christina and Chanut. Already in 1646 he had given her the *Méditations métaphysiques*, and since 1647 the philosopher himself had been in correspondence with the Queen. That year had been marked in Christina's mind by Mathiae's forced apologia for his *Idea boni ordinis*, her own struggle over the "*Liber Concordiae*" and the Riksdag's protests against Mass being celebrated in Chanut's house. As a result of this display of bigotry, Christina began to widen her contacts with the intellectual world of Europe and, disillusioned by the narrow intolerance of Swedish Lutherism, to study in secret the other great religions of the world as well. She later admitted that as a result of this, while keeping up outward observances, she evolved a creed of her own. But in time Christina found even this belief difficult to maintain. The impact of contemporary science, including the discoveries of Copernicus and Galileo, had revolutionized the conception of the universe.

Something of this attitude emerges in a further note, added by the Queen's secretary at the end of the chapter for 1648 in the synopsis of her biography. He wrote: "With regard to becoming a Catholic, the Queen says elsewhere, addressing God, as can be seen in her own hand 'All the respect and admiration that I have had for you all my life, Lord, did not prevent me from being very unbelieving and not at all devout. I did not believe in the religion in which I was brought up. All that they told me did not seem worthy of you. I believed that they made you speak after their fashion, and that they wished to deceive me and made me believe them so that they could govern me, according to their will. I had a mortal hatred for the long and frequent sermons of the Lutherans; but I knew that I must let them have their way and be patient, and that I must hide what I thought. When I was a little older I formed a kind of religion of my own, awaiting that with which you would inspire me, for which I had naturally such a strong inclination. You know how many times, in a language not known to the commonality, I asked for the grace to be enlightened by you, and I vowed to obey you even at the price of my life and fortune.'" This passage corresponds with others in which the Queen described her religious views, and is of particular interest as it reflects Christina's spiritual and mental state at the end of 1648.

It seems probable that Chanut read some telling passages from Descartes's work to the Queen during their journey, and the fact that the great philosopher had succeeded in reconciling faith with reason inspired her with the hope that if only she could talk to Descartes, she might find the answer to her problems. For, shrewd observer that he was, Chanut had realized that Christina's passion for exhausting hours of study sprang from an unquiet mind. He thought she wore herself out because she did not wish to think. But for all this, in his famous word-portrait of the Queen which he had sent to France early in 1648, Chanut had stressed her profound religious feeling, showing by inference how the influence of her upbringing remained with her. With such a sincere man, his insistence on this point would have been a matter of conviction, not just a courtly gesture in describing one sovereign to another; particularly because Christina was a Protestant and the recipients of this pen-portrait were the Most Christian King and his mother and, of course, Cardinal Mazarin.

Indeed the reason that Chanut gave for writing this profile of Christina was that although at the King's request he was sending her portrait to France, this could give no indication of the fine qualities of her character, more particularly because the mobility of her expression changed her face from one moment to another. Nevertheless he began with a cautiously flattering description of the Queen's appearance. Honesty compelled him to admit, even when describing one sovereign to another, that at first one did not perceive "so many marvels in the beauty" of this twenty-two-year-old princess as when "one considered them at leisure." This was a very polite way of saying that at first glance Christina seemed downright plain, which is confirmed by many other observers. Like Chanut, they all also found that after a while her vivacity made them forget the ugliness.

According to Chanut the Queen's face in repose was pensive; though agreeable and serene. On the rare occasions when she was roused to anger her expression could strike terror in the beholder. In the same way, although she normally spoke with firmness, her voice had the softness of a young girl's, but it could suddenly change to a robust tone much stronger than that normal in her sex. He said that Christina was below average height, though this would not have been apparent if like other women she had worn high-heeled shoes; but for comfort at home, and for walking or riding in the country she wore flat shoes like a man's, made of black morocco leather.

Chanut went on: "She has a great feeling for God and a sincere attachment to Christianity. . . . She does not approve if in scientific discussion anyone disregards the doctrine of grace to philosophize in the pagan fashion; what does not conform to the Gospel seems to her to be but delusion. She shows no bitterness when discussing the differences which exist between Protestants and Roman Catholics. It seems that she has studied these points of disagreement less than is usual among the philosophers, the Jews and Gentiles; her devotion to God is more evident from the consciousness which she shows of being under his protection, than in anything else. For the rest, she is not strict, she does not at all affect outward demonstrations of ceremonial devotion, but what is most remarkable about her is her incredible love of virtue which is her whole joy and pleasure. To this is added an almost excessive passion for glory. From what one can judge, she wishes to have virtue accompanied by honour. Sometimes she likes to talk like the stoics of this pre-eminence of virtue which is our sovereign good in this life—she is marvellously strong on this—and when talking with people whom she knows well she shows her true feelings about the things of this world. It is a great pleasure to see her place her crown beneath her feet and state outright that virtue is the one possession to which all men should be absolutely attached, irrespective of their condition in life. But in the midst of all this she does not forget for long that she is Queen. She is quickly conscious of her crown and, while recognizing its weight, realizes that the first step to virtue is to acquit herself well in her profession. She has great natural talents for achieving success in this, because she has a marvellous facility for understanding and getting to the bottom of affairs, a memory which serves her faithfully, but which she sometimes abuses. She speaks Latin, French, German, Flemish and Swedish and is studying Greek. She has savants in her employ with whom she discusses in her leisure hours all that is most interesting in the sciences, and with that spirit which wishes to know all, she asks about everything. Every day of her life she reads a passage of Tacitus, which she calls a game of chess. . . . She loves discussing debatable questions, particularly with savants who hold contrary views, upon which she never gives her opinion until everyone else has spoken, and then in a few well-chosen words sums up the whole matter."

Chanut then described Christina's penetration and capacity for taking time to arrive at a measured judgment before revealing her own opinion. He noted that she made particular use of these tactics in dealing with the government—letting all the ministers speak first and reserving her opinion to the end, so that they did not know on which side she would ultimately throw her weight.

He said that these characteristics made her appear distrustful: it was true that she was suspicious and a bit slow to reveal the truth and (no doubt judging others by herself) quick to suspect craftiness; but she was reasonable, particularly in dealing with affairs. Chanut also noted that Christina did not discuss matters concerning her own household or anything to do with persons depending in a private capacity on her absolute power; but that she debated in the Senate all questions concerning the government of the state, and that it was "incredible how much power she has over her council."

Referring to Christina's personal life, Chanut remarked her extraordinary physical endurance, how she was indifferent to heat and cold and could stay ten hours in the saddle in the hunting field, and shoot a hare with a single shot better than any man in Sweden. He noted particularly that she never talked to women, being too much taken up with affairs of state or sport to be bothered with them. If anyone bored her, she would cut the conversation short. He said, however, that she was kind to her servants and would chaff them, though they were a bit nervous about this. He confirms that Christina slept for only five hours at night and was little interested in her clothes or appearance—taking only a quarter of an hour to dress in the morning. Except on state occasions, her coiffure consisted only of a rapid combing of her hair and tying it up with a ribbon, and she never wore a hood or mask, as the custom then was, to protect her complexion, but when riding wore a plumed hat. In fact, Chanut said, that if any stranger saw Christina out hunting, wearing a masculine type of coat with a small man's collar, he would never have imagined that she was the Queen. With sound common sense he noted that she carried this personal neglect to excess, especially as there were occasions when it could affect her health. However, he concluded that none of these things mattered to Christina, who was only taken up with her conception of honour and virtue, so much so that one could say that her real ambition was to "make her name famous by her extraordinary merit."

Although this is admittedly a partial portrait of the Queen, for whom Chanut quite evidently entertained a strong esteem and affection, and was written for the personal consumption of young Louis XIV and his mother, whose chief European ally Christina was, it is nevertheless a most revealing document. For in describing the extraordinary qualities of this curious and versatile young woman of twenty-two, Chanut's eye lighted unerringly on the ones which were most significant in her make-up, and those, moreover, which were to bring about her strange destiny. Dominant among them all, as he so clearly realized, was that passion for glory, for "virtue" in the classical, mediaeval and renaissance sense as representing excellence in every form, so far removed from our limited interpretation of the word as applying mainly to sexual morality. This, and the desire to make her name famous in the whole world, were to play a dominant role in Christina's conception of her abdication as the grand gesture which she felt sure would make her name known to all posterity. In her own copy of the *Mémoires de Chanut*, which were published after his death, the Queen made a marginal note on his observation about placing her crown beneath her feet; to the effect that she put beneath her feet what other kings placed upon their heads. Also, on another occasion she noted that the only sovereigns who had laid down their crowns were Diocletian, Almansur, the Emperor Charles V and Christina!

Nevertheless she planned this dramatic gesture with consummate caution and cunning, working it out step by step over a period of six years. She used to the full a quality which Chanut had recognized in her: that of maturing an idea over a long period before she revealed her purpose. At no other time in her life did Christina display this quality so clearly. Even if she was sometimes assailed by doubts, she pursued her secret aim, successively overcoming the opposition to each step of her successor, her ministers, the Råd and the Riksdag.

The first inkling that we have of Christina's plan is her having told Charles Gustavus, in 1647, that she would marry him only if made to by reasons of state. He forced the issue by insisting on seeing her, before he took up the High Command in Germany in 1648, and made her reveal her future intentions by telling him that he would be appointed her successor. But obviously nothing could be done about this until the peace, which she had been striving for, was finally established.

The ink was barely dry on the signatures to the hard-won treaty, before the Queen took the first step. When the Riksdag was summoned in January 1649, she proposed that Charles Gustavus should be nominated her successor. The very idea created a furore, the Queen had publicly agreed to marry her cousin (it was on this understanding that he had been made Generalissimo). What possible need was there for him to be recognized as her successor? He was four years her senior, and even if she died prematurely without children, as her widower he would obviously be her heir. The Government and all the Estates, except the clergy, with whom the Queen was now not popular, were bitterly opposed to the idea and insisted on holding Christina to her promise to marry Charles Gustavus. One cause of this strong opposition was probably the fear of raising up two rival dynasties if, as now appeared possible, Christina might want to marry someone else. Consequently yet another rival branch of the royal house might be raised up to add to the threat of the claims of the Polish Wasas, which had not been forgotten.

At the end of February a deputation of the Riksdag went to see the Queen, but she held firm. The Riksdag were equally firm, and Christina saw that in this impasse the only thing to do was to tell half the truth. She said that she did not wish to marry at all. The Queen's aversion to marriage had already been known for some time, to a widening circle, so that to the members of the Råd it cannot have come as a surprise. But as nobles and extensive landowners they had their own reasons for not wanting Charles Gustavus's succession to be assured if Christina died suddenly. If this were the case, they could not bring pressure to bear upon him to confirm their privileges and ownership of lands before acquiescing in his accession. The shadow of the old elective kingship died hard in Sweden. It will be recalled that the existence of the Polish Wasas and Charles IX's provision that his nephew Duke John must waive his claims before his own son Gustavus Adolphus could succeed, added to the fact that Gustavus Adolphus was under age, had enabled the nobles to wrest very considerable privileges from the young King, before he was officially acclaimed. Christina's own accession at the age of six had posed no problems about whether she would confirm the nobles' rights and possession of their lands; in fact during her minority many of the demesne lands had been sold to the nobility. But if she died young and was immediately succeeded by a young and active king, he would be within his rights in calling for an examination of the whole *status quo* of privileges and land tenure, and of rescinding many of them, by a process known as a Reduction. The next two reigns were to provide ample confirmation for the nobles' fears in this respect.

It was in the face of the Råd's refusal, and even that of the Riksdag committee, that Christina now displayed to the full her extraordinary capacity for political manœuvring. With the help of Bengt Skytte, the son of Gustavus Adolphus's old tutor, who had been ennobled by him and appointed a member of the Råd, Christina succeeded in getting the question of the succession submitted to the Riksdag. At first only the clergy were agreeable but, with the assistance of her uncle Gyllenhielm, who feared an aristocratic oligarchy and knew probably better than anyone else Christina's determination not to marry, she won over the Estate of the bourgeoisie. The peasants followed suit. The Estate of nobles was now in a minority of one, but given the strength of their voting power, their opposition must at all costs be overcome. This the Queen achieved by gaining the Råd's approval by imposing some very stringent conditions upon her successor's status during her own lifetime and the terms for his accession after her death. While Christina reigned, Charles Gustavus would be obliged to follow her directions concerning his personal status. When he succeeded he would have to keep to the Lutheran form of Protestantism, abide by the laws and *not diminish or reduce any privileges already granted.* This last clause was the key to the matter as far as the nobles were concerned. When the diet of the Riksdag closed at the end of March, Charles Gustavus, who was four years older than the reigning Queen, had been declared her successor. Thus, in two months, Christina had succeeded in imposing her will upon the Råd and Riksdag. She said herself that it had only been achieved "with great difficulty, everyone being opposed to it."

No one seems to have dreamt of discussing the matter with the person most concerned. When the news reached him at Nuremberg, Charles Gustavus was quietly and efficiently applying his remarkable capacity for organization to disbanding the unruly mercenary armies in Germany. Immediately he realized that Christina's success in carrying through her plan had almost certainly put paid to all hopes of his marrying her, this faithful but unwelcome suitor wanted to refuse the honour thrust upon him. He appealed to Christina's mother, his own father and even to Bengt Skytte. They counselled silence and patience; in the end Charles Gustavus never even acknowledged the official intimation that he was now to all intents heir to the Swedish crown. He still wrote pathetically to Mathiae, but at the official peace banquets of the executive committee of the Treaty of Westphalia at Nuremberg he was observed to be drinking heavily, possibly to drown his sorrow.

There was one other factor that undoubtedly played a part in Christina's success in this matter. During the last few years the winds of change, and even revolution, had been blowing strongly through Europe. Since 1642, civil war had raged in England, and the very month in which the Riksdag had opened had seen the trial and execution of Charles I. 1647 had brought the popular revolt of Masaniello in Naples against the Spanish crown, and the summer of 1648 the beginning of the Fronde, which was to paralyse France for close on six years. No wonder that as a patriotic Swede, and the last surviving member of the older generation of the Swedish Wasas, Carl Carlsson Gyllenhielm urged his niece to secure the Swedish succession, and that she herself recognized that here for once, personal inclination and duty marched in step. Therefore she summoned all the remarkable forces at her command to achieve a single end.

In March Chanut reported that the Scots General "Reduving" (Patrick Ruthven, Earl of Forth and Brentford, who had served under Gustavus Adolphus) had come to Stockholm as an emissary of the Prince of Wales to seek aid for his father; but in the same month the news of Charles I's execution finally reached the capital. Apparently in Sweden the progress of the English Civil War had been watched with mixed feelings. Chanut found that even at court "there were some who did not think it a bad thing that there should be a public example made of a King by his being deprived of his authority, because he had used it badly and not according to his subjects' wishes," but he added that Charles's execution had "destroyed whatever advantage the English had enjoyed up to now." The French Minister noted that the Queen "suffered such sorrow from it that she decided to contribute personally as much as possible to the chastisement of the criminals, and to re-establish the King of England"; however, this deep impression appears to have been short-lived. On the same day Chanut noted that Christina was overjoyed when she received the news of the ratification of the Peace of Westphalia.

Indeed Charles I's death appears to have been quickly forgotten. No court mourning seems to have been observed. On 4th April a ballet was given in honour of the Queen Mother. The theme was "Victorious and Vanquished Passions," and it is interesting to note that in spite of Christina's recent declaration that she wished never to marry, the verses included overt suggestions that she should find a husband. Possibly this was due to Maria Eleonora's unjustifiable optimism about her own influence in this respect, as she naturally wished to see her daughter settled in a normal married state. In any case it must have been a very splendid occasion, as it was the first time that the new court theatre was used. This had been built into a great hall—normally used for balls and banquets—on the top floor of Stockholm Castle. In 1647 Magnus De la Gardie had brought back from Paris the Italian architect Antonio Brunati, who was probably responsible for the décor, which was typically Italian in style, as well as for the complicated stage machinery that was so popular in the seventeenth century. This stage-machinery enabled gods and goddesses to appear floating in clouds and to descend from them on to the stage. The theatre had separate seating accommodation for the nobles and the bourgeoisie. It was hung with rich tapestries and lit with oil lamps while the seats were covered with costly carpets. The curtains were of white satin trimmed with silver cords, there was also a veil of blue and yellow—the Swedish national colours—and a drop curtain with a painted landscape. The proscenium was painted in the Italian style to represent marble pilasters and statues. The sets included a scene with the sun rising over a city and a wood, a typical Italian water-garden filled with lime, pomegranate and orange trees. There was also a splendid palace set with painted columns of lapis lazuli.

What a dream world this evocation of far-distant Italy must have seemed in the mud and slush of a Stockholm April, more particularly because it cannot have been a very happy month for Christina. News had come that her old and trusted friend Chanut had been raised to the rank of ambassador, but was to be transferred to Holland as mediator at the peace negotiations being carried on there between Sweden and Poland.

The natural modesty and good sense with which he received the news of his promotion becomes very clear in Chanut's own descriptions of his reactions to the new appointment. Not being a rich man he was worried about the extra expense involved, and also about the protocol which he should observe in taking official leave of Christina, now that he represented his own King in person. *A la rigueur* he was entitled, like a king, to keep his hat on in the presence of the sovereign to whom he was accredited, but despite the importance attached at that time to protocolaire privileges, his own good taste made him remain uncovered in the Queen's presence. Noticing this, Christina begged him to be covered. Chanut replied with ready wit: "I would do so Madame, if it seemed to me that the King my master would wish it in an Ambassador accredited to your Majesty, but as he is so polite a Prince and so well brought up, and your Majesty is so worthy to be served, he would not himself wish to appear in your presence other than uncovered, and for this reason I must do the same."

A few weeks after Chanut's departure, the last days of May brought Christina one of the great moments of her life—the arrival of the treasures from the Emperor Rudolf's collection in Prague, which had been seized by Königsmarck for the Queen. When the Swedes captured the Hradschin palace, its great doors were barred and locked and the unfortunate custodian, Eusebius Miseron, was tortured before he would reveal the hiding place of the keys. Although Miseron had managed to conceal a few of the most important pictures, putting copies in their place, the vast bulk of this fabulous collection, including genuine works by Titian, Tintoretto, Veronese, Correggio, Andrea del Sarto and a host of lesser artists, as well as some mistakenly attributed to Mantegna and others, were stripped of their frames and packed to be sent to Sweden. There were nearly 600 pictures, statuettes of bronze, marble and alabaster, cases of silver, pearls, and semi-precious stones, embroideries, majolica, scientific instruments and ancient manuscripts, including the famous silver Gothic codex of Ulfila (now at Uppsala).

All these bales and cases of loot had been loaded on to a flotilla of barges in frantic haste, to be towed up the Elbe and away before the news of the Peace of Westphalia reached Prague, which might have put a stop to this rape of the treasure. The convoy left on 6th November, with only three days to spare. Its progress was so slow that in the end ice blocked the river. Everything had to be off-loaded and taken overland to Wismar; with it went a live lion, also the booty of war. Christina had been following the progress of this—her personal "gratification," as it was euphemistically called—with anxious interest. She wrote frequently to Königsmarck to try to hurry it up; finally in the spring it was all embarked for Stockholm. Her excitement at its arrival can be imagined, for hitherto some hundred works by minor German, Flemish and Swedish painters had been all that the royal gallery could boast of. The glowing light and colour of the Italians—especially the Venetian school—came as a revelation to Christina. They were given pride of place in the *Chambre des Arts* in Stockholm Castle, and remained her preference all her life.

Naturally the lion's share, and the lion, went to the sovereign, but the loot of the Thirty Years War had for some time past been seeping into the castles and manors of Sweden, bringing with it a revolution in the lives of their owners. The aristocracy had seen the luxury and splendour in which their continental compeers lived, and were determined to emulate it. Indeed ever since the sixteen-thirties the great nobles, and those who had been ennobled after making fortunes in the war, had been building new castles and town and country houses. At first the interior decoration and furniture retained the traditional Swedish simplicity. Though rich with inlaid woods and fine tapestries, the rooms were furnished in sober, solid style. Now, with the influx of looted treasures, walls were covered with painted and gilded Spanish leather, and German and Italian cabinets, enriched with marquetry and inlaid semi-precious stones, stood in rooms filled with ornate, gilt furniture. Raftered ceilings were replaced by painted and stucco decoration in somewhat clumsy imitation of the contemporary baroque style of the rest of Europe. Jacob De la Gardie's town house in Stockholm called Makalös, the Swedish for Nonesuch or Nonpareil, was the epitome of this nouveau-riche Sweden.

This changing world of mid-seventeenth-century Sweden lives before our eyes today in two rooms in the Nordiska Museum in

Stockholm. The first, transported bodily from Tynnelsö Castle in Lake Mälaren, contains the traditional, sober, solid furniture—the table and chairs once belonged to Axel Oxenstierna. The second, brought from Ulosunda Castle, was decorated for Count Anders Torstensson and his wife who were married in 1665. Here the bed alcove, with its pilasters, swags and trophies, might have been made for an Italian palace; the gilt torchères, crystal chandeliers and candelabra, for a French salon. It is scarcely surprising that in this atmosphere, which was accelerated by the Peace of Westphalia, Christina's own way of life changed, and that, especially after the arrival of the Prague collections, her interests began to veer from erudite subjects to the study of the arts.

This change, combined with her curiosity about foreign countries, had led the Queen to take a particular interest in a young Pomeranian, Matthias Palbitzki, who had been in the Swedish service for some time and had recently returned from his travels to the Mediterranean and Levant. Palbitzki, who was also an enthusiastic antiquarian, had indeed accomplished a remarkable journey for those days. During an absence of three years he had got as far as Egypt, though he had not been able to continue on to Persia as he had hoped. Instead he had returned to Italy, staying eleven months in Rome, and because of his knowledge of the country the Queen now dispatched him on an official mission to Venice. She also instructed him to return to Rome to buy drawings and antique marbles, also to bring back an Italian sculptor and the architect Jean de la Vallée, who had written to say that his debts prevented him leaving the Eternal City. On his way Palbitzki stopped in Florence, where he was well received by the Grand Duke of Tuscany and introduced to one of his kinsmen, Paolo Giordano Orsini, Duke of Bracciano. Palbitzki and Orsini had much in common, for the Duke was a traveller who had been as far afield as Norway. He was also a man of parts, being a poet, artist, engraver, musician and inventor. Evidently Palbitzki's descriptions of the intellectual Queen of Sweden stirred Orsini's interest, for in June he wrote to her, a letter which was to be the beginning of a long epistolary friendship.

Christina's interest in Palbitzki, the various commissions which she gave him on his journey, and the enthusiasm with which she entered into correspondence with Orsini, show clearly the feeling of intellectual suffocation which she was evidently beginning to feel in Sweden. Like Catherine the Great of Russia, who in the next century was to commission a French artist to draw for her the classical ruins of Sicily, Christina evidently thirsted to know more of the world outside; particularly about those legendary, sunlit countries of the Mediterranean whose glory and beauty had been familiar to her from childhood through the writings of the classical authors. Her friendship with Chanut had introduced the Queen to French intellectual circles, but now her spirit roved more widely, avidly seeking to hear and to know more about contemporary artistic developments, especially in Italy. Christina's later letters to Orsini show clearly how she tried to keep herself abreast of all that was going on there, and how the revelation of the paintings of the Italian school had kindled her interest in the arts.

The most revealing of these letters was actually written in May 1652, but it shows how for years past the Queen had been studying the Italian scene:—"I will send you my portrait when it is finished, also a miniature of a Titian, and if you like will send you other copies of Italian pictures from Prague which include Veronese, Polidoro, Correggio, Tintoretto, etc. All the Prague Gallery is here and is very beautiful, there are Albert Dards (Dürer) and other German masters of which I do not know the names; which anyone but I would admire very much. I swear to you that I would give them all for a pair of pictures by Raphael, and think that I was doing them too much honour. I would like to know if there is any better composer than Carissimi or anyone who approaches him? What are the best Roman and Italian poets? They say that Balducci is good, I don't think so. Is Guarini [Girolamo Grazzini, author of *La Conquista di Granata*] good? He seems so to me, and would seem wonderful to anyone who has not read Tasso or Ariosto, but I only read him after them; what is the judgment of your academies on him? Please excuse my curiosity . . . this is the only amusement that I have, to nourish my spirit with these beautiful things in the hours from which my other occupations allow me a breathing space, and I would rather lose my life than give up these innocent pleasures."

On 26th July of the same year Orsini wrote to Christina, evidently in answer to yet another of her letters filled with questions. He gave a detailed chronology of Pietro da Cortona's major works, including the frescoes in the Barberini and Pamphilj palaces in Rome and his work for the Grand Duke of Tuscany, which Palbitzki had probably seen. He added that the artist was now engaged on mosaics for St Peter's and that he was very good, but so also was Guercino although he was now an old man. The Duke continued "there are good sculptors other than Cavaliere Bernini, mentioned by Your Majesty, and Cavaliere Algardi." He listed some of their works and then turned to the musicians, saying that Horatio Benvolo of St Peter's was as good as Carissimi, and mentioned other famous musicians of the day.

Christina may have picked up information about Italian composers from an Italian musician called Tommaso (no record of his surname has survived), who had spent some time at her court. After he returned to Rome, Tommaso told the Vatican librarian, Holstenius, that the Queen had constantly questioned him about life in Rome and especially about its monuments. One of the best Italian singers, Baldassare Ferri, was also in Sweden for some time, and Brunati too, as a stage designer, would have been well informed about the Italian theatrical world. By 1652 Christina also had two Roman sculptors at her court, G. Peroni and N. Cordier, and yet another agent in Italy scouting for acquisitions for her collections. This was Nicholas Heinsius, son of Daniel the famous Dutch philologer and himself a philologer, who had already been in Stockholm in 1649. In May 1652 Christina wrote to Heinsius in Italy asking him for catalogues of books for sale, for descriptions of medals that might be on the market, and particularly if he could buy any of the letters of the famous antiquarian Cassiano dal Pozzo for her. She assured Heinsius that he could have all the money he needed for his travels, adding "and again you must not leave Italy without seeing Sicily, and stay as long as you like anywhere that may be useful for my service."

The summer of 1649 was to bring another excitement for Christina. In August there arrived a couple who were to give added impetus to her longing for another world, and indeed to open her eyes to the existence of one which she had hitherto only glimpsed through Magnus's descriptions of his Paris triumphs. These new visitors were Nicolas de Flécelles, Comte de Brégy, and his wife Charlotte, who although she was the niece of the learned and celebrated Claude de Saumaise, was famed for frivolity rather than learning.

Until now foreign visitors to Stockholm had come for the most part on business—official or otherwise—and although they might become valued friends as Chanut had done, they were inevitably of a serious turn of mind. The Brégys were birds of a very different feather. He was tall, handsome and distinguished, and instantly appealed to Christina, who liked men of a commanding presence; the Comtesse has been variously described as "a finished coquette, affected but very amusing," and as a "provocative beauty." In the Brégys the Queen met for the first time the polished products of the Paris salons, and was completely fascinated. This sophisticated couple had come to Sweden simply as tourists returning from a diplomatic post in Poland, but in no time they became the centre of court life. Although Brégy made no secret of his amused surprise at the simplicity of the northern capital, Christina tried her very best to tempt him to stay there. She suggested that he should become chamberlain of the court or even that he might command a corps of French guards, to be recruited specially for the purpose. But the Brégys had no intention of forsaking the flesh-pots of Paris for these honours. No matter how complimentary they might be to Christina herself, like rare birds of passage, which they so closely resembled, at the first threat of a northern winter they were in a fever to be off. In vain did Christina try to hurry on for their benefit the first performance of the grandest ballet yet staged in Sweden. John Ekeblad, a gentleman of her court, wrote to his brother in the country on 23rd October saying that the Queen had not even attended the funeral of Axel Oxenstierna's wife because she said that she was ill. Though really she was too taken up with the ballet for the Brégys, and they were trying to get away before the sea froze over.

This ballet, which was first given on 1st November, was adapted from the French *Le Vaincu de Diane* by the famous Swedish librettist and poet Georg Stiernhielm, and is considered to be his masterpiece. This versatile man, who was also the Antiquarian Royal and keeper of the archives, called his adaptation *Then Fångne Cupido* (The Captured Cupid). The theme—no doubt much appreciated by the star performer, Christina herself—was the story of Cupid's defeat by the chaste Diana, a suitable role for the huntress Queen. The ballet was a long one, comprising twelve scenes, and the costumes were magnificent confections of gleaming silks and satins, lavishly ornamented with embroideries, ribbons and gold and silver lace. All of these luxuries had to be imported, and the bill for the dresses alone amounted to 16,850 riksdaler.* Some of the accounts for items bought for Christina's own costumes survive; they include twenty-two ells of wide silver lace, twenty-eight of silver gauze, twelve of white satin ribbon and one pair of English gloves.

The Queen Mother came specially to Stockholm as the ballet was given in honour of her birthday; her daughter met her at Södertälje. But all was in vain. The much sought-after Brégys fled on the earliest boat, leaving the Queen disconsolate; so disconsolate that although she received him ceremoniously, she had little time to spare for a much more illustrious and long-awaited French guest, the great Descartes himself.

Pathetically, in the light of later events, the hermit of Egmond had displayed such enthusiasm in accepting the invitation of the Pallas of the North (as Christina was now beginning to be called in Europe), that instead of coming in the spring or early summer as she had suggested, he had insisted on arriving at the beginning of the arctic Swedish winter. To the astonishment of friends who saw him before he left Holland, Descartes had prepared himself for the encounter dressed as a courtier, with curled hair and lace-trimmed gloves. One of them wrote to Chanut saying that he was reminded of Plato, who was not so divine that he did not wish to know what humanity was like. But it seems likely that all this *empressement* was due in part to his hope of enlisting Christina's aid for the distressed family of his beloved pupil Princess Elizabeth Palatine.

This beautiful and intellectual princess was the daughter of Charles I's sister, Elizabeth Stuart, and the Elector Palatine,

* In the first half of the seventeenth century the Swedish riksdaler weighed twenty-five grammes of silver, the French écu twenty-seven grammes, the Roman scudo 26·42 grammes. In England today one Troy ounce of silver equalling thirty-one grammes is worth 9*s*. 4*d*. The value of the riksdaler may therefore be roughly estimated at 8*s*. 3*d*., the écu at 8*s*. 10*d*., and the scudo at 8*s*. 6*d*., though their purchasing value in the seventeenth century would have been considerably higher.

Frederick V—the ill-fated Winter King and Queen of Bohemia. Her brother Charles Lewis—of the motto "*Cedendo non cedo*"—had fared worse than anyone at the Peace of Westphalia and Elizabeth herself had recently had to leave the refuge of The Hague. Owing to Chanut's partial descriptions, the philosopher probably expected to find in the Queen, if not the beauty of Elizabeth, at least something of her brilliant and steadfast spirit. In youth Elizabeth had refused the crown of Poland, because she would not forsake the Protestant faith in which she had been brought up, and she was to end her days as the Abbess of the Lutheran Abbey of Hertford, which she converted into a retreat for philosophers of all creeds.

What Descartes could not have known was that Christina had changed greatly since Chanut had left Sweden. It must have come as something of a shock to find on his arrival in Sweden the "Pallas of the North" so occupied with the preparations for a ballet (this time to celebrate the Peace of Westphalia) that although she received him ceremoniously, she had little time to spare for other matters and actually suggested that he should take part in it. At the age of fifty-four Descartes's refusal was polite but firm. It was instantly met by the suggestion that he should instead write the libretto. Another "no" was unthinkable in the face of what amounted to a royal command. So Europe's most famous philosopher set to work to compose verses on the *Triumph of Peace* which was the title of the ballet performed on 8th December, Christina's twenty-third birthday. On his return to Stockholm shortly afterwards, Chanut prevented the embarrassed author from destroying his work.

At first, in spite of Christina's neglect, and the unexpected suggestion that he should take five or six weeks holiday in order to get to know Sweden, Descartes' reactions appear to have been favourable though mixed. Shortly after his arrival in October, he wrote to Elizabeth Palatine extolling the Queen's generosity, (she had given him the considerable sum of 400 écus) and described her "gentleness and goodness" which, he said, made everyone devoted to her. But with characteristic frankness Descartes also informed his correspondent that as far as he could make out the Queen had as yet no knowledge of philosophy. He was not sure that she would prove to have a taste for it. Then, more ominously

Christina about the age of fifteen, painted by J. H. Elbfas in 1641.

Count Magnus De la Gardie, painted by M. Merrian in 1649.

Countess Ebba Sparre, called Belle by Christina. Portrait by S. Bourdon.

Overleaf: The old Castle of the Three Crowns in Stockholm.

for the future of his relationship with Christina, he continued "but the virtue which I see in this Princess will oblige me to put my desire to be of use to her before that of pleasing her, which will not prevent me from telling her frankly what I think. If this is not agreeable to her—which I do not expect—I will at least have the satisfaction of having done my duty and I will be able to return all the sooner to my solitude." The very much more worldly Elizabeth may well have wondered what would be the outcome of so frank an attitude towards the imperious Queen, and she would have been right.

After the performance of the *Triumph of Peace* Christina only saw Descartes four or five times before she left for Uppsala, at the end of December. These meetings took place in the very early hours of the morning in the Queen's library in the presence of Freinsheim, her Protestant librarian; it is, therefore, unlikely that any religious subjects were discussed. Even after returning from her fortnight's absence at Uppsala, Christina was evidently in no hurry to resume the discussions, as in a letter written to Brégy on 15th January Descartes told him that he had not seen the Queen. The two men evidently knew each other well and Descartes could not conceal his disillusionment with Sweden. He wrote, "I have seen no one and I think that men's thoughts freeze here in winter, like the waters. . . . I assure you that my desire to return to my solitude grows every day more and more . . . I am not in my element here."

The meetings in the Queen's library, beginning at five a.m. in arctic winter weather, were, however, resumed. Nothing is known of what transpired, or if Freinsheim was again present, but Christina now seems to have seen Descartes more frequently. She requested him to draw up a scheme for the creation of an academy of savants. This was barely completed when Descartes fell ill with congestion of the lungs, of which he died on 11th February. The Queen displayed considerable grief and wanted to erect a magnificent monument to the great philosopher; but at Chanut's insistence he was buried simply, according to the rites of the Roman Catholic church, in the cemetery reserved for foreigners. From there his remains were removed to Paris seventeen years later.

Christina's encounter with Descartes is one of the mysteries of her life. She admired him for years from afar, but when this man who was one of the greatest brains in Europe actually arrived, over a period of some four months she only saw him on a few occasions. It is true that her intellectual orientation appears to have changed during the summer of 1649 (on his arrival Descartes observed that she was now absorbed in the study of letters and Greek literature) and that her preoccupation with the Brégys revealed a much more frivolous side of her character than had hitherto been apparent. Yet it seems that when the Queen actually met Descartes she took a personal dislike to him.

Several factors probably contributed to this unexpected reaction, among them Descartes's unimpressive appearance—he was dark, short and rather rotund. Much more serious was his belief that Christina would regard plain speaking as a compliment; on her own admission she had been unable to bear correction of any kind even in childhood. Apart from his intellectual brilliance, Descartes's dominant trait was his restless and independent character. His entire life had been devoted to his work, and his pursuit of abstract truth seems to have robbed him of realism and humanity to some extent. Elizabeth Palatine had recognized his estrangement from emotion and practical problems, of which her own family's misfortunes had made her only too well aware, and it was under her influence that Descartes had made his study of the passions of the soul. But study was one thing, personal experience another. When confronted with the lively and enquiring mind of the young Queen of Sweden, although Descartes was immediately aware of her shortcomings in philosophy, he apparently failed to perceive her almost boundless self-esteem. Unfortunately for him this was allied to an innate sharpness which would have made Christina quickly aware of his reservations about her accomplishments, even if the philosopher's "plain speaking" was couched in courtly language. At the back of her mind there may have lurked the odious suspicion that perhaps, in his eyes, the capacities of the Pallas of the North did not quite match up to those of Elizabeth.

To Christina's credit it must be admitted that, in one thing at least, her humanity and practical knowledge were far in advance of Descartes. His philosophical detachment had led him to the conclusion that animals had no reasoning powers; because of this they were simply complicated mechanisms resembling clocks and their cries of pain when hurt had no more significance than the creaking of a cart-wheel. Christina's consummate mastery of horses gave her a practical advantage over the philosopher. In her autobiography she said that she loved horses and dogs, and that although she loved hunting she had "never killed an animal without having felt a lively compassion for it."*

Just as Elizabeth Palatine's troubles had made her aware of Descartes's detachment from human feeling, so too the twenty-three-year-old Christina, with all the burdens of a reigning sovereign upon her shoulders, may have felt some disillusionment over her expectation that Cartesian philosophy might provide an answer for her own very real problems.

Thus, this eagerly awaited encounter between the Queen and the philosopher brought disappointment upon both sides. Descartes, probably partly misled by Chanut's descriptions, found a very different woman and a very different welcome from that which he had expected. His nature was such that he could not conceal it. Christina, on the other hand, for the first time in her life was confronted with one of the greatest brains and most independent personalities of the century. Remarkable though some of them were, hitherto the ministers, ambassadors and savants she had known were all, to some extent, dependent upon her favour. The uneasy suspicion raises its head that when the Queen was confronted with someone whom she had the wit to realize was more than a match for her, she did not care for it—the centre of the stage was hers by right. Her resentment and boredom in childhood over the obsequies of her father, provides an early indication of this, so later does her reaction against Axel Oxenstierna, who only when he was safely long dead did she admit to have been one of the outstanding men of the age. In this connection Christina's autobiographical remark about the impression she believed herself to have produced upon the Russian embassy at

* Another philosopher's shortcomings in practical observation of natural life had been noticed by the mediaeval Emperor Frederick II of Hohenstaufen, himself an experienced falconer and bird-watcher. In his treatise *The Art of Hunting with Falcons*, the Emperor wrote "We have followed Aristotle when it is opportune, but in many cases, especially in that which regards the nature of some birds, he appears to have departed from the truth. That is why we have not always followed the prince of philosophers, because rarely, or never, had he the experience of hunting which we have loved and practised always."

the age of seven, "I made the ambassadors feel that which all men feel when they approach something greater," is revealing—she had evidently experienced this sensation herself. Thus, although she did not acknowledge it for many years, it seems that Descartes had made his mark on the Queen. The founder of modern philosophy—the great mathematician and physicist of the seventeenth century who had not dared to publish his work *Le Monde, ou Traité de la Lumière* because its findings were too similar to those of the condemned Galileo—was a convinced Catholic. His faith had stood up to those scientific truths before which Christina's quailed. Years afterwards the Queen recalled that her own conversion had been helped "by certain things Monsieur Descartes had said."

On 31st March 1650, Christina was taken with a shivering fit in the night, but insisted on attending a meeting of the Råd next day. However the fever mounted and she had to take to her bed. By 4th April she was better and sat up in bed to receive the Brandenburg Ambassador, talking to him gaily; her court were very relieved as apparently she had been so worried about herself that they had sat up all night. Still, all through April the Queen was ill with fever and abscesses and in such a weak state that she could not eat. By now Christina appears to have been seriously alarmed, especially as her weakness continued into May. So were the people around her, for she had told them of her fears. Rumours spread and the superstitious Swedes began to see evil omens. Spirits were said to have been seen at night in the royal park. Chanut reported all this to his government with the shrewd comment that the Queen was not so ill as was imagined, and although her doctors were bad, a tertiary fever was not really dangerous in someone of her age. It was her own alarm that was creating the panic. Christina herself probably realized the deficiencies of her doctors. These deficiencies seem to have been common court gossip, for John Ekeblad wrote to his family that the Queen "could not eat and has no appetite. This troubles her as she cannot get better. The only reason for this is the many silly doctors who have demolished her stomach with their medicines, if it hadn't been for this she would have been all right as her ague left her long ago." Still, two months' illness, evidently accompanied by great weakness and depression, to someone of Christina's basically strong constitution and great energy must have been alarming. It seems probable that if the famous vow to become a Catholic was made during an illness, this was a more likely moment, especially after Descartes's recent, sudden death.

Very significantly Chanut reported to his government in April and again in June, though in very guarded terms, that there were suggestions that Charles Gustavus might take over the government and the Queen retire to private life. This would have been a terrible blow to French diplomacy, as Christina was definitely pro-French whereas her cousin was not and, cautious though he was, he had shown his sentiments in Germany. Just how much Chanut knew of Christina's secret plans it is difficult to estimate. Probably she hinted something (possibly even as early as 1648) and he had guessed the rest. Certainly in June Chanut was already acting on the supposition that Charles Gustavus would be the rising star, and was preparing the way for France to enter his good graces on his return to Sweden. The Ambassador enlisted the help of Christina, and the principal ministers of state, to counter any suspicions Charles Gustavus might entertain that France had behaved badly over the peace treaties.

The spring of 1650 was definitely a time of rumours: even Chanut seems to have been a bit ruffled by the extraordinary success of the frivolous Brégys the previous autumn. With some satisfaction, he reported that Axel Oxenstierna had never even replied to the letter that Brégy had written to him, a letter which commented that the Chancellor was one of the shrewdest men alive. After a trip to the country to see her mother, at the end of May, Christina was evidently recovered and beginning to take an interest in the plans for her coronation. Apparently it was not yet decided whether this would be held, as was the tradition, at Uppsala, or as it eventually was, in Stockholm. Ekeblad recorded that the Queen went to Uppsala to see a triumphal arch being built there, possibly the one which was finally erected in Stockholm. In any case the preparations were getting under way. On 28th May a ship filled with fireworks arrived in Stockholm together with a "castle," the gift of General Wittenberg. Evidently this was similar to the "fortress" of cardboard, that went up in a blaze of fireworks at the celebrations concluding the Nuremberg negotiations in June. Ekeblad, however, who retailed all these excitements to his country brother, added that although the Queen had presented fine new liveries to her pages, he himself had not seen a penny of his pay.

Indeed, when the Riksdag met in July the dismal state of the country's finances was foremost in people's minds. They were still paying the same taxes as during the war. Although foreign ambassadors could not be present at the debates, Chanut evidently had a good idea of what was going on. He even tried to get the official reports of matters discussed from Salvius, who had recently returned from Germany and was in high favour with the Queen. Chanut was well aware that the three non-noble Estates were discontented. He reported to Paris that there was talk that at her coronation the Queen might make a Reduction like some of her predecessors, and "take back everything that had belonged to the demesne, though everyone knew that the nobles would never agree to this as they would thus lose their best lands." Chanut added that it was even said that during Christina's minority the Regency had purposely sold these demesne lands so as to weaken the royal power.

What was actually happening was that, to gain her own ends, Christina was using the idea of a Reduction to win the favour of the non-noble Estates and hold it as a threat over the heads of the aristocracy. How successful she was may be estimated by Chanut's later report that in the Riksdag "Her Majesty has absolute control over the peasants, bourgeoisie and clergy who are zealous in her favour."

On 25th September, like a rabbit out of a hat, the proposal was presented to the Riksdag that Charles Gustavus should be appointed not only the Queen's successor, but her heir, and that his male children should succeed him. The aristocracy and the bourgeoisie would not agree; but Christina countered this by absolutely refusing to discuss any question of marriage until the matter was settled. On 9th October she pulled it off. Charles Gustavus became her heir, and from now on was granted the style and title of His Royal Highness, the Prince of Sweden.

Charles Gustavus had returned to Stockholm on 28th September, while his fate still seemed to hang in the balance, but he was given a royal welcome; like "a triumphant king," according to Chanut. A public holiday was declared, the shops were shut and to salvoes of cannon the Queen, ambassadors and the entire court went in procession to meet him. Christina, who appreciated the importance of external pomp, was doing everything to pave the way for Charles Gustavus's acceptance as her heir. The shrewd Chanut had evidently seen for many months which way the wind was blowing, for long before he had asked his government about the all-important question of what protocol he should observe towards the Prince. The reply had come back to "please the Queen in every way." In view of this Chanut decided, on his own initiative, that when he made his ceremonial call on Charles Gustavus he would not mention the embarrassing fact that the Prince had not taken France's interests to heart at Nuremberg, but instead he would praise his activities in Germany.

These were indications that the able diplomat had a much clearer idea of what the Queen intended than did her heir, who probably had not realized that this extraordinary woman had achieved the initial step towards her abdication, eleven days before her coronation. How slowly and carefully Christina had pursued her secret plans must by now have been evident to Chanut. More than three years had passed since she had made her sibylline remark that "time would enlighten" him about her reasons for delaying her coronation. To Charles Gustavus she had also kept her word, given in the summer of 1647, that he would have her final decision before she was twenty-five and the time for her coronation had come. On 8th December 1650, as a crowned, unmarried and anointed Queen, Christina would enter her twenty-fifth year.

By the middle of October, however, all serious matters appeared to have been forgotten in the pageantry and carousel of the coronation. Christina withdrew to Jacob De la Gardie's country house, Jacobsdal, prior to making her state entry into Stockholm. This was a splendid affair with guards, pages, heralds and trumpeters preceding the members of the Råd in their carriages. Charles Gustavus's brother, Adolphus John, came next and then the ambassadors of Brandenburg, France and Portugal. After some heart-searching Chanut agreed that Charles Gustavus should have the place of honour usually reserved for ambassadors, immediately in front of the Queen, because he had noticed that the Prince was now accorded the nordic symbols of royalty—his arms were displayed on his house and stables and he had the same escort of halberdiers as the Queen. In the procession Christina herself drove in a carriage covered with black velvet embroidered with gold. She was surrounded by halberdiers, pages and footmen; her mother's equipage followed after, and then, rather curiously, six camels and twelve richly caparisoned mules, with carts filled with Christina's baggage.

On the mainland, opposite the bridge leading to the castle, stood the triumphal arch erected in the Queen's honour by the Råd. It is probable that the idea of copying the classical Roman tradition was due to the fact that Jean de la Vallée's design was inspired by the Arch of Constantine, which in common with other Roman triumphal arches had been dedicated by the Senate to the various emperors. It will be recalled that Palbitzki had been instructed to hurry the architect's return from Rome in preparation for the coronation celebrations, and it is likely that he came bringing his plans with him. Although it was only a temporary edifice of wood and painted canvas, the arch cost 16,000 écus and was a splendid affair. The decorations were painted in *trompe-l'œil* to represent reliefs in the classical style, and illustrated the Swedish victories in the Thirty Years War. These were surrounded by painted vines, crowns and other royal emblems such as the Lion of the North with a thunderbolt in his paw, and Christina's personal device of the sun. The whole thing was surmounted by the battle standards captured in Germany. After the entry there was a firework display over the water. During the next two days the Queen remained in the castle giving audiences and receiving presents.

Fortunately, 20th October, the day of the Coronation, was one of the few fine ones that autumn. After the usual struggles about precedence, in which the members of the Råd and the great officers of state had flatly refused to give up their place of honour to the representatives of any foreign powers, the knotty problem was, as usual, solved by Chanut's good sense. He declared that as no foreign sovereigns had been invited it would be simpler for the ambassadors to watch the coronation procession from a house on the route. In recognition of this, Christina sent two of her gentlemen to say that a special place had been reserved for Chanut in the church and, as the coronation was a political act, his presence would be regarded as a visit to a palace not to a (Protestant) church!

All participants in the coronation ceremonies gathered in the castle at eleven a.m. and most of them then walked through the streets in procession to the Storkyrkan or Great Church. The members of the Råd and the great officers of state, however, went in carriages. They filed into the church two by two, the great officers of state carrying the regalia. They were led by the Grand Treasurer carrying the golden keys. As Grand Chancellor, Axel Oxenstierna followed bearing the orb, followed in turn by the Grand Marshal, Jacob De la Gardie, who had to be led because he was now blind. The Grand Admiral, Carl Carlsson Gyllenhielm, had recently died and in his place Gustavus Horn carried the sceptre; Per Brahe, the High Steward, came last with the crown. Finally the Queen arrived. Clad in a purple velvet robe made in Paris, she descended from a carriage covered with crimson velvet embroidered with gold. Surrounded by pages and halberdiers, with officers holding a canopy of state over her head, she entered the church. Immediately behind her came Magnus bearing the royal banner, then the heir to the throne followed clad in ermine robes. Charles Gustavus's royal state was further emphasized by his curious broad-brimmed hat being encircled by a high pointed crown. The procession finally wound up with the Queen Mother, John Casimir, the Landgrave Frederick of Hesse and the ladies of the court.

John Mathiae preached the sermon, and after Christina had taken the oath she was anointed, crowned and invested with the rest of the regalia as a herald cried out "the most powerful Queen Christina has been crowned and no other person." The beautiful, delicate silver throne, which is still used by the kings of Sweden and was given by Magnus De la Gardie for this occasion, was now placed in front of the altar. With four generals holding the canopy over her head, and Charles Gustavus standing beside her, Christina received the oaths of allegiance of the members of the Råd. Emerging from the church, the Queen mounted a golden triumphal chariot, drawn by four white horses. With the treasurer walking before her, throwing gold and silver medals to the crowd, she returned in procession to the palace. There, immediately upon her arrival, salutes of guns were fired which lasted two hours.

That night, and for the two nights following, great banquets were held in the palace. The Queen dined in solitary state at the high table, with Adolphus John serving her as cup-bearer and Count Charles Lewenhaupt as carver. There were so many guests that the great hall was literally filled to overflowing and tables had to be placed in adjoining rooms. During these three days all the Estates took the oath of fealty to the Queen, and the nobles knelt and had their fiefs confirmed to them, which must have been a great relief after the threats of a Reduction.

On 24th October the celebrations started again with two of the curious Swedish Upptags. These resembled the contemporary English "barriers" but were more elaborate. They consisted of a masque, a procession in fancy dress and a joust, and usually ended up with a torch-lit procession and dancing. Four were held during October and November, of which the most famous was the *Pompe de la Félicité*, which was apparently given both in French and Swedish. The theme, which was aptly chosen to flatter the Queen, extolled the fact that true happiness is not to be found in love or war, but in virtue, amity and concord.

As usual John Ekeblad reported these doings of the court to his family in the country, giving an amusing insight into what went on behind the scenes. He said that Count Lewenhaupt's cavalcade was not a very grand affair. He himself took part in it and would not even have had a horse if Lennart Torstensson hadn't lent him one. Moreover the trappings of the horses were poor and the triumphal cars not very cleverly decorated; the best was one "drawn" by two pasteboard elephants. Wachtmeister's, on the other hand, was very fine. Ekeblad had been invited to take part in it by Klas Tott; it took place on a beautiful cold day and they were all mounted on fine horses from the Queen's own stables. At the jousting and games afterwards Magnus took a toss when tilting at the Turk's head, but this did not prevent him from presiding on the same evening at his magnificent banquet, where Charles Gustavus was present and everyone drank a great deal.

On 10th November, Christina's cousin and old companion of her studies, Eleonora Palatine, was married to the Landgrave Frederick of Hesse and a banquet was given in the evening. This appears to have been a more intimate family affair, as it was held, not in the great hall but in a salon known as the square room where the court often met. The guests were mostly the court ladies, with a sprinkling of the grander cavaliers. On the same day three of Torstensson's maids were married. Ekeblad's description of a party being given for them in one of the small salons in the castle, where he himself helped serve the crowds of guests, casts an interesting light on the intimate feudal atmosphere which still reigned at the Swedish court.

Two days afterwards there followed one of the most ambitious entertainments given for the coronation. Evidently, like the senators' triumphal arch, this was an attempt to model the celebrations on the grandeur of ancient Rome. A series of fights between animals was arranged, of the type that used to be given in the Roman Colosseum. (Possibly the arrival of the famous Prague lion had given rise to the idea.) For all her alleged love of animals, Christina was present on this occasion and so was her mother, but barbarously cruel as the whole spectacle seems to us today, none of the combatants were allowed to fight to the death.

Ekeblad, who was evidently much affected by the whole affair, gave a detailed account of how first an unfortunate calf was chased by a lion, but was not apparently killed. After this a bear was loosed into the arena and tore a mannikin, made to represent a man, into a thousand shreds, before giving chase to the lion. The bear jumped on this unfortunate beast's back, hanging on with his claws and giving him terrific buffets, until the lion succeeded in getting free and savaged the bear with its talons. Ekeblad says that the poor bear cried so terribly that the lion was returned to its cage, but its trials were not at an end. A buffalo and a horse were now loosed in the arena. The buffalo butted the bear and the horse kicked him. Finally, to Ekeblad's relief, the bear was left alone and jumped into a pool and took a bath. Ekeblad said that everyone was surprised at the poor showing put up by the lion.

The bread-and-circuses atmosphere of the capital was, however, on the wane after the first week of November. On 6th November another diet of the Riksdag had begun, which was to prove to be the longest and one of the most significant in Swedish history. The non-aristocratic Estates had evidently not forgotten the taste of power which they had enjoyed during the diet in the summer, when their alliance with the Queen, together with the threat of Reduction, had forced the aristocracy to accept Charles Gustavus as heir. Apparently they had now realized that they need not always follow obediently in the wake of the aristocracy. This was something new in Swedish politics. Often now, under the leadership of the Archbishop of Uppsala, and with Christina's tacit support, they challenged the aristocracy, even reverting to the question of a Reduction. They succeeded in wresting promises for better conditions, and the clergy actually were given new privileges which became law in November. To save themselves from the Reduction, the nobility were forced to give in to the Queen's conditions for Charles Gustavus's recognition as heir and eventual successor, though some of these included a measure of reassurance for them. A list of twelve articles governing the whole matter was now drawn up, the most important of which preserved all the power in Christina's hands as long as she reigned. Curiously, in view of the bad state of the country's finances, most questions of taxation were put off till the next meeting of the Riksdag; possibly this was done so as not to mar the festive occasion of the Queen's coronation by acrimonious discussion. Christina was evidently determined that there should be no mistake about Charles Gustavus's new status. At the last meeting of the Riksdag he sat in a chair of state on her right hand, though, with a nice distinction noted by Chanut, not under her canopy or on her raised dais. However the Prince was now accorded the use of the Swedish royal arms, with those of Palatine placed in an escutcheon *en surtout*, and the style *Carolus Dei Gratia Regni Sueciae Princeps Electus*.

The last spectacle of the coronation celebrations took place on 9th January. This was the ballet *Le Parnasse triomphant*. It proved to be the most expensive and elaborate ever given in Sweden, rising to new heights of sophistication in that it abounded in complicated mechanical devices and was almost certainly performed in French. Efforts were evidently made to give it a very cosmopolitan character: an Indian, a Persian and a Castilian poet were included among the dramatis personae. The theme, as might be expected, was chosen to flatter Christina. The first scene showed the flourishing empire of the Muses, the second their destruction in time of war and unrest, and finally their triumphant restoration, thanks to the victorious peace treaty and the happy coronation of the Majesty of Sweden. The sets were very elaborate. The nine

Muses appeared seated on an imposing Mount Parnassus with the well of Hippocrene before them, and at the end of the first act Mount Parnassus burst open, revealing six shepherds who came on to the stage and sang, accompanying themselves on the lute. In the final scene Aurora and the Muses stepped down from the sky to carry Virtue up to the heavens, and Mount Parnassus was lit with a blaze of light.

It is not surprising that on 15th January, after the celebrations had finally ended, Ekeblad wrote to his brother that the court was empty. Everyone had gone to the country to recover, and there were only two gentlemen left to serve the Queen. Nevertheless Christina apparently expected to receive the same service from these two as from the whole court when it was present. Poor Ekeblad complained that his arms were so tired from carrying food that he could scarcely hold a pen, and that he had no need to play tennis as "the stairs in the palace give me enough exercise."

Ekeblad was not the only person discontented with Christina, early in the New Year of 1651. Her high-handed tactics in forcing through the succession had alienated many members of the Råd, and more particularly Axel Oxenstierna, who had retired to his estates with feelings not unmixed with jealousy. Clearly he realized that Salvius had now become the Queen's chief adviser. At the end of January Christina replied to this gesture by taking the leadership of the Chancery and Riksdag away from him. On 4th March he openly criticized her government in the Råd, though she was not present. In the same month the Queen even allowed Salvius to recall Oxenstierna's son Bengt from Germany, without his knowledge. Reporting all this to the French government, Chanut said that Christina now exercised practically absolute power, but public opinion would make it impossible for her to continue in this course for long and that she must be intending to abdicate within the space of a year or two.

However at the end of the month the Queen's attitude suddenly changed completely. She started to make advances to Oxenstierna, agreeing with his policy in dealing with the Church. This action probably sprang from her desire to get a free hand to send Salvius to Lübeck for negotiations with the Poles. The astute Oxenstierna must have agreed to this with concealed mirth, as the Polish question was a political quagmire in which any man could lose his reputation. But Christina's conciliatory tactics had a far more profound cause. She now wanted to stand well with everyone because, as she told Magnus in April, she had definitely decided to abdicate and she knew that this would be no easy matter. Her favourite was very naturally horrified at her intention because he stood to lose more than anyone—his posts as Riksmarskalk and as Governor of Livonia as well as remunerative diplomatic ones. But no matter what protests he made, Christina ordered him to write to Charles Gustavus at the end of April, telling him to meet Magnus at Uppsala as he had an important communication to make. Christina could not herself be present at this interview as she was again ill. This made secrecy easier, as discretion indicated that the meeting should take place away from the prying eyes and ears of the capital.

In the event, the meeting did not take place at Uppsala. Christina learnt from his brother that Charles Gustavus was planning to go to the Island of Öland. On 7th May she wrote to the Prince saying that Magnus would see him, and would tell him of her decision: all she asked by way of recompense was that he would not oppose her. Charles Gustavus had not wanted to go to Uppsala; he hated mixing with court circles and was only too conscious of the fact that he did not shine in them. The last time he had been to court he had got hopelessly drunk. In the end the two brothers-in-law met at Gripsholm on 9th or 10th May. In that grim, old castle whose walls had witnessed so many dramas of Swedish history and the Wasa dynasty, Charles Gustavus learnt from Magnus of Christina's intention to abdicate within a few months.

In his dismay at this astonishing news, Charles Gustavus decided to go and see his father and ask his advice. John Casimir's health was not very good now, and he lived in retirement in the Castle of Stegeborg, on the coast south of Nyköping. Charles Gustavus got there in the middle of May, and the advice that John Casimir gave his son was consistent with Axel Oxenstierna's estimate of his wiliness; but it also seems to have coincided with Charles Gustavus's natural inclinations. The Prince was to show himself very unwilling to accept Christina's offer, thereby making it plain that the whole initiative was hers. He was to take the line that he was her loyal subject who would only accept the crown if it were forced upon him, and the country in general accepted his accession. Charles Gustavus then wrote a letter to Mathiae (who seems to have retained his old position as secret go-between, and friend, to the two cousins) saying that Christina's project would be very difficult to carry out and that he still hoped that she would marry him.

It was now rapidly becoming essential for Christina and Charles Gustavus to meet and talk matters over. As a cover plan it was decided that the Queen should accompany her mother, who had recently been ill, to her new residence in the castle of Nyköping which was close to Stegeborg, and that a family council should be held there.

Unaccountable, as it must have seemed to the others, Christina delayed her departure for Nyköping. At the beginning of June, her mother went there alone. After further consultations with his father, Charles Gustavus arrived there on 18th June, and the next day the Queen also set off for Nyköping. Chanut, who saw her there when he came to kiss hands on his departure for Lübeck, seems to have guessed the reason for her journey. He informed his government of his belief that the Queen intended to abdicate, adding that it was possible that she might retire to live on Öland (Christina had at this time been talking of making an expedition there or to Gotland). Chanut was also mystified by Christina's delay in leaving Stockholm and, no doubt naturally influenced by the Fronde in France, he mistakenly believed that she was afraid to leave the capital. Apparently he saw the innocuous Charles Gustavus in the role of a potential Swedish *frondeur*. That so able a man as Chanut could entertain such a belief goes to show not only how wise John Casimir had been in the advice he gave to his son, but also how well Christina was able to keep her own secrets.

The Palatines were, in fact, in a very embarrassing situation. They could not bring themselves to believe that Christina really intended to give up her throne. Despite all that she had said, they thought that at the last moment she would change her mind. No mention whatsoever had yet been made of her leaving Sweden and going abroad after her abdication. To these men who had known her all her life, the prospect of the very active and imperious Queen being content to live in retirement on a small and isolated island must, understandably, have seemed improbable.

They also knew that if Charles Gustavus did become king, he would be faced with a country nearing bankruptcy and be forced to put through many unpopular financial measures, including a Reduction. Nevertheless Christina had been right when in February 1649 she had disagreed with Torstensson's protests against making Charles Gustavus her successor. Torstensson said that Gustavus would marry no one but Christina, and she replied: "Oh but yes, love does not burn exclusively for one person and a crown is a very pretty girl." When it came to the point, neither Charles Gustavus nor John Casimir really intended to refuse outright if Christina was prepared to abdicate, though they still hoped that the matter would be solved by marriage.

Curiously enough Chanut also believed that Christina would ultimately be forced to this, in spite of the fact that he well knew the utter repugnance with which she regarded marriage. She had once told him that she could not bear the subjugation of being a married woman. The idea disgusted her. She would never contemplate the idea of someone behaving to her "as a peasant does with his field." Here no doubt there was something of the same attitude as that recognized in Elizabeth of England by a Scots Ambassador, who said to her, "Madam, I know your stately stomach; ye think that if ye were married, ye would be but Queen of England, and now ye are King and Queen both; ye may not suffer a commander." But there was more to it than that in Christina's case. Apart from the early infatuation with Magnus, there had been no signs of a Robert Dudley in her life, nor had she ever considered marriage for reasons of state. Elizabeth had contemplated marrying both the Archduke Charles of Austria and Alençon, her last suitor, for whose premature death she had wept for days.

Evidently none of Christina's *démarches* by letter, and through third parties, had prepared Charles Gustavus and Adolphus John Palatine for the firmness with which she informed them—on 23rd June—of her intention to abdicate. No documents have survived to tell us what Christina actually said, apart from a letter which Charles Gustavus sent by his brother's hand to his father. In it he wrote that Adolphus John would explain by word of mouth exactly what had passed, which he himself had been "horrified to hear, let alone mention" in writing. Charles Gustavus had, it seems, protested violently, and so did John Casimir to Magnus, whom Christina had sent to see him for the purpose of giving him a detailed report of her plans. To Magnus, John Casimir said that he could hardly draw breath. To the Queen he wrote a letter saying that he could not agree with her plans.

John Mathiae was also called in to reason with Charles Gustavus. But like the Palatines themselves, he was evidently very nervous of the innuendoes and intrigues that would result, to the detriment of the family, if any report of these secret negotiations leaked out. Charles Gustavus was so much afraid of this that, although he had to go to Stockholm early in July for Torstensson's funeral, and willy-nilly the abdication was again discussed, he took the precaution of sending all his suite and baggage to Öland, so that he had a valid excuse for not staying long in the capital. Christina had an even more unwelcome plan in store for him. She tried to persuade her cousin to become engaged to a German princess who was then staying at the court, so that when she came to make the public announcement of her abdication she could present her heir as well on the way to being married and ensuring the succession.

Christina's return journey from Nyköping had provided yet another reason why the succession should be firmly settled. One evening she fainted at supper. For an hour she lay unconscious with a pulse so weak that no one could feel it. The attack was a very sudden one and evidently terrified her, for as she collapsed Christina said "Goodbye my dear Count" to Magnus, who was sitting next to her. Everyone was so appalled that they completely lost their heads and did not even try to revive the Queen. She remained semi-conscious until after midnight and only regained consciousness when the doctors, who had been hurriedly called, arrived from Stockholm which was about five miles away. However, Christina was sufficiently recovered when she saw them to say, with grim humour, to her French doctor Du Rietz, "I thought I would never see you again." For six hours she remained in severe pain, but by the next day she was well enough to return to Stockholm with Charles Gustavus.

Too much work had not been the only reason for Christina's collapse on the way back from Nyköping. In addition to mental strain she must also have been suffering from great emotional tension, which was not only caused by her plans for abdication.

During March and April Axel Oxenstierna had been negotiating the terms of a commercial agreement with the Portuguese Ambassador, Pinto Pereira, whose mission to the Swedish court had included this task, as well as that of representing King John IV at Christina's coronation. Earlier, while Oxenstierna had been away in the country, the Queen herself had discussed the agreement with the Ambassador, through his interpreter Gomez de Serpa: apparently Pinto Pereira knew no language but his own. As chance would have it, when the negotiations were reaching a crucial phase and Christina again took a hand in them, the official interpreter fell ill and Pinto Pereira took with him to the audiences his Jesuit chaplain instead. The chaplain was Antonio Macedo, who had been a missionary in Africa, a teacher of humanities and morals, and was a good Latinist. Christina quickly spotted that Macedo was a priest, in spite of his being dressed as a layman. Feeling her way cautiously, she began by asking him questions about literary subjects, as well as discussing the agreement with the Ambassador. Later she started to discuss religion, and Macedo's ready replies confirmed the Queen's suspicions about his real identity. Gradually their discussions became more profound, and Pinto Pereira realized that these exchanges were a good deal longer than what was actually required for his negotiations with the Queen. He questioned Macedo, but the Jesuit replied that Christina was also asking him about literary matters, to which, in courtesy, he was bound to reply. Knowing the Queen's curiosity about all things, the Ambassador was satisfied for the moment. It was, of course, a situation that would have appealed immensely both to Christina's delight in intrigue and her wry sense of humour.

These curious conversations with Macedo began in the spring or early summer of 1651. As they progressed the Jesuit noticed that the Queen always spoke very respectfully of the Pope and was interested in, and not at all hostile to, Roman Catholicism. Seizing on this almost incredible opportunity, Macedo tried to explain and to teach Christina as much as possible, despite the extraordinary circumstances in which they were conversing, about his faith. Both the Queen and the priest now tried to find excuses for private conversation without arousing suspicion. People, however, were beginning to talk and the Ambassador was suspicious that Macedo was betraying him politically. Worse still, Christina knew that the embassy must come to an end when the commercial negotiations were finished, and that this was likely to occur in August or September.

The encounter with Macedo was fortuitous, but for years, first unconsciously and then consciously, the Queen's mind had been preparing for it. As we have seen, from childhood, her restless and enquiring intelligence had made her question much in her own religion, even that which was told her by the well-loved John Mathiae. Like her father, Christina was naturally unbigoted; as she grew up the increasingly narrow sectarianism of the Swedish Church evidently alienated her; when she had displayed an interest in Protestant syncretism it had been ruthlessly quashed, so she had turned instead to learning, to contacts outside Sweden and the study of other religions, gradually evolving a creed of her own. Not daring to show her feelings too openly, she had nevertheless discussed religion with Chanut. By his own account, she was interested to find that the Roman Catholic faith was very different from what she had been led to believe. Then came the encounter with Descartes which, even if not seemingly successful, had, together with his works, made Christina realize that this man who was one of the most daring thinkers of his time was nevertheless a believing Catholic. The conspiratorial discussions with Macedo, therefore, did not resemble the light on the road to Damascus, but were the culmination of a long sequence of events in Christina's life.

With the threat of Macedo's imminent departure before her, Christina was now forced to make a decision. According to Macedo's own account the Queen summoned him to the castle on 2nd August and "withdrawing with me into the most remote rooms of her private apartment, she informed me that she wished to tell me something of the greatest importance. Drawing close and speaking into my ear she said 'Padre Macedo you are the first Jesuit I have known, and from the knowledge and experience I have of your goodness I think I can rely on your fidelity and prudence. As you are going to leave, I want you to arrange, without fail, that two Italians of your Company be sent to me, experts in all branches of knowledge, who under cover of gentlemen seeing the world, can stop at my court, so that without suspicion I can make use of them, to which effect I will give you a letter to your General.' "

Macedo went on to relate how at this tremendous news he thanked the Queen and offered to serve her faithfully, swearing secrecy to her. He returned home filled with jubilation, wondering what excuse he could find to get away, and in the end he asked the Ambassador's permission to go to Hamburg. This was evidently refused, as Christina now told Macedo to leave without saying anything more. After he had been warned that a ship for Lübeck was already at the "Port of Balen about thirty-five miles away" (possibly a misinterpretation for Dalarö), Macedo went to say a last goodbye to the Queen. She gave him the promised letter of credence for the General of the Jesuits, written in her own hand and, although Macedo does not himself mention it, a special passport, money and a gold chain. Macedo's last words to Christina were to beg her humbly to fulfil her "holy inspiration," to which she replied that if she "knew the Roman religion to be the right one, she would embrace it." Again she asked him to send the two Jesuits, with whom she could discuss matters without suspicion, and again she recommended him to secrecy.

After this leave-taking, Macedo related how he "left the palace by the back door which gives on to the sea, and on a *felucca* arrived at a rock." Here he stayed the night, as he could not reach his ship that day. The next day, he got to "Balen," where an agent of the Queen's had arrived, because of the Ambassador's protests about Macedo's flight. Ostensibly this man had been sent to arrest him, but Christina had given secret orders that if he found Macedo he was to let him go, and pretend that he had not discovered him. Macedo boarded his ship safely and set sail for Lübeck at the end of August. By the end of October he was in Rome reporting to the General of the Order, who consulted the Secretary of State, Cardinal Chigi, before acting on his momentous news.

For Christina the die was now very nearly cast. It was illegal for a Swede to be a Roman Catholic, and even if she had not absolutely committed herself to Macedo, in her own mind she knew that she was playing with fire. The mere fact that she had entered into correspondence with the General of the Company of Jesus—those arch-priests of the Counter-Reformation—meant that there was now no real possibility of turning back. On 7th August the Queen summoned the Råd to tell them of her intention to abdicate, and of calling the Riksdag on 22nd September to inform them of this fact.

CHAPTER 5

Conversion: 1651–1654

The Queen's announcement of her intention to abdicate took many of the Råd by surprise, although Axel Oxenstierna and Magnus had, of course, known of it beforehand. She gave three reasons for her decision: that her abdication would be best for the country because a man was needed to rule and to lead the army in war, that it would also be best for Charles Gustavus, and that she herself longed for peace and calm. She said that she had been thinking of abdicating for five or six years (in fact since the crucial year of 1645) and added that there were other reasons which she could not mention.

As she said this Christina's thoughts must have gone to Macedo aboard his ship, awaiting a fair wind for Lübeck. His escape was not to be so easy. Chanut learnt of his presence in Lübeck and of his later arrest in Hamburg. Evidently he was aware that Macedo was a Jesuit, although rumours were circulating that he was a traitor who had defected to Spain in the midst of his own country's struggle for independence. Anyway, on his arrest Macedo was found to be in possession of a passport, money and a gold chain, which Christina had given to him.* From this, Chanut concluded wrongly that the Portuguese Ambassador must have been aware of the Jesuit's activities. He was nearer the truth in guessing that Christina was a party to them, and in noting in his dispatch

* In the seventeenth century passports were not necessarily issued by heads of state or their representatives only to their own nationals, as is the custom today.

that, seemingly, she bore little hostility towards Roman Catholics.

When informing the government of her intention to abdicate Christina took the same line with them as she had with Charles Gustavus, saying that she wanted assent not advice. She very well knew that without their backing it would be impossible to win over the Riksdag in the autumn. Curiously, even after her long battle to get Charles Gustavus nominated her successor, she seems to have underestimated the opposition which so serious a proposal was bound to arouse. In any event, the reaction of the Råd was rapid and firm. They evidently realized, much more clearly than the Queen, that her project would meet with absolute refusal from the Estate of the nobility in the Riksdag, especially through fear that Charles Gustavus would be bound to make a Reduction. The Råd were also completely at a loss to understand Christina's reasons—she, the daughter of the great Gustavus Adolphus, give up the throne of Sweden without any apparent reason! It was a situation entirely beyond their comprehension.

Axel Oxenstierna now asked the Queen's permission to discuss the matter in council. The upshot of this was that, on 12th August, Christina was presented with a letter signed by fourteen members of the Råd. In this document, which had been drafted by the Chancellor, the signatories pointed out to their Queen that her birth imposed grave responsibilities upon her, and that it was the duty of people in her position to accept their work and if need be sacrifice themselves for it. Nevertheless, if she felt the burden to be too much for her, it could be shared by Charles Gustavus and others. The letter concluded by begging her not to abdicate. Although this plea did not alter Christina's decision, she saw that nothing could really be done before the Riksdag met in the autumn. Therefore she agreed that the members of the government could retire to their country estates, as was customary at this time of year. She herself prepared to go to Nyköping where she could see Charles Gustavus. He had wisely kept clear of the capital at this critical juncture.

September brought two totally unexpected and ill-assorted people to Stockholm. The first, whose arrival made a great stir, was the disgraced Danish minister, Corfitz Ulfeld, and his wife; the other was Godfried Francken, a Jesuit attached to the suite of the Spanish Ambassador in Copenhagen, Bernardino de Rebolledo. Ulfeld had until lately been the all-powerful minister of Frederick III of Denmark and was married to the King's step-sister, the beautiful Leonora Christina, one of Christian IV's numerous offspring by his morganatic marriage to Christina Munk. While Ulfeld was absent negotiating a treaty in Holland, charges of peculation, and even of having tried to poison the King, were brought against him. The poisoning charge was proved to be false, but fear of being indicted for peculation led him to flee with his wife, first to Holland and then to Sweden. The Ulfelds' journey had been an adventurous one, and Madame Ulfeld arrived in Stockholm dressed as a man. The Swedes, not unnaturally, found her behaviour very strange, as she persisted in walking about Stockholm attired in this fashion which, far from affording her a disguise, must have made her highly conspicuous as she was six or seven months pregnant.

On his arrival Ulfeld had made contact with Magnus, but evidently Christina was in something of a quandary. She did not know what to do about him; punctiliously she informed the Danish Resident, wrote to Frederick III and sent a message to Ulfeld to say that he must wait eight days before she could see him. However, at the end of September, she agreed to receive him formally, sending her carriage for him and remaining closeted alone with him for two-and-a-half hours. Christina also received Madame Ulfeld, who presented herself on both occasions still dressed as a man. It would have been unlike the Queen to be put off by oddity of dress. Evidently she took to the beautiful Leonora Christina, for she offered her an apartment in the castle in which to live during her confinement, justifying her reception of the couple on the grounds that the Danes had also accepted Swedish political refugees. The French Resident, Picques, who had replaced the absent Chanut, reported to Paris that the Ulfelds had evidently not felt altogether secure as they had left Stockholm; some said for Danzig, others to join the Queen Mother at Nyköping. When the King of Denmark's letter finally arrived, it did not request their repatriation, but simply stated that his former minister's trial for peculation would be continued *in absentia*.

A chance incident had given rise to the Jesuit Father Francken's journey to Stockholm. The celebrated Calvinist philosopher and historian Claude de Saumaise had followed his flighty niece Charlotte de Brégy on a trip to Stockholm in August 1650. He came at the Queen's invitation, as a result of the suggestion of both Descartes and Vossius. Saumaise (or Salmasius as he was often called, according to the contemporary custom of latinizing names) was sixty-three, and Christina was evidently afraid that he, too, might succumb to the rigours of the Swedish climate, for she gave him and his wife a comfortable suite in the castle. She also apparently took a great personal liking to him, though this may not have been entirely due to his erudition.

A tale is told of how once, when Saumaise was ill, she and Belle went to see him in his room. They found him reading a book which was not of the type that might have been expected in so serious a scholar. It was in fact the *Moyen de Parvenir*, then regarded as a shocking exposition of scepticism. Quickly realizing what it was, Christina took the book and invited the ingenuous Belle to read it aloud. Poor Belle was so shocked that she threw it on the floor and fled. Whether this story is true or not, Saumaise's company was so much appreciated by the Queen that she kept him in Stockholm for a year. When he left in August 1651, he stopped en route in Copenhagen, and there evidently called upon the Spanish Ambassador, for in describing to him his life in Sweden, he mentioned that Christina was interested in Catholicism. Francken was present during the conversation, and afterwards said to Rebolledo that a good theologian could "give so illuminated a mind the true light of faith."

The Ambassador was quick to seize the drift of Francken's thought, also to realize that if there was anything in what Saumaise had said, it could have important political implications. He therefore dispatched the Jesuit secretly to Stockholm, where he succeeded in making contact with the Queen. Christina received Francken well and ordered him to stay. Although she was cautious, the Jesuit soon realized that Saumaise had been right and that Christina was definitely interested in Catholicism. After waiting for a short time, however, he evidently felt that he could go no further without consulting his Ambassador, so he returned to Copenhagen. Rebolledo now lost no time. By the end of October Francken was on his way back to Stockholm, armed with a letter from King Philip of Spain, written in 1649, declaring the Spanish ports open to Swedish ships. There was also one from the Ambassador himself and an essay on morals.

To Christina, Francken's return was doubly welcome. She was in the thick of the struggle to try to push through the abdication, but she had as yet heard nothing from Rome of the result of Macedo's mission. She must have felt the need for some other line of communication with the Catholic world acutely, especially in those days of slow and precarious travel. Moreover, if after her abdication, she was to travel and live abroad as a Catholic convert, she would need the political support of some powerful figure. The alacrity which Rebolledo had shown evidently inclined Christina to think that the King of Spain would fill this role admirably. In view of Chanut's shocked reaction to her hints of abdication, she knew that with the French government the political advantages of the Swedish alliance would far outweigh her personal concerns once she had ceased to rule. Therefore, her conversion to his own faith might not be so favourably received by the Most Christian King of France and his advisers.

Christina tried to persuade Charles Gustavus to come back to Stockholm in September to help her prepare for her abdication. As usual he avoided doing so and she had to carry on alone. Her determination was well equal to the task ahead, but she now realised it was going to be a much harder struggle than she originally anticipated. On September 30th, the entire Råd, led by the High Steward Per Brahe, went to see her, armed with yet another petition signed by nineteen senators. This united front impressed the Queen, though it did not make her change her mind. She saw that if she was unable to divide them by some means, she could not present her plan of abdication to the Riksdag. She therefore gave them a temporizing answer, playing upon their sympathies and reiterating that she could never marry: the burden of government was too much because of her ill health, whereas Charles Gustavus would marry and provide heirs. But, led by Axel Oxenstierna and Per Brahe, the Råd remained adamant.

It is interesting to note that Christina's fresh avowal at this grave juncture that she would never marry, did not apparently weigh at all with the Råd as a reason for her abdication. Possibly they were swayed by their fear of a Reduction if Charles Gustavus succeeded or possibly, like Elizabeth of England's advisers, they felt that a young woman's preference for the virgin state would disappear, if only the right man came along. Therefore, although in later life Christina gave her determination not to marry, and the general unfitness of women to rule, as her reasons for abdication, the Råd evidently did not share this view. Nor for that matter did Christina herself later consider either of these things to be an impediment to her attempting to become Queen of Poland. But then she also concealed the fact that she was still equally determined not to marry. It seems, therefore, that her desire to abdicate from the throne of Sweden cannot be attributed to this one cause. Nor can it have been due wholly to her intended conversion. On her own admission she had been thinking of abdicating since 1645, and had definitely been paving the way for it since 1648; but although Catholicism had evidently interested her for some time, her first overt step towards conversion was only made in the summer of 1651.

Christina returned to the charge on 15th October by summoning the Råd to her presence. Picques reported to the French government that this meeting lasted for five-and-a-half hours. The Queen was again confronted by the unbroken unanimity of all the senators. Although she herself appeared to be equally unyielding and was still determined upon abdicating, Christina evidently began to waver about the possibility of doing so now. Axel Oxenstierna and Magnus, who were seeing her daily, probably sensed this change and every means of persuasion was brought to bear upon her. They told her how Swedish prestige abroad would be affected if the news of her impending abdication was known. These conversations confirmed the warnings that Chanut had already given to the Queen. The Palatines, too, continued their absolute resistance to her plans. At last, in the middle of November, Christina gave way and agreed to go on ruling.

Her decision was greeted with enthusiasm by both the Råd and nobility. Yet in their jubilation at what they regarded as a political victory, they apparently chose to disregard the Queen's warning that she would make no guarantees for the future. In this, Christina was being more than usually frank, for she had determined on a step which would make abdication inevitable. As proof of this, she dispatched Francken to Copenhagen in December with a letter for Rebolledo. The terms of this were decisive enough to make the Ambassador report the whole matter to the Spanish Foreign Minister, Luis de Haro, who informed the King. As a result of this, Philip IV himself took up the question of Christina's conversion.

Francken now returned for the third time to Stockholm to report progress, but ostensibly as a master of mathematics. This was to provide an explanation for his visits to the Queen. He remained until January, and at last Christina told him of Macedo's mission. Francken replied that she could have found what she wanted in the Low Countries as easily as in Italy. When he left Sweden at the end of January 1652, Christina apparently had no news of the result of Macedo's mission, although the acting head of the Order, Goswin Nickel, had written to her on 4th November. She therefore decided to use Francken as her agent to the Spanish authorities, giving him a letter to Antonio de Brun, the Spanish Ambassador at The Hague, and instructions to discuss matters with the Archduke Leopold, Governor of the Spanish Netherlands. She had already asked Francken to have someone sent to her who was really well-versed in mathematics, and could instruct her in the Catholic faith. Was it the shade of Descartes—the great mathematician who had reconciled faith with reason—that inspired this request?

Abdication apart, the year 1651 had also brought further problems for the Queen. In December Charles Gustavus had received a lampoon which attacked her in violent terms. Discreet enquiries in the Island of Öland, where the Prince then was, revealed that it had probably originated in Stockholm—it was said in the Chancery itself. Charles Gustavus dispatched one of his gentlemen to Magnus with the lampoon and a letter for the Queen. Both were at once laid before her, and Christina, who evidently had suspicions as to the lampoon's authorship from the start, ordered the various secretaries of the chancery to be shown both it and the address on the outside, which was written in another hand. One of them immediately recognized the handwriting of the address as that of one of his clerks. The man was summoned to the Queen's presence, and without any demur admitted that the address had been written by him. He explained that the lampoon had been sent to him already sealed, by a friend who had asked him to address it, as he did not know how to write Charles Gustavus's titles, or how to get it sent to him in Öland. On being asked who this friend was, the clerk replied "the son of Messenius, Your Majesty's historiographer."

In fact Arnold John Messenius the historiographer, and not his son Arnold, who was a mere youth, was the man whom the Queen had instantly suspected. Both father and son were now arrested, though this was done quietly by a ruse; Christina was not sure that they alone were involved in the affair. As a matter of fact the Messenius family had a long record of sedition. Arnold John's father, John Messenius, had been condemned for high treason and had ended his days in prison. Arnold John had been imprisoned for sedition, but was released at the time of Christina's majority and befriended by her, receiving the appointment of official historiographer.

When the Queen questioned young Arnold Messenius, in the presence of the chancery secretaries, he at first denied his guilt. Then he broke down and admitted that he was the author of the lampoon, but said that it was based on statements made by his father, who was quite unaware that he had written it. Arnold John was then questioned. At first he also denied all knowledge of the lampoon. In the end he admitted that his son might be guilty of the offence, but that he could not be held responsible for what his son might have written.

Many hours of questioning did not move either father or son from their original statements. It was then decided to try torture. Upon seeing the instruments prepared, the father broke down and asked that the Queen should be present while he made his confession. He admitted that his son had shown him the lampoon, and that he had not done his duty in preventing him from sending it to Charles Gustavus; for the lampoon incited the Prince to rise against the Queen, to encompass her death and take over the government. It also attacked Axel Oxenstierna, Magnus and Jacob De la Gardie and other members of the government. Messenius said that the Mayor of Stockholm, Nils Nilsson, a Stockholm writer and a clergyman of Västerås had helped to compose the lampoon, as well as others whose names he would not mention. By these last words he evidently meant to convey that important personages were also involved; later he is said to have made the threat that if he was put to the torture he would reveal names which Her Majesty would not like to hear, and the story went the rounds that some of the nobility were involved. The other three accomplices he named were arrested but, as Nilsson was particularly popular, they were ultimately pardoned. Arnold John Messenius realized that he could not escape the death penalty and asked to be allowed the privilege of kissing the Queen's hand once again. When she reproached him for his ingratitude, he justified himself by saying that she had caused him to lose a court case, this had poisoned his mind against her. Both father and son were beheaded and the son's body was broken on the wheel.

Although it made a tremendous stir, especially abroad, where it was regarded as being an indication of internal weakness in Sweden, the Messenius incident did not really merit the name of conspiracy. Its main effect was to bring about better relations between the Queen and the government, as they had all been attacked. The puerile lampoon did, however, touch on one very sore spot—the chaotic state of the national finances, to which the Queen's extravagance and complete lack of any financial sense had contributed.

Though before Christina's majority her own expenses and those of the court had only absorbed 3·1 per cent of the national income, they were now well on the way to being quadrupled, and within a year her own, the Queen Mother's and Charles Gustavus's households together absorbed twenty per cent of the state revenue. Early in 1652 one of her gentlemen in waiting, John Ekeblad, wrote to his brother in the country: "We at court have now taken a new manner of writing on our doors—*point d'argent*, or no money for our creditors. We haven't seen a penny of our wages." Many thinking people in the country must already have been aware of the situation and have regarded the future with alarm. Even Christina, who normally considered finance to be below her consideration, realized that something must be done, and tried to curb her own and the court's expenditure, though needless to say in one of her temperament these good resolutions could not last for long. Nor was the step she took officially—that of putting the spendthrift Magnus in charge of the Ministry of Finance—calculated greatly to improve the country's economy.

A chance remark at supper at the end of February 1652 ushered in one of the most hectic periods of Christina's life. Someone at the table remarked upon the appalling cold, whereupon General Wachtmeister, who had lately returned from Germany, said that on his way back he had travelled for some time with two Italians, who did not seem to be afraid of it. Christina immediately pricked up her ears and asked if they were musicians. Wachtmeister said no, they were gentlemen travellers, whereupon the Queen said she would like to see them.

The next morning the two Italians, Don Bonifacio Ponginibio and Don Lucio Bonanni were informed of this, and Zaccaria Grimani, a compatriot resident in Stockholm, took them to see Magnus to arrange for them to be presented to the Queen. The same day, about dinner time, they went to the castle, and when Christina came into the square salon where the court assembled, they were told to approach her. After kissing her hand, the elder of the two, Don Bonifacio, made a compliment to the Queen in Italian, to which she replied in French. They then proceeded to dinner. Don Bonifacio walked just before the Queen, and when nearly everyone had left the room she said in a low voice "perhaps you have letters for me?" Without turning his head, he replied "yes" and Christina hastily whispered "do not give them to anyone." She was sure that they were the two long-awaited Jesuits from Rome.

The two travellers were, in fact, Father Francesco Malines, a Piedmontese of noble family who taught theology at Turin and had been specially chosen for his knowledge of languages, mathemathics and theology, and Father Paolo Casati of Piacenza, who taught mathematics and theology in Rome and was the author of various works on physics, optics and theology. They had been personally selected with great care by Father Goswin Nickel for their adventurous and important mission.* They had received their marching orders in the middle of November. As might be expected of Nickel, who was a German, these orders were most precise, including such details as written instructions to Malines to

* Nickel had become vicar of the Order during the interim period since the death of the General Piccolomini and before the election as General of Alessandro Gottifredi. After the latter's sudden death Nickel himself was elected General.

let his hair and beard grow. This would enable him to disguise his true identity when he put on secular dress, after making his rendezvous with Casati in Venice on 8th December. Malines was also told that if he knew Greek he was to refresh his studies in that language during the arduous journey that would confront him across Europe in mid-winter. However when he arrived in Venice he knew little of his mission until he met Casati and read Nickel's instructions. These indicated that the Queen was to be referred to in letters as Don Teofilo, and that the two Jesuits were themselves to take the false names under which they travelled to Sweden. During their journey they were not to make contact with any other Jesuits, but were to study Greek literature and such controversial questions as were likely to arise in their discussions with the Queen. On their arrival in Sweden they were to put themselves entirely at Christina's disposal and "to accommodate themselves to the will and talents of Don Teofilo," making no attempt to convert anyone else or to enter into religious or political discussions, or to accept any benefices or honours. They were also given a letter which would serve as their credential to the Queen, and a cypher and list of pseudonyms for people whose names might have to be mentioned in their correspondence with Rome. Nickel was to be referred to as Amiano, Macedo as Apollonio and so on.

The two Jesuits left Venice on 12th December, travelling on horse-back, via Innsbruck across Europe to Hamburg. They were delayed on the way by bad weather and Malines had a fall from his horse, which kicked him. His injuries held them up for a few days and he continued to feel the effects for some months. They stopped for a couple of days at Hamburg, where they had a letter of credit for the same Jewish banker who had helped Macedo and with whom he had left Christina's gold chain in pawn. Macedo had written to this man, asking him to let them have this chain; possibly he was the same Diego Texeira, a Portuguese Jew, who afterwards became the Queen's banker, and who had agents both in Rome and Venice. From Hamburg the two Jesuits proceeded by way of Schleswig-Holstein, where at Rendsburg they encountered the Swedish Senator and diplomat Schering Rosenhane, travelling in his company to Roskilde.

The Queen afterwards told Casati that this had been a most

useful encounter. In order to see if Rosenhane had entertained any suspicions about them, she told him that she did not know what to make of these two Italians. He replied that she had nothing to fear; they were good people who had always treated him with the utmost courtesy. The Fathers now went on to Copenhagen, making another fortunate acquaintance in General Wachtmeister, and finally arrived in Stockholm on 14th February.

After dinner in the castle, Casati was approached by one of the company—a plump, dark, not very attractive-looking individual who spoke French—who asked him if he had a letter for the Queen. Casati not unnaturally gave evasive replies until the man repeated to him exactly what had passed between Christina and himself, adding that his name was John Holm. Casati was now convinced that the request really did come from the Queen, having evidently been informed that Holm, who had begun life as a tailor, was now the Queen's confidential factotum, so he handed Nickel's letter over to him. Next morning the priests received instructions from Holm to go to court two hours before the usual time. They were shown into the square salon where they had been presented to the Queen the night before, but found it empty except for the soldier on guard. However, scarcely had they entered, when the Queen appeared and, feigning surprise at finding them there alone and at such an early hour, started to talk to them about their journey. After a while she asked the guard if any of her secretaries had arrived, and on being told not, used this as as a pretext to dispatch the guard to look for one of them. During his absence, which lasted about an hour, she thanked the two Jesuits for coming and, assuring them that they had nothing to fear, promised that she would allow no ill to befall them.

However, Malines later reported in Rome that the Queen had warned them "to be secret and not to confide in anyone," telling them the names of certain people "to whom she feared we might give our confidence in process of time." Christina was apparently particularly anxious that none of the Germans or even the French at court should penetrate their disguise. Afterwards she told Malines that she had specifically asked for Italians for this reason. Malines later described how "she encouraged us to hope that, if she were satisfied, our journey might not have been in vain. She questioned us respecting the arrival of Father Macedo and how we had come to be selected to visit her court, and related to us the manner in which Father Macedo's departure had taken place."

Neither Malines's nor Casati's full reports of their mission have survived, so the exact circumstances in which their secret talks with Christina later took place are not known, but from fragments which have been published, the gist of their conversations emerges. As might be expected, both Jesuits reported the Queen's early dissatisfaction with Lutheranism. She also confirmed that during five years she had undergone great uneasiness of mind, examining all religions, including those of the Jews and Moslems, judging each religion by applying what it said about the others to itself. As a result of this she anticipated Karl Marx by coming more or less to the conclusion that "Religion is the opium of the people," or a "political invention for the restriction of common people," as she phrased it.

According to Casati, Christina admitted that all of this was the result of her desire to judge everything by the light of human reason and that although she never "fell into such blindness as to doubt the existence of God, or His unity," she had been "too profane in desiring to investigate the most sublime mysteries of the divinity, for she did not permit one mystery of our religion to escape her examination, while she sought to give rest to her mind by the final discovery of a religion." But that "finally she had arrived at another conclusion, that it was expedient to proceed in externals as others did, believing the whole to be a matter of indifference, and that it mattered nothing whether she followed one sect or another. It was sufficient, she thought, if she did nothing contrary to the dictates of reason, or for which having done it she would have cause to blush. . . . She went on in this way for some time, and seemed even to have found repose for her mind. Especially having discovered others (summoned from distant lands) who seemed to be learned and wise, were of opinions but slightly different from her own—they being without the pale of the true Catholic religion which they considered to be mere childishness. . . . She had the most perfect will and desire to know the truth. She was guided by the light of sound reason, for she frequently assured me that she never suffered herself to do anything for which she ought to blush (that being her form of expression). . . . She reverted to the thought that there must be some religion and, having granted that man must have some religion, then among them all she knew in the world none appeared to her more reasonable than the Catholic, and on reflecting found its tenets not so absurd as the Lutheran pastors say."

Malines also reported that the Queen had invited foreign scholars to her court, making them generous offers under the pretext of wishing to learn from them, but in fact cleverly making them reveal their own beliefs. Christina adopted somewhat the same tactics with the two Jesuits. For he says that "At first she dissimulated her perfect disposition" (to become a Catholic) but that both he and Casati were impressed by a twenty-five-year-old princess's complete disregard for human greatness and her "just estimate of all things, which seemed only to be nourished by the marrow of moral philosophy." However they soon realized that Christina intended to become a Catholic and to abdicate, although at one stage she apparently asked the Jesuits if it would be possible for her to profess Catholicism in secret but perhaps, by a special dispensation of the Pope, to take the Lutheran communion once a year. Upon being told that this was impossible "because the simulation of a false cult is intrinsically an act injurious to God," Christina "with great magnanimity of soul, said 'then I must descend from the throne and leave the realm.' "

In view of the fact that the Queen had been contemplating abdication now for seven years, had been actively preparing for it since 1648, and had lately emerged unsuccessfully from her tussle with the Råd to achieve it, this sacrifice of leaving throne and country for the sake of her conversion, cannot quite be accepted in the pious light in which she presented it to the two Jesuits. Though in the circumstances, given Christina's love of dissimulation and grandiose gestures, it is understandable that she wanted it to appear thus. It would also greatly enhance her prestige in Rome and enable her to extract even greater privileges and more help in the Catholic world when she actually came to abdicate and leave Sweden. Her question about a secret profession was obviously made as a safeguard, not because she wanted to go on reigning, but so that she might have breathing space to arrange her money affairs, possibly even after she had reached a settlement and left the country; for already she feared that her conversion might result in Sweden cutting off supplies.

From all this it is evident that Christina's active brain and shrewd sense of her own interests did not for one moment desert her, even when making what, on the face of it, seemed the spiritual and emotional decision of changing her faith. In fact, the enthusiastic Jesuit fathers give no indication of any mystic leanings on the part of their remarkable convert, nor is there any allusion to discussions about dogmatic difficulties which had to be overcome or solved.

In view of some extraordinary remarks which the Queen made after she had been ceremonially received into the Catholic Church, and been greeted by what amounted to a triumph on her arrival in Rome, there appear to be grounds for the supposition that Christina took the lead in these conversations with the Jesuits, and that in meticulously following their instructions to "accommodate themselves to the will and talents of Don Teofilio," Malines and Casati did not raise too many awkward questions. Just how embarrassing this might have been is shown by the fact that even after her conversion Christina said to an astonished French scholar, who had made her a graceful compliment on her conversion, "My religion is the religion of the philosophers, which I prefer to all others . . . it was very well defined by Lucretius in his books *De Rerum Natura*, it is only that which I approve." Notwithstanding the grandeur and passion of Lucretius's poetry, this praise of the advocate of materialism and epicurean philosophy rings strangely in the mouth of a recent convert to Roman Catholicism.

The only other indication of what went on in these secret discussions between Malines and Casati and their neophyte, is that they sent all the way to Italy for Father Daniello Bartoli's book *Dell' uomo di lettere*. The author was a fashionable writer on religious, philosophical and literary subjects. Although unexceptional from the Catholic point of view he was not profound, being a typical exponent of the rather worldly, religious humanistic movement. He was witty and no pedant, and defended the liberty of the creative intellect (he had the courage to defend Galileo after his condemnation). That the trouble was taken to get so superficial a book all the way from Italy, seems to indicate the tone of the discussions with the Queen, who, Descartes believed, knew little about philosophy. Probably the book was produced to show what freedom of thought existed in the Catholic world—a fact that would have greatly appealed to Christina—and it seems that her questions may have been directed more along these lines, than upon a profound study of articles of faith. In view of her life at court and the circle of people who now surrounded her, this is not very surprising: the witty French doctor, Guy Patin, can be excused for laughingly accusing Christina of having "adopted the Catholic religion as being the most convenient for travelling."

Nevertheless, at the beginning of May Casati left for Rome to bring the great news of the Queen's conversion. Christina gave him a letter for the General Nickel and other detailed instructions, for she had already decided that after her abdication she wished to live in Rome. This choice was probably not entirely due to her change of religion, nor to the strong attraction which Italy, since the arrival of the loot from Prague, had come to hold for her. In any other country she would have to play second fiddle to some other monarch—and his queen—whereas in Rome she would incontestably be the first lady, and all Catholic sovereigns naturally bowed before the Pope. Malines remained with Christina; possibly because he had some experience of court life—having been page to the Duke of Savoy—and would therefore be less conspicuous.

At the end of May the Queen had a narrow escape from drowning, when inspecting a warship in Stockholm harbour. Both she and the Admiral went overboard when stepping on an unsecured plank. With great presence of mind he kept hold of the Queen's skirt as she went under, but she was actually saved by Anton Steinberg (one of her household and afterwards a great favourite) who dived in after her. It was a close shave, but Christina took it in very good part, dining afterwards in public and recounting her adventure to everyone.

What opinion Malines can have formed of life at the Swedish court is a mystery. Already it had changed a good deal in the last few years, but the same month of February 1652, when he and Casati were introduced to it, saw the arrival of a man who was to transform it out of recognition. He was a French doctor who had much in common with Guy Patin and whose name was Pierre Bourdelot. Ever since Magnus's return from his embassy to Paris in 1647, when he had brought with him not only French servants, but artists such as Antonio Brunati and craftsmen as well, many foreigners had come to Stockholm and the Swedish court. The number of French increased greatly after 1649. They found that in the troubled world of the Fronde there was little hope of leading their former comfortable lives as the petted favourites of Parisian salons. They now looked towards Sweden with the fascination of prospectors surveying the discovery of a new gold-field. The purveyors of the luxuries and graces of life, who had also been hard hit, followed suit. These immigrants to Sweden ranged from André Mollet, the famous gardener, right down to Champagne who had been Queen Maria Luisa Gonzaga of Poland's coiffeur—though it is to be feared that Christina can have given him little occasion to exercise his art on her behalf. There were also Italians in the Queen's household other than the musicians and artists already mentioned. One of these, Alessandro Cecconi, apparently held a confidential post similar to John Holm, for he was mentioned not only by Malines and Casati, but also by ambassadors. One of his compatriots referred to him scathingly as "a servant now become a gentleman." But this motley company, which at various times had included Saint-Amant and lesser lights, such as the libertine poet Marigny and the adventurous Gascon, Hercule de Lacger, was small when compared with the full flood of the foreign invasion which only reached its strength after Bourdelot's arrival.

There were very good grounds for another doctor being summoned to the Queen. Ill health had dogged her since 1645. To her old troubles of monthly pains, palpitations, fevers and headaches, were added abscesses and increasingly frequent fainting fits. By common consent her doctors seem to have been recognized as incompetent—their favourite panacea was doses of pepper-corns in brandy. It is not surprising to find, therefore, that from the very beginning the new French doctor was given an enthusiastic welcome, at first by Magnus and then by Christina herself. For the Queen he possessed the added attraction of having served the great Prince de Condé, probably the only one of her contemporaries whom she considered to be on a par with the classical heroes she so much admired.

Although Bourdelot had been doctor to Louis XIII and was a privileged member of the Condé household, his origins were undistinguished. He was born in 1610, the son of a barber—probably a surgeon-barber—in Sens, and his name had originally been Pierre Michon Bonnet. He was fortunate, however, in having become the heir of his maternal uncle Jean Bourdelot, who had been in the service of Queen Marie de Medicis, and together with his fortune the uncle bequeathed to him his more distinguished name. Pierre Bourdelot soon learnt to make his way in the world. He accompanied François de Noailles on his embassy to Rome, where the young attaché distinguished himself by pelting passers-by with snowballs from the embassy windows. He returned to France saying that Cardinal Barberini had promised him ecclesiastical preferment.

Bourdelot was to become the most criticized and most hated physician who ever attended a Swedish sovereign, but even judging by modern standards he was evidently an able one. He possessed, above all, the invaluable gift of common sense and undoubtedly had a good bed-side manner. Although his diagnosis of Christina's state of health when he examined her was inevitably couched in the baroque Latin, intermingled with some Greek, which was then considered proper for such purposes, and was filled with learned disquisitions on the qualities of the "humours" in the Queen's body and their effect upon her present state of health, he immediately perceived that much of the trouble arose from the impossible life she was leading.

Shorn of seventeenth-century, pseudo-scientific language, his diagnosis boils down to this: "The Queen works too much and does not sleep enough or take care of herself. She eats things which are bad for her, as a result her appetite is ruined. She does not want to eat and the normal functions of her body are affected. For the past seven years she has been subject to recurrent fevers and lassitude, and each month she suffers from acute pains in the left hypochondriac region, sleeplessness, headaches, fainting and sometimes even convulsions."

At the time of his first examination Christina's lips were dry and cracked, and her skin harsh and freckled. Bourdelot's treatment was to put the Queen on a light diet which included nourishing veal broth, plenty of fruit, cooling drinks, barley water and extracts and essences of lemons and oranges. The usual heavy

Swedish dishes of greasy, smoked, salted and highly spiced foods were rigorously excluded. He also encouraged her to drink mineral waters and a tonic containing iron. He prescribed frequent warm baths and foot-baths. Naturally, according to the custom of the time, this treatment was accompanied by blood-lettings and the use of clysters. But above all Bourdelot insisted that the Queen must study less, rest and sleep longer, and take life less seriously and strenuously.

Not very surprisingly, as a result of this sensible treatment, Christina's health began to improve rapidly and within a few months she was well on the way to recovery. Her gratitude to Bourdelot was measured by the fact that with characteristic exaggeration she believed him to have saved her life, and he could do no wrong in her eyes. From that time her whole way of life underwent a revolution. Meticulously she followed Bourdelot's instructions, including those for taking more leisure and amusing herself, and she found that she took to the new regime as a duck to water. Her new physician was also well equipped to assist her in this aspect of her cure; he was evidently very amusing and good company, and had a malicious sense of humour akin to Christina's own. He sang well, accompanying himself on the guitar, was used to life among highly sophisticated people, and must have brought to the Queen a whiff of a society which she had only so far enjoyed with the Brégys. Although not learned, Bourdelot could more than pass muster in the literary world of the Paris salons. He had held cultural meetings in the Hotel de Condé—and, which was rare in Sweden at the time, could cook excellently. He even prepared some of the broths and dishes which he prescribed for his royal patient, and dabbled in perfumery. All in all, few men were better gifted with qualities suitable to Bourdelot's new role, which was not only that of doctor, but very soon leader of the Queen's revels as well.

Bourdelot also brought with him an apothecary and a very suitable assistant—young Clairet Poissonnet. He was a gay, handsome youth and a good raconteur who was to remain in the Queen's service all his life. But the same year of 1652 also found some Frenchmen of serious worth at the court, though inevitably they fell foul of Bourdelot's gay troupe. Among these was Samuel Bochard, the Protestant pastor of Caen, author of the *Geografia*

Sacra and a great authority on oriental languages, especially Hebrew. One of Bochard's tasks was the classification of the oriental manuscripts which the Queen had bought when Mazarin's famous library was sold during the Fronde. He was accompanied by the young intellectual prodigy, Pierre Daniel Huet, who at twenty-two had already distinguished himself as a poet, mathematician, chemist and physician. He was later to become tutor to the Dauphin, an academician and Bishop of Avranches. This very learned young man, who had come to study a manuscript of Origen in the Queen's library, apparently found that in spite of its new *réclame*, the Court of Sweden did not quite come up to his intellectual standards, for he left in September of the same year.

Another well-known figure was Gabriel Naudé, an authority on classical dances who had studied in Paris and Padua. He had travelled widely, especially in Italy, and had been librarian to Cardinal Barberini and to Mazarin. He was now to perform the same service for Christina, and was helped in his work by a less serious character, Raphael Trichet Du Fresne, whose main task was to draw up a catalogue of the famous collection of pictures. This he completed in 1653, with not very illuminating results. Although he had written a book on Leonardo da Vinci, Trichet Du Fresne contented himself with counting the works in groups —these sometimes included drawings as well as paintings—giving their provenance and a description of the subject. He made no mention whatsoever of the artists' names. The justly celebrated French artist Sebastien Bourdon, who arrived with his wife in October, was soon commissioned to paint the Queen's portrait and those of other members of the court, and was appointed her painter in chief.

The turn of the year saw the arrival of Urbain Chevreau, a fit companion for Bourdelot. Witty and frivolous, a novelist and a dabbler in the theatre, he was set to work to compose the ballets and other diversions which were the rage at court. Then there was the solemn young German from Schleswig, Mark Meibom (usually known as Meibomius) who was an authority on antique music, and the cultivated and able Conrad Van Beuningen, the new Dutch resident in Sweden. Van Beuningen tried to regain Christina's favour for his compatriot and her erstwhile professor of Greek, Isaac Vossius, who had disgraced himself by having a row with the favoured Saumaise. Finally there was an Italian poet called Vincina, of no great renown, but witty enough to make the Queen laugh.

These are only a few of the more conspicuous foreigners who were flocking to Sweden in the hope of making their fortunes; they were noticed because they played a part in court life. Just how numerous they were, and how cosmopolitan Stockholm had become, may be judged from the fact that it now boasted not only a French tavern, called the Croix de Lorraine, but also an Italian *osteria*. It was a changed city from the days of Christina's childhood only twenty years before, and even from the time of her accession. Needless to say the arrival of frivolous heretical Latins, ever on the lookout for the patronage of newly-rich nobility and thereby taking the bread out of the mouths of sober honest Swedes, was far from popular. All the more so because it was becoming increasingly evident that the Queen preferred them to her serious, God-fearing subjects.

It is against this background of envy and gossip that the *potins* and descriptions of the life now led by Christina's court must be judged. It is, however, true to admit that in the midst of the smoke-screen of scandal, there were some very glowing embers, if not an actual fire, which gave rise to what was said. With the exception of such serious men as Bochard, Naudé and young Huet, many of these foreigners, particularly the French, were free-thinkers or libertines who did not dare to express their opinions openly. They maintained a façade of Catholicism, but really believed in nothing. They were typical representatives of the libertine intellectuals of the period, many of whom in France and Italy were often priests of the type for whom a benefice represented a comfortable income and nothing more. Their opinions and their way of life were the ultimate result of the effects of the Renaissance, with its love of classical learning and hedonistic pagan pleasures, which had disrupted the centuries-old world of mediaeval beliefs.

The new scientific discoveries had added fresh fuel to the fire which began in Italy. There, in the fifteenth century at Padua, a revival of the study of Averroes' commentaries on Aristotle, particularly by Pietro Pomponazzi, had led to discussion on the immortality of the soul. Church censure was avoided by Averroes' own theory of the double truth, which postulates the theory that faith should be accepted, while it recognizes that it cannot be justified on philosophical grounds. Giulio Cesare Vanini, who had also studied at Padua, went much further and, although he became a Carmelite monk, taught a pantheistic philosophy; he was ultimately executed and burnt in Toulouse in 1619.

It was from such philosophical undercurrents that French, libertine thought took its inspiration, though its practitioners were careful to keep on the right side of the establishment as represented by Church and State. They usually managed to combine their secret free-thinking with the maximum enjoyment of life. From Christina's conversations with Malines and Casati, it is evident how closely related her own thinking had been to the intellectual side of libertinism. What is a great deal more difficult to understand is that while she was engaged in her discussions with the Jesuits—discussions leading to her final decision on conversion—she went still further and wholeheartedly embraced the frivolous *joie de vivre* of libertinism as well.

The paradox of this situation has puzzled historians for centuries. Some have tried to explain it on the grounds that the Queen used this frivolity as a cloak to conceal her intended conversion. But as she continued to behave in exactly the same way, giving rise to great scandal and embarrassment, after she had left the country and even in Rome when she was an acknowledged daughter of the Church, this argument scarcely holds water. The only explanation seems to be that Christina believed that in accepting Catholicism she had escaped into a far freer world than that of Lutheran Sweden—the request for *Dell' uomo di lettere* appears to indicate this—and in "giving up a throne to become a Catholic" she had made such a demonstration of faith and piety that almost anything could be permitted to her.

Whatever the underlying thoughts were in the Queen's own mind, it is certain that in 1652 her court at Stockholm justly came to be regarded as the gayest in Europe, and by many as the most risqué as well. In the midst of a serious financial crisis fortunes were squandered on parties, balls, ballets and entertainments of all kinds, by both the Queen and the aristocracy. This frittering away of money was so widespread that careful diplomats with small private means begged not to be posted to Stockholm, for they knew they would be ruined financially if they were to put up any kind of a show.

But gradually another side of the life at court came to be whispered about at first and then gradually to be spread by gossip round Europe, giving not only her companions but also the Queen a very equivocal reputation; so much so that even the level-headed Madame de Motteville believed in the stories of her immorality. A good deal of this was certainly the result of Christina's and Bourdelot's peculiar sense of humour. There was one famous episode when they made the elderly and learned Naudé give a demonstration of the antique dances, upon which he was an authority. The serious young Meibom had to provide the musical accompaniment for this performance because of his scholarly knowledge of classical music. Jokes of this kind are not usually calculated to appeal to serious scholars, and to hold up their learning to such ridicule was regarded as unpardonable. Meibom punched Bourdelot in the nose and left the court in disgrace. Naudé remained to nurse his wounded feelings and finally he spoke to Saumaise, describing the extraordinary behaviour of this Queen whom he had originally so much admired. Even Bochard did not escape Bourdelot's twisted ideas of humour. The doctor administered a purge to his royal patient on the very day she was to listen in state to Bochard's reading of his great work *Phaleg*. These buffooneries aroused the fury of the savants, but they did not have the serious repercussions that were produced by another ill-judged joke made by one of Christina's circle. Bochard—that serious Calvinist pastor of Caen—was asked by one of them what he thought of "a certain book called the Bible," and when earnestly the good man started to give a learned dissertation upon Holy Writ, he was greeted with roars of laughter.

If this had been an isolated incident it might not have provoked too much of a scandal in all but pious circles. Unfortunately, the subjects of the debates which now took place every Wednesday at the meetings of the Queen's academy—the academy for which Descartes had drawn up the plans and over which Bourdelot now presided—were almost as shocking. In a discussion of what would seem an innocuous subject today—the existence of demons—Bourdelot was reported to have said that in France and Italy no intelligent man believed in the Scriptures. After this there followed rumours that the Queen herself gave voice to even worse blasphemies—that she believed in neither heaven nor hell, nor in the Incarnation nor in the resurrection of the dead, nor even in the immortality of the soul. That the most personal beliefs were the best and that the ordinary ones accepted by most people were just superstition and error, also that "what is believed today to be religion is simply the illusion of men who wish to be deceived." Finally, without having been able to read the notorious work *The Three Impostors*, she was convinced of the untruth of Moses' passage of the Red Sea.

Much of this can be put down to exaggeration and hearsay. In fact, even during Christina's lifetime but particularly after her death, many tendentious memoirs about her and the life of her court were printed in Europe. However the fact remains that some of these sayings attributed to her coincide closely with what Christina herself had told Malines and Casati of her religious doubts. Other statements made by Christina, such as her jokes about the execution of Charles I, which were for long discounted as malicious inventions, were mentioned in his diary by the reliable Imperial Ambassador, Count Raimondo Montecuccoli. It seems that Christina made these remarks in the course of conversation with him. The excuse could also be advanced that Christina made these provocative statements in order, as she had told the Jesuits, to test other people's beliefs. But most of the meetings of the Queen's academy, presided over by Bourdelot, took place after Casati's departure, by which time Christina had declared her intention of becoming a Catholic. Moreover, after this event, certainly as late as 1653, the Queen was continuing her search for books which were commonly regarded as the gospels of disbelief.

This search had begun as long ago as 1651 with her trying to obtain Gassendi's *Philosophie d'Epicure*, and Bodin's *Heptaplomères*—reputed to extol Judaism at the expense of Christianity. In 1653 Christina's agents were still trying to obtain a copy of Garasse's *La Doctrine Curieuse*—a treatise that appeared to attack atheism but really defended it. The most prolonged pursuit of all was undertaken in order to unearth a copy of that infamous book *The Three Impostors* which, without any pretence at all, named them: Moses, Mohammed and Jesus Christ. Of this legendary work, whose existence had been rumoured as far back as the twelfth century in Italy, no copy has ever been discovered by Christina or anyone else. But it is interesting to note that his alleged belief in its subject was one of the causes of the first excommunication of the mediaeval Emperor, Frederick II of Hohenstaufen. At his court Michael Scott introduced the works of Averroes to western Europe—that same Averroes whose works had been again studied at Padua in the fifteenth century and had ultimately given rise to the libertine philosophy professed more or less openly by some of the members of Christina's circle.

As might be expected, accusations about this libertine circle surrounding the Queen did not stop short at matters of pagan philosophy and religious disbelief; to them were soon added allegations of gross immorality as well. To the jealous ministers and nobles, who had been forced to swallow cavalier treatment at the hands of her new favourite, Bourdelot's ascendancy over Christina could not simply be explained by the gratitude of his patient, or her sudden discovery of the joys of living a gay life. They thought that he must also be her lover as well. Bourdelot was not, however, the only man of whom this was suspected, his "rival," who in the end was widely believed (even by the sensible Madame de Motteville) to have shared Christina's bed, was the Spanish Envoy, Don Antonio Pimentel de Prado. His arrival in Sweden was to provide the last act in the drama of her abdication.

CHAPTER 6

Abdication: 1652–1654

The Envoy of His Most Catholic Majesty, Philip IV of Spain, arrived in Stockholm in the middle of August 1652. Don Antonio Pimentel, who came of one of the old, aristocratic families of Leon, was born in 1604 in Palermo, then the second capital of the Neapolitan Kingdom owned by Spain, and was educated in Italy. He was an excellent soldier and looked like one; he was tall, stately and of striking appearance, which was enhanced by his erect carriage. Pimentel was in fact the forceful military type of man which Christina admired and she took an instant liking to him. But the Envoy was not an impressionable youth to be bowled over by royal favour, he was nearly fifty—quite old by seventeenth-century standards—moreover, he was "no carpet knight" and was a happily married man. It must be admitted, however, that the circumstances surrounding Pimentel's mission and sojourn at the Swedish court were such as to lend colour to the rumours of the Queen's attachment to him, which subsequently spread round Europe.

Pimentel had only been second choice for this appointment. A regular soldier, he had never before undertaken a diplomatic mission, and was suddenly ordered to do so because he was the best man available in the Spanish Netherlands. He expected his mission to be of short duration, as it was ostensibly only concerned with the negotiation of a commercial pact with Sweden, and a return of the courtesy of Palbitzki's mission to Madrid in the previous year.

The situation confronting Pimentel was a difficult one, because

Spain and France were at war and France was Sweden's ally. It was further complicated by the fact that French susceptibilities were exceedingly delicate at the time because of the Fronde. Moreover Christina had not been tactful in suggesting that Palbitzki, on his way back from his mission to Madrid, should act as mediator between Louis XIV and his rebellious subjects. Palbitzki was informed that as a foreigner he could never be accepted as a mediator in France's internal affairs; moreover he was asked why Her Majesty of Sweden had allowed so long a time to elapse without appointing a diplomatic representative to the court of her old ally, the King of France. This was a particularly pointed remark, in view of Palbitzki's recent mission to the King's enemy—Spain. There was yet another complication. King John IV of Portugal had a diplomatic representative at the Swedish court, but as far as the King of Spain was concerned he had no right to this, as the self-styled King was none other than Philip IV's own rebellious subject, the Duke of Braganza, who had been fighting to free Portugal since 1640.

It was into this whirlpool of diplomatic intrigue that, without any previous experience of such things, Pimentel was precipitated on his arrival in Sweden in August 1652. Nor was his mission quite so straightforward as it seemed. He had secret instructions to inform himself about any marriage projects the Queen might have which would affect the European balance of power; and to assess Sweden's political propensities and military strength. This last task was probably the reason for his choice as a substitute for Estevan de Gamarra, who had originally been appointed to the post.

Nor was this all. When, at the end of January, Christina had dispatched the Jesuit Francken to The Hague and Brussels, with a letter for Brun and instructions to discuss matters with the Archduke Leopold, she had also given him a letter addressed to the City of Antwerp. In this letter she expressed the wish for better trade relations between Antwerp and Sweden. Francken also had instructions to discuss this matter with the Archduke Leopold and to tell him clearly that Christina, who was much interested in Catholicism, believed that these trade relations with a Catholic city, like Antwerp, might provide a means for infiltrating Catholicism into Sweden. The Archduke examined the question very soberly, but came to the conclusion that although there was no doubt that Antwerp would reap great financial advantages at the expense of Amsterdam, nevertheless, the proposal was directly contrary to a clause of the Treaty of Westphalia which closed the Scheldt to trade. Therefore it could not be accepted without a probable break with Holland, which was out of the question as long as Spain was at war with France. The Archduke was also very uncertain whether the cause of Catholicism could be furthered by this means, or whether he could trust the Queen of Sweden. She might have been prompted to make this offer by some deep-laid French intrigue. Pimentel was, therefore, warned to treat any further proposals of this kind with the utmost caution.

The Archduke had been quite wrong in suspecting French finesse as the cause of Christina's astonishing proposal about Antwerp. The spider sitting in the middle of this web of intrigue was the Queen herself. By mid-May, however, she must have been beginning to realize that she had brought on herself more than she had bargained for. As a result of her impatience and her appeals both to Macedo and to Francken, she now had four Jesuits on her hands. On 1st April Philip Nutius had arrived from Belgium, in answer to Francken's request for a teacher who was also versed in mathematics.

In May, Francken returned to Stockholm. This was probably one of the reasons for Christina's prompt dispatch of Casati to Rome in the same month, and although she had told him and Malines of her contacts with Francken, she studiously avoided informing Nutius of the two Italians' presence in Sweden. She even asked Nutius—on his return to the Netherlands—to have a message sent to Rome to stop them coming, nor did she give Nutius any indication of her definite intention of conversion. This extreme caution was probably induced by the fact that Nutius's presence, and even his name, had been reported to the Swedish Chancery. In any case his stay in Stockholm was short—he was only there for five weeks—but he may just have seen Francken before he left, as their stay overlapped for one day.

Looking back, after an interval of three centuries, there is something irresistibly comic—reminiscent of the atmosphere of a contemporary theatrical farce—about the repeated entrances and exits of the men charged with the task of converting Christina. At the time, however, this was not only a very serious matter but a very dangerous one as well. The Jesuit General, Goswin Nickel, was only too well aware of this and had issued orders recalling both Nutius and Francken.

Christina was evidently now more than a little alarmed. Information had come back from the Swedish representative in Vienna, Matthias Biörenklou, that no less than four Jesuits were known to be in Stockholm. Earlier in the year the Queen had felt reassured that no one had any real suspicion of her intended conversion, because when Charles Gustavus had heard rumours that his sister Eleonora's husband, the Landgrave Frederick of Hesse, was going to become a Catholic, he had at once turned to Christina for help. The irony of the situation would have appealed to her. It also provided her with an excellent means of counter-propaganda to still any doubts about her religious beliefs. She took the opportunity to write a most tactful letter for the Landgrave, which she sent to Charles Gustavus. Very wisely the Queen did not attempt to present herself as an orthodox Lutheran, but said "as I belong to a third religion . . . it is right that I should speak to you as a neutral person." Her arguments for dissuading the Landgrave were based upon the discredit it would bring his house, she said that he would regret such a decision all his life. In the event the young man's intended conversion proved to be a false alarm, and the Queen's letter was never sent; but the whole episode did avert suspicion from herself.

This incident had arisen in February or March. But by midsummer, with the reports coming from Vienna, and Nutius's presence having been so rapidly discovered by the Chancery, it must have been becoming clear to Christina, that as a Catholic neophyte she could not remain for long upon the throne in a country where Catholicism was illegal. The arrival of the King of Spain's representative, who could be of such assistance to her in arranging the material aspects of her conversion and her life abroad, was therefore eagerly awaited by her. It was to be a very important event in her own life and affect her plans for the future. Pimentel, who had been Governor of Nieuport in Flanders, passed through The Hague on his journey to Sweden. He was briefed there, by the experienced and capable Spanish Ambassador de

Brun, on the latest developments in north-European diplomacy.

On his journey, Pimentel had a rather unwelcome travelling companion in Conrad Van Beuningen, the new Dutch Resident in Sweden. Although their respective countries were now at peace, the traditional suspicion had not abated. In fact it had, if anything, increased. King Philip IV of Spain had been the first to recognize the Commonwealth government in England after the Civil War, and since June Cromwell's England had been fighting sea-battles with Holland. Pimentel presented his credentials to Christina at the Royal Castle in Stockholm on 19th August. In accordance with the protocol of the time he made his oration in Spanish, which was translated by his interpreter into Latin. The Queen replied in Swedish, which her interpreter then rendered into Spanish.

There is a curious story that during the ceremony Pimentel turned pale and seemed to have lost the ability to speak, and that at a subsequent audience he apologized to Christina for his behaviour, saying that it was due to the overwhelming impression made upon him by her personality. This has rather naturally been pooh-poohed by historians, as part of the Christina-Pimentel legend. But the English Ambassador Bulstrode Whitelocke, who was personally and politically allied to Pimentel and was an eye-witness of his official leave-taking of the Queen, said that the same thing also occurred on this occasion. Whitelocke noted marginally in his journal that this was "odd for a man of his parts, but some say he acted this part to please the Queen, who thought by her majesty and presence to daunt foreigners." Christina had apparently tried to do something of the same kind when Whitelocke had presented his credentials. As she "came close to me and by looks and gestures . . . she tried to daunt me." However, as Whitelocke stoutly remarked, "those who have recently passed through the late great affairs in England [the Civil War] are not likely to be appalled by a young lady and her servants."

Whitelocke had every reason to marvel that a man of Pimentel's "parts"—a seasoned soldier and a proud Spanish aristocrat representing the might and majesty of His Most Catholic Majesty—should behave in such a way. It can easily be imagined how this later came to be woven into the legend that Christina and Pimentel were lovers, even giving rise in the twentieth century to the plot of a romantic film. As so often in history, the circumstances behind the story were a great deal more prosaic. The situation was complicated by two factors. Firstly, the Queen was determined to obtain the King of Spain's support for her conversion. This made her keep Pimentel in Sweden, where she treated him with marked favour, for nearly two years, although his original mission should have been completed in two months. Secondly, her treatment of Pimentel aroused jealousy and political suspicion among the representatives of powers hostile to Spain and members of the court in Stockholm.

Christina had evidently expected that Pimentel would be fully empowered to treat on all questions between herself and King Philip IV, including the very secret and personal one of her own conversion. The first indication that the mission might not come up to her expectations was that Pimentel was only an envoy. Then came the disappointment. At the end of their first private audience, after Pimentel had outlined the official scope of his mission as the negotiation of the commercial treaty, she asked him if his King had anything more to tell her. The answer was "no": Philip IV was being cautious. Pimentel had received very circumscribed and limited instructions, and had not been given a secret hint of Christina's personal intentions. The Queen at once sensed this and saw that she must keep Pimentel with her as long as possible, as a line of communication if nothing else. Then she could try to win him over gradually as a personal friend.

Pimentel had arrived with an entourage of fifty people. It included his chaplain Charles Alexandre Manderscheydt, a Jesuit from Luxembourg, who was later to act as postman for Christina's communications with Rome. By the middle of September, the main object of Pimentel's mission—the negotiation of the trade agreement—was completed and he expected to leave shortly. Playing her cards very cleverly, however, the Queen persuaded him to stay until December when the Imperial Diet would open at Regensburg. To persuade him to do so she promised to support the election of the Emperor Ferdinand III's son as his successor and King of the Romans, if the Emperor's anti-Swedish policy in central Europe ceased. To this promise Christina added protestations of the need for closer relations with Spain and the exchange of permanent residents. In time she was to add the bait of calculated indiscretions about Sweden's foreign policy. So, feeling that he could well serve the interests of both branches of the House of Hapsburg,* Pimentel agreed to stay. For economy he sent his large retinue back to the Netherlands and took up a more suitable permanent residence in the mayor's house in Norrmalm.

The Emperor's son, Ferdinand King of Hungary, was only elected as his father's successor in May 1653. But meanwhile Christina had been employing all the wiles at her disposal to win Pimentel's sympathies and keep him in Sweden. There was not a banquet, ball, ballet or hunt at court to which he was not invited and showered with favours. He was invested with the Queen's newly instituted Order of Amaranth, supposed to be founded in honour of the nymph of that name. The insignia consisted of a gold medal on a crimson ribbon, the medal being inscribed with two "A's," interlaced and surrounded by a laurel crown. As Mars Pimentel appeared in a ballet or masque in which the Queen took the part of Amarantha. Corfitz Ulfeld was Jupiter and a new protégé of the Queen's, the Polish *émigré* Hieronym Radziejowski, was Bacchus. Although wildly extravagant, (at one of these entertainments, the jewels sewn on Christina's dress were cut off and given away as presents) these gay diversions were probably perfectly innocent. Even the puritan Whitelocke later found them so. But already it was being whispered that the second A on the order of Amaranth stood for Pimentel's Christian name Antonio.

One of the most splendid occasions of the whole winter was the reception given by Magnus for his brother Jacob's marriage to Belle. On 11th January 1653, Ekeblad wrote to his brother: "Just think, as I write, Count Jacob is taking the reward from the red mouth of the beautiful Ebba Sparre for all the pain and anguish he has suffered these last three years." The last phrase was a reference to the fact that for a long time Belle had been engaged to one of the Oxenstiernas. Even after her marriage to Jacob De la Gardie she continued to live with the Queen.

* The Emperor Ferdinand III and King Philip IV of Spain were both great-great-great-grandsons of the Hapsburg Emperor Maximilian I, but also first cousins, as Ferdinand III's aunt, Margaret of Austria was Philip IV's mother.

Beneath the brilliant social surface Christina was hard at work to tempt Pimentel, and through him his master Philip IV, into her web of intrigue. Although Sweden's foreign policy was traditionally anti-Spanish, the Francophobe Axel Oxenstierna was not averse to seeing Spain brought into play to counterbalance French influence. The Swedish Chancery even gave Pimentel to understand that the Scheldt question might be arranged to Antwerp's advantage, as Holland was hard-pressed in the war at sea against England. The Queen too kept talking of arbitration in the Franco-Spanish war and a possible Swedish-Spanish alliance. But as time passed Pimentel noticed that the Portuguese had asked the Swedes to arbitrate in London over Anglo-Portuguese relations, a sure indication that they regarded Sweden as friendly to Portugal. He told Christina that such support of the Duke of Braganza would not help her relations with Spain, and reported to his own government that the Queen was very subtle and clever and they must be wary in their negotiations with her.

Although Christina had known by November 1652 that the Jesuit General in Rome had approved her conversion, evidently she did not tell Pimentel about it until March or April 1653. By then he had realized that she really did want to conclude a treaty with Philip IV, the offer had already been communicated to Madrid. Once Pimentel knew of the Queen's intended conversion, the whole problem of her puzzling behaviour resolved itself. He now understood that she had really been in earnest about the treaty all along, as she needed the King of Spain's help personally.

At the end of the month an extraordinary meeting was held in great secrecy, consisting of the Queen, Pimentel, his chaplain Manderscheydt, Malines and Bourdelot, whom Christina had now also told of her conversion. It was decided to send Malines to Philip IV to make all arrangements, and on 7th May he set out. Not long afterwards Philip's refusal of the Spanish-Swedish treaty arrived and, realizing the impossibility of continuing negotiations because of the time-lag in communications, Pimentel finally got the Queen's agreement to his returning to Spain. She even put one of her best ships at his disposal to take him there directly. It seems that during the last hectic days before his departure, Christina and Pimentel were so indiscreet as to remain alone for hours in her room at night on more than one occasion. The necessity for long secret discussions is the probable explanation for this behaviour; but it was not an explanation that could be given to suspicious and watchful courtiers, and these conversations, *tête-à-tête*, were not unnaturally given a very different interpretation. Finally, at the beginning of August, Pimentel sailed from Gothenburg, but a violent storm nearly wrecked the ship, forcing it back to port.

Pimentel had taken independent action in leaving Sweden without having received his King's order of recall. In fact his last official instructions, dating from December which had arrived in March, had told him to remain and he was now in a complete quandary about what he should do. Finally he decided that his only course was to return to Christina's court. He found her at Vadstena Castle on Lake Vättern, where she had gone for the funeral of Adolphus John Palatine's wife. Pimentel's unexpected reappearance caused a terrific scandal and the French Resident, Picques, was not alone in thinking that the shipwreck was a put-up job. To Christina and Pimentel his forced return was a really serious blow. They were already preparing plans for him to return to Spain by land, when further definite instructions for him to remain in Sweden arrived from Philip IV. Time was pressing and already the Queen had started to ship her most valuable possessions out of the country. In August the *Fortuna*, whose master was a Dutchman, had set sail with a collection of tapestries, manuscripts, books and other valuables to the value of 500,000 livres.* Storms and the war at sea made the journey a perilous one, but the ultimate destination of these treasures, and that of the Queen, was now settled in her mind; it was Rome. On 26th July, Goswin Nickel had written from there to say that he would "conserve them with the greatest care and faithfulness until the arrival of the person I am anxiously awaiting."

In view of the King of Spain's explicit orders, Pimentel had to remain at his post, but another reliable messenger to the court of Spain was found in the Dominican Juan Baptista Guemes, whom Rebolledo had sent from Copenhagen to Sweden. At the end of September Guemes left for Spain, briefed by Christina and Pimentel in all the details of her plans for abdication and her subsequent movements.

* Three livres equalled one écu. See note p. 127.

Pimentel's unexpected return, and his evident intention of now remaining in Sweden, had been viewed by many as the final and flagrant confirmation of his liaison with the Queen. That their relations were illicit in a very different sense—Catholicism being illegal in Sweden—was a secret shared only by Bourdelot and Father Manderscheydt, who now continued Christina's religious instruction. As he saw her frequently in private, his description of how she appeared to him at the time is particularly interesting. He wrote: "There is nothing feminine about her except her sex. Her voice and manner of speaking, her walk, her style, her ways are all quite masculine. I see her on horse-back nearly every day. Though she rides side-saddle she holds herself so well and is so light in her movements that, unless one were quite close to her, one would take her for a man." He goes on to describe Christina's total disregard for her dress and appearance, remarking that he had seen her chemise splashed with ink and that her linen was often torn.

During the last few years the Queen's portraits had begun to depict the signs of the plumpness which was to become so marked in later years. Even in court portraits, such as those by David Beck and Ehernstrahl, the tendency to a more than double chin was now marked. It is true that Sebastien Bourdon at this time painted one immensely attractive portrait of the Queen (now in the Swedish National Museum) but, because he was a consummate portrait painter, Bourdon could flatter even while providing a striking likeness. Another of his portraits of Christina, in the same pose and dress, is not nearly so complimentary. In his famous equestrian portrait (now in the Prado), which in spite of its size she took with her to Rome, the Queen is portrayed in a rather shabby riding habit, with a masculine coat and stock fastened with a black bow. In the painting, although the Queen quite evidently had her fiery charger very well in hand, her seat looks a trifle awkward owing to the somewhat hunched position of her shoulders, which was probably due to her deformity. Apart from fine eyes, her face is definitely plain. All in all, neither Manderscheydt's verbal description nor the very large range of portraits of the Queen which were painted at the time, portray her as the type of woman for whom a staid, cautious, reserved and happily married man of nearly fifty, like Pimentel, would throw his cap over a windmill.

Nevertheless this was the story which was spreading through Europe, greatly to Pimentel's own embarrassment. In December 1652 he was aware of the rumours and wrote to Brun in The Hague, hoping for his recall. The main purveyors of the story were not just gossiping courtiers or outraged savants, but the diplomatic representatives accredited to Christina's court. There were, of course, strong political and other reasons for these defamatory reports. Christina's position as a young unmarried Queen, who swore like a trooper, was given to jokes in very doubtful taste and preferred almost exclusively the company of men—some of them of doubtful reputation—would give rise to scandal and slander even today. In the seventeenth century sovereigns ruled as well as reigned, therefore any personal preferences or favourites they might have were of political interest to diplomats and their governments.

Peder Juel, the Danish Resident, was the prime source for the now widely-held belief that Christina and Pimentel were lovers. His dispatches to the Danish Chancellor, Christian Thomesen, and letters to the Danish Resident Peder Charisius, at The Hague, represented the Queen as a dissolute woman, surrounded by a dissolute court. There were excuses for this view even allowing for his anti-Swedish bias.

To the mystery of Pimentel's prolonged stay was added the fact that life at court had indeed become exceedingly extravagant in the midst of terrible want in Sweden—a fact which did not pass unnoticed or uncommented upon by the Lutheran clergy. Magnus, although vain and a spendthrift, was at least a Swedish noble of some standing. But owing to his intermittent illness, his place at court had been filled by foreigners such as Bourdelot and Pimentel and a set of gay, handsome, swashbuckling and irresponsible young men such as Klas Tott, Anton Steinberg, Adolphus John Palatine and another foreigner, Christopher Delphicus von Dohna. While in the background there lurked the refugees Corfitz Ulfeld and the Pole Hieronym Radziejowski, both intent upon trying to stir up trouble between Sweden and their respective countries. Altogether it must be admitted that the Queen's circle provided justification for innuendo.

The curious thing is that Juel, who was to make such adept use of this situation, was not a loud-mouthed gossip or a scandalmonger. He was a rather dry unimaginative man, on good terms with the Queen Mother, who had become very devout with her advancing years. His main correspondent, the Danish Chancellor, was honest and religious, and not a person who would have had much time to spare for mere unsupported court gossip, but Thomesen accepted and apparently believed Juel's dispatches. Over a considerable period of time, and rising to a crescendo in the year 1653, these reported that not only life at court, but also the Queen herself, was extravagant and immoral. Juel said that Christina openly blasphemed God, had immoral relations with both Pimentel and Tott and an otherwise unidentified "young Burs," and more particularly, that she had "hidden the beautiful Ebba Sparre in her bed and associated with her in a special way." There were even accounts of how Christina got drunk at a party with Pimentel, and allowed men at the court masques to undress down to their underwear in front of her. Juel also reported that Axel Oxenstierna was furious about the Queen's behaviour with Tott, and the Råd even more so over the *déshabillé* in which she appeared in public, while the Estates were filled with indignation about her lack of religion and her open misbehaviour with "young Burs."

Not surprisingly, in an age of almost absolute monarchs, no hint of any of these accusations has survived in any Swedish document. For one of her subjects to put such allegations on paper—and fail to see that it was destroyed—would have been courting disaster. Such documents could only have survived in a foreign chancery, taken out of Sweden under cover of diplomatic privilege. Of the less serious allegations, that of Christina's drunkenness seems to be particularly unlikely, given her life-long antipathy to wine and spirits. The allegation that men undressed before her may be explained by the *Värdskaps*, masquerades resembling the French *Hôtelleries*, in which the participants, in masks and fancy dress, danced and mimed the parts of people meeting in a country inn. After the performance they removed their disguise. The puritan Whitelocke wrote that these entertainments were perfectly innocent, with "no offence or scandal."

Among the more serious allegations, that of irreligious behaviour does seem to have some foundation in fact, especially according to the customs of the period. Maria Eleonora was so disturbed that she personally taxed her daughter. The interview resulted in Christina's fury and her mother dissolved into floods of tears which lasted for hours on end. The stories about Pimentel are, in the circumstances, easily understood and can almost certainly be discounted. But the favour shown by the Queen to Klas Tott was so marked that even the discreet Ekeblad referred to it in two letters to his family. In both cases he mentions the jealousy of other young men, "because Her Majesty likes Tott very much," or "too much." This swashbuckling young man's career as royal favourite was drawn to the attention of all by Christina accepting the compliment of being proclaimed his lady at a joust, at the turn of the year 1652–53. He managed to keep himself in the public eye by picking quarrels and fighting with everyone, although duelling was strictly forbidden. Indeed it was frowned upon by the Queen unless it was practised by Tott, who received the title of Count of Karlberg and commensurate lands after a particularly notorious bout in 1652. Although she was now older, Tott does seem to have awakened in the Queen something of the attraction that she had felt for Magnus, seven years before; but though she loaded him with honours and gifts, she apparently had no compunction about leaving him behind when the time came.

The allegation about Belle, who although now a married woman still lived with the Queen, travelled with her and shared her bed, was much more serious. Belle was useful to the De la Gardie family, particularly Magnus, as a go-between, but he does not seem to have liked her. After his fall from favour he once made a very cryptic comment about the fact that she constantly accompanied the Queen, saying "I find it amusing that my brother Jacob allows her to travel. This would not be to my taste, if for no other reason than the gossip to which it gives rise among so many people." Not only did Christina regret the loss of Belle after she left Sweden, but in 1661 Belle planned to try to go and see her in Hamburg.

What foundation, if any, ever existed to support these very serious allegations that Juel made about Christina will surely now never be known. She said herself that she had strong passions and that if she had been a man they would have been her undoing. She was also reliably reported to have said to the Queen Mother of

France, in very coarse language, "Faith, Madam, it vexes me to be a woman, it spoils the most tender pleasures, if I was a man it would be a very different matter." To Christina's pursuit of dubious books and her enjoyment of broad jokes and salacious comedies, was added a preference for paintings of ample nudes in the Rubenesque style. It is worth noting that Rubens was one of the few Flemish or German artists whose works were well represented in her collection. Admittedly many of these pictures were by the greatest masters such as Titian and Veronese, but Giulio Romano also appealed to her, while the works of great contemporary artists such as Poussin and Claude Lorraine, who preferred more ethereal subjects, did not. Christina's taste for the "noble and nude" may have been purely personal, the result of intellectual honesty in an age of false prudishness, or of her desire to shock; though today it might equally be attributed to repression. Certainly it did not escape the notice of her contemporaries, as was evident from their shocked horror when she ordered the fig-leaves to be removed from the Farnese marbles.

Even if Christina's own behaviour may have been above reproach, throughout her life she had an unfortunate habit of collecting individuals around her whose conduct was far from exemplary. It is difficult to believe that she was altogether ignorant of their activities. One very damaging reference to the life led at Christina's court—infinitely more damaging than Juel's allegations in view of its disinterested source—has survived. It comes in a letter written by Corfitz Ulfeld's eldest daughter Anna Caterina to a family friend, Dr Otto Sperling, at the time of her father's death in April 1664. Sperling was in charge of the youngest Ulfeld child, Leon, then aged thirteen, whom the other brothers wanted to send to live with Queen Christina in Rome. Anna Caterina secretly enclosed a letter with the one containing her brother's suggestion, protesting strongly against the plan. In it she said, "I knew well how in Sweden children of good family were ruined at her court, at that time when she had a whole kingdom." Addressing Dr Sperling in the third person she continued: "I am, however, sure about the friendship the Doctor always had for my dear father, and the Doctor knows well that he never wanted to send any of his big children to stay with Christina, much less the little innocent Leon."

Corfitz Ulfeld and his family had reason to be grateful to Christina, the Leon in question was probably the child that his wife was expecting when they arrived as refugees in Stockholm in 1651. But in spite of his gratitude to Christina, his willingness to engage in her politics and to maintain friendly relations with her after she had left Sweden, it is evident that Ulfeld held very different views about her court being a suitable place for his children. This is all the more remarkable because it was the custom of the age to send adolescents of good family to court as pages, to learn manners and the social graces.

By the beginning of 1653, the whole situation at the Swedish court had got far beyond the understanding of the unfortunate French Resident, Picques. For some time the activities of Bourdelot, the protégé of the *frondeur* Prince de Condé, had occupied his mind almost to the exclusion of everything else. But now the sinister machinations of the Spanish Envoy Pimentel were also filling his anxious dispatches to Paris. These were highly coloured because Magnus and his supporters kept Picques well supplied with information derogatory to both Bourdelot and Pimentel and to the court. Ever since his embassy to Paris Magnus had been regarded as the leader of the French faction, and his recent partial eclipse in royal favour, owing to ill-health and absence from court, and the rise of new favourites, was taken seriously both by Picques and himself.

As a result of Picques's increasing anxiety, Chanut was sent on a short mission to Stockholm in April–May 1653. Although he found Christina ill, (but trying to conceal it out of loyalty to Bourdelot, whose sensible regime she had been neglecting) she apparently welcomed Chanut with all her old enthusiasm and told him that there was no change in Sweden's friendship for France or her foreign policy. This the Ambassador believed because it was borne out by the assurances he received from Axel Oxenstierna and the Råd. He realized that Picques's reports on Bourdelot had been alarmist. He even promised the Queen to request Mazarin to grant the doctor a benefice, which would conveniently remove the recipient from Sweden. In fact Bourdelot left in June, shortly after the Ambassador. Chanut did not display quite his usual perspicacity about Pimentel, believing the Spaniard simply to be on very friendly terms with the Queen. This was not so disquieting for France as it might have been, as it was evident from Christina's behaviour that she was really going to abdicate very soon.

The Queen was now completely occupied with her own future, to the exclusion of the national interest, and wanted to sell Swedish ships worth 300,000 riksdaler to France, so that she could be paid the money as a pension after she had left Sweden. Realizing that the Queen was not going to be very popular in Sweden after this event, Chanut was not at all sorry about the apparent diminution of French influence, or that most of the French contingent at court were preparing to leave. A good deal of the blame for her actions was bound therefore to be laid on Spain. Now that he was certain where France's future political advantage lay, Chanut paid a call on Charles Gustavus in Öland on his way back to The Hague, and was kindly received. Chanut's correct summing up of the situation received further endorsement in November. Trichet Du Fresne passed through The Hague and let slip that, although the Queen's treasures had been shipped to France, they were to be sent on from there to the General of the Jesuits in Rome. Spain might then reap the glory of the Queen's conversion, but the Franco–Swedish alliance was safe.

Although Christina's interest in her country was slackening, one last drama of her life in Sweden remained to be played out before the curtain came down on the final scene of her abdication at Uppsala. Her relations with Magnus had been changing for some time and had further degenerated since the rise of Bourdelot. Nevertheless, especially after Bourdelot's departure, ostensibly friendly relations had been resumed between him and the Queen. However Magnus's pride and vanity had received a severe blow and the situation rankled, particularly because, after Bourdelot had left, he did not regain the Queen's favour. In this he had been replaced by Pimentel, whom both he and Picques considered to be politically dangerous. He was also jealous of the new favourites who had arisen. Among them were the young courtiers Klas Tott, Anton von Steinberg and Christopher Delphicus von Dohna.

Even when Magnus had been at the height of favour seven years before, Chanut had perceived the basic weakness and vanity inherent in his character. These defects were fully revealed when he joined the court at Uppsala in November, where it had moved for fear of the plague spreading in Stockholm. At the first opportunity Magnus complained to the Queen about her changed attitude, and her preference for other ministers. He even told her that it had been reported to him that she had accused him of treachery; she had reputedly said that she would never take him back into her favour or protect him, and that if anyone wished to harm him she would just laugh.

Far from receiving the reassurances and denials that his past situation as a spoilt favourite had led him to expect, Magnus instead found himself confronted by a furious Queen who wanted to know who had dared to say such a thing. In his surprise and confusion Magnus blurted out that it was Count Anton von Steinberg, Master of the Horse. Christina subsequently questioned Steinberg, who hotly denied the story. Now thoroughly roused the Queen determined to investigate the whole matter, and demanded that Magnus should tell her who had really said this to him. Magnus now said that it had been Colonel Schlippenbach, in a *tête-à-tête* conversation at Ekolsund. Schlippenbach received a written summons from the Queen to present himself at court. Magnus must have got to hear of this and lost his nerve, for he took the fatal step of writing to Schlippenbach and begging him to admit to the conversation. Schlippenbach refused, and in a dramatic confrontation Magnus threatened him in the Queen's presence. Christina was now convinced that Magnus had lied to her, right from the beginning. In her fury and disgust she banished him from court, until he could produce proof of the truth of his allegations.

Even now Magnus would not accept his disgrace nor would he withdraw with dignity. He asked Axel Oxenstierna and Charles Gustavus for their help. Unwillingly, Oxenstierna suggested that Magnus should persuade his mother and his wife to intercede for him with the Queen. It must have been a curious and painful interview for all three women, whose lives were so closely interwoven by family ties. It even occurred at a time when they would normally have met to celebrate the birth of another De la Gardie—Belle's first child. Only fear for her favourite child could have induced the proud Ebba Brahe to beg favours from the outraged Queen. For Maria Euphrosyne the task can have been scarcely less painful. However Christina received them kindly and, though they did not move her, she gave them an assurance that she would proceed no further against Magnus. With the Messenius plot still fresh in mind this must have been a relief.

But even now the culprit could not bring himself to accept the fate which his foolishness had brought on him. With the help of the Scotsman, Colonel Hugo Hamilton, Magnus made an attempt to see the Queen. This she answered by a searing letter written on 4th December, which was made public. In it Christina said "I cannot, without contradicting myself, pardon you for the crime which you have committed against yourself, do not believe that I am offended, I assure you that I am not, I am now incapable of feeling anything for you but pity . . . you have yourself made public a secret about which I resolved to remain silent all my life, by making it obvious that you are unworthy of the fortune you have received from me." Christina's fury was doubled by the fact that Magnus had shown up not only the weakness of his character, but also her own lack of judgment. With bitter self-revelation she wrote: "I have done too much for you during nine years, I have always blindly taken your part." In a lesser degree she had made the same mistake with Messenius, and in the future she was to err much more seriously and to extract a commensurate revenge. Now she contented herself with depriving Magnus of his office as president of the finance ministry, and he was replaced by Herman Fleming. In view of the country's appalling financial position this was a wise move, but the manner in which it was effected was constitutionally incorrect and gave rise to misgivings, especially on the part of Axel Oxenstierna.

Within a few days of these events, the English Ambassador, Bulstrode Whitelocke, arrived at Uppsala. The measure of the consternation caused by these incidents may be judged from the fact that although Whitelocke in his journal gives an account which is substantially correct, he himself did not believe it and described it as "a piece of romance which may, for diversion's sake, be here inserted."

Although Whitelocke's trained legal mind afforded him remarkable powers of detailed observation, and his journal gives a fascinating picture of life in Sweden, his sketches of people are often limited to externals. He seems to have lacked Chanut's

The peace banquet given by Charles Gustavus at Nuremberg on 25th September, 1649, engraved from a painting by W. Kilian.

The leader of the peasants in the Riksdag, by P. Olsson.

The great philosopher René Descartes, by D. Beck. He died in Stockholm in 1650.

Right: Stockholm in 1650, by W. Hartman.

HOLMIÆ INSIGNIA
Thet Konungzlige Slottet
Thet Konungzlige Amiralitetet.
Bodar.

Count Raimondo Montecuccoli, Imperial Ambassador to Christina's court in Stockholm and Antwerp. Portrait by E. Griessler painted in 1665.

capacity for evaluating their characters and motives. He also lacked the quick perception of the Imperial Ambassador, the Italian Count Raimondo Montecuccoli. Montecuccoli also kept a diary, but unlike Whitelocke's journal, which was evidently meant for publication or at least private circulation, this was a personal record consisting of brief, incisive jottings on daily events, discussions and personalities. Between them, these two journals present a remarkable record of life at Christina's court in the months before her abdication, Whitelocke's for the general background, Montecuccoli's for greater inside knowledge and candid reporting and comment.

Owing to his sophisticated and attractive personality, and the close links existing between the Hapsburg court of Vienna and that of Madrid, Montecuccoli quickly gained far greater intimacy with the Queen and her friends than Whitelocke could ever hope to achieve. Montecuccoli was observant and shrewd in his judgments. It is remarkable that his summing-up of Whitelocke after their first meeting was much the same as that of the editor of Whitelocke's papers, made in 1855. He noted that Whitelocke was pleasant and courteous, but that in talking of war and religion he could be ridiculous. In fact when Charles Gustavus paid the Ambassador the signal honour of a personal call, only twelve days before his accession, Whitelocke treated the future "Napoleon of the North" to a discourse on the lack of Sunday observance in Sweden.

Possibly, Whitelocke's incapacity for seeing much below the surface sprang from the trait in his own character which caused his facile acceptance of events during the Civil War and Commonwealth. It was he who drew up the ordinance for the abolition of the royal power, though he was honest enough not to hide the fact that he preferred a monarchy. He could defend the legality of his government, although he did not really believe in its principles. But for the job in hand Whitelocke had been an excellent choice. His stately looks and nice appreciation of appearances and the finer points of etiquette, together with his experience of court life, were well-calculated to impress foreigners with the dignity and solidity of what amounted to a revolutionary government in England. His learning and real connoisseurship of music had a special appeal for Christina. On the business side, he had been given clear-cut instructions for the negotiation of a trade treaty with Sweden, and to prevent her from giving any assistance to Charles II. He had also been commissioned to buy arms from Sweden. To carry out his mission, Whitelocke was provided with a suite of one hundred persons and an allowance of £1,000 a month.

Whitelocke had a rough crossing from Gravesend to Gothenburg, from where he started for Uppsala on 30th November. The roads were appalling, ice causing injuries to men and horses, with only four hours daylight, fourteen miles a day was good going. Few details of Swedish life escaped the Ambassador's attention, they were all noted in his journal in which, like Caesar and Pope Pius II before him, he referred to himself in the third person. He was struck by the poverty, but also by the honesty of the people and their frugal way of life. Even gentlemen's houses were still usually built of wood—huge tree trunks calked with moss, the roof boards being covered with birch bark and then turf. He noticed that the peasants pastured their sheep and goats there. More than anything else, Whitelocke complained about the appalling food and bad beer, though he was an abstemious man who refused to accept the Swedish custom of constant toast drinking and consequent drunkenness. This caused a tussle over protocol and considerable ill feeling after he got to Uppsala on 20th December.

The English Embassy was lodged in "a fair brick house in the market," one of the few not built of wood in the whole town. It was furnished with the Queen's own hangings and plate and, as was customary, for the first three days she provided the entertainment—food, drink, and even musicians. In the withdrawing-room there was a canopy of state and a carpet of cloth of gold. Whitelocke's own bedroom was also very fine, with a bed hung with blue velvet—embroidered with gold and flowers—and crimson and Turkey carpets. Etiquette required that the official corresponding to the Marshal of the Diplomatic Corps should fetch him from there, to take him in the Queen's carriage to present his credentials.

Whitelocke gives a minute description of every detail of this ceremony. He himself was dressed in "fine black English cloth" with a diamond hat-band and buttons worth £1,000. He completely outshadowed Queen Christina. The Ambassador related how he would never have known who she was, if she had not risen from her chair of state when he entered the throne room. He described her dress as being of "plain grey stuff, her petticoat reaching to the ground, and over that a jacket, like men wear, and of the same stuff, reaching to her knees. On the left side she wore the order of Amaranth with a crimson ribbon. Her cuffs were ruffled *à la mode*. She wore no gorget or band, but a black scarf tied round her neck and tied with a black ribbon in front, like that of soldiers and sailors. Her hair was braided and hung loose on her head. She wore a black velvet cap lined with sables and turned up in the Swedish fashion, which she put on and off as men do their hats. Her face was sprightly, but somewhat pale. She had much majesty in her demeanour and although small, a very noble mien and carriage."

After making three bows and kissing the Queen's hand, Whitelocke read his oration in English. Most noticeably he drew a parallel between Queen Elizabeth and Christina herself. This was then translated into French by his chaplain; although Whitelocke himself had a good command of the language it was not etiquette to make his oration in any language other than his own. Throughout this ceremony, at appropriate moments, Christina and the Ambassador doffed their hats to each other. At one time she came close to Whitelocke and "by looks and gestures Whitelocke thought she was trying to daunt him." The Ambassador received this demonstration with truly English phlegm and was much astonished when later he saw Pimentel play up to her. His credentials had evidently been most carefully examined by the Queen before their official presentation and, characteristically, she sent a message to ask why she had not been accorded the style of *potentissima donna* which was given to her by the Emperor and other sovereigns. Before she would receive him, Whitelocke had to explain that this was a mistake.

The Ambassador had come well briefed about the personalities at court. Among the four foreign diplomatic representatives he made a note that the French one was to be spied on, but that Pimentel, because of his "very great favour with the Queen and because his master was a good friend of England" was the most important. Of the Swedish nobles, "Greve Tott, the Queen's favourite and a gallant young gentleman" headed the list, which included "Senators Vanderlin, [Lorenz von der Linde] Bond [Karl Bonde, the correct spelling of Swedish names and titles was not Whitelocke's forte] and Greve Eric Oxenstiern"; though the most important of all was, of course, the Chancellor Axel Oxenstierna, who was then away in the country.

On Christmas eve Pimentel came to call. He acknowledged that he enjoyed the Queen's favour and offered to help in any way, advising Whitelocke not to ask for official audiences through the Secretary of State. He should ask for private ones with Christina herself. Pimentel said that he had always transacted his business in this way, and as he knew that the Spaniard "enjoyed extraordinary favour with the Queen and her servants," Whitelocke realized this was good advice.

On Boxing-day Whitelocke had his first private audience with Christina. On this occasion she wore a black velvet dress. This was cut in the same curious style as before. They talked French and during the whole audience paced up and down the room together. Poor Whitelocke, who was lame, was very tired at the end. The conversation lasted for two hours behind closed doors, no one else was present. Christina professed great admiration for Cromwell—"Your General hath done the greatest things of anyone in the world." This was not just fulsome flattery; the manner of Cromwell's rise to power and his dictatorial tendencies appealed to her personally; at the time of her death she still had his portrait in her palace in Rome.

No business was transacted, however, the Queen's main interest seeming to be in the state of religion in England, and the custom of the Commonwealth army officers preaching to the troops. At one stage Christina turned to Whitelocke and said "Methinks you preach very well and have now made a good sermon." The Ambassador took this as a compliment, obviously being unaware of her hatred of sermons and that she was pulling his leg. But although he was strict about Sunday observance and shocked at Swedish laxity in this respect, and at the crucifixes in Churches and clergy's use of copes and other vestments, Whitelocke was not a bigot. It is evident that he met Pimentel's chaplain, Father Manderscheydt, quite often, and although he must have known he was a Jesuit, he liked and admired him, describing him as "a man of excellent parts, wit and behaviour. He spoke fluent Spanish, Latin, French and High Dutch. He was very learned and Whitelocke liked to converse with him because he never mentioned anything of religion that might cause dispute."*

Before the Ambassador had his second audience with Christina, in which they began to get down to business, Pimentel called on him and suggested that Spain, Sweden and England should make an alliance as it seemed likely that France, Holland and Denmark were intending to make one against Spain and England. In fact both Spain and France were at that time angling for an agreement with England, and this was evidently an attempt by Pimentel to spike the French guns. Whitelocke replied very guardedly as his instructions were limited, and grand strategy of this sort was definitely not included in them.

From his conversation with the Queen on 29th December, however, it is plain that she must have had a very good idea of what these instructions were, for she very soon broached the question of the opening of the Sound, which formed part of them. She even referred to the very delicate subject of Charles II's approaches to Charles Gustavus, and the rumours that she was supposed to be going to marry him! This time, because Christina now knew of Whitelocke's lameness, they sat on two stools—a great concession on her part and an indication of her estimate of how important English friendship could be to her. It is fascinating to note that when they reached the confidential part of their conversation, Christina drew her stool right up to Whitelocke's so that she could speak more softly. The Queen now asked for the particulars of the proposed trade treaty, and Whitelocke, "having resolved as to the best way in his judgment to deal with a Princess of honour," told her all the articles. He kept back only three clauses for subsequent negotiations, and gave her copies of the document. Christina was careful to ensure that he came to hear her remark that "the English Ambassador had dealt with her, not as a merchant but as a gentleman and a man of honour."

The following day Whitelocke was again summoned for an audience, as the Queen had received news that the peace negotiations between England and Holland had been broken off. She

* Here as usual Whitelocke referred to himself in the third person.

then produced Pimentel's suggestion for an Anglo-Swedish-Spanish alliance. Upon receiving Whitelocke's guarded answer, to the effect that England might not agree because Spain had failed to give satisfaction for the murder of an English minister, Christina adroitly turned the conversation again to religion in England. In the midst of this, a large mastiff burst into the room, and Whitelocke had to admit that he had brought it with him as a present for the Queen from Mr Peters, a simple Englishman who was a great admirer of hers and had also sent her a letter and a cheese; whereupon the Queen said she would accept both gifts, and "they parted in much drollery." Not, however, before Christina had found out from Whitelocke how he communicated secretly with his government. The Ambassador told her that he employed two waters which he made himself: "one to write and the other to bring up the writing."

The days passed pleasantly enough, with Pimentel coming frequently to call (Whitelocke found him very good company), and with a ball at court, at which the Ambassador particularly admired Christina's dancing. Whitelocke even went to call on the ladies at court (he notes this was useful, presumably for gossip); these included Lady Jane Ruthven, in spite of her royalist sympathies. Lady Jane was the daughter of Gustavus Adolphus's General, Patrick Ruthven, and Christina was evidently much attached to her and other members of the family. At home the English Embassy entertained themselves with music, which was evidently of a high order, for Whitelocke himself had been a composer and had organized masques for royalty. Both Swedes and foreigners came to listen to these concerts, including Christina's Italian musicians and singers, of whom several were the highly esteemed castrati.

Although he went frequently to see the Queen and found her minutely informed not only about England but his own family, and full of hints about England having plenty of money, Whitelocke realized he was not getting any further with the negotiations for the treaty. Axel Oxenstierna's arrival on 8th January was therefore a very important event. Even so Whitelocke would not budge an inch on protocol: the Chancellor, because he was a subject in Sweden, must make the first call on Whitelocke who was Ambassador of England.

Oxenstierna arrived in considerable state, and was received by Whitelocke in a ground-floor room, specially prepared with his own gold and silken hangings. This was done to save the seventy-one-year-old Chancellor from having to climb the stairs. Whitelocke found that Oxenstierna was having trouble with his eyes and could not sit facing the fire. Nevertheless the Ambassador described him as "a tall, proper, straight old man, wearing a habit of black cloth, a close coat lined with fur, a velvet cap furred, no hat, and a cloak . . . his hair was grey, his beard broad and long, his countenance sober and fixed and his carriage grave and civil." They spoke Latin because, although they both knew French, Oxenstierna did not see why that nation "should have the compliment of their language being used by others, though Latin was more honourable and copious and fitter to be used, the Romans having been masters of so great a part of the world, and yet their language not being particular to any people." Whitelocke noticed that he mixed business with "pleasant stories" and liked talking of his past life, calling this "*senilis garrulitas*," also that he reminisced a good deal about Gustavus Adolphus. Whitelocke asked him to get the treaty settled as soon as possible, to which the Chancellor replied that he had to take his orders from his mistress, the Queen.

A few days later the news broke that Cromwell had been declared Lord Protector, making Whitelocke somewhat apprehensive about Swedish reactions, more particularly because he had some trouble about it with his own suite. He need not have bothered, as Christina received the news with enthusiasm. She said she was sure that Cromwell would later become king, and drew a parallel between his situation and that of her own ancestor Gustavus Wasa. She also told Whitelocke, in confidence, that during her minority Oxenstierna would have liked to assume a similar office. As usual, the Queen reverted to the question of religion in England, asking why the laws were so severe against Roman Catholics. Oxenstierna, however, had some very searching questions to ask about the legality of Cromwell's step. He reminded Whitelocke of the disasters which the election of emperors by the army had brought on Rome, and remarked on the instability of Sweden's own previously elective monarchy. But in the end he agreed that the treaty was being negotiated with

England, rather than any particular government, though he asked to examine Whitelocke's credentials again.

On 21st January Christina, who had returned from a visit to her mother, summoned Whitelocke to a private audience. She now told him in the greatest secrecy about her abdication, making him promise not to mention it to anyone except Cromwell and then only by word of mouth when he got back to England. The Queen justified her action on the grounds that it would be much better for Sweden to have a man to rule. She also admitted that she wanted to retire into private life. When Whitelocke rebutted this on the grounds that it was her duty to God to go on ruling, since he had called her to this state, the Queen replied "I am resolved never to marry."

It seems that Christina's revelation did not come as a great surprise to Whitelocke. He must have been aware of her previous abdication attempt in 1651, and with his legal caution he at once gave her some shrewd advice about her money affairs. He illustrated this by a fable of an old man, who had arranged to make over all his goods to his son, but when friends came to witness the deed the son told the old man to go into the kitchen because he was smoking and spitting in the parlour. When the moment came to sign, and the father was called back into the parlour again, he would not do so because he said he was resolved to spit in the parlour as long as he lived. Christina appreciated the story and said that she would also "arrange to spit in the parlour."

February brought two new ambassadors to Uppsala—one a Russian, who had to excuse himself from an audience because he was already drunk at ten a.m., and his complete opposite, the very polished, shrewd and attractive representative of the Emperor, Count Raimondo Montecuccoli. This able soldier, aged forty-five, had been in the Imperial service since he was sixteen, and was friend and confidant of both Ferdinand III and the Archduke Leopold, Governor of the Spanish Netherlands. Although the purpose of his mission was a secret, we know that Montecuccoli had arrived with the astounding proposal that Christina should marry the Emperor's eldest son, Ferdinand, whose election as King of the Romans she had helped to secure: she would be the future Empress. In spite of her aversion to marriage and of her own self-esteem, even Christina's vanity must have been tickled, especially because the envoy was a personable unmarried man. Although she had been ill in bed and that morning had been bled, she received Montecuccoli the same day with her arm bandaged.

Immediately the Imperial Ambassador was received into the Queen's intimate circle. Two days later he went with her, Pimentel, Tott and Ulfeld on a bear hunt in the country. After this they supped and danced in a hunting lodge until midnight. Montecuccoli noted that Christina danced exquisitely and that, driving back in her carriage in the small hours, her conversation was very witty and amusing. He described it as being on the whole amorous, but noted that she made jokes about religion and the execution of Charles I. She said also that she was in love with Belle.

The next day, at a private musical party in her own room, with Montecuccoli present, Christina introduced Belle to Whitelocke with the words "Discourse with this lady, my bed-fellow, and tell me if her inside is not as beautiful as her outside." The staid Englishman seems to have found nothing shocking in this remark, and described Belle in his journal as being "modest, virtuous, witty, of great beauty, and excellent behaviour." The Queen now proceeded to take off Belle's gloves and to give one to Whitelocke as a favour and, tearing the other into four, divided it between Pimentel, Tott, Montecuccoli and an Italian of his suite.

By the middle of February Whitelocke found out that the news of the Queen's abdication was beginning to be talked about. General Sir George Fleetwood, who had been with Gustavus Adolphus on the field of Lützen, came to see him and mentioned it. Nevertheless the gay life at court continued. On 16th February there was another ball, where Montecuccoli was invested with the Order of Amaranth—just three weeks after his arrival. However Christina sent a gift of a herd of reindeer to Whitelocke, apparently as a present for Cromwell. (Unfortunately they were all eaten by wolves or died while boarded out at a farm.) The English Embassy had now been in Uppsala for two months, and Whitelocke was beginning to get restive about the treaty; he went to see the Queen and insisted that he must go home as her forthcoming abdication was generally known. However Christina promised that the treaty would be settled before she abdicated, and said she was going to see Charles Gustavus and would discuss the matter with him.

As his secret mission had obviously failed, Montecuccoli was also beginning to think of leaving. He started on a round of ceremonial calls, collecting some interesting opinions as he went. Ulfeld explained Sweden's precarious financial state to him, pointing out that Stockholm, where the customs used to render an income of from 200,000 to 300,000 thaler annually, now afforded less than 50,000. He attributed this to the fact that Sweden's main exports were copper, iron and pitch, useful in war but not in peace. In the opinion of this Danish ex-minister, Sweden's economy could only be geared to war. He added that the soldiers would like Charles Gustavus because he was militarily minded—events were to prove Ulfeld not far wrong. The High Steward, Per Brahe, said that no honourable official in Sweden would ever accept the Queen's abdication—there was a mutual obligation between princes and their subjects—and that Christina could never abdicate, except by exercising autocratic power.

A few days later Montecuccoli went to see the Queen in the evening. He described her as being attired in her night-dress. Christina told him that as she was sure of his good faith, candour and chivalry, she wished to confide in him about a matter of the greatest importance to herself and that she believed that it was God's will that he had come. The Queen went on to say (not very surprisingly in the circumstances) that if they stayed and talked together for some time they would be regarded with suspicion. She asked him, therefore, to go and see Pimentel the following morning at eight, saying that he would explain everything. In his diary on the following day Montecuccoli only made the cryptic entry "Go to Pimentel's rooms and he confides in me the great secret." There is good reason to believe that this entry was made on or about the same day that Christina wrote her famous "abdication" letter to Chanut, in which she said "others do not know my reasons or my turn of mind, as I have never declared myself to anyone but you and another friend." It is clear that as her intention to abdicate was already known, the secret must have been her conversion to Catholicism.

Christina evidently persuaded Montecuccoli to put off his departure, for some days later he left with her, Tott, Steinberg and Adolphus John Palatine to go and see Charles Gustavus at Västerås. The first two days were taken up with discussions between the Queen and her heir about the abdication, and Montecuccoli was tactfully sent off to see a horse-breeding farm near by. Herman Fleming, however, was present, and probably gave financial advice during the meetings, so too was Charles Gustavus's friend, Lawrenz von der Linde, the Marshal of the Diplomatic Corps who was a member of the Råd. Von der Linde had in fact been appointed by the Queen the previous autumn, together with other personal supporters of herself and the Prince. It was part of her policy to weaken the Råd's opposition to her abdication. It was a cautious move, but in the event the Råd's resistance was not nearly so strong as in 1651.

During the last three years Axel Oxenstierna and many of the senators had become aware of Christina's dwindling interest in her own country, and her preoccupation with the world outside. Moreover, they—and the Chancellor particularly—had had occasion to appreciate Charles Gustavus's qualities, especially his wisdom and loyalty. So when, in February, the Queen announced her intention to the government of abdicating immediately and placing her cousin on the throne, although a minority protested violently, Axel Oxenstierna and his supporters realised that opposition was fruitless. All they could hope for was that the Queen would reflect once more before taking so drastic a step, and possibly of arranging a compromise which would relieve her of some of the burden of ruling.

An address to this effect, signed by twenty-five senators, was sent to her, but in vain. In the middle of February, to make her position absolutely clear, Christina summoned the entire Råd to the Castle to tell them of her irrevocable decision. She said that her reasons would soon be known. A stiff tussle ensued between her and Per Brahe, but Axel Oxenstierna knew that nothing was to be gained, and in the end the Råd agreed that the Riksdag should be called on May 1st to be informed of the Queen's abdication. So when Christina arrived at Västerås she was able to tell Charles Gustavus that the whole matter was settled, only her own financial arrangements remained to be discussed.

Faced with this *fait accompli* Charles Gustavus agreed to accept the crown. That evening at supper, the Queen was in good humour; she told Montecuccoli that when he came to Spa—where she was supposed to be going for her health after her abdication—he must come and see her and bring his Italian friends Hercolani and Caprara, whom she already knew. By now Montecuccoli probably had a shrewd idea that Spa might not be the Queen's ultimate destination. But the project of Christina's health cure in Protestant Germany would obviously be more acceptable to the future King of Sweden than any other plans his cousin might have in mind. The next day the party broke up; Charles Gustavus went to Eskilstuna to take counsel with Axel Oxenstierna, whom he had kept informed of the Queen's propositions. Christina returned to Uppsala, to begin the financial negotiations which would ensure that even after her abdication she could "spit in the parlour"—Peder Juel had already told Montecuccoli that she intended to do so to the tune of 200,000 riksdaler a year.

Although several people told Whitelocke that it was very doubtful if the Queen would be able to abdicate, she herself evidently entertained no such fears, and during the whole of March was taken up with the financial arrangements. Very cleverly she suggested that her appanage should consist of lands which Sweden had gained during her own reign, such as the islands of Ösel and Gotland and estates in Pomerania, also those belonging to Adolphus John Palatine (for whom his brother could now be expected to provide) and the vast estates which she herself had given to the fallen favourite, Magnus. With the exception of Per Brahe, most of the Råd agreed to this and that the Queen should receive lands capable of bringing her in an income of 200,000 riksdaler.

Had he but known it, there was no need whatsoever for Whitelocke to advise the Queen about her appanage, and to make sure that the lands from which her income was to be derived should be firmly in her own possession. Christina might be extravagant, but she was well able to look after her own interests. Whitelocke was evidently beginning to regard her with a more perceptive eye, possibly because she had offered to sell the Swedish colonies in West Africa to England. He made no mention of who was to receive the money for them, but the inference is that it was to be the Queen herself. About this time too, the Ambassador made one cryptic comment in his journal which might suggest a suspicion of the Queen's Catholic leanings. He noted that he was anxious to get the treaty through before Pimentel left, "because of his great favour with the Queen; which with her respects to Montecuccoli, both great Papists, caused Whitelocke to have more doubt of her inclinations."

Montecuccoli had now become almost as much the Queen's confidant as Pimentel. He told an amusing story of how he received a message that he would be asked to dine with Adolphus John Palatine at the castle in Uppsala, and that he would see many pictures there. He was to admire them very much and say that they were the best of those which came from Prague. As Montecuccoli was well aware, the best pictures had already been shipped out of the country, but an Italian's judgment of Italian pictures would of course impress the ignorant Swedes. On the same day as he went to this dinner, Montecuccoli went driving with the Queen, and afterwards she gave him a case of medals to be taken to Hamburg where they were to be deposited in Pimentel's name. Nor was this all: a few days later Christina also gave the Imperial Ambassador a box of jewels to take out of the country, which he left at the beginning of April, bearing a personal letter from the Queen to the Emperor.

Pimentel finally left about the same time for Spain. Before her abdication Christina gave one more extraordinary sign of her wish to please him and honour Spain. This was made at the expense of the unfortunate Portuguese Ambassador, now Antonio Da Sylva. Apparently Christina felt no debt of gratitude towards Macedo's nation, although he had served her so faithfully, nor did she worry about embroiling Sweden with a friendly country if by doing so she could make absolutely certain of currying favour with Philip IV of Spain. Her own financial arrangements were far from settled and she was becoming increasingly aware of the fact that she would need strong political support once she had left Sweden. Accordingly she sent Lawrenz von der Linde with a letter to Da Sylva's house. The letter was addressed to von der Linde himself, but he had instructions to open it and read it aloud to the Portuguese Ambassador.

In the letter the Queen stated that she now considered the Duke of Braganza (John IV of Portugal) to be a usurper, and that in consequence Da Sylva was no longer *persona grata* at her court. The unfortunate Ambassador took counsel with Axel Oxenstierna, who told him to be patient and to pay no attention as within a few weeks the Queen would have left the country. In defence of Christina's action it must be admitted that she was probably very well aware that this was what would happen, and that Swedish–Portuguese relations would not be disturbed, but she would have scored a trump card with Spain. She had also given Pimentel a diamond ring worth 10,000 crowns. He told Whitelocke that she had handed it to him in her mask, apparently as a joke, at the last Värdskap or Masque danced at court before he left; and then had told him to keep it. Whitelocke had particularly admired Christina's dancing on this occasion. He described the Masque as being designed to show "the vanity and folly of all professions and worldly things," and said that it was "genteel without the least offence or scandal."

Towards the end of April, Christina and Charles Gustavus met for the last time before the abdication, in the Queen Mother's residence at Nyköping. Maria Eleonora was miserable about the whole situation, not only because she could not understand her daughter's action, but because she had grave doubts about its possible effect upon her own finances. However, Christina promised her mother that these would be provided for, before she left the country. Indeed the Queen had arranged this meeting with her cousin to settle the details of the abdication and tell him about her own financial plans. In his customary gentlemanly fashion Charles Gustavus agreed to all her proposals, subject to confirmation by the Råd and Riksdag. Afterwards he told Axel Oxenstierna that in the circumstances he could not do otherwise. Charles Gustavus was doing everything possible to smooth Christina's path, even to the extent of persuading his silly and tactless brother Adolphus John (whom the Queen rightly did not like or trust—she had deliberately cut him out of the succession by making it applicable only to Charles Gustavus and his male heirs) to give up his post as Grand Master of the Queen's very much reduced court.

Although the two cousins would see each other subsequently at the abdication and at Christina's formal deposition of the crown, this meeting at Nyköping was the final parting of the ways for them both. It was the end of a relationship that had endured through many vicissitudes since childhood. To the Queen, in the midst of her feverish intrigues and preparations for her abdication and life afterwards, this probably meant little; it can scarcely have been the same for Charles Gustavus. The clearest indication we have of his feeling for Christina is the attitude of dignified consideration with which he always treated her, both personally and as King of Sweden; though he had ample cause to regret many of her subsequent actions. His attitude may be explained by past affection, gratitude or his own idea of honourable behaviour. Certainly it presented a marked contrast to that of Magnus and other former favourites, and shows that in her estimate of the confidence that she could repose in him, Christina was for once not at fault. It was a far greater tragedy for her than for her cousin that she had not continued to return his affection, though she evidently appreciated his gifts. The portrait that Bourdon had painted of Charles Gustavus only two years before shows a remarkably clever face, though with a sensual pouting mouth not unlike Christina's own, and a slightly cleft chin. Its outline is already blurred by the fleshiness that was later to mar his whole appearance. This may well have been brought on by excessive drinking, but neither this nor his corpulence—about which the Queen was later to make such derogatory remarks—were to affect his brilliant career as a soldier or to make Charles X of Sweden a less effective ruler.

Christina's abdication was by now being openly discussed in Europe; and more serious from her point of view, her conversion to Catholicism was being discussed in France. The result of this was an exchange of letters between the Queen and Chanut. The French government were as anxious to clear themselves, beforehand, of responsibility for the conversion, as Christina was to conceal it altogether until her finances were settled and she was out of the country. Her money worries were increased by the fact that the lands which she wished to have in Pomerania had been awarded to Swedish commanders for the part they had played in the Thirty Years War. Understandably they were putting up a stiff resistance and they were being backed up by most of the nobility, who saw in this expropriation the thin end of the wedge which would serve as a precedent for Charles Gustavus to make a general much-needed Reduction once he was on the throne.

The resistance was something which Christina had foreseen and feared, and she now tried to circumnavigate it by proposing to Whitelocke, even before she went to Nyköping, that a secret clause in her favour should be inserted into the treaty with England. This clause laid down that Cromwell should revoke the treaty if Sweden did not fulfil her obligations with regard to the Queen's appanage. Whitelocke was nonplussed; he was afraid that if he did not agree Christina would prevent the treaty going through at the eleventh hour. Of course he had received no instructions for such an eventuality. He temporized, therefore, by saying that all he could suggest was that Christina should prepare such an article and sign it. On his return he would submit it to Cromwell. The Queen replied that she would send Ulfeld to discuss it with him while she was away, but he was on no account to mention it to any of the Swedes, because she could not trust them.

Whitelocke's comments on it in his journal are eloquent of both their points of view. He wrote that he "agreed, but said that he was afraid that if this clause was later invoked it would make the Queen more unpopular than before. She thought that it would keep the Swedes still in fear of her, for fear of the treaty being broken. Whitelocke secretly thought that it might be convenient for the Lord Protector to have the means of breaking the treaty, but he doubted the honour and clearness of it, and felt that the less said the better. He reflected to what a condition the Queen had brought her affairs that she dared not trust her countrymen in this business, and that even before her abdication distrusted their keeping their agreement of how she should be treated." He again counselled Christina to be very sure of those in charge of her revenue, and to get out of Sweden quickly.

Fortunately, when Ulfeld came to discuss the matter with Whitelocke, they both agreed that it would be most inadvisable for the Queen to include the secret clause. In the end it was agreed that she should write a personal letter to Cromwell asking him to be her friend. As a comment on the Queen's own behaviour and contemporary political morality, it should be noted that at this interview with Whitelocke, Ulfeld made proposals to him about the Orkneys—then a Danish possession—to the detriment of his own country. On another occasion he suggested how the Sound could be passed, again to the detriment of Denmark. In her present situation, Christina had grown accustomed to taking Ulfeld into her confidence; she told Whitelocke that she hoped that he and his wife would accompany her abroad.

When the diet of the Riksdag opened on 11th May, neither the question of the Queen's appanage nor the proposed financial settlement had been definitely agreed with the Råd. To make a good impression Christina was, for the first time in her life, trying to economize and keep within the budget limits laid down by Fleming; she saw to it that Holm, now ennobled as Leijoncrona and Intendant of the court, did so as well. The really chaotic state of Christina's personal finances and her efforts to economize were all reflected in thc sad letters which Ekeblad wrote to his family in March. He said that everyone at court was unsure of their position. They had no money and could get no credit; if they went out to eat, they were told after three meals that they would be served no more unless they paid cash. His letters at this time show Christina in an exceptionally bad light. Admittedly she was battling for her own financial security, but she made absolutely no provision for those who were dependent on her. On 15th March Ekeblad wrote that "Today Her Majesty started to dismiss all her chamber servants and already she has told all the women that they could get out. [He uses a word which indicates that she did this in an unpleasant fashion.] Only two or three maids will remain with her." Ekeblad's feelings were obviously coloured by his own anxiety, but previously he had admired the Queen and now he was completely disillusioned. He compared his own condition and that of his fellows, who were all being dismissed with nothing, with their feelings four years ago at the time of the coronation. In May he wrote about this. He described how the future members of Charles Gustavus's court were all smartening up their clothes with new lace and galoons "just as we did four years ago for our Queen's coronation," but now, he wrote, members of "our own court haven't even got bread."

Her servants were not the only people to criticize the Queen at this time. When Charles Gustavus got to Uppsala on 16th May, Axel Oxenstierna complained to him that Christina was working for the Hapsburg interest against that of Sweden. The clergy were also becoming very suspicious. Some of the rumours of the Queen's conversion must have reached them, for they wanted to insert a clause into the agreement for her financial settlement, stipulating that she should remain a Lutheran. Christina flatly refused, maintaining that this showed an insulting mistrust of her solidarity with her country and people.

When the diet of the Riksdag opened on 11th May, the Queen had still not been able to get the Råd's definite agreement to her financial settlement. Contrary to the expectations of some, there was no difficulty about the Riksdag's acceptance of the abdication. The financial question was to be a very different matter. The crux of the situation was the expropriation of the Pomeranian estates, which the nobles realized could be used as a precedent for a general Reduction. There was also the question of compensation to the present owners of these estates. How Christina finally pushed this vital matter through is obscure, but Picques reported to his government, and he was probably right, that she gave the nobles to understand that the Råd had already sanctioned her financial settlement. At the same time she led the Råd to believe that the nobles had agreed to it. However, she had to agree to recompense the owners for the improvements they had made, and to rule these estates according to the law of the land. Militarily and politically they still formed part of Sweden. Christina could neither sell nor pledge them, and on her death they would return to the Swedish crown. Apart from estates and the town of Norrköping in Sweden itself, these lands included the islands of Öland and Gotland. In the Swedish possessions overseas there was the Estonian island of Ösel, the estates of Pohl and Neukloster in Mecklenburg, the town of Wollgast and the estates "of the table" in Pomerania. When the act of abdication was finally drawn up, it stipulated that the Queen was subject to no authority, and answerable only to God for her actions. She had full jurisdiction over the members of her court and her guards, and could at her pleasure submit them to the normal courts of justice, or have them tried by a special court.

In order to pacify public opinion about the extent of her financial settlement and the extraordinary powers which she had been granted, Christina took care that it was generally understood that after her cure at Spa, she would return to live in Sweden, or in one of the Swedish possessions. Possibly she would go to Pomerania or to one of the islands, as Charles Gustavus had done. The nobles were still worried about the possibility of a Reduction, so their representative, Per Brahe, went to see the Queen at the end of May, accompanied by Marshal Wrangel. At their request, she promised them that the expropriations made in her favour would not constitute a precedent for a further Reduction. However a few days later Christina wrote a secret letter to Charles Gustavus, specifically stating that he need not be bound by any of her donations. In fact, she left the way clear for him to carry out a Reduction, as indeed he did after his accession.

Now there was nothing left to do, but to give due ceremonial form to the abdication. Whitelocke described how on 10th May mounted trumpeters and drummers paraded through Uppsala, announcing in various parts of the town that the Riksdag was due to meet on the morrow; everyone was to present themselves at the castle at eight a.m. or be fined half a riksdaler. The same night, between ten and eleven p.m., Whitelocke had been invited by the Queen to the wedding of Baron Horn and the Lady Sparre; he does not mention if the bride was a relation of Ebba's. But she seems to have been well-liked by Christina, as the magnificent diamond tiara and the necklace and girdle she was wearing were reported to be the Queen's own, lent for the occasion. Both bride and groom were dressed in white, and after the ceremony there was a ball. It was opened as usual by dancing the "brawls" (from the French *branle*, a round dance or farandole led by the senior person present) and the Queen asked Whitelocke to dance with her. At first he refused, saying he was not worthy, finally they took the floor together. Before the Civil War, with his experience of court masques, Whitelocke had evidently learnt to dance well. Christina now complimented him on his dancing, telling him that the Hollanders had lied in saying that all the nobles of England were for the King. She knew from the way Whitelocke danced that he had been brought up as a gentleman. After the ball there was a banquet. The whole entertainment lasted seven hours, and Whitelocke returned home in one of the Queen's carriages at about seven a.m.

Little more than an hour later the Ambassador was back again at the castle. This time he was to witness the meeting of the Riksdag at which the Queen's abdication was to be announced. The presence of a foreign ambassador was quite exceptional. In view of the special circumstances, it had probably been agreed that Whitelocke should be present as a witness. The meeting was held in the great hall of the castle which, with its plain raftered ceiling and simple brass candelabra, was reminiscent of the austere Sweden of the past that was fast disappearing, at least in royal and noble residences. On this occasion, however, the walls were hung with tapestries and other hangings. Whitelocke was amused to recognize some that had been lent to furnish his own embassy. The middle of the hall was filled with benches covered with red cloth. At the upper end there was a dais reached by three steps and covered with rich carpets; on it stood Christina's silver throne. It was the same one that Magnus had given her for her coronation. The canopy was of embroidered crimson velvet, and to the left of it were five crimson velvet chairs for the great officers of state; before it was a semi-circle of velvet-covered stools for the senators or members of the Råd. The eighty representatives of the peasant's Estate entered first, at nine a.m. They were preceded by their leader, whom Whitelocke described as "a plain lusty man in boor's habit, staff in hand" (he habitually referred to the peasants as boors). They filed into their seats on the right and sat down and put on their hats. Next came 120 representatives of the boroughs and cities, then 200 richly dressed nobles; whereupon everyone stood and took off their hats. Last of all came the clergy; the same ceremony was again observed by all.

A quarter of an hour later the Queen's guards and gentlemen arrived, the senators and great officers of state, all bare-headed. Then finally the Queen arrived, also bare-headed, and surrounded by pages and attendants. After the Queen was seated on the throne, everyone but the government and actual members of the Riksdag left the hall and the doors were closed. Christina was silent for a few moments, then, Whitelocke says, "rising up with mettle she came forward to the utmost part of the foot-pad, and with good grace and confidence spoke to the Assembly." Her speech was short and to the point. In it the Queen extolled "her most dear cousin's" good qualities and, said that it "sufficeth that all may be done for the good of the country and the prosperity of my most dear cousin." She also said that if by the ten years of her administration she had merited anything from them, she hoped that they would "consent to my resolution, since you may assure yourselves that none can dissuade me from my purpose."

Addresses by the Archbishop of Uppsala and the Marshal of the nobles followed, finally there came an honest and touching appeal from the leader of the peasants asking the Queen not to leave them. Without ceremony he then walked up to the Queen, shook her hand and kissed it and returned to his place in tears. The speech from the throne followed. This was a review of the events of the reign and included the Queen's plea that the Riksdag "will consent to her quiet in retiring herself from so heavy a burden." When this was over, Christina left the hall.

At eleven that night Whitelocke was again summoned to the wedding festivities at the castle; he was very tired, having like the Queen and the court been up all the previous night. However, with his usual eye for detail he described the curious old Swedish custom of a silver-headed spear, decorated with ribbons of the bridegroom's colours, being carried in procession in front of the bride. How the groom then made a speech of thanks, in which he announced the dowry and present of 2,000 crowns which he had given to the bride, for herself and her children if they outlived him. It was customary in Sweden for this to be announced after the wedding night, to show how satisfied the groom was with his new wife. The spear was then laid on the floor in front of the bride and subsequently thrown out of the window. The waiting crowd fought for the silver head and the ribbon favours. After dancing had again got well under way, Whitelocke escaped as soon as he could "wondering that the Queen after so serious a work as she had been at all morning, could be so pleased with this evening's ceremonies."

On 16th May Charles Gustavus made his state entry into Uppsala. Whitelocke, who had already made his official adieux to the Queen, watched the procession from his window. He described Christina as being "gallantly mounted, habited in her usual fashion in grey stuff, her hat on her head, her pistols at her saddle-bow, and twenty-four of the Gardes-du-Corps about her person." Charles Gustavus was "in a plain grey cloth suit of a light colour, mounted upon a very brave grey horse, with pistols at his saddle and sword by his side." Whitelocke noticed that he rode bare-headed, sometimes beside the Queen, who would call to him to come and talk to her.

The following day Whitelocke was received by Charles Gustavus. The etiquette to be used on this occasion caused the Ambassador some heart-searching: the situation was so extraordinary that it had few if any precedents. Even the question of the language they should use was earnestly debated. Whitelocke suggested that they should speak English, because he had not been accredited as an ambassador to the Prince; Latin was inappropriate because they were not to negotiate a treaty. Finally at the Prince's suggestion they agreed upon French. Charles Gustavus's good sense and modesty emerges very clearly from his behaviour at this interview, also the importance of Cromwell's England in Swedish politics. In every way Charles Gustavus deferred to Whitelocke, trying to make him take precedence—to walk through the doors first, to sit on the right—quite a struggle of politeness ensued about this. In the end, one of the Prince's court whispered to Whitelocke that he must give way, as it was his master's desire thereby to do honour to the Lord Protector and Commonwealth. After a few moments of ceremonial exchange of compliments, the two men retired to Charles Gustavus's study, there to discuss affairs.

When the Prince returned Whitelocke's call, they sat solemnly with their hats on, in the Ambassador's bedroom and discussed the religious situation in England. It was on this occasion that Whitelocke addressed his exhortation on Sunday observance in Sweden to the Prince. Charles Gustavus seems to have been both surprised and amused, for he replied that he had not heard any soldiers discourse on this theme! However they did also touch on serious state business. Charles Gustavus stressed the importance of the Protestant powers keeping together in face of the designs of the Catholics, particularly the House of Austria. This must have been reassuring for Whitelocke, after his suspicions of the influence of those "great Papists," Montecuccoli and Pimentel, on Christina.

When Whitelocke made his informal farewell visit to the Queen, she talked of her journey to Spa and said she would write a personal letter for Cromwell. Whitelocke again advised her to leave Sweden as soon as possible—he had already told her that if she did not he feared for her liberty. In saying goodbye Christina twice gave him her hand to kiss, but the Ambassador thought she was not so cheerful as before. One last adieu remained, and for the Ambassador of the English Commonwealth it was perhaps the most moving. Axel Oxenstierna was the senior Protestant statesman in Europe, the man to whom Sweden's great part in the Thirty Years War was largely due; Whitelocke habitually addressed him as father, in recognition of this fact. Nevertheless, at this last meeting, both men courteously agreed to differ about the superiority of their respective parliamentary systems. Whitelocke upheld any English member of parliament's "liberty to propose anything in our Parliament," as the safeguard of the nation's liberties. Oxenstierna replied "That hath been a great occasion of all your troubles." Three months later the great Chancellor died. Christina believed that her own abdication had been too much of a blow for him.

The news of the actual abdication ceremony, which took place on 6th June, was brought to Whitelocke in Stockholm by Marshal Wrangel the same night. Although he had so bitterly opposed many of her recent actions, Per Brahe afterwards remembered Christina as looking "beautiful like an angel," when she entered the great hall of Uppsala Castle wearing her purple velvet coronation robes and all her regalia. No matter what they may have felt about the Queen during the last few years, when actually faced with her laying down the crown, which she had worn since her father's tragic death twenty-two years ago, many of those present wept. The sword and sceptre, the orb and the keys were deposited upon as many cushions on a table beside the throne. There remained only the crown, but before being divested of it, the Queen made a short speech.

She acknowledged the unwillingness with which her desire to abdicate had been met, and concluded by wishing Charles Gustavus every happiness. Instead of Axel Oxenstierna, the abdication document was read by Schering Rosenhane, the same man who had told Christina that Malines and Casati were courteous gentlemen. Now came the moment for the Queen to be divested of her crown. No one was willing to do this, although she apparently asked both Tott and Steinberg. Finally at her express and repeated command the deed was done. She then also laid down her royal robes. Thus relieved of all the emblems of royalty, Christina curtsied to her cousin and the company, and retired. Charles Gustavus then walked with all the company in procession to Uppsala Cathedral, where the Archbishop was waiting to crown him Charles X, by the Grace of God King of the Swedes, Goths and Vandals.

That night there was a great banquet in the castle with Christina present. Years afterwards, in Rome, she added a note in her own handwriting to the synopsis for her biography. She said that even on this occasion, after her abdication, the King handed her the napkin at table; also that he held her stirrup for her to mount her horse. Since the Middle Ages these courtesies had been the symbols whereby potentates acknowledged the rank of their superiors (holding the stirrup had been a bone of contention between the popes and emperors for centuries). This behaviour on the part of the newly-crowned King was, of course, exceptional, but typical of the man and his conduct to Christina. It was the last time in her life that she was to be accorded precedence over a reigning sovereign and, after she had lost the reality of power, the symbols came increasingly to mean more to her. But now Christina was so filled with excitement and a sense of anticipation, that she could not rest, even for a night, before she left. After the banquet was over, between eleven o'clock and midnight, on one of those white nights of a Swedish June, the Queen set out from Uppsala to Stockholm. Charles accompanied her to the first staging post at Flottsund where the road passes an arm of Lake Mälaren; here they made their last farewell.

Christina stayed several days in Stockholm. Some say that she deliberately attended Holy Communion, receiving the Sacrament in public, according to the Lutheran rite, while she was there, in order to still the rumours of her conversion. Certainly while she was at the castle she arranged to take four more sets of the royal tapestries with her, including that of Diana which had been woven for the wedding of her parents. Was this last-minute decision due to mere acquisitiveness or did Christina suddenly feel the need for these familiar things? They had been in the room which had witnessed the sorrows of her childhood and the gay times of the last few years. Did she perhaps wander for the last time in the gardens so recently laid out for her, where the tulips were in flower, and myrtles and lemon and orange trees in wooden caissons struggled to survive in the northern climate? Probably if she did it was with the thought that soon she would see these plants growing in luxurious profusion in the Mediterranean sun. This dream-world of cultured classical Italy had contributed much to her vision of herself making the incomparable gesture of sacrificing a throne.

But the Queen was in a fever to be off. Disregarding the fleet which Charles had put at her disposal to take her to Germany, she travelled post-haste across Sweden to Halmstad on the west coast, near the border of the Danish provinces. Here Christina sent away the few officials who had accompanied her, including her Lutheran chaplain. Either here or actually at the Danish frontier, Lawrenz von der Linde is said to have offered for the last time, on Charles Gustavus's behalf, his heart and hand. Christina is said to have replied, somewhat abruptly, that it would have been more decent to marry before the abdication, and that her cousin was too prudent to need her councils.

In Laholm the Queen stopped, cut off her hair and changed into men's clothes. The royal party was now reduced to four gentlemen, including Steinberg and Christopher Delphicus von Dohna—the son of the Prussian Viscount who had served Frederick and Elizabeth Palatine as Ambassador to England. Possibly because of a certain personal resemblance, and to add to her disguise, Christina now took von Dohna's name. She had not needed Whitelocke's advice to make very sure of protecting her liberty until she was out of Sweden. At last she reached the little stream that formed the border between her own country and Denmark. Here (Picques reported to his government, on what authority is not known) Christina "got out of the carriage and jumped to the other side with incredible joy, saying 'Here I am at last at liberty and out of Sweden, where I hope never to return!' "

CHAPTER 7

The Road to Rome: 1654–1656

A disguise, a false name, the company of four carefree young men. Once she was out of Sweden, Christina's journey must have seemed to her the very essence of adventure, the first step on the way to freedom and the sunlit countries of the south which she had dreamed of since childhood. Although she may have felt lost to the world, far from a censorious court, and able at last to give rein to impulse and to behave and do exactly as she liked, this was of course not so. A Queen can never really escape even if she abdicates, and in fact as Christina travelled she was surrounded by the invisible web of the intelligence services of Europe. All the powers had alerted their agents to keep track of her, and to try to find out her ultimate destination. Many of these reports still lie gathering dust among the old secret files of chanceries.

Thus Cromwell's Foreign Secretary, Thurloe, soon received a copy of an intercepted letter which the Dutch agent at Elsinore had sent to the States General in Holland. It was dated 7th July 1654, and read: "The Queen of Sweden arrived here this morning in disguise, being in man's apparel. She came from Elsenberg, [Hälsingborg] having only twelve persons to attend her and among them the Earl of Dohna. The Queen, when she came into the inn, had boots on and a carabine about her neck, but she put off her boots, before she got up again into the waggon."

It would seem that her adoption of men's clothes was already attracting more attention to Christina than almost anything else, and what must have appeared to her to be a sensible (and exciting) step, was in the end to lead to notoriety and scandal. Gossip had surrounded the Queen while she was in Sweden, but it was nothing compared with the rumours that now began to circulate, increasing in volume when she arrived in the Netherlands. They were to surround her for the rest of her life, creating the Christina of legend which has survived to our own day.

Quite early on the Queen's journey an insignificant incident provided a good example of how fact could be embroidered into fiction, thereby making a much more intriguing story. The Danish government had been informed in advance of Christina's route, but when the King and Queen of Denmark arrived at Kolding to greet her, they found only her retinue and baggage. Christina was already five days' journey ahead. As a result of this abortive meeting the legend arose that the young Danish Queen, Maria Amalia, had been so eager to see such a sensational character, that she had disguised herself as a maid in the inn where Christina was to stay. The story continues that Maria Amalia was instantly recognized by Christina but, concealing the fact, she treated the "maid" to some very unflattering comments upon their Majesties of Denmark.

It must, however, be admitted that often there was no need to invent stories about Christina's behaviour in order to shock the sobersides of the seventeenth century. She arrived at Hamburg decorously enough, accompanied in her carriage by two of her gentlemen. But the other two occupants were Portuguese Jews—the Queen's doctor, Benedict de Castro, and her immensely rich banker, Abraham or Diego Texeira. It was in Texeira's house that Christina now took up residence and there she received the Emperor's representative. As if this were not enough, the Queen welcomed the worthy diplomat attired in a coat "such as men wear, and a woman's skirt put on for the occasion on top of the man's trousers. Her hair hung free, cut like a man's." In a century when protocol was the very breath of life, it is not surprising that these shocking details were privately conveyed to the Emperor in a personal letter.

To Christina it was all no doubt a joke, part of her old game of shocking people, and even more now of demonstrating her freedom and that she did not give a fig for anyone. Later she told Montecuccoli with glee that on her journey a girl had taken her for a young man and tried to flirt with her. Needless to say this incident, and others, were construed by gossips as lesbian adventures. To us Christina's lack of racial prejudice seems as admirable as her desire for religious freedom for everyone. But her contemporaries viewed it in a very different light. They were even more shocked by her adoption of men's clothes and her free and easy behaviour. This is clearly shown in the intelligence reports reaching Thurloe. It is in one of these that the allegation of hermaphroditism first appears; "We hear stories of the Queen of Sweden and her Amazonian behaviour, it being believed that nature was mistaken in her, and that she was intended for a man, for in her discourse, they say she talks loud and sweareth notably."

Christina was either blissfully unaware of, or simply did not care about the impression she was making. In any case she proceeded to enjoy herself in Hamburg, seeing old friends and relations and all the German notabilities including her cousin Eleonora, now Landgravine of Hesse. She was loaded with gifts and entertained royally. But in the midst of all this gaiety she did not neglect what must have been a welcome duty, that of making sure that Charles Gustavus got married at last. For she travelled to Neumünster to arrange his engagement to Hedvig Eleonora, daughter of Frederick III of Holstein-Gottorp. This accomplished, the Queen felt free to move on, and a few days later after returning from a farewell banquet at Wandsbek at one a.m., she quietly left Hamburg. Mr Bradshaw, the English agent in Hamburg, reported to Thurloe that the city gates had twice to be specially opened for Christina in the middle of the night and that "very privately attended only by the 'grim Steinberger' [Steinberg] . . . she is said to have gone to Zell."

Cromwell's government was mainly concerned about Christina's relations with Charles II, in particular because she had originally announced her intention of going to Spa, where he was living in exile. It must have been with relief, therefore, that early in August they heard that her next stopping place was to be Antwerp—though their informant added anxiously that there were plans afoot for Christina to marry Charles II "if he be so virile." But by now Thurloe was probably aware of the truth, for on 3rd July Longland, his astute agent in Leghorn, had written "advised hither from Rome, that after the Queen of Sweden has been in

France she intends to go to Rome to embrace that religion," though he continued cautiously "how lykely I know not."

Whether it was due to the watchfulness of the "grim Steinberger" or to her own more decorous behaviour, Christina managed to cross Holland in a carriage without anyone being aware of it except the two distinguished savants, Gronovius and Anna Maria Schurman, whom she visited on the way. By the beginning of August she had arrived in Antwerp, and was installed in the palatial house of Garcia de Yllan, also a Portuguese Jewish banker and an associate of Texeira. Here in the Rue Longue Neuve Christina settled down, apparently for some time, as some of her treasures shipped on the Fortuna were taken out of their packing cases, including several of the Italian masterpieces looted at Prague. Christina, who barely if ever worried about her own appearance, evidently felt an acute need to be surrounded by beauty and splendour. Possibly this was more the case now that she was no longer a reigning sovereign, and these treasures took on something of the character of status symbols, reminders of her royal estate. In any case they provided a splendid background for the gay social life that she was now leading.

Hardly a day passed without visitors arriving at the Rue Longue Neuve. With the Franco-Spanish war in progress, Flanders was living up to its name of the cockpit of Europe, and was the meeting place of nobles from all the Hapsburg domains—soldiers, diplomats, adventurers and political intriguers from half Europe, upon whom the sensational Queen and her unpredictable political future acted as a magnet. In her new-found freedom Christina seems to have kept open house for this somewhat mixed company, also going almost daily to the theatre and to parties in country houses.

It was in the midst of this gay world that Montecuccoli found Christina when he arrived in Antwerp on 16th September, as the Emperor's envoy. Actually he encountered her driving in the town, and immediately she invited him into her carriage, where he found the young Prince of Lüneburg and Corfitz Ulfeld's wife's brother-in-law, Hannibal Sehested, sometime governor of Norway, but who had been disgraced. When they reached her lodging, Montecuccoli presented to the Queen a personal letter from the Emperor, and then like old friends they sat down to discuss her plans. Christina said she really wanted to go straight to Rome, but before she declared herself openly, she was sounding out the reactions of the King of Sweden. Steinberg had already been sent to Sweden to say that Christina did not intend to return, but was going to settle in Italy. Christina foresaw however, that this would really not be possible until the following year, and asked Montecuccoli to wait and accompany her. After this serious interlude they both went off to the play—a comedy by Desmarets—where Montecuccoli learnt that the Queen had hired the entire company, which had previously been in the service of the Prince of Orange. This diversion was costing her 4,000 francs or about £300 a month in modern currency.*

Montecuccoli's diary of this period, as at the time of his mission to Sweden, was filled with daily jottings of events and, as much of his time was spent with Christina, it provides an extraordinarily vivid record of her life in the Spanish Netherlands. He mentions frequent expeditions to a "casino," which was probably Garcia de Yllan's country house at Groeninghof. Often they were accompanied by Count Carlo Hercolani, (member of a noble Bolognese family and therefore from the same part of Italy as Montecuccoli) who had been both in Christina's and Montecuccoli's service in Sweden and to whom she now gave the order of Amaranth. The Neapolitan Marquis Spinola was also a constant companion.

Although Christina told him about it ostensibly as a joke, Montecuccoli was evidently somewhat startled when she informed him that there were rumours that the King of Spain intended to give the Netherlands to her for life, to govern as his aunt the Infanta Isabella had done. Christina said that this was all pure invention or make-believe, but that really the only unfulfilled desire which remained to her in life was to lead an army—therefore if this make-believe could be true, she would choose Flanders rather than Naples because the army was there.† Was the shape of things to come already taking form in the Queen's mind, together with a shadow of doubt about the wisdom of abandoning a throne? Montecuccoli did not ultimately rise to be a Marshal and Prince of the Empire for nothing, he was a very shrewd man and a faithful

* The franc, unless being specifically mentioned as gold, weighed five grammes of silver and was therefore roughly the equivalent of 1*s.* 6*d.*

† The Kingdom of Naples then belonged to Spain and was governed by a viceroy in the same way as the Netherlands.

servant of the Emperor, who reposed great confidence in him. Moreover he was surely well aware that his master's cousin, the King of Spain, had no intention of handing over one of his domains to a foreigner. But he also knew Christina's capacity for intrigue, and realized that this "make-believe" required a firm answer.

In replying to her he adopted ostensibly forthright military tactics. He reminded her of something he had previously said—that when she was a Queen regnant she could dispose of an army as she pleased, and could have invaded Denmark with imperial support and sure success during the Anglo-Dutch sea war. Evidently realizing that this was a courteous but decisive manner of rebutting the tentative feelers which she had put out, Christina took the hint. She replied tactfully, explaining the limits to which Swedish sovereigns were subject in declaring war and governing the country: even her father, she said, had had cause to rue it in his own day. No further reference was made to any "make-believe" kingdoms.

Possibly this incident was not wholly unconnected with Montecuccoli's visit two days later to Brussels to pay his respects to the Archduke. After watching him dine in state in the old palace of the dukes of Brabant, Montecuccoli was received by Leopold William in his famous picture gallery. The two men had been companions in arms in the Thirty Years War, and the Archduke evidently stood on little ceremony with his brother's personal envoy to Christina. For he told Montecuccoli very frankly what he thought of her—he had visited her in Antwerp shortly after her arrival. Although Leopold William praised the Queen's spirit and vivacity, he said straight out that he wished that Christina would show greater restraint in her way of life, and that he had doubts about the firmness of her resolution (of becoming a Catholic); he thought that she sometimes repented of it.

Montecuccoli says that he explained everything to the Archduke, praising Christina's virtues and reminding him of the good will that she had shown the House of Austria. Two days later he had another audience with Leopold William, and Montecuccoli then told the Archduke that Christina had asked him to remain with her until the arrival of Pimentel, who was coming as the King of Spain's envoy. This explained his continued presence in the Netherlands, as originally Montecuccoli's mission had been expected to be a brief one, of little more than a month. At the same time he asked the Archduke for a passport for a short trip to England. His diary shows that this was evidently just for pleasure. Before he left he had to take temporary leave of Christina. He found her in a gay mood, and driving in her carriage they discussed the indivisibility of love. The Queen's comments were evidently of the type that Montecuccoli had described in Sweden as "*per lo piu amorosi*," for he says: "I bet Amarantha [Christina] that within a year she would be passionately in love." He was not so very wrong. Christina told him that Chanut, who had recently been to see her, said that "the natural sentiments of man are to be recognized in dreams." However, Chanut's visit had also put more serious ideas into her head, or at least resuscitated the old one of acting as mediator in the war between France and Spain (a curious *volte-face*, after her recently expressed desire to stay in the Netherlands and lead an army). To Chanut's extreme chagrin and discomfiture Christina allowed it to be understood that his visit to her had been made with this end in view. In actual fact it was she who had invited him and procured a Spanish safe-conduct for him to enter enemy territory. As Louis XIV's Ambassador at The Hague, Chanut asked the Queen officially to deny the story of peace negotiations, but she never did so, and in the end he was forced to publish her invitation, which led to an exchange of acrimonious letters between them. Nevertheless Christina now gave Montecuccoli to understand that the French would welcome her good offices as mediator, and that Chanut had said that if only she had gone to The Hague, the King of France would have had many interesting proposals to make to her. Apparently by these tactics she was trying to play Austria and Spain off against France, in the hope of reaping some reward for herself.

When Montecuccoli returned from England he found Tott in Antwerp, as Charles Gustavus's envoy to Christina. Tott told Montecuccoli that his King wished that she would return to Sweden, "because of the tender love the King had for her," or at least that he hoped she would not go as far away as Italy. On 3rd November Pimentel had arrived and was received as the King of Spain's Ambassador Extraordinary to the Queen. After the official audience he went incognito to see her, and then no doubt con-

John Holm, who started life as a court servant and tailor and became Christina's confidential aide.

Charles Gustavus, as Generalissimo of the Swedish army, painted by S. Bourdon.

Christina, by S. Bourdon, painted about a year before her abdication.

Right: Christina's abdication at Uppsala Castle on 6th June, 1654, drawn by W. Swidde.

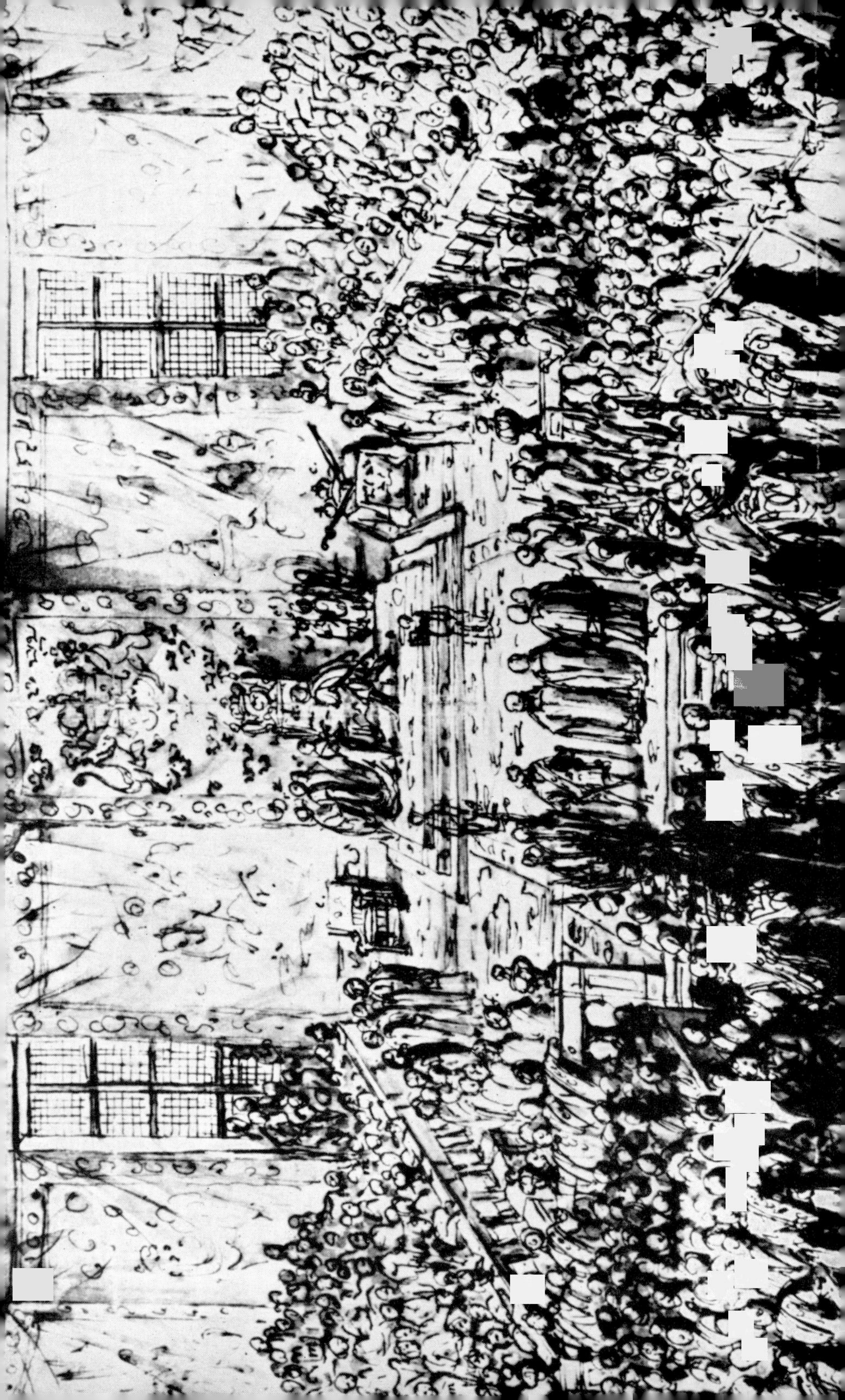

The main street of Antwerp at the time of Christina's residence there in 1654, by E. de Bie.

veyed Philip IV's message to her in more suave terms than those which he later employed to Montecuccoli. Briefly, the King did not want Christina to make a public profession of the Catholic faith immediately, but to do it in secrecy, and certainly not to do it in Rome during the reign of the present Pope, Innocent X. He added that the King would "see she lacked nothing." It had in fact already been arranged that the Archduke would invite Christina to be his guest in Brussels and that she would make her profession of faith while she was there, in the deepest secrecy in the presence only of Leopold William, Pimentel, Montecuccoli and two high officials.

Thus for once the views of the Kings of Spain and Sweden coincided. Neither of them wanted Christina to leave the Netherlands. To be constrained in her actions must have annoyed her considerably, but she put a good face on it and gave Montecuccoli to understand that she had decided upon this step herself, talking about the possibility of peace negotiations, but adding that if they did not come off she could go to Italy earlier. When Montecuccoli went to see the Archduke in Brussels early in December, the latter evidently realized that Christina was not best pleased at this enforced change in her plans. He began by chaffing Montecuccoli about reports in the press that Christina was going to marry him, saying: "I wonder if I ought to call you Maestà?" Then he questioned Montecuccoli as to whether he had been able to glean anything of Sweden's intentions from the Queen, because the Emperor wanted to know. Montecuccoli replied that he did not think that the crown of Sweden now communicated its secrets to the Queen, to which the Archduke answered: "I think the same. But thank God that she continues with her intention to embrace the Faith. I will give her these apartments, and I have written to the Emperor that I have commanded her to remain here until the declaration can be made. I think it will displease the Queen that the King does not approve her voyage to Italy as she much wanted to go there, but these long journeys cost a lot of money."

Apart from the financial aspect, the King of Spain's wish to delay Christina's going to Rome for the duration of Innocent X's reign may be partly explained by the fact that the aged Pontiff was known to be failing and was totally under the influence of his sister-in-law, a circumstance which was scarcely edifying for so distinguished a convert. But there was also the consideration that the Queen might arrive in Rome during an interregnum, or worse still after the election of a pro-French Pope, when all the trouble and expense the House of Hapsburg had incurred over her conversion would not receive its due meed of religious and political credit. The Archduke's reference to the expense that would be involved in the Queen's journey shows that he knew something about her finances. By the middle of December these were in fact in such a parlous state that Christina had sent orders to John Holm-Leijoncrona, her Intendant in Sweden, to send her services of gold and silver plate to the mint to be melted down, while in Antwerp she was forced to pawn a large part of her jewels for 46,000 écus; she was never to see them again.

Although she affected to despise such matters, the astuteness and tenacity with which Christina had negotiated the arrangements for her appanage before she left the throne, show that she had not failed to appreciate the difference that money would make to her future. Her estimated income of 200,000 crowns (the equivalent of some £100,000 today but with a much higher purchasing value) was indeed a royal dower, but as the months passed it became evident that there was a considerable difference between the paper calculation of the revenues due from her vast but scattered domains and the money which eventually actually arrived in her pocket.

Thus although Christina had to swallow the pill of Hapsburg interference with her plans, it was gilded by the fact that they were offering immediate and lavish hospitality for herself and her suite, which would help her out of her embarrassment for the present. Her journey to Brussels on 23rd December was a splendid occasion, the Archduke going to meet the Queen at Wilbruck, where they dined together in state. They then drove part of the way in Leopold William's carriage, with Pimentel and Montecuccoli in attendance, but the triumphal entry into the capital of the Spanish Netherlands was made in the Archduke's gilded state barge. It was nine at night when they finally arrived; the whole of Brussels was illuminated and the city resounded to the roar of fireworks. Exactly twenty-four hours later Christina abjured the faith of her fathers and was received into the Roman Catholic Church.

As he was present at this ceremony as the Emperor's representative, and would shortly have to give an account of the proceedings to his Imperial master, Montecuccoli obviously watched proceedings with a careful eye. His record in his diary is more detailed than that for any other ceremony he witnessed during his missions as the Emperor's envoy to Christina but, curiously for an Italian, neither on this nor on any other occasion does he give a sign of any emotion or personal reaction. On the contrary, a true son of his age, he was evidently more concerned with protocol and observed that as the Count de Fuensaldana had been Philip IV's Ambassador to Charles I in England, he had precedence and could keep his hat on in the Archduke's presence.

The excuse given out for the intimate gathering together in Christina's room of such important personages as Leopold William, Fuensaldana, Don A. Boreno Navarra, Pimentel, Montecuccoli and the Dominican Guemes (ostensibly as a secretary of Pimentel's embassy) was that they were holding a discussion about the election of the new King of Rome, necessitated by the death in July of the Emperor's eldest son. This matter was of course of the highest political importance and would have justified the absolute secrecy with which the meeting was surrounded. Montecuccoli's use of the word *camera* makes it plain that all these notabilities were actually gathered together in Christina's bedroom, but as the Archduke had apparently relinquished to her his own apartment, and was a bishop as well as being a soldier and statesman, it is more than likely that there would have been a small private chapel attached to it. In any case it was in an atmosphere of intimacy and seclusion that the Queen now took the final step on the road which she had avowedly been following since 1651 and probably secretly in her own mind long before.

Christina had wished to make her act of faith in Rome, sanctified for all Catholics as the scene of apostolic martyrdom and the seat of the papacy, but policy considerations had robbed her of the emotional support of this splendid background. What must she have felt now that this supreme spiritual action of her life had to be carried out behind closed doors, in the presence of five men (three of whom she hardly knew) who were there as official witnesses almost as if this were a purely political event? No indication has survived that gives any clue to Christina's state of mind, but it is perhaps permissible to wonder if in the end the sheer stark simplicity of the occasion may not have been what she preferred—later she was to show very clearly that she loathed and despised a parade of religion, or any kind of playing to the gallery about her conversion. In any event, in the ritual that followed the Queen first read the Creed and specified that she believed in transubstantiation, in the Lord's Supper, in the Roman Catholic Church, purgatory, indulgence, the infallible authority of the Church, the interpretation of the Scriptures according to the Roman Catholic Church and especially in the findings of the Council of Trent. Christina then promised and swore to be a Catholic, after which she knelt down while Father Guemes recited a psalm and some prayers and gave her absolution from heresy. Those present now gathered round her to make their congratulations on this happy event and at that moment all the cannon in the city boomed out a salute, while the sky was rent by the blaze and crackle of fireworks.

The good burghers of Brussels must have wondered at this demonstration, which was clearly most carefully timed. Although he does not say so, Montecuccoli evidently felt some relief that the solemn act was finally accomplished; perhaps in spite of his protestations to the contrary he had shared some of the Archduke's misgivings. In his diary, by way of light relief, he makes an untranslatable play on the words *colazione* for supper and *collazionare* for collating or attesting the documents concerning Christina's conversion (which was actually done on 6th January) and ends his description of the scene by saying that he then went off to have supper with Pimentel and Navarra. Afterwards Montecuccoli returned to accompany the Queen to hear midnight Mass from a gallery, after which, according to his diary, they stayed up until the small hours watching ceremonies and listening to music. On Christmas day Montecuccoli again accompanied Christina to the gallery of the church, while the Archduke and the others attended Mass.

From now on Christina's visit to Brussels took on a public and social character. On Christmas Day she dined alone in state in public, afterwards receiving the Duke of Lorraine in public audience, likewise the Duchess of Arschot, who was the wife of the premier Grandee of Spain in the Netherlands. With his customary sharp eye for the finer points of etiquette, Montecuccoli noted that the Duchess sat in front of the Queen on a low chair, while Christina had a royal one; Christina then retired to her suite where less privileged ladies and gentlemen waited on her. In the evening she went to hear vespers, where a motet was sung of the Magnificat, and afterwards the Archduke joined her to watch the fireworks and take supper with her. Even now the full Spanish etiquette was observed, only four people being seated at the table —Christina, the Archduke, the Duke of Arschot and Pimentel— while the rest of the company stood around and watched. However the news that arrived shortly afterwards, that the French armies were massing at the frontier, broke the ice of protocol as far as the Archduke was concerned. He spent the rest of the evening chatting as one old soldier to another with Montecuccoli, complaining of the state of the army—poor intelligence, bad discipline, lack of money to pay the troops and poor quarters for them—and concluding that he would be happy to be recalled from his command.

Nevertheless festivities succeeded one another during the seven weeks that Christina remained as the Archduke's guest at the palace, where in addition she had the leisure to enjoy one of the greatest art collections in Europe. Leopold William's pictures are still treasured in the Künsthistorisches Museum in Vienna. To all appearances therefore the Queen's life at this period seemed to be one of carefree enjoyment. Only one slight incident clouded the horizon, her disagreement with the Prince de Condé.

As a great general in the Thirty Years War, Condé had been one of Christina's heroes since she was a girl, they had exchanged admiring letters and she had used her influence to help him when he was imprisoned for his part in the Fronde. Condé was still hostile to the French government and was now in the Netherlands fighting on the Spanish side, but as was to be expected he had been one of the first to wish to greet Christina on her arrival in Antwerp. However this projected meeting, which might have been supposed to be so ardently desired by both parties, broke down on a matter of etiquette. Laughable as it seems today, the whole question hinged upon what kind of seat should be provided for Condé when he called on Christina. In accordance with the custom of the time such knotty points of etiquette were discussed beforehand when two exalted persons were to meet; as a French prince of royal blood Condé expected to be received with the same ceremony as the Archduke, Governor of the Netherlands, and to this Christina flatly refused to give her assent. After some recrimination Condé called on Christina as a private person. He was kept standing all the time, with the result that their relations were afterwards less cordial, although the Prince sometimes attended the festivities in Brussels.

Although admitting to this small contretemps and to missing her friend's company, Christina certainly intended to give the impression that she was having the time of her life in Brussels in a letter she then wrote to Belle in Sweden. In it she says: "My happiness would be second to none if I was allowed to share it with you and if you could witness it. I swear to you that I would merit the envy of the gods if I could enjoy the pleasure of seeing you; but since I cannot hope to possess what I love, you must at least give me this satisfaction of believing that in whatever place in the world where I may be I will keep for ever the memory of your worth, and that I will carry with me even after death the noble passion and tenderness that I have always shown to you. At least keep me in your memory and do not lessen my happiness by an undeserved forgetfulness of the person who honours you most.

"I beg you to give my good wishes to all my friends, you know who they are. Do better, and give the same even to those who do not wish to be, I forgive them with a good heart, and am no worse off for it. I forgot to tell you that my health is wonderful, and that here I am up to my eyes in honours, also that I am well with all the world except the Prince de Condé, who I only see at the play and at court. My occupations are to eat well and sleep well, study little, chat and laugh a lot, go to see French, Italian and Spanish comedies and pass the time agreeably. Finally, I don't listen to sermons any more, I despise all orators, as Solomon says all the rest is but wretchedness, pity and folly, as everyone should live content, eating, drinking and singing . . . Adieu Belle, you understand me, and remember your Christina."

In February the Queen took up residence at the Palais d'Egmont. Montecuccoli had left some weeks before to report to the Emperor and from his notes on their discussions, it emerges that beneath the brilliant surface Christina's life was marred by money troubles. One of the matters which she had evidently asked Montecuccoli to take up with his master was the question of the payment of instalments of the war indemnity which the Empire owed Sweden under the terms of the treaty of Westphalia, and which apparently had been reserved to Christina as part of the financial provisions of her appanage. It must have been a slightly embarrassing matter for the now Catholic Queen, living under Hapsburg protection in a Spanish province, to have to broach at this precise moment, but the need was pressing. As time passed it was becoming increasingly evident that the collection of the revenue from Christina's vast but scattered domains presented a serious problem. Although her political acumen had enabled her to obtain the title, as it were, to what appeared to be great potential wealth, with her total lack of capacity for financial administration Christina had failed to set up any efficient machinery to deal with it. Admittedly this was not an easy task; much of the Queen's Swedish revenue was drawn in kind—in wheat, wood, tar, lime and building stone, which had to be marketed before she could collect the cash—while many of her Pomeranian lands were still devastated by war, or if they were in working condition they had been rehabilitated by the men to whom they had been granted for their war services. By the terms of the financial agreement made between the Queen and the Swedish government at the time of her abdication, the government was responsible for buying out these owners and recompensing them for the money they had spent, but the government now found that it lacked the cash to do so.

When Montecuccoli arrived in Vienna the Emperor told him that Sweden was also claiming the war indemnities. Ferdinand III evidently questioned his envoy very closely about the reality of Christina's conversion for he asked "did she really believe in her heart" and how many times had she taken Communion? His Minister, Prince Auersberg, was more outspoken, asking Montecuccoli not only about Christina's conversion but also about her morals, even going so far as to say that it would have been much better if she had stayed in Sweden.

From Montecuccoli's account of these highly confidential

conversations in Vienna, one thing emerges very clearly, and that is the disparity which existed—beneath all the ceremonial trappings—between Christina's own view of her abdication and conversion as a great and dramatic action which must win her the admiration and gratitude of Catholics, and that of Ferdinand III and his advisers. Like his brother Leopold William, the Emperor and his ministers were sure that Christina now knew nothing about Swedish policy, and they were understandably anxious to be better informed as to what the martial Charles Gustavus's intentions might be—Ferdinand gave point to this by saying that the King of Spain would be better advised to keep an ambassador in Sweden rather than accrediting him to Christina. Devout Catholics though they might be themselves, these sober statesmen saw things in terms of power politics, and a Christina friendly to the House of Hapsburg and sympathetic to Catholicism, still sitting on the throne of Sweden, was a far greater asset to them than an ex-Queen whose conversion was likely to lose her any influence she might still possess in her own country. In the circumstances, therefore, they may perhaps be forgiven for having some private reservations about a woman who, to judge from her behaviour and circumstances, might become a future source of political and financial embarrassment.

Although also a realist where others were concerned—had she not written to warn Frederick of Hesse that converts "are despised by those whose opinions they embrace"—Christina's opinion of herself often blinded her to the outcome of her own actions. After the first careless rapture of her early months of freedom, she had now been brought up against the hard facts of money shortage and the Hapsburg veto on her continuing her journey to Rome. Although this last had been coupled with a great show of courtesy and the King of Spain's promise that she should "lack for nothing," Christina had received no spectacular offers (such as those she had told Montecuccoli that Chanut had hinted to her) by way of recompense for her having "sacrificed a throne to become a Catholic," nor had anything very definite been done even to help her out of her present financial distress. To an imperious woman who had enjoyed almost absolute power the realization of her changed position might be slow to dawn, but when it did, she could be expected to be ruthless in the pursuance of her ends. It is in this light that Christina's actions during the next few years must be judged.

In the meantime, life in Brussels did not lack variety. In the midst of less serious pursuits Christina visited Bolland the famous Jesuit scholar and author of *Acta Sanctorum*, or Legends of the Saints, and gave him access to some of the precious mediaeval manuscripts which she had brought from Sweden. Nevertheless the spring of 1655 must have been an anxious time of waiting for the Queen. For one thing she was now the object of the most vicious and defamatory attacks in anonymous pamphlets, which gave rise to a whispering campaign against her. One of the chief accusations raised against her were allegations of atheism. On this charge Christina was of course vulnerable; although she was still ostensibly a Protestant her household included no minister of that faith, while her free use of bad language naturally did not help matters. The old stories of the Queen's libertine beliefs and behaviour in Sweden were revived, but this was far from being all. The most virulent of the pamphlets, which was circulated as a copy of a private letter, contained repulsive descriptions of her appearance and habits and accused her outright of promiscuity and lesbianism.

The fact remains however that these libels would have been unlikely to have gained wide credence if the Queen's tactless (to say the least of it) behaviour, added to her past record, had not lent colour to the stories. The fact that so serious a man as the Archduke, occupied as he was with public affairs and the war with France, was worried about Christina's conduct, indicates that she had given her detractors some ground on which to build. The Governor of the Netherlands would not depend for information on scurrilous pamphlets. Apart from the more secret sources available to him, he had loaned one of his own gentlemen, the Marquis de Tourlon, for service in the Queen's household.

The carefully concerted manner in which these attacks were launched show that someone was making clever capital out of the Queen's failings, exaggerating and distorting them, in order to discredit her. The fact that this campaign would cause embarrassment, apart from Christina herself, primarily to her Hapsburg protectors, points to their enemy France as the instigator. French hostility to Christina personally would also be understandable at this juncture. In Sweden she had forsaken her old friendship with France to make advances to Spain, but of more immediate importance was the fact that she had countenanced the rumours that Chanut had visited her to ask for her mediation in a Franco-Spanish peace. This campaign of denigration could be simply dismissed as an insignificant incident in Christina's life, were it not for the fact that two of the printed pamphlets were clever and salacious enough to achieve extensive circulation, being reprinted many times during her lifetime. Indeed both then and afterwards they gained wide acceptance, affecting the Queen's reputation so seriously that their contents have become part of the Christina legend which still exists to this day.

That Christina was painfully aware of this campaign is shown by her impatience to get to Rome, and her having said to Pimentel that the Swedes would rather know her to be a Catholic than believe her to be an atheist. However by April she could foresee the end of this anxious period of waiting, for on the seventh of that month Cardinal Chigi was elected Pope Alexander VII. No news could have been more welcome to Christina. As Secretary of State, Chigi had been informed by the Jesuit General when Macedo arrived in Rome bringing his momentous news. Subsequently the Cardinal had followed the progress of the Queen's conversion, though he was not as yet aware of her secret abjuration.

Although Chigi had not belonged to the Spanish party among the Cardinals but was supported by a neutral group of younger men, led by Cardinal Azzolino and known as the "Flying Squadron," the French faction had for long tried to block his election. Thus his accession, if not an outright Spanish triumph, was nevertheless very welcome news to Christina's protector the King of Spain and to his cousin the Emperor.

Though there could now be no doubt of the welcome which would finally await the King of Spain's protégée in Rome, Christina's way there was as yet far from clear. Already harassed by financial problems, she was increasingly afraid as to what effect the public acknowledgment of her change of faith would have in Sweden, in fact that it might result in her income being cut off altogether. The political news from the north only added to her anxieties, as there were persistent rumours that Charles Gustavus was preparing for war.

Christina in fact was torn between her desire to get to Rome and make a declaration of her faith and the fear that by so doing she would render herself penniless. Although in the past she had displayed remarkable skill in maturing her designs over a long period, in the end impatience and the fear of her Catholicism being discovered in Sweden had got the upper hand, for speed rather than caution had characterized the final financial negotiations for her abdication. It might have been imagined that if the Queen feared public knowledge of her Catholic sympathies while she was in Sweden, she would also have foreseen the effect that her actual abjuration might have upon her country's willingness to honour the agreement about her appanage. But it seems that this was not really brought home to Christina until she had tasted "freedom" for some months and realized that it too had its disadvantages—she could no longer call upon the revenues of a kingdom for her expenditure, and in her dealings with other sovereigns there was a difference in not being the head of a powerful state.

Two courses now lay open to the Queen, and in her anxiety she tried them both. One was to sound out the ground to see if the Pope would agree to her coming to Rome before she had made a public renunciation of Protestantism. For this task she enlisted the good offices of the King of Spain to explain to Alexander VII her fears about the effect of her conversion upon Sweden's willingness to honour the financial terms of her abdication. The other course was to get Charles Gustavus to agree to give her a sum of ready money in exchange for part at least of her lands before her conversion was made public.

When Montecuccoli returned to Brussels at the end of June, now ostensibly on a private visit but in actual fact on a mission for the Emperor with explicit instructions to report all conversations with Christina to the Archduke, he found the Queen awaiting the result of her *démarches* to the Pope and to the King of Sweden. She had evidently tided over her immediate financial problems by raising a large loan from her French banker, Bidal, making over to him as security some of her lands in Pomerania and the Bishopric of Bremen. As this was contrary to her agreement with the Swedish government—that she should administer her own lands and that at her death they should return to the Swedish crown—

Charles Gustavus was unwilling to give his consent to the transaction. This, coupled with her cousin's evident intention of attacking Poland, bringing war perilously close to Christina's Pomeranian domains, had understandably aroused in her even greater apprehension about her financial future and, less forgivably, hostility against Sweden and Charles Gustavus.

The fact that although East Pomerania belonged to Sweden it was still a fief of the Empire, now inspired the Queen to tell Montecuccoli that he should suggest to his master that if the Swedes confiscated her Pomeranian lands when they knew she was a Catholic, the Emperor should come to her aid. There were legal grounds for this, as according to the provisions of the Treaty of Westphalia no one could be deprived of property for religious reasons. Still, that the daughter of Gustavus Adolphus should appeal to a Hapsburg to intervene in a province for which her father had risked his life, does leave an extraordinarily unpleasant taste in the mouth. So too does Christina's somewhat wild proposal that if the war became one of religion and the Swedes confiscated her lands, she would have cause to raise a force by selling what she possessed and to lead it against the enemy —her own country Sweden. Nor was she above indulging in petty spite at Charles Gustavus's expense, declaring that he was so fat that two men had been required to hold him on his horse at his coronation, and that therefore he could not possibly be an efficient leader in the field.

Such childish spite directed at a man who had always behaved well to her and was to be called by future historians "the Napoleon of the North" for his lightning speed in attack, was as laughable as some other political ideas that Christina aired to Montecuccoli about this time. These, like her former project for giving Benefeld to Magnus De la Gardie, show how ludicrously wide of the mark, for all her astute political intrigues, Christina could sometimes be. The choicest of her suggestions was that Cromwell could become the legitimate King of England by turning Catholic, giving England to the Pope and receiving it back again as a papal fief on condition of granting religious freedom! In the same breath she even discussed her own return to Sweden after her public declaration of Catholicism, adding that in the event of Charles Gustavus's death she could resume the crown, introduce religious liberty, and declare a Prince of the House of Hapsburg her successor.

While Montecuccoli knew Christina well enough to season these two last astonishing proposals with several grains of salt, it is significant that he took the trouble to record them among the very succinct entries in his diary. As an Italian he also understood Christina sufficiently well to realize that such political persiflage was not indulged in for nothing. The point was to impress upon the Emperor's representative, even by slightly facetious means, her enthusiasm for the Catholic cause, her attachment to the house of Hapsburg and her own wide-ranging view of the political world that would fit so remarkable a woman for many roles. Once Christina realized that her means of subsistence and therefore her independence were threatened—as they undoubtedly were when Charles Gustavus invaded Poland on 11th July—she was prepared to use any means, fair or foul, to protect her own interests. For the realization was being forced upon her that without money or power the life of spiritual and religious freedom, of escape into a world of art, learning and sunshine, for which she had schemed for years and really given up her throne—could vanish like a rainbow.

After some delay, on 1st July Malines had presented to the Pope Christina's own letter announcing her secret abjuration, but also stating the difficulties of making it public. Philip IV's letter to the Pope explaining the financial difficulties involved did not arrive until September. Long before then Christina had received the Pope's reply. He expressed his joy at her news, but regretted that owing to the state in which he had found the papal finances he could be of no "temporal" assistance to her. Alexander advised Christina not to make her conversion public while travelling through non-Catholic countries, but only to do so on her arrival in Italy, so that he could receive her with all the solemnity that was her due. Although graciously phrased this letter made it very clear that the Pope would not receive the Queen unless she had first publicly abjured Protestantism and been received into the Roman Catholic Church.

Christina, who had been hoping to leave for Italy in September, now definitely decided to do so and to make her formal profession of faith at Innsbruck. She told Montecuccoli of her plans and once again he set out for Vienna to inform the Emperor, and to tell him that the Queen had specially requested that he might accompany her on her journey to Rome. Montecuccoli took with him a long exposé of Christina's views on the present political situation. Although she said she did not wish it to be known that it had been drawn up by her, but rather simply by "a well-informed person," the nature of its contents and the fact that the Emperor would obviously question Montecuccoli about the source of this information, would make it scarcely possible for him to conceal the identity of the author.

This document, going even further than her previous informal suggestions to Montecuccoli, reflects no credit on Christina. It shows clearly that she was perfectly prepared to reveal Swedish state secrets and instigate attacks on her own country if by doing so she could protect her personal interests. For the aim of the whole exposé was an elaborate plan to get the Emperor to invade Pomerania as soon as possible, thus making sure that the province would be in the hands of a friendly Catholic power—and a large part of Christina's own income safe—before Sweden could expropriate her estates upon hearing that their erstwhile Queen had become a Catholic. To achieve this, Christina was prepared to suggest to the Emperor that he should incite the Dutch and Danes "who hate Sweden" to attack her, to reveal the existence in the past of secret agreements between Sweden and the inhabitants of the Inn valley in Upper Austria to allow the passage of Swedish armies to the Danube, and also the contents of secret documents in Swedish State archives. Even allowing for the seventeenth-century lack of nationalistic spirit, these revelations by Gustavus Adolphus's daughter are the measure of the lengths to which Christina was willing to go in the defence of her own interests. The Queen had now very obviously woken up to the facts of life in a cold hard world, and although later in her "Maxims" she might affect and preach an elegant disregard for money, she now knew that its possession, or the power to obtain it, were the only sure bases for independence, which she probably valued more than anything else, in the life that she had chosen.

If after having taken this, as she no doubt hoped, decisive step, Christina felt any lingering qualms about revealing her country's secrets to its traditional foe, her last day in Brussels brought a sharp reminder of her financial position. On 21st

September she signed an IOU in favour of Garcia de Yllan and his heirs for 136, 437 Swedish riksdalers, 88,000 of which were to pay for her journey, the rest to be held in reserve for future expenses. The next day the Queen set out for Rome accompanied by about 250 people. These included Pimentel, as the King of Spain's personal Ambassador, his compatriot Antonio della Gueva y Silva and his wife, the Queen's newly-appointed Marshal of the Court and Mistress of the Robes, Father Guemes, in disguise, as her Chaplain, Gilbert the French secretary, now in charge of the Chancellery, and David Beck the court painter. The rest of the company were of mixed nationalities: Spaniards, Flemings, Portuguese and Italians—the three Italian musicians who had followed the Queen from Sweden were making sure of a free trip home. But of the Swedes only two remained, Gustavus Lilliecrona the chamberlain and Erik Appelgren, a page. What, one wonders, did these two faithful servitors make of the rest of the polyglot throng which accompanied their Queen on her progress across Europe? Or did the fascination of foreign travel, of seeing for themselves the great battlefields of the Thirty Years War, the riches of Augsburg and at last, at the end of October, Innsbruck itself, absorb them so completely that it never occurred to either of them to wonder about the why and wherefore of Christina's journey? They could well be excused if this was so, as the secret that it was at Innsbruck that Christina was at last to make her public abjuration, had been so well kept that when she arrived there the Governor of the Tirol, the Archduke Ferdinand Charles, his wife and his brother Cardinal Sigismund Francis, had no idea of it.

Although they were poor, the Archducal couple had done everything in their power to make Christina's visit a splendid occasion. Borrowed silver, and probably borrowed money, had been gathered together so that Ferdinand Charles could entertain his guest according to his own estimate of his "high archducal reputation." But as no one had any idea that this was to be anything other than a purely social occasion, only banquets, a gay Venetian comedy, and a visit to the famous art collections and gardens of the Castle of Ambras had been arranged. However, Christina found waiting for her in Innsbruck Father Malines and the Pope's specially appointed Internuncio, Lucas Holstenius, who was empowered by him officially to receive the Queen into the Roman Catholic Church.

Alexander VII's choice of these two men as his first emissaries sent to greet Christina even before she set foot on Italian soil, shows that this devout and kindly Pope was concerned not only with the political importance of the Queen's conversion as a triumph for the Church but with the human aspect as well. This was after all a young woman who had left her own country to enter a strange world, and his humanity and consideration led him to send the two people who would be best calculated to make her feel at home. One was Malines whom she already knew well, the other Holstenius, himself a convert and a northerner, a native of Hamburg who had been famous for his learning long before he became an apostolic protonotary, a Canon of St Peter's and Vatican Librarian. Their meeting here in Innsbruck was in fact to be the beginning of a life-long friendship.

Montecuccoli also joined Christina in Innsbruck, and wrote to his brother, who was a priest, describing the festivities. In this letter for once he gives rein to enthusiasm, saying, "The secret is revealed, the Queen has made her public abjuration, it is a great event for the Church, an event that has no equal." Naturally Montecuccoli had been present at the impressive ceremony on 3rd November when Christina, dressed in black silk with a diamond cross as her only ornament, had knelt in the choir of the Hofkirche and read the Catholic confession of faith in a "clear, distinct and loud voice," before the celebration of the Mass and the singing of a Te Deum culminated with the booming of cannon and the ringing of church bells.

The Queen wrote immediately to inform the Pope and the King of Sweden of her action, and to Charles Gustavus she said: "I have received His Holiness's permission and command to declare myself openly for what I am and have been for a long time." Did this confession come as a surprise to her intelligent but secretive cousin, now the master of defeated Cracow? It is very doubtful that it did. But the letter written three days later by the faithful Gustavus Lilliecrona, who now clearly doubted if he should or could carry out his King's instructions and accompany Christina to Rome, speaks for what must have been the reactions of countless simple Swedes when they heard of Christina's conversion.

Lilliecrona thus described his reactions to a friend in Sweden: "I assure you that my surprise was so great that I could not see the ceremonies in the church, nor even the Queen for three days. It was then that I grasped her (hand) and with many tears entreated her to grant my dismissal." Christina must have persuaded Lilliecrona that it was his duty to remain, but this evidently did not calm his anxiety as to what the King and people in Sweden would think, for he assures his correspondent that he wishes "to live and die in the faith for which I have my fatherland to thank in faithfulness to H.M. the King of Sweden."

On 8th November Christina set out for Italy, stopping at Trent where she was met by the Bishop, Prince Carlo Emanuele Madruzzi. There she attended Mass and went to see the church of S. Maria Maggiore, listening to the famous organ and being shown a painting of the Council of Trent, in which one of Madruzzi's kinsmen had played an important role. From there the Queen's journey took her across Venetian territory to Mantua, where she was honourably entertained by the Duke at Revere. But all of this was a mere prelude to the welcome that awaited Christina once she entered the Papal States.

Ever since the middle of October, various departments of the papal administration had been busily engaged in making preparations for the Queen's arrival. Within a few days her journey had become common knowledge and the talk of all Rome, so much so that the French diplomatic representative, Hugues de Lionne, reported home in disgust "at present the entire occupation of this court is the arrival of the Queen of Sweden." Apart from the purely practical questions of preparing ceremonies, lodgings, festive decorations, entertainments and gifts—no mean matter for so singular an occasion—there was the even more onerous task, in the seventeenth century, of examining the records in order to establish the exact protocol to be observed at each moment of what promised to be a long series of ceremonies, both religious and secular, in connection with an event which was really without precedent. No wonder that it was decided that the Queen's road to Rome must be as roundabout as possible, in order to allow time for all these preparations before she actually arrived.

In letters, instructions, reports, ledgers, bills and other papers still preserved in the Vatican and other archives, the Queen's progress through the Papal States can be followed in every minute detail—where she slept, what she ate, how she was entertained, whom she met and whether the arrangements went well or badly. Thus we know that no less than four nuncios, carefully chosen to represent four Italian provinces, were to await the Queen on the further bank of the Po, with the Pope's sedan chair ready for her to be carried in it to the gilded barge or bucentaur in which she was to cross the river. We know also that the bucentaur was to be well decorated and accompanied by a fleet of boats for the rest of the company. All of this the Cardinal Legate at Ferrara (who was responsible for the arrangements) was carefully instructed must be carried out "without confusion."

It was perhaps too much to ask in Italy at any time—let alone three hundred years ago—that anything should be arranged without confusion. In the event the weather was far from favourable and what actually happened was that in pouring rain the hardy northern Queen had crossed the frontier and already got several miles within the Papal States before she was met by the unfortunate ecclesiastics, who naturally had to descend to meet her and stood waiting up to their knees in mud. Graciously the Queen also got out of her carriage and conversed with them in the downpour. The Pope's letter of welcome having been presented, the company returned to its coaches and made the fastest time possible to Figarolo, where they were to dine in the house of a local worthy. Again the weather intervened, the supplies for the banquet had failed to arrive and although their host did his best, they now pushed on to Occhiobello where the Cardinal Legate was waiting in person to receive them. Here, although the decorated bucentaur and boats were all there waiting for the Queen to cross the Po, perhaps by now Christina was a little mistrustful of the actual efficiency of the arrangements made for her. Seeing a wide and turbulent river in full autumn flood, she rather wisely preferred to cross it by a solid bridge of boats intended for her baggage train. The chronicler to whom we are indebted for this description of Christina's first welcome in the Papal States, does not relate whether, while she was being carried across in the Pope's sedan chair, the Queen was saluted with the musket fire, trumpets and caracoling of the horses of the cavalry escort, which the papal instructions said were to have enlivened her more stately arrival in the bucentaur.

From now on, however, Christina travelled in one of the Pope's own carriages, specially dispatched from Rome for her use, together with two sumptuous beds, two canopies and matching chairs of state upholstered in cloth of gold, a complete outfit of silver-gilt plate, table services and the late Innocent X's celebrated chef, Luigi Fedele. In the midst of all this splendour Christina characteristically stuck to her severe mannish dress of a black hongreline, or tight-fitting long-skirted coat with a man's collar. It was thus attired that she was received by the Cardinal Legate and made her state entry into Ferrara. After suitable religious and civic ceremonies the Queen proceeded to her lodging in the castle and supped in private. The next day, however, she dined in public. For such occasions the official instructions from Rome—which had evidently been drawn up with an eye to those whose knowledge of royal protocol might be rusty—had stated firmly that only one place was to be laid at the table, but that if Her Majesty honoured the Cardinal Legate by inviting him to her table, he should not seat himself alongside her, but at the side of the table. However on this occasion Christina graciously insisted that the two Cardinals present should sit on either side of her, and the observant chronicler noticed that even though they were a slight distance away "they also both participated to a small extent" in the honour of sitting under the Queen's canopy.

For this feast Luigi Fedele had exercised all his art. The *trionfi* (elaborate confections with statues, scenes and flowers made of sugar, marzipan or aspic and often gilt with real gold leaf) were considered to be particularly ingenious, while the dishes themselves were described as being "so delicate and with a thousand different flavours in them, that sometimes it was difficult to know exactly what they were." This is not surprising as in the fat volume of accounts for the expenses of Christina's journey which were, on the Pope's express command, finally presented to the Apostolic Chamber for payment, some of Fedele's shopping lists appear. They include an amazing list of spices, scented essences and waters and even musk pellets. Bourdelot would have shuddered at the thought of his patient being regaled with such fare, and the unfortunate Christina had to clear her plate at each course before the Cardinals would even begin. She had, too, by now evidently departed from her usual custom not to drink wine, for she complimented the Cardinals on the Italian vintages, though they noticed that she always added water.

The conversation at table turned to contemporary art in Rome, the Queen extolling Pietro da Cortona and Bernini, evidently being delighted to air the inside knowledge gained from her correspondence with Paolo Giordano Orsini (this desire to surprise people with an intimate knowledge of what was going on in their country was one of Christina's foibles). Probably from the same source of information Christina was able to name the most fashionable of the castrati singers of the day—Bonaventura, who was in fact to take the leading role in an opera dedicated to the Queen and performed in her honour after her arrival in Rome. After a visit to the fortress, where the Queen personally assisted in firing the cannon, and to churches and monasteries, she witnessed a moral drama composed in her honour, describing the romantic idyll of the nymph Oritia and the North Wind, from whom her own illustrious pedigree was inevitably traced.

Bologna was the next stop on Christina's triumphal progress. Here she was regaled with a spectacular joust in an open-air theatre, fireworks, dancing and, as was to be expected at the seat of the oldest university in Europe, learned panegyrics and discussions. Proceeding along the ancient Via Emilia, the Queen was fêted at Imola and Faenza. Arriving at Forlì at night, she found the main piazza decorated in the classical and Renaissance fashion with green garlands draped to form an open evergreen pavilion lit by great bowls of flaming oil and wax. The arms of Sweden and Roman trophies were grouped around an allegorical figure of the River Rubicon, extolling Christina's spiritual triumph in comparison to Caesar's military one. After crossing the historic stream on 1st December, the Queen continued by slow stages to Cattolica. Here, as she had now left the province of Emilia and was entering the Duchy of Urbino, she was met by another Vice-Legate, Luigi Gasparo Lascaris, and a new escort under the command of Count Ludovico Santinelli. As the company approached Pesaro, the Legate—Cardinal Luigi Homodei—came out in his carriage to receive them.

Although Christina on this occasion only stopped in Pesaro for two days, this little town on the Adriatic coast and some of the men she met there were destined to play a dramatic role in her life. After a visit to the Cathedral, the Queen went to her lodging in the old palace of the Sforza and the Della Rovere dukes, which was now the Cardinal Legate's residence. Here Christina supped privately, afterwards being entertained by the performance by Ludovico and his brother Francesco Maria Santinelli of a galliard and the *canarino*. The next day the Queen dined in public with the Cardinal, probably in the great hall of the palace—the second biggest room in Italy—magnificently decorated with the Della Rovere emblems. Afterwards Christina was again entertained by Count Ludovico Santinelli's expert dancing, this time of a Spanish chaconne, followed by a show by strong men and acrobats. In the evening the ubiquitous Santinelli brothers made a further display of their virtuosity, both of them appearing in a combination of opera, ballets and academic meeting entitled *Festive Preparations on Parnassus* of which Francesco Maria was the author and impresario. Festini, the chronicler to whom we are indebted for the tragi-comic description of the Queen's crossing of the Po, dismissed this entertainment as "learned rubbish."

Christina, however, seems to have appreciated it, and the handsome and ingratiating brothers who acted as her escort. They were in fact the Italian counterparts of the irresponsible but amusing Duncan de Cerisantes, the swashbuckling Tott and versatile and entertaining Bourdelot, in fact the sort of company she enjoyed and had been deprived of for some time, travelling as she was with a court of grave Spaniards. It is not surprising, therefore, that after another highly diverting entertainment improvised when the Queen stopped the night in the remote little town of Senigallia, where the Santinellis excelled themselves by improvising a comedy, fake duels and acrobatic feats, she felt that the brothers would be an asset to her entourage. Unfortunately the shrewd Montecuccoli had gone on to Rome by a more direct route. As an Italian who knew the world he would have been much better at summing up the characters of these young men whom the Queen now suggested to Cardinal Homodei she might take into her service. Either through ignorance, a desire not to cross the Queen, or provincial pride—the Santinellis came of quite a well-known local family—the good Cardinal agreed with her; he could not have done her a worse service.

From Ancona Christina now went on to Loreto, one of the great places of pilgrimage since the Middle Ages, when the house of the Virgin Mary was believed to have been miraculously transported there from Nazareth after the Moslems had threatened it with destruction at the end of the thirteenth century. As the great basilica, which shelters the holy house, came into sight perched on its hilltop, Christina descended from her litter to pray in the snow. The weather was by now so bad that she did not make the traditional pilgrim's approach to the shrine on foot, but after Mass had been celebrated in the Basilica, Father Guemes placed her votive offering of a jewelled crown and sceptre at the feet of the famous black Madonna, which is traditionally believed to have been carved by St Luke.

The journey now continued in hard winter weather across the Appennines, with a stop at another shrine—that of S. Nicola at Tolentino—then through the high mountains via Camerino to Foligno in Umbria, where again festivities had to be curtailed because of the weather. From Foligno a deviation was made in order to allow the Queen to visit Assisi. Here rather inappropriately in the last resting place of the *poverello,* Christina was regaled with the most spectacular banquet of the whole journey. The *trionfi* were so remarkable that pages were devoted to their description in the printed accounts of Christina's progress, and indeed she herself was so struck by them that she asked for them to be brought to her room for her to admire at leisure.

The royal route now followed the valleys of the Tiber and its tributaries, branching off at Otricoli to enable the Queen to spend the night at the palatial Farnese villa at Caprarola. The Spanish Ambassador in Rome, the Duke of Terranova, came thus far from the capital to greet the Queen, but here again the pouring rain ruined the decorations and festivities so carefully prepared by the Marquis Giandemaria, resident in Rome of Ranuccio II Farnese, Duke of Parma. But looking out of the windows of the Farnese villa at the fabulous view, with Soracte rising blue and mysterious in the distance as it does in countless paintings of Claude

Lorraine, Christina saw at last the classical landscape of the poets and, recognizing its pagan enchantment, exclaimed: "I dare not say the name of Jesus lest I break the spell!"

The Queen had finally arrived in the world she had dreamed of and, appropriately, the day after she left Caprarola she was met by Paolo Giordano Orsini, Duke of Bracciano, whose letters to her in Sweden had provided a link with this land of art and music. Christina spent that night at Bracciano Castle, which towers majestically above a lake surrounded by olive groves. The Duke and Duchess had displayed the art treasures of their ancient house in honour of the Queen and, knowing her love of music, had arranged a concert for her. It was Sunday, 19th December, and the last stop on Christina's long journey. The following day she would be plunged into the arduous ceremonial of her arrival in Rome. In the meantime in the quiet of the Italian countryside, did she pause to think that she had just passed the threshold of her thirtieth year and wonder what the future held for her? Had she but known it, three men she was to meet in the next few days were to provide an augury for her future life. All three were cardinals. Two, whom she was to meet that very day, were but incidental symbols of the change in her status which fourteen years of intermittent effort and intrigue were to do nothing to alter. The third was to become the dominant figure in her life.

The Villa of Olgiata some few miles to the north of Rome had been designated as the place where the four nuncios, who had accompanied the Queen from Ferrara, were to be replaced by the two Cardinal Legates who came out of the city to meet her. The façade of the villa was elaborately decorated, according to the custom of the time, with allegorical figures painted in *trompe-l'oeil* on canvas. Here significantly we hear no more mention of the arms of Sweden but now only of Christina's personal ones, consisting of the Wasa sheaf of corn emblazoned on an escutcheon with two bendlets sinister. For all his paternal benevolence, Alexander VII had a long career behind him as nuncio and secretary of state, and he knew as much as anyone about the etiquette appropriate to the occasion. So, again significantly, although the two Cardinal Legates welcoming Christina were scions of the ruling houses of Medici and Hesse (the Cardinal Landgrave Frederick of Hesse-Darmstadt was in fact the Queen's distant relation), they were only cardinal-deacons, not cardinal-bishops as would have been de rigueur for the reception of a reigning sovereign. If Christina noticed this nice difference, she gave no sign of it, and after an exchange of complimentary addresses the long procession, swollen now by trumpeters, drummers and an increased military escort, set out for Rome.

It was dark before the company reached the city, so as this was supposed to be a purely informal and incognito arrival, the Queen entered the Vatican by a short cut through the gardens, descending from her carriage in the Cortile del Belvedere. Simply dressed as she was in grey with her habitual black scarf around her shoulders, Christina was led by Monsignore Farnese, the Pope's majordomo, up through the torchlit staircases and galleries of the palace. To her astonishment these were packed to overflowing with interested crowds, so that at one point she turned round laughing and said: "Is this the usual way of entering Rome incognito?" Finally the Queen arrived at the Pope's apartment and was received by him in private audience for a quarter of an hour. Alexander VII was fifty-six, a small delicate man, whose face plainly showed the sufferings of ill-health, the bristling moustache and goatee beard of the period contrasting strangely with his gentle expression. Although he loved learning and the arts, preferring the company of poets and scholars, Alexander was well versed in diplomacy and politics and had been an able secretary of state. He does not, however, appear to have known a great deal about Christina personally, as at the Consistory when he had read to the cardinals her letter announcing her public profession of faith at Innsbruck, he admonished the Sacred College to look to their behaviour in the presence of the Queen, so that she should not be shocked. He told his listeners that when he was Nuncio in Münster for the Peace of Westphalia, he had learnt how critically northerners watched the Romans.

The Pope himself must have been curious to see what this distinguished convert was like. A somewhat flattering description of Christina, written by one of the chroniclers of her journey, gives some idea of how Italians reacted to her. The writer was most struck by the Queen's vivacity, the mobility of her expression and the beauty of her eyes. Except that her hair was now rather cautiously described as "appearing to be brown and curly" (she was in fact wearing a dark wig) the rest of the description is already familiar from Chanut's famous pen portrait of many years before, describing how Christina ate, slept and drank little—nearly always water—and was very learned, though it is interesting to note that even to the Italians she seemed small.

After the ritual three obeisances at the beginning of the audience, the Pope invited Christina to be seated on his right on a chair which was euphemistically described as a "magnificent royal seat" placed under the papal canopy. Here again Alexander behaved in the manner which his biographer and friend, Monsignore Sforza Pallavicino, described as "very circumspect, containing himself within the just mean of honour and prudence, doing enough but not too much." The "royal seat" had indeed posed a difficult problem: none but a ruling sovereign could sit in a chair with arms in the presence of a pope. The question had been solved by giving Bernini carte blanche to design this important piece of furniture, and no doubt the result was magnificent to look at, but the back was low and the arms rounded—Christina would indeed have been mortified to know that in the papal account books it featured as "a large stool for the use of Her Majesty."

If, however, Alexander was not going to depart from time-honoured public protocol for the reception of this royal convert, the circumstances were so unique that he resolved to honour her in another way. For the first time in recent history, officially at any rate, a woman guest was to be lodged in the Vatican. When the Queen left the Pope she was conducted to an apartment which had been specially prepared for her, not in the palace itself, but in the Torre dei Venti which rises above the Cortile del Belvedere, adjacent to the Vatican library and archive. Probably few lodgings could have appealed to Christina more than this eagle's nest, consisting of a suite of eight exquisitely frescoed rooms occupying the three top stories of the tower. Although it commands the most superb views of Rome and the surrounding countryside, the building is not known as "the tower of the winds" for nothing, but on this occasion it was warmed by silver braziers and logs blazing on hearths furnished with silver firedogs, pokers and tongs. There was even a silver bed-warmer for the Queen's bed. Weeks of careful planning, directed by Bernini's brother, had gone to make this apartment really fit for a queen.

Apart from the splendid furnishings, tapestries and pictures, sheets of the finest cambric edged with lace from Arras had been especially made for the Queen's bed, which was draped with crimson Flemish brocade, while white satin canopies, sprinkled with gold-embroidered ears of wheat, hung in her audience chamber and over her seat at table.

Even when surrounded by such luxury after a long journey, Christina did not change her usual custom of sleeping little. In her excitement and desire to see everything, she was down early to see the famous Cortile del Belvedere and, evidently warned beforehand of her habits, the Pope had arranged that his personal gifts to her should be ready there on display. These were a magnificent carriage, litter and sedan chair, upholstered in sky-blue velvet and gleaming with silver decorations which had been designed by Bernini himself. With this splendid gift went the six coursers to draw the carriage, two mules for the litter and, what Christina probably appreciated most, a beautiful palfrey superbly saddled and housed in blue and silver. The Queen mounted at once, putting her horse through its paces and demonstrating her undoubted mastery of horsemanship. Among the admiring onlookers there ran the whisper that there had not been a man in Sweden who could ride even a charger better than the Queen.

Montecuccoli now presented Bernini to Christina as the designer of the decorative figures on the carriage. He said modestly: "If there is anything bad it is mine," and Christina replied with ready wit in Italian: "Then there is nothing of yours." Although unfortunately no drawings or prints have survived to give any precise idea of what this splendid equipage was like, Christina evidently cherished it, as its worn remains were still there in her coach house twenty-two years later—a reminder no less of her triumphant arrival in Rome than of the great artist who became her friend. After displaying her expertise as a horsewoman and her ready command of Italian, Christina went off with Holstenius to see the Vatican library, surely one of the sights of Rome which she had been most longing to see. Later in the day she had the honour of being received by the Pope and of chatting with him for a whole hour. When Alexander came, carried in his chair through the long galleries of the palace, to pay the Queen a return visit in her own apartment, something of Christina's youth and excitement—after all she was only just twenty-nine—is reflected even in the staid pages of the official chronicle of her arrival. For the writer describes how as soon as the Queen heard of the Pope's approach "she ran with long strides through several rooms to prostrate herself at his feet."

On 23rd December came the great day of Christina's state entry into Rome. For this she left the Vatican in one of the Pope's carriages, attended by the two Cardinal Legates and a large retinue, and drove to the historic Ponte Milvio. Here the Senator of Rome was waiting to welcome her with a company of nobles, pages, trumpeters and a cavalry escort, all in their finest clothes and uniforms. The procession halted at Pope Julius III's beautiful villa on the Via Flaminia, magnificently decorated for the occasion, where the Queen was offered a light collation. Here the Pope's gifts were officially presented to her with much ceremony, but just as she had done in private in the Belvedere, Christina now mounted the palfrey, although the weather was still bad, and took her place in the interminable procession that continued on its way to the Porta del Popolo. No doubt she had been told that the old gate had been specially decorated in her honour by Bernini and that Alexander VII had himself composed the inscription *Felice Faustoque Ingressui* which (in abbreviated form) with the date is still to be seen today.

Just inside the gate the entire college of Cardinals was waiting, mounted on their mules, to welcome the Queen. As it was Advent they did not wear their customary scarlet, but the *paonazza* or bright magenta appropriate to a time of vigil. As their doyen, Cardinal Francesco Barberini delivered an address of welcome. Here too the leading members of the Roman nobility were drawn up to welcome the Queen, all dressed in the most splendid clothes, the grandest being the nephews of the two last popes, Prince Barberini and Prince Pamphilj. As the latter was still in mourning for Innocent X, there was some doubt as to the suitability of his presence, but he came dressed in black velvet embroidered with diamonds valued at 100,000 scudi, with three even bigger diamonds in his hat. He was however eclipsed by his wife, Princess of Rossano in her own right, who was covered with jewels estimated to be worth seven times as much as her husband's.

For once Christina was right in claiming for herself "a good taste in dress." In the midst of this barbaric and overwhelming display, at a time when Rome had lived through a surfeit of papal nepotism, she, the centre of the whole scene, the focus of all eyes, appeared without a single jewel except a little gold ring, and wearing a simple grey dress, her usual black scarf and plumed hat. It was, of course, just as Christina loved to present herself, surrounded by splendour but all the more remarkable for her apparent scorn of such vanities. It was convenient too, for, with half her jewels in pawn, it is doubtful if she could have matched, let alone outshone, the fabulous wealth that the Barberini and Pamphilj had accumulated during the reigns of the last two popes; while the austere Alexander VII, who had been elected by the efforts of the Flying Squadron to put an end to nepotism, would be certain to approve of such simplicity.

With a long train of glittering princely carriages now added to the procession, and surrounded by cardinals, Christina continued on her triumphal way to St Peter's. They wended their way along the Corso, flanked by splendid palaces, the scene of the races of the Roman carnival, and turned right beside the grim Palazzo Venezia. Here they plunged into that warren of narrow streets, grown up among the ruins of classical Rome, where since time immemorial popes and pilgrims had gone on their way to the great basilica, built according to the Catholic belief over the tomb of the Prince of the Apostles. As the Queen dismounted in the piazza in front of St Peter's, the cannons of Castel Sant' Angelo boomed a salute. What would Gustavus Adolphus have felt if he had known that his little daughter, who had clapped her hands at the cannons of Kalmar, would one day kneel in front of St Peter's to the sound of those of Sant' Angelo?

After Christina rose from the golden cushion, upon which she had knelt to kiss the cross, she entered the porch of the basilica. This was hung with magnificent tapestries, while above the central door there hung a curious painted allegory of a royal crown and the Wasa sheaf of corn floating on a stormy northern sea. As Archpriest of the basilica, Cardinal Francesco Barberini had caused the whole nave to be hung with his family's wonderful collection of tapestries, with gold-embroidered draperies and trophies and crowns representing Christina's triumph. To the sound of chanting, the Queen made her way to the high altar, where she knelt to pray before the Blessed Sacrament; then passing by a private stair she entered the Vatican Palace, where the Pope was waiting to receive her in consistory surrounded by the cardinals.

Not very surprisingly, on the following day Christina was exhausted. She went incognito, carried in a chair, to see the traditional Christmas Eve banquet which the Pope gave to the cardinals, but by the evening she had taken to her bed and was not present at the night's religious ceremonies. Christmas Day was to see the climax of the Queen's long pilgrimage. In St Peter's on that day she received the sacrament of confirmation from the Pope himself. She took Alexandra as her second name in honour of her new "father" and also at the Pope's request the name of Maria. Cardinal Medici stood proxy for the King of Spain as her sponsor at this ceremony, because neither Pimentel nor Terranova would agree that the other should have this honour. In the afternoon Christina went to Santa Maria Maggiore, to see the relic of Christ's crib which is kept there and only exposed at Christmas.

On St Stephen's Day the Queen was to leave the Vatican to take up residence in the Palazzo Farnese, but before she left the Pope accorded her the extraordinary honour of inviting her to dine with him. According to the protocol laid down in the *Caerimoniale Romanum* no woman may eat in the presence of a pope, and only twice, on the occasion of royal or imperial weddings, had the rule been broken during the last century. With loving care contemporary chroniclers dwelt upon each minute detail of the protocol observed, how the Pope's and Queen's individual tables were separated by about half a yard, the Pope's being about four inches higher than Christina's and raised on a dais, while hers simply stood on a carpet under his canopy—the famous "royal seat" again coming into use. Both Pope and Queen were very abstemious, but a fabulous series of dishes—aspics, jellies and blancmanges set in wonderful shapes and gilded—were placed before them, while the famous *trionfi* were not just the work of a skilled chef. Artists and sculptors who were Bernini's assistants had designed and cast in sugar and painted and gilded these allegorical groups of statues which represented Abundance with the Wasa sheaves of corn, also, as a compliment to the learned Christina, Minerva surrounded by the liberal arts. This stately repast was enlivened by the Jesuit Father Oliva preaching a sermon—the Pope was delighted when Christina afterwards made a learned allusion to a passage from the Scriptures which he might also have used to advantage—and music provided by members of the choir and orchestra of St Peter's.

That night as dusk fell, the Queen was accompanied by a cavalcade of ambassadors, nobles and princes to the Palazzo Farnese, the most superb Renaissance palace in the city, which had been placed at her disposal by the Duke of Parma. She may not have known it, but the impecunious Frederick of Hesse-Darmstadt, or the Cardinal Langravio as he was usually called, had been forced to leave in order to make way for her. Until Christina's arrival the Landgrave had been the most distinguished convert in Rome, but now he was forced to take refuge in Prince Pamphilj's remote villa on the Janiculum. The new tenant was welcomed with bonfires and torches flaming in the piazza before the palace, of which the entire façade was covered with splendid painted decorations, where Old Testament virtues, classical allegories and a plethora of crowns and banners, bore witness to the Duke of Parma's hopes that the Queen would influence the Pope in his favour and bring about some modification of the terms imposed upon Parma at the end of the War of Castro.

CHAPTER 8

The Phantom Crown I: 1656–1658

Christina was enchanted with the idea of her new home and all excitement to see it. Hardly had she said goodbye to the Spanish Ambassador, who had accompanied her from the Vatican, than she insisted on being shown the whole of the first floor of Palazzo Farnese, or *piano nobile* as it is usually called in Italy. The honours were done by the same Marchese Giandemaria who had arranged the Queen's reception at Caprarola. As a result of the War of Castro, begun by Urban VIII in an attempt to wrest this fief from the dukes of Parma for the benefit of his own nephews, the Farnese no longer came to Rome (though a member of the family was Alexander VII's majordomo), but their extensive possessions in the Papal States necessitated their keeping a representative there, and this office had for some years been filled by Giandemaria.

Christina's curiosity about the Palazzo Farnese is understandable as it is exactly the type of Roman residence she must have dreamed of in Sweden when imagining her future life in Rome. The building was begun by Antonio Sangallo the younger for Cardinal Alessandro Farnese before he became Pope Paul III, was continued by Michelangelo and completed by Giacomo Della Porta. Although it had not been a family residence for some time, the famous Farnese collections of antique sculptures, cameos and engraved gems were still housed in the palace. Nevertheless, furniture and the ordinary necessaries of life were lacking, and Giandemaria had a busy time preparing for the Queen's arrival, for the Cardinal Landgrave Frederick of Hesse, who had lived in part of the palace, was only finally evicted at the end of October. Now, in high hopes of what the Queen of Sweden's influence with the Pope might be able to achieve for him in modifying the terms imposed at the end of the War of Castro, the Duke of Parma had sent orders that the whole palace was to be opened up and put in order for her, tapestries, furniture and pictures even being sent from Parma for the purpose. But the result of years of neglect had to be made good, probably only Giandemaria's own apartment under the garden terrace leading to the Tiber was really habitable, and in some of the vast halls parts of the decorative friezes and mouldings had crumbled into decay. This damage was ingeniously concealed by canvas painted in *trompe-l'oeil* to fill the gaps, the existing gilt and marble-topped consoles and tables were restored, and the rooms furbished up with new hangings and curtains of red velvet and green or scarlet damask edged with gold.

Giandemaria had arranged four principal apartments on the *piano nobile*, each consisting of a bedroom and three other rooms. The huge Hall of the Emperors* was converted into a throne-room for the Queen's official audiences, and provided with a crimson chair of state and canopy. Curiously, to modern minds, there was no state dining-room; at that period in Rome a table was simply set up in the room in which it was decided to eat. After making her inspection, Christina selected for herself what is undoubtedly the most attractive suite of rooms in the palace, in a corner overlooking the Tiber, choosing as her bedroom the room opening on to the garden terrace. As Master of the Court and Mistress of the Robes, the della Guevas were given the corresponding apartment on the other side of the famous gallery frescoed by Annibale Carracci, while the rest of the Queen's suite were lodged on the other floors of the vast palace.

All these details, and indeed every aspect of his activities during the last two months and in the months to come, Giandemaria reported to the Duke of Parma or his Minister, Marchese Lampugnani. In these dispatches Giandemaria emerges as a highly conscientious administrator, keeping a sharp eye on his master's

* The palace is now the French Embassy, and the hall is called Le Salon d'Hercule after a copy of the Farnese Hercules standing by the entrance.

interests, also as a shrewd observer, though not above retailing some spicy gossip. What he has to say about Christina and her household is of particular interest, as he lived at close quarters with them under the same roof for seven months. The mere fact that the main interest this meticulous man had in them was purely administrative—unlike the majority of people who came into contact with the Queen, the larger canvas of international politics were no concern of his—makes the Marchese's picture of Christina at this time probably the most unbiased source available.

Although Giandemaria quickly realized that Christina was not going to be an easy or peaceful tenant of the Palazzo Farnese he evidently liked her, and although he must have found the total lack of order in her way of life highly irritating, he accepted it with considerable humour. But this precise little man was quick to spot Christina's strangeness and restlessness—he found she changed her bedroom almost every night—as well as her sudden enthusiasms and equally rapid switches to boredom, which rendered her completely unpredictable. Giandemaria soon got to know of the Queen's ferocious sense of humour, and displayed considerable agility in avoiding becoming the object of it himself, but he also soon learnt to respect her quick understanding and to fear her swift judgment, while her wit appealed to his own sense of humour.

On one point his testimony is exceedingly valuable, especially in view of the rumours that were soon to circulate in Rome. Although Giandemaria was shocked by Christina's freedom of behaviour, and the fact that she would wander chatting in a room full of men without a single woman attendant, he was emphatic that in spite of this the Queen never forgot for an instant who she was and "there has never been the slightest sign of any liberty." In fact from the first Giandemaria noticed that as far as ambassadors and the nobility were concerned Christina stood very much on her dignity, exacting the utmost protocolaire ceremony from all of them. This was markedly different from the way in which she received the cardinals, and particularly the cardinals of the famous flying squadron who had brought about Alexander VII's election. This group, mainly composed of the youngest and most brilliant of the cardinals and including the formidable Cardinal de Retz, one of the leaders of the Fronde, was remarkable in that its members were unattached either to France or to Spain, a position almost unique in the Roman politics of the day. Giandemaria had also noticed very early on that the Queen singled out a particular member of the group for special favour.

Cardinal Decio Azzolino came of a family from Fermo in the Marche that could already boast of having produced two cardinals, but was only of the lesser provincial nobility and not well off. Azzolino (he was then only thirty-three) had in fact got on in the world through his own intelligence. He had shown marked diplomatic and—infinitely more rare in an Italian—administrative capacity. In fact by 1656 he was very much of a figure in Rome, and was known to be the moving spirit of the flying squadron.

Judged by modern standards, Azzolino was not good-looking. His face was plump and he had too prominent a nose, but his portraits leave no doubt as to his force of character and his ability. He had a broad high forehead, expressive eyes, a strong chin and a firm yet mobile mouth. In Bernini's masterly bust the mouth is particularly noticeable, and indeed it was at once Azzolino's most distinctive and revealing feature, indicating wit and humour, decision not unmixed with subtlety, and unmistakably that he was an Italian. According to the Venetian Ambassador Azzolino was attractive to women, Cardinal de Retz described him as "one of the finest and readiest spirits in the world." Evidently he possessed that elusive but invaluable gift—charm. It was a charm, moreover, which was well-calculated to appeal to Christina—soft, subtle and sophisticated—the opposite to herself and unlike anything she had encountered hitherto.

On his side, the young Cardinal could not fail to be flattered at being singled out by a Queen whose conversion and arrival in Rome had created such a sensation. Nor would he and his colleagues of the flying squadron have been slow to appreciate what an asset Christina could be to them politically. But there was more to it than this. The flying squadron were the intellectual élite of the Sacred College, they very genuinely shared the Queen's tastes for art, learning and literature, while Azzolino was also personally interested in science and even in engineering projects such as rendering the Tiber navigable. Thus a natural rapport was added to political interest, but there was also the fact that a young woman of twenty-nine found herself in a strange city with an entourage of people she hardly knew. It was not surprising, therefore, that Christina welcomed visits from the sympathetic young Cardinal. In fact by the end of March these had become so frequent and so prolonged that even the higher powers in the Vatican began to be seriously alarmed. For on the 22nd March Azzolino found it necessary to write to the Pope's confidant, Monsignore Sforza Pallavicino, assuring him that his friendship with the Queen was completely innocent.

In the meantime Christina was plunged into a concentrated programme of sight-seeing and festivities. Naturally the great basilicas of St Peter's and St John Lateran were among the first sights. There the famous relics were exposed for the Queen to revere. This was followed by visits to the Spanish national church of St James, the Bernini fountains of the nearby Piazza Navona and the famous Jesuit church, the Gesù, where the General, Father Nickel, did the honours. After that, it was the turn of Castel Sant' Angelo, where a military parade was followed by a collation. Curiously to modern minds, this consisted of huge bowls each holding sixty pounds of nougat, sugared almonds and crystallized fruits, served with wine and soft drinks. At the Sapienza—the University of Rome—the blue-stocking Queen was welcomed with addresses in Hebrew, Greek, Syrian, Arabic, Chaldean and given 112 books. This was rivalled by the reception at the Propaganda Fide, when the Queen was greeted in twenty-two languages, and by the learned display put on by the Jesuit Collegio Romano. Here the erudite Father Kircher displayed to the Queen the marvels of modern science, medicine and nature, including the apparatus for making Theriaca—a famous specific since the days of Nero, and the Balsam of Life, a sample of which was presented to her.

During a short breathing-space between this gruelling programme of visits and the opening of carnival, Christina found time to open her own Academy, which met each week in the Palazzo Farnese. It must, however, be admitted that as a learned body this was a little disappointing, although the list of the foundation members includes some famous names, and the Santinelli brothers were assiduous in their attendance. The topics discussed were the virtues of the Pope; that ladies' apparent indifference and cruelty often indicate the craft and finesse of love;

whether night or day is more suitable to poetry; and which love lasts longest—the *coup de foudre* or that which comes from long acquaintance.

However, before these profound discussions had given place to religious disquisitions more appropriate to Lent, the Roman Carnival was in full swing, and it was a carnival long remembered for its splendour as "the Carnival of the Queen." One of the earlier and most magnificent performances was the opera entitled *The Triumph of Piety* or *Human Life*, which had been specially composed for the occasion. The libretto was written by Monsignore Giulio Rospigliosi—the future Pope Clement IX—and dedicated to Christina, the music had been composed by Marco Marazzoli, while the leading role was taken by the Queen's favourite castrato, Bonaventura. This splendid entertainment, for which the famous Bolognese artist, Giovanni Francesco Grimaldi, had been designing the sets and costumes since the end of November, was given by the Barberini family in the private theatre of their palace.

Judging by engravings which still exist, the settings, costumes and scenic effects were splendid. Real fountains flowed in front of the proscenium arch and there were sparkling cascades on the stage itself, where in the opening scene night changed gradually into day. There were garden and woodland scenes where storms thundered and gods and goddesses appeared sailing into sight on clouds before descending on to the stage, where the action was frequently enlivened by ballets. The final scene took place against a Roman background, with St Peter's in the distance and a grand firework display in progress on Castel Sant' Angelo. This was a realistic reproduction of the famous *girandola* which celebrated great events and had welcomed Christina's arrival. It was customary in the prudish atmosphere of Counter-Reformation Rome for separate performances of opera or plays to be given for ladies, but it was impossible for the Queen not to be present at the first performance of such a spectacle given in her honour. So a special box was prepared for Christina, with its own private staircase, from which she could watch without being seen.

Meanwhile, although the Barberini put on two other operas for the Queen, the Pamphilj, as relations of the last Pope, had also of course to provide splendid entertainment. Though, probably because they were in mourning, this was of a more private nature, it was also spectacular and particularly complimentary because the Prince had himself composed the libretto of the entertainment. A room in the palace had been converted into a theatre for a pageant, where not only Venus and Cupid again descended from the clouds to sing and dance, but the ladies of the Princess's household also danced, covered with jewels and holding flaming torches in their hands.

Afterwards the versatile Prince presented Christina with a song he had written on her abdication. This entertainment came as the culmination of several lesser ones, which Christina may have enjoyed even more, as during all her life in Rome she was an enthusiastic spectator of the carnival, and on this occasion the Pamphilj more or less kept open house for her to watch it. A splendid box was erected in front of their palace in the Corso, from which the Queen could watch all the races and processions. She went constantly to see the various events, and each time was feted with music, dancing and singing and the customary collations of sweets and crystallized fruits. Remembering the rose-water episode of Christina's childhood, many of the drinks served on these occasions must have appealed to her. They were simply water delicately flavoured and scented with flower essences, extracts of oranges and lemons and aromatic spices.

More serious celebrations were not lacking, however. The Queen went to see the "noble apparatus" at the Gesù, of which the theme was naturally purely religious. It was in fact one of those curious shows for which a *trompe-l'oeil* painted setting was set up in the street and, by means of ingenious stage machinery, allegorical painted scenes and figures were made to appear and disappear. Very much more to Christina's taste, one would imagine, was a performance of *The Sacrifice of Isaac*, with music by the famous Carissimi, given by the German seminary.

However the Barberini had one more fête in store for the illustrious guest, and this was the most magnificent of all. Grimaldi had also been burning the midnight oil since November for its preparation, designing for it not only an open-air theatre which held 3,000 people, but also some of the most fabulous triumphal cars and costumes that had ever been seen even in seventeenth-century Rome. This tremendous entertainment, called the *Giostra delle Caroselle*, which was held after dark on 28th February, was part joust, part pageant. Triumphal cars accompanied by horsemen and filled with singers dressed as gods, goddesses and nymphs processed round the arena and serenaded the Queen in her box. Then, to the blare of trumpets, rival teams of mounted cavaliers and "amazons" charged each other and engaged in mock battle. Pistols were fired and the riders dashed around the arena showing off their horsemanship, which must have been quite consummate as one and all wore fabulous costumes topped with ostrich-feather head-dresses as tall as their mounts and themselves. Suddenly a huge dragon, breathing flame and spurting rockets from its mouth, appeared, provoking yet another battle which of course the "amazons" won and, to the music of an orchestra and singing, all the performers lined up in a vast procession to salute the Queen. The bills for a large part of all these entertainments given for Christina still exist in the Barberini archive, adding up to 7,285 scudi, 86 baiocchi, approximately six and a half million lire or £3,100 of today's currency.*

Although if she knew of the vast sum expended Christina would undoubtedly have admired the extravagance of this princely expenditure in her honour, it must surely also have caused her a pang, as she was herself in desperate straits for money. The loan she had been able to raise from Garcia de Yllan was exhausted and of the war indemnities owed by the Empire she had only been able to realize 70,000 écus on a debt which ran into millions. So, as early as the end of January the Queen dispatched her secretary Appelman to Sweden with instructions to negotiate with Charles Gustavus. The plan he was to expound was not new, Christina wanted her cousin to buy from her all the lands of her appanage, for which she asked a million and a half écus. No one knew better than the Queen the impoverished state of Sweden's finances at the time of her abdication, and to the normal expenditure had now been added the burden of the war in Poland. So, realizing that her project was not likely to be accepted, Christina had given instructions for alternative offers. The first was that the King should begin at least by buying back the islands of Öland,

* The fact that at the time 24 lb. of macaroni could be bought for one scudo (about 900 lire) and today this would cost about 3,000 lire, gives an indication of the difference in actual values.

Gotland and Ösel. Christina evidently had no great hopes of this either, as she also offered to accept an exchange of her Pomeranian estates for others in Poland, a Catholic country even if conquered by the Swedes. If no satisfaction was forthcoming from any of these suggestions, Christina asked for the only thing which she probably really believed that she had any hope of obtaining: this was the King's agreement that she herself could sell or raise loans on some of her lands.

If Charles Gustavus would agree even to this last suggestion, the Queen would be able to raise enough money to enable her to settle down in Rome in something like the style appropriate to her station. This was very far from being the case at the moment. Christina's exchequer was so depleted that although she felt she ought to make some return for all the hospitality she had received—she wished to give a performance in the Palazzo Farnese of one of the minor operas which the Barberini had put on for her—she was forced to let Cardinal Francesco Barberini shoulder the major part of the expenses. Nor was this all. Christina's rather motley crowd of followers and servants had not been paid, and already in January they had begun to steal the silver and the furnishings of Palazzo Farnese and even a carriage, and to break up and burn the doors to keep themselves warm. Poor Giandemaria was at his wit's end, writing anguished letters to Parma. Later he was to take much sterner measures, appealing to the Queen and even to the Pope.

How lonely Christina could feel with all her pressing financial worries in the midst of the splendours of her Roman welcome, transpires from a letter she wrote to Belle on 6th January. This time there is not a word about the honours that were being paid to her or of the gaiety of her life; the lack of a single soul in whom she could confide evidently outweighed all else. In her loneliness Christina stands revealed as a very different person from what all those around her must have believed the haughty, self-willed and already slightly shocking Queen of Sweden to be like. The actual letter has survived, and all that is written on the outside by way of name and address is the rather pathetic superscription "A la Belle"—to the beautiful one. The letter reads: "How happy I would be if it was permitted for me to see you Belle, but I am condemned to the fate of loving you always, esteeming you always, but seeing you never, and that envy of the stars for human happiness prevents me from being entirely happy, as I can never be that when I am so far away from you. But never doubt the truth of this, and believe that wherever I may be in the world you have there someone who belongs to you as much as ever. But is it possible that you still remember me? Am I still as dear to you as I used to be? Or did I deceive myself when I thought that I was the person whom you loved most in the world? Ah, if that is true, do not undeceive me. Leave me my error, and don't be jealous of my imagined happiness, which allows me the belief that I am dear to the most amiable person in the world. Leave me this blessing if it's possible, and do not allow time or my absence to deprive me of the comfort of being loved by you. Adieu, Belle, adieu. I embrace you a million times, Christina Alexandra."

With the *Giostra delle Caroselle* the "Carnival of the Queen" was drawing to an end. It had, of course, been the talk of all Rome, but the entertainment that the Queen attended on the last night before Lent began, set the tongues of those politically in the know wagging a great deal more furiously. This was the performance of Corneille's *Heraclitus* given by Hugues de Lionne, the French Ambassador to the Italian Princes, but with only the grade of Chargé d'Affaires to the Holy See. It was staged in Lionne's residence, the Palazzo Mazarin, and not, as Christina's Spanish entourage had tried to insist, in the Palazzo Farnese. That the Queen should wish to see the play at all was a sad disappointment for them, but realizing her utter determination to do so—and possibly not just for its dramatic and literary merits—Pimentel, della Gueva and the Spanish Ambassador, the Duke of Terranova, had done all they could to prevent the Queen from going publicly to the French diplomat's residence: after all Spain was at war with France and the Queen had come to Rome under Spanish protection.

On this point, however, Christina was adamant, and behind her determination lies the history of her relations with the Spaniards since her arrival in Rome and possibly her memory of her meeting with Chanut, all those months ago in Flanders. Chanut had then reported that the Queen did not seem to be so pro-Spanish as she was said to be, and Christina had told Montecuccoli that the King of France would have had many interesting proposals also to make to her if she had stayed in neutral territory in Holland instead of going to the Spanish Netherlands. One thing anyway is certain, the Duke of Terranova was not the man to win the favour of the spirited Queen, and her old friend Pimentel was on a very different footing from that which had obtained in Sweden when, together, he and Christina plotted to arrange her conversion and life after her abdication.

Not for nothing did Spanish etiquette earn its reputation for being the most rigid in the world. The right of the Spanish grandee to wear his hat in the presence of the King of Spain was a major factor of life in the most exalted circles. Christina was not only exigent as far as etiquette towards herself was concerned, she was also a past master at using it as a weapon against others. It was in fact about the only weapon she now possessed, as a Queen without a country and, worse still, without money. But in the seventeenth century etiquette and protocol were no mean weapons and, all alone with not a single disinterested friend upon whom she could rely, Christina used this one advantage to the top of her bent. She had made a slight slip at the beginning at Bracciano, by allowing Paolo Giordano Orsini to wear his hat in her presence because he was a grandee of Spain, and for this the Pope had remonstrated with her, saying that he himself gave no preference to the Roman nobility who were also Spanish grandees, and that the Queen must do the same. Christina had also to conform to the Roman etiquette that gave precedence to cardinals over ambassadors.

This was delicately conveyed to the Duke of Terranova but this gentleman still felt that his own King would be affronted if he himself did not receive from the Queen preferential treatment over the cardinals—especially, need it be added, the cardinals of the hated flying squadron who thronged the Palazzo Farnese. But Terranova had also received explicit instructions from Philip IV that he must see Christina as often as possible, so call on her he must. The problem was how to do so without receiving a slight in public. Finally he asked for a private audience, only to be received by the Queen, without his hat, and given a stool to sit on. The Spanish Ambassador's rage and mortification can hardly be imagined when he heard that Lionne, not even a properly accredited ambassador to the Holy See, had been received by the

Queen *with his hat on his head.* Like poor Giandemaria, Terranova also sent anguished reports to his sovereign about the behaviour of this remarkably difficult Queen.

It is plain that one of the prime causes of Terranova's predicament was that he was not a very intelligent man, and almost certainly a bore, whereas his rivals—the cardinals of the flying squadron and Lionne—were just the reverse (the latter did not finally rise to be a French foreign minister by employing Terranova's tactics). To Christina independence was paramount, she had often said that she had been born free and intended to remain so and now that she was in Rome she had no intention of being dictated to by the Spaniards. So gradually the Queen came to ally herself with the opposite party whose representatives were personally much more attractive to her. There was also the inescapable fact that the sacrifice of her throne for religion (as Christina felt the Most Catholic King should view her abdication) had not brought any commensurate recognition from Spain and, in spite of promises, no financial assistance in her present crisis, while even from the Empire the Queen had not succeeded in extracting anything like her due in the matter of war reparations.

In view of this situation it is not surprising that Christina's thoughts turned to the rival party, who were courting her so assiduously. If the King of Spain did nothing for her, she would see what the King of France had to offer. In order to curry favour in this quarter Christina apparently even indulged in an elaborate intrigue to settle the problem raised by the refusal of that notorious *frondeur*, Cardinal de Retz, to waive his rights to the Archbishopric of Paris, but in the end this came to nothing. It would have seemed that in her present predicament the Queen's most obvious source of aid would have been the Pope himself, even if he had previously warned her that he could give her no "temporal" support. But here too her passion for independence had closed the door.

It had not taken Alexander VII long to realize that this most spectacular of all converts was not going to be a very docile daughter of the Church. No doubt he had heard indirectly of his majordomo's recent discomfiture. Monsignore Farnese had heard that some very audacious pictures had been hung in his family palace and all the fig leaves and discreet draperies removed from the Farnese marbles, and had considered it his duty to protest to the Queen. Curtly Her Majesty had replied that she was not going to be bound by "considerations worthy only of priests." There had also been criticisms of Christina's attire, not for its mannish style, quite the opposite; the usually uncoquettish Queen had suddenly taken to very low-necked dresses (it is tempting to wonder if Azzolino's undoubted attraction had something to do with this) and thus attired had been receiving cardinals. In any event Christina's reaction to this criticism was characteristic—she simply covered her bosom with pearls.

Evidently her conversion to Catholicism had not abated Christina's loathing for false piety and prudishness. Apart from observing the essentials of her new religion, she had no intention of allowing anyone to dictate to her how she should live now, any more than she would have done when she was Queen regnant in Sweden. It was an extremely awkward attitude to adopt in seventeenth-century Rome, where appearances were everything and women were expected to lead a life of semi-oriental privacy. As an illustration of this, a turn-table for serving their food without entering their apartment had actually been installed for the women of the Queen's household in the Palazzo Farnese.

Papal remonstrances about her behaviour, and particularly her lack of religious observance in public, had been tactfully conveyed to the Queen, but without result. In the end Alexander VII himself told her frankly that there was more virtue in reciting publicly an Ave Maria than the whole rosary in secret. Thus the Pope's unwillingness further to tax his already over-burdened exchequer by contributing to the Queen's maintenance can be well understood. It is also possible that he believed that financial stringency might bring her to heel in the end. If so, he could not have made a greater mistake.

Since the days of Suetonius Rome has been a whispering gallery, and its inhabitants were no more charitable in the seventeenth century than they had been in the first. Thus it is not surprising that they regarded Christina's extraordinary behaviour as confirmation of the rumours that had been floating around even before her arrival—that she was not a normal woman, but a hermaphrodite. The Queen's masculine voice, manner and walk, which Father Manderscheydt had noticed in Sweden, were doubly conspicuous when compared with the delicate feminine Roman women. Later, even the staid Giandemaria reported to Parma the current rumour that Christina had been in love with a nun in a convent in the Campo Marzio, where she had made a retreat, and had afterwards sent the object of her affections a superb present.

Needless to say all these stories and rumours were grist to the mill of the outraged Spaniards, who were not slow to report the Pope's genuine disapproval in their dispatches to Madrid. They went much further, however; in order to revenge themselves for the affronts which they considered Christina had put upon them, they nurtured and spread even more offensive rumours, and the Queen was informed of the fact. Things had reached such a point that both Pimentel and della Gueva had asked Madrid to be posted back to the army in Flanders, and this had been agreed to. Christina had by now replaced nearly all the Spaniards in her household by Italians, appointing Francesco Maria Santinelli as della Gueva's successor, and one day while her husband was away, she ordered Madame della Gueva to ride in her carriage with Santinelli. This was regarded by the Spaniards as an appalling affront, and the della Guevas left Palazzo Farnese to live in the Spanish Embassy.

Worse was to follow when at the end of May the della Guevas came to make their formal adieux of the Queen. To his apology for not having served her as he would have wished, Christina replied, in the presence of some Italian members of her court, that she knew how to reward a gentleman and punish a knave and if she ever learnt that della Gueva had slandered her, her punishment would reach him wherever he might be. Accounts vary as to whether Christina then actually said to della Gueva's face that only her respect for the King of Spain prevented her having him beaten, or whether she said this to the pro-Spanish Cardinal de' Medici, but in any event the rupture between the Queen and the Spaniards was complete.

Christina had, however, by no means finished with the Spaniards. She was thirsting for revenge. Giandemaria had reported to Parma that della Gueva and his followers had published abroad that the Queen was "the greatest whore in the world" and no doubt she had heard this too. Chance favoured Christina at this difficult moment. Alexander VII had been away staying at Castel

Gandolfo when her quarrel with the Spaniards reached its height and he now returned to make a surprising announcement. This was that, although after his accession he had declared that there would be no nepotism during his reign and he did not intend to summon his family from Siena or give them any high offices, he had invited his brother Mario Chigi and his nephews Flavio and Agostino to Rome.

The news must have come as a bombshell, especially to the flying squadron who were particularly hostile to nepotism and had supported Alexander VII's election for this very reason. Nor could they or the Romans generally be blamed for fearing the arrival of yet another papal family to be enriched as the Borghese, Barberini and Pamphilj had been. It was in fact the bare-faced manner in which Innocent X's sister-in-law, Donna Olimpia Pamphilj, had drained the papal exchequer and lorded it over Rome, which had caused the final revulsion from such practices and even influenced the King of Spain in delaying Christina's arrival in the city. With an ancestor so famous as a banker as the original Agostino Chigi, it might have been supposed that the family were rich, but in fact Agostino's vast fortune had not survived him very long and Alexander VII's relations were no better off than those of his predecessors had originally been.

In the circumstances it is not surprising that the Pope now turned to a foreigner and not to a Roman for support, instantly sending his brother and nephews to pay their respects to Christina upon their arrival in Rome. To everyone's amazement the Queen, that stickler for etiquette, received them with the honours that she normally only accorded to cardinals. Where a Queen led it was very difficult for others not to follow, and in his gratitude for her support it was natural that the Pope should lend a very sympathetic ear to Christina's complaints about the Spaniard's outrageous behaviour. The upshot of this was that a cardinal was instructed to administer a stiff rebuke to Terranova, while the Queen actually published a manifesto about the dispute, stating that she enjoyed papal support for her actions. Even with this her virago spirit was not appeased: in June Father Guemes was to be dispatched to Madrid to obtain redress from the King of Spain himself.

To the outside world it must have seemed that the Swedish

Queen had succeeded by her clever diplomacy in extracting the utmost that could be expected by way of reparation. But not so Christina. It is probable that for some time now she had been meditating in secret an even greater revenge, or at least an action that would solve for ever her distressing financial problems. No documents have survived to tell us anything about the early stages of this plan, their secrecy would have been such that they were probably immediately destroyed, as indeed were many of the papers connected with the Queen's conversion, which otherwise might have survived in the Jesuit archives in Rome. So all we have to guide us in the early stages of this story is a series of inferences. Already on her journey south through Italy in 1655, Christina had befriended the Prince of Gallicano, who was very *mal vu* by the Spaniards in her entourage because he had been involved in one of the Neapolitan plots against Spain. There were protests about this, but the Prince was a literary figure and the type of man who would quite naturally appeal to the Queen on totally unpolitical grounds. In fact he became a member of her Academy.

Of far greater future consequence was another man whom the Queen had also met on her journey. This was Marchese Gian Rinaldo Monaldeschi, who began to frequent the Palazzo Farnese in February and by April had been appointed one of Christina's equerries. Monaldeschi came of a well-known and once powerful family of the little town of Orvieto in the Papal States. He was a sprig of the provincial nobility like Azzolino and the Santinellis and, like them, had his way to make in the world. But Monaldeschi's past had been much more stormy than any of theirs. He appears to have been both a conspirator and a soldier of fortune, for he had led an armed band to support the abortive French attack on Naples in 1654. There is no doubt that both Monaldeschi and the Prince of Gallicano had maintained contact with the rebel faction in Naples, and the Spanish diplomats were probably right in saying that they had fanned the flames of Christina's resentment against Spain.

Precisely at what stage the activities of these two men changed from simply encouraging the Queen's indignation to letting fall suggestive comments, and finally to making definite proposals, we do not know. But Christina could not have failed to be aware of the disaffection that was rife in the Kingdom of Naples against the Spanish vice-regal government, and also of France's more or less overt encouragement of it. At the end of Masaniello's revolt in 1646–47, the Duc de Guise had attempted to take power, and he had been the leader of the overt French sea-borne attack in 1654, when Monaldeschi had led a band of supporters from the Abruzzi. This Italian irregular supporting force had been surreptitiously raised and equipped by Cardinal Antonio Barberini—a member of the famous flying squadron. Now Christina's desperate financial situation combined with her *rapprochement* with France and her final break with Spain, would have made her welcome a plan that at one blow would solve her money worries, seal her friendship with France and wreak a really spectacular vengeance on Spain. All this—and her dream of leading an army—could be achieved if she headed another expedition against Naples and became its Queen.

At the end of June Christina wrote to Mazarin asking for agreement to her proposal for crossing France on her way to Sweden. That she was already in secret communication with Mazarin is very likely (she had certainly made contact with his intelligence network and given one of them a cipher) but this was a perfectly straightforward letter as there were good reasons for her journey and choice of route. Christina's finances made it imperative that she should come to some arrangement with Charles Gustavus. The King had replied kindly to her about Appelman's mission, but he said frankly that he had no ready cash and told her that her estates were a safer investment than anything else. It was sound advice but not much help to the Queen at this juncture. The shortest route to Sweden, across Austria and Germany, was closed for quarantine owing to an outbreak of plague in Rome, so France was the only alternative. In her letter Christina told Mazarin that as she would be travelling in haste she wished to do so incognito, and asked him not to arrange any formal reception.

The wish for haste and anonymity is understandable, in view of the fact that the Queen had to sell her carriage and horses and Monaldeschi and Francesco Maria Santinelli had pawned or raised private loans on eight large diamonds, but only raised part of her travelling expenses. Christina appealed to the Pope for a loan, and he generously sent her a gift of 10,000 scudi, a purse filled with gold and silver medals coined to celebrate her arrival in Rome. He also offered her the use of galleys of the papal fleet to take her to France. He was probably glad to be relieved of the responsibility of Christina's presence, as the plague was spreading fast; he himself courageously remained in Rome, directing with remarkable efficiency such measures as were available to stop the epidemic. Whatever her plans might be, Christina was desolate at leaving. She wept, and Giandemaria noticed that she kept on taking a miniature out of her pocket and looking at it; he thought it was a portrait of Azzolino. Finally the Queen departed on 20th July still weeping. It was twenty months since Montecuccoli had laid his bet with her that "Amarantha would be passionately in love within a year"—he seems to have lost it by a margin of eight months.

The Queen and her suite were accommodated on three galleys. They sailed from Palo which was not a port but simply an anchorage near one of the Orsini castles and probably chosen to avoid infection, though its choice also indicates that the galleys cannot have been very large. In fact Christina's departure from Rome could not have presented a greater contrast with her arrival; there were no ambassadors and no ceremony, she and her suite travelled in carriages hired by Cardinal Francesco Barberini, while the suite itself was now reduced to a not very distinguished company of whom all but two were Italians. Francesco Maria Santinelli was Marshal of the Court, his brother Lodovico, Monaldeschi and Count Thiene equerries. There were two secretaries, the Frenchman Gilbert (one of the Queen's last links with her Stockholm household) and Davidsson, a Swedish Catholic recruited in Rome who was to remain in Christina's service all her life, as was also young Captain Landini, one of the guards. A chaplain, gentlemen, guards, three maids and other servants made up a company of about sixty.

After a hot and stormy voyage the little fleet arrived at Marseilles at dawn on 29th July. Seeing the Papal flag, and being in terror of the plague reigning in Rome, the populace demonstrated violently against the Queen's landing. However Mazarin had sent one of the King's gentlemen, M. de Lesseins, a cousin of Hugues de Lionne, with instructions that throughout France Christina was to be received with the honours of a reigning sovereign. As a result the royal salute of the cannons of the Château d'If mingled with the yells of a hostile crowd gathered on the quay to prevent the Queen landing. It was a farcical situation, to which characteristically Christina made her own contribution. M. de Lesseins had boarded her ship to tell her of the royal honours awaiting her, but at the same time begged the Queen to make a discreet landing with a few persons in a boat, because the mooring of the galleys at the quay had been forbidden by the municipal authorities. The Queen however was adamant, it was to be the quay or nothing. After a long parley she won, she and her suite were allowed to disembark but afterwards the galleys were to be moored at a safe distance. This initial contretemps over, all went well, as the three days' festivities planned in the Queen's honour made the Marseillais forget their terror of the plague, and there followed a succession of fêtes and banquets. Christina must have found the twenty-four courses of some of the latter slightly overwhelming, but it seems that in the midst of all this gaiety she found time to visit François Malaval, later famous as the blind mystic of Marseilles. Malaval was not a churchman but, rather surprisingly in view of his infirmity, a lawyer and also interested in the natural sciences. This interest was probably the reason for the Queen's visit, they kept in touch and years later Malaval dedicated to her the Italian translation of the *Pratique Façile*, the book on prayer that made him famous.

Honours were showered upon Christina in every city, town and hamlet in her triumphal progress across France. But the state reception really only began in earnest in Lyons where she was met by the King's personal representative, the Duc de Guise, the Comte de Comminges, acting in a similar capacity for the Queen Mother, the Archbishop, Mgr de Villeroy, and her old friends Chanut and Bourdelot. Christina was very well aware that all the honour shown to her had a political motive, and it is unlikely that she entertained any doubts as to what that might be. But if she had, the choice of the Duc de Guise—twice leader of expeditions against Naples—as the King's representative, would have provided her with a clear answer.

Even the highest circles in France, it seems, were full of curiosity about this extraordinary Queen of whom they had heard such diverse accounts and rumours. In downright, soldierly language the Duc de Guise wrote a letter to a friend at court describing his charge, and the Queen Mother's friend and confidante, Madame de Motteville, recorded in her memoirs how this very frank description was read aloud to the King and his mother. The Duke made no pretence whatsoever about his feelings in the letter which reads: "At a time when I am dreadfully bored I would at least like to amuse you by sending you a portrait of the Queen I am accompanying. She isn't tall but has a well-filled figure and a large behind, beautiful arms, white hands, but more like those of a man than a woman; one shoulder is higher than the other, but she hides this defect so well by her bizarre dress, walk and movements, that you could lay bets as to whether it exists or not. Her face is large, but not to a fault, also all her features are marked: the nose aquiline, the mouth big but not disagreeably so, teeth passable, her eyes really beautiful and full of fire; in spite of some marks left by chicken pox her complexion is clear and quite good; the shape of her face is fair but framed by the most extraordinary coiffure. It's a man's wig, very heavy and piled high in front, hanging thick at the sides and here it's fair at the ends, the top of her head is a mass of hair and at the back there is some slight resemblance to a woman's coiffure. Sometimes she wears a hat. Her bodice, laced up cross-wise at the back, is made practically like our pourpoints, her chemise showing all round between it and her skirt, which she wears badly fastened and not very straight. She is always very heavily powdered over a lot of face cream, and practically never wears gloves. She wears men's shoes and her voice and nearly all her actions are masculine. She loves to show off her mastery of horses and she glories in it and is quite as proud of it as her father the great Gustavus might have been. She is very civil and full of flattery, speaks eight languages, but mostly French and that as if she had been born in Paris.* She knows more than all our Academy and the Sorbonne put together, understands painting as well as anyone and knows much more about our court intrigues than I do. In fact she is an absolutely extraordinary person."

The Duke was not the only person in France to find Christina

* This was not just flattery: in his official dispatches Hugues de Lionne had said that Christina's French was as good as his own, and this at a time when she had not yet patched up her quarrel with France.

odd and masculine. This journey too brought its crop of rumours of lesbian affairs. It must be admitted that the Queen asked for trouble by her extraordinary behaviour. It shocked even her fellow amazon, Anne Marie d'Orleans, usually called the Grande Mademoiselle, who had taken part personally in the battles of the Fronde, and was now living in exile from the court in consequence. When she heard that Christina was travelling nearby Mademoiselle rushed to see her. She admitted in her diary that she had heard so much about the Queen's odd clothes that she was "dying of fear lest I should laugh when I saw her." Christina was watching a ballet when Mademoiselle arrived, wearing a flame-coloured jacket embroidered with gold, a gold-embroidered grey skirt and, to Mademoiselle's surprise, looking not at all funny but quite attractive. She admired the Queen's complexion and her blue eyes and in fact described Christina as looking more than anything else "like a pretty little boy." But the Queen's behaviour during the entertainment left Mademoiselle aghast: "She swore to God, slouched in her chair, stretched her legs this way and that, hung them over the arm of her chair; I've never seen anyone except Trivelin and Jodelet, the Italian and French clowns, take up such postures. . . . She fell into deep reveries, let out profound sighs, then all of a sudden collected herself like someone who waked up with a jerk," Mademoiselle recorded in her diary, adding, like the Duc de Guise, "she's completely extraordinary."

Mademoiselle saw Christina only a few days before she arrived in Paris. The Queen had been travelling for over a month, constantly attending ceremonies and parties in great heat, and her health had been troubling her. Fatigue may have accounted to a certain extent for Christina's curious fits of absent-mindedness at the play, certainly she was very tired by the time she arrived in Paris. The splendours of the reception staged in her honour, however, put even those of her arrival in Rome in the shade. Guns boomed and the gates of the city and all the streets were decorated and thronged with crowds variously estimated at 200,000 or 500,000 people. With an escort of 15,000 troops, Christina rode through the city on a grey horse. His name was Unicorn and he was loaned for the occasion by the Duc de Guise, but even such an expert horsewoman as Christina was unable to persuade him to walk under the superb gold and silver canopy, given to her by the City, so instead this had to be carried before her. Although the procession ended at night by torchlight, the Queen went to Notre Dame to hear a Te Deum and was afterwards driven in a gilded chariot to the Louvre, and must have been very thankful to get there as her attendants noticed she was exhausted and irritable. A week of pompous ceremonies followed but from these Christina was able to escape for long enough to see some of the people who were congenial to her—such as the libertine poet Saint-Amant, whom she had known in Sweden, the Scuderys and the Duc de La Rochefoucauld, author of the famous "Maxims."

The court was at Compiègne, and on 15th September Christina left Paris to go there. Cardinal Mazarin came to meet her halfway at the Château de Chantilly where the Queen was to dine and stay the night. Like everyone else in France, the eighteen-year-old Louis XIV was so curious to see his extraordinary guest that he and his brother rode off to Chantilly and, mixing with the crowd in the castle, tried to get a look at her without anyone knowing. Of course the two brothers were spotted by Mazarin, who presented them to Christina as "two of the most accomplished gentlemen in France." She was not deceived however, and replied that to her they looked as if they were "born to wear crowns." Although Louis XIV was then a shy young man he got on well with Christina, and after a friendly conversation returned to Compiègne.

When Christina arrived at Compiègne the next day, Louis, the Queen Mother and the entire court were waiting on the terrace in front of the château to receive her. In her memoires Madame de Motteville gives a vivid description of the scene, with this magnificent assembly grouped against the background of the superb château and the green velvet lawns stretching away in front of them. Shrewdly she noted that Christina was being received not only as a Queen, but "as a Queen well-liked by the Minister [Mazarin]." Christina on her arrival obviously took Madame de Motteville's breath away—here was a royal visitor coming to the most splendid court in the world without even a lady-in-waiting, with her wig uncurled and her hair blowing over a face bereft of powder. Madame de Motteville also noticed that Christina's clothes were absolutely extraordinary—more like a man's than a woman's, with skirts so short that her feet showed, while her bodice was so badly put on that it had slipped off one of her shoulders, showing that her man's shirt was only fastened at the neck with a pin; even her hands were grubby! Christina was travelling light and was evidently wearing her usual grey dress, but as she certainly also possessed the beautifully embroidered jacket admired by Mademoiselle, it seems that she may well have chosen deliberately to arrive *en déshabillé*, for she knew full well that she could not compete with the French court in matters of dress and probably preferred to show her splendid indifference to the whole matter.

But now, more astonishingly perhaps than on any other occasion in her life, by sheer personality Christina triumphed. For Madame de Motteville admits that gradually, as she became accustomed to this extraordinary woman, she ceased to notice her strange appearance and realized instead that she had beautiful eyes and that in her face pride was mixed with gentleness: "In fact," she said, "I found to my surprise that she pleased me." The Queen Mother too, told Madame de Motteville that at first, like everyone else, she had been terrified of Christina, but that gradually, hearing her talk, her own attitude had changed completely; it is true that Christina had admired in the most graceful manner the beauty of the Queen Mother's hands and arms. Even the wags of the court, who were expecting to make hay of this "Gothic Queen" as they all called her, were evidently impressed by Christina's personality and the dignity with which she treated them, though, as the astute Madame de Motteville realized, the good impression Christina had made on the King and Queen Mother and the Cardinal's favour probably also had something to do with this. But Christina's entourage made a poor showing, the Santinellis and Monaldeschi Madame de Motteville dismissed as "two or three men of poor appearance to whom for courtesy she [Christina] gave the title of counts." Christina's two women "were more like shop assistants than ladies of standing." In fact Madame de Motteville was horrified to learn that the Swedish Queen actually shared her bed with them, and apparently in private also her meals.

The next day, however, Christina herself rose even more in everyone's estimation. She had taken considerable trouble with her appearance, her wig was freshly curled and powdered and she was wearing the dress that Mademoiselle had admired. It must have suited her well as Madame de Motteville even went so far as to say that if the Queen "had been interested in compliments about her appearance, that day she certainly deserved them." On this day too Christina appears to have been exceedingly discreet, at first talking hardly at all and then only to make polite comments. Obviously she was feeling her way in what she knew full well to be the most intelligent and sophisticated court in Europe, but also the most sarcastic and full of gossip. Later Christina relaxed a bit and amused everyone by showing that she knew all the *potins* just as well as they did, twitting some of the men about their love affairs, but also, as she loved to do, making people realize that she knew more about French art collections than some of the actual owners who were present.

It is understandable that even Christina should have been nervous at the beginning of her visit. This was the critical moment of her whole journey, her secret negotiations with Mazarin were about to begin and inevitably the result would be a turning point in her life. During eight years the Queen had prepared her abdication, vowing that she wished to retire into private life. Now the astonishing woman was seeking another crown, and one that could not be attained without bloodshed. Naples was no easy prize, two unsuccessful French expeditions had already proved that. But to Christina her whole future depended on the success of this venture. So with a smiling face she embarked upon the week of festivities arranged in her honour—fêtes, banquets, hunts, ballets and plays—evidently gathering assurance as she went along. But all the time behind this brilliant social façade the secret discussions went on, and Mazarin evidently found an able negotiator in this strange Queen.

On the face of it, Christina had little to offer. She was penniless and Mazarin knew it—during the last two years instead of receiving 400,000 riksdaler from Sweden she had received only 100,000—and anyway his spies must have told him of the jewels pawned and the horses and carriage sold in Rome. Nevertheless she held one trump card. The Neapolitan project formed an important part of the Cardinal's overall strategy in the Spanish war at that moment. Already in March an agreement had been made with Daniele Spinola as representative of the Neapolitan nobility which wished to cast off the Spanish yoke, one of its conditions being that Louis XIV's young brother Philippe, Duc d'Anjou, should become King of Naples. But as Louis XIV was only eighteen and not yet married, Philippe was heir apparent to the French throne, and until the succession was assured by Louis having children there would be strong opposition in France to Philippe's going to Naples. In vain had other candidates, including nearly all the Italian princes, been suggested to the Neapolitan leaders, they refused to accept as their future kings men whose ancestry and position they considered to be little superior to their own. Moreover in the eyes of the world, the French royal family had a legitimate claim to the Neapolitan throne.*

This somewhat farcical situation had placed Mazarin in a quandary, until evidently his agents in Italy had informed him that Christina was already in contact with the dissident Neapolitans. This Queen without a throne suited the Cardinal's book perfectly, she was extremely unlikely ever to get married and have heirs of her own, but in the meantime she could keep the throne of Naples warm, as it were, for Philippe d'Anjou or one of his children. Also, conveniently, the Neapolitans were quite accustomed to Queens regnant, for they had already had two. Through her Neapolitan contacts Christina must have been well aware of all this, with the result that in the treaty which was now concluded between her and Mazarin, she was able to extract very favourable conditions for herself.† After making quite certain of the reversion of Naples to the French crown in the event of Christina's death—Christina, the

* In 1266 the saintly King Louis IX's brother, Charles Duc d'Anjou, won the battle of Benevento in which Manfred, the last Hohenstaufen King of Naples and Sicily, was killed. Charles d'Anjou had been offered the Neapolitan throne by the Pope who was suzerain of the realm, and the Angevin dynasty ruled both Naples and Sicily until the famous Sicilian Vespers in 1282. As a result of their hatred of the French the Sicilians then offered their island to Ferdinand of Aragon, because his wife was Manfred's only surviving legitimate child, and eventually the Aragonese recovered Naples as well. It was as heir of the Angevins that Charles VIII invaded Italy in 1494 in order to recover the Neapolitan kingdom for the French crown. He was, however, unable to consolidate his conquest, which afterwards became a Spanish dominion governed by viceroys. This was still the position when the Franco-Spanish war broke out in 1635.

† Although the existence of such a treaty was for long denied, a copy of it still exists in the archive of the French Foreign Office. The original document was held by Louis XIV himself.

nobility and the people were to make a declaration to this effect, and in taking their oath of allegiance the two latter parties were also to swear to accept Philippe d'Anjou as heir—Mazarin left the Queen a free hand, both as titular leader of the expeditionary force and as sovereign afterwards. Naturally the treaty provided for a permanent alliance between Louis XIV and the future Queen of Naples, but the entire burden of placing her on the throne rested with France. On his King's behalf Mazarin undertook that all France's influence should be used to this end, promising an invasion fleet superior to anything that Spain could put into the Mediterranean, with a landing force of 4,000 infantry and 200 cavalry, as well as raising a cavalry force of 400 to escort the Queen on her dash to Naples. To Christina it must have seemed that at last her dream of leading an army was coming true.

Future glory did not, however, distract the Queen from the practical problems of the present. The French Ambassador in Sweden was instructed that Louis XIV felt bound to regard Christina's interests as his own, and to press for a financial settlement for her with the King of Sweden as "a matter of vital importance to Franco-Swedish friendship." The Queen must also have managed to get some ready money out of Mazarin (probably as part of the sums she claimed as her share of French war subsidies still owing to Sweden), as she now abandoned all idea of going to Sweden. But as her financial reasons for going there had been the excuse for her leaving Italy, to avoid suspicion she and Mazarin gave it to be understood that while in France Christina had received a latter from Charles Gustavus agreeing to a settlement. On 23rd September, the day after the treaty was signed, the Queen left Compiègne for Italy.

The Queen Mother accompanied her departing guest for the first two leagues of the way, then taking leave of her with considerable signs of affection. Her confidante, Madame de Motteville, was sure that a good deal of this was genuine. Madame de Motteville was herself evidently surprised at her own reactions to Christina. Before the Queen arrived she was not well predisposed toward her because she had heard all the European gossip that Christina "had left the throne because she was forced to and because of her frivolity, and that in Sweden and Flanders she had loved Pimentel." After she had seen Christina at close quarters for a week, Madame de Motteville was prepared to admit that "nearly all her actions are in some way extravagant . . . in no way does she resemble a woman, she hasn't even the necessary modesty . . . she seems rough, brusque and libertine in all she says, about religion and on matters in which feminine propriety should oblige her to be reticent, she swears by the name of God and her libertine ideas affect all her actions." Nevertheless Madame de Motteville found that when one had actually seen Christina and particularly heard her talk "it was not difficult to pardon all her irregularities."

This is a most illuminating comment upon the charm that this extraordinary woman could exercise when she wished—a charm that none of Christina's portraits have ever conveyed, with the possible exception of one by Bourdon. It is all the more telling in that it comes from a woman who was a shrewd observer and enjoyed a very privileged position at the French court. What is even more remarkable is that when later Christina's reputation reached its nadir as far as that court was concerned, Madame de Motteville, whose own virtue was beyond question, was convinced that in spite of the apparent looseness of her behaviour, Christina was also virtuous, at least while she was in France. Living as she did in a highly sophisticated and often licentious world, Madame de Motteville was not likely to be hoodwinked over such a matter, and she is categorical about it. She says "there was nothing in her [Christina] that was contrary to honour, I mean to the honour that depends from chastity." She backed up this assertion, with the sarcastic shrewdness of one long accustomed to court life, with the words "had she [Christina] laid herself open to insinuations in this respect, charitable people at court would never have omitted to let everyone know about it."

Nevertheless two incidents on Christina's return journey to Italy show only too clearly how she brought upon herself accusations of libertinism in both faith and morals. At Lagny she stopped to see the notorious courtesan Ninon de Lenclos, succinctly described by Madame de Motteville as "celebrated for her vice, her libertinism, her intelligence and exquisite wit." Ninon was more or less incarcerated in a convent, but Christina is alleged to have written to Louis XIV recommending her to him as a suitable ornament for his court.

A short stop at Dijon produced another disquieting incident. In conversation with the Queen, the erudite author C-B. Morisot found occasion to make her a graceful compliment about her conversion. Christina brought him up short, saying "My religion is that of the philosophers, I prefer it to all others. This religion is indeterminate, its limits are uncertain, but it was well defined by Lucretius in his *De Rerum Natura*. It is the only one of which I approve." That a classical scholar such as the Queen should admire the wonderful verse in which Lucretius described the material nature of the universe was understandable, but that a recent convert to Catholicism should uphold the beliefs of a poet who thought that immortality was simply an empty dream, and preached something very like present-day materialism, naturally caused shocked astonishment in the seventeenth century.

Before she quitted French soil on 8th October Christina wrote a letter of thanks to Mazarin. Even at the remote little frontier town of Pont de Beauvoisin rumours had evidently reached her of Franco-Spanish peace negotiations. Although only two years before Christina had been busy representing herself to the warring nations and the world in general as the ideal intermediary for such a laudable purpose, she now wrote to Mazarin: "The news today threatens the world with a great calm, I love the storm and fear the calm. . . ." Peace was all very well if it served Her Majesty's purposes. From Turin Monaldeschi was dispatched to rally the Duke of Modena to the Neapolitan cause, and with further instructions to return to Paris to keep Mazarin on the *qui vive*.

By 19th November the Queen was installed in the old Della Rovere Palace at Pesaro, where nearly a year ago she had been so gaily entertained on her way to Rome by the Santinelli brothers. The plague still raging in Rome was the reason given for the choice of this remote little town in the province of the Marche as Christina's winter residence, but money shortage and the fact that Pesaro was a less conspicuous base from which to keep contact with Mazarin and the north Italian princes involved in the Naples project, were much more likely reasons. As Pesaro was in the Papal States and the Queen was living in a palace belonging to the government, the Pope's sanction must, of course, have been obtained. However this would not have been difficult in view of Christina's friendship with Azzolino, who was a native of the province, on excellent terms with the Legate, Cardinal Homodei, and an old and close friend of the Vice-Legate, Monsignore Gasparo Lascaris.

All the splendours of her reception in France and the excitement of her secret negotiations do not seem in any way to have modified Christina's feelings for Azzolino. The Venetian Ambassador in Paris had been so struck by her enthusiasm for the young Cardinal and her constant references to him that he reported the matter to his government. They had kept up a constant correspondence, but it was not until she was safely back in Pesaro that Christina wrote to tell Azzolino her real impressions of the economic and political situation in France and of the court. Naturally, in view of her present situation, these were very favourable, and she even went so far as to warn Azzolino that his friend Cardinal de Retz had less support in France than he led people to believe. Interestingly, Christina shared the view of modern historians, which is contrary to the beliefs of many contemporaries, that although the Queen Mother was much attached to Mazarin, and by her faith in him had made him absolute master of France, they were not lovers. Curiously, for a woman who had once said that she had never experienced love, Christina had a good deal to say on this subject in her letter, and she said it with considerable perception. Rightly she foresaw that Louis XIV's head would in the end always rule his passions, adding that in spite of his three years infatuation for Mazarin's niece Marie Mancini "he has probably never even touched her fingertips" and that it would pass. Characteristically she also declared that Mazarin would never be such a fool as to allow the King to marry his niece, because "marriage is the sovereign remedy against love and the marriage bed its tomb" and the wily Cardinal would not thus jeopardize his influence over the King who adored him. Marie, Christina considered to be intelligent and adroit, "she knows very well how to appear cruel and takes great pleasure in seeing the greatest King in the world languishing at her feet, although I am sure she has no intention of allowing him to die of love, but you know the wiles of the Roman ladies." For a Queen whom most people regarded as being almost entirely masculine because of her manner and behaviour, this is a surprisingly feline and feminine letter.

Lascaris, who was Christina's constant visitor, in his letters to Azzolino throws further sidelights on this usually carefully concealed aspect of Christina's character. The Vice-Legate came of the ancient Constantinople family, his uncle was Grand Master of the Order of Malta, and he was able, cultivated, worldly and probably bored in provincial Pesaro, so that the Queen's arrival and Azzolino's obvious attraction for her must have provided him with a good deal of welcome amusement. Lascaris kept his friend the Cardinal well posted as to what was going on. Although he may have exaggerated a little to flatter Azzolino about his conquest, this worldly Italian prelate's letters show that Christina could be attractive to men. Lascaris found her provocative, even seductive, and in the manner of the time did not hesitate to say so in the broadest terms to Azzolino. In one of his letters he wrote: "Her Majesty is more beautiful and devoted than ever.* Yesterday she was wearing a black velvet dress with blue ribbons and a beautiful collar. It was enough to turn one's head, especially when she took from the table a French comedy and began to read it by the light of a single candle. She read the part of Diana making love to Endymion, and read it so well. . . ."

But for all their joking these two friends were not happy about Christina because, as sensible men of the world, they had immediately taken the measure of her entourage. Their disdain of Monaldeschi and the Santinellis equalled that of Madame de Motteville—in his letters Lascaris refers to them as ruffians, and his descriptions of Christina's "ladies" are scarcely more flattering. To his credit, Azzolino worried about Christina's circumstances, and through Lascaris he tried to influence her to run her affairs in a more orderly and economical fashion. Lascaris even tackled Francesco Maria Santinelli about the extravagance of the Queen's household, remonstrating with him about the needless expense of so many guards, only to receive the braggart retort "better to do without bread than guards"—this economy would not have suited Santinelli's pocket.

Both Lascaris and Azzolino would have been a great deal more anxious had they known what was really going on. But apart from undue extravagance Christina seemed to be leading a sensible life at Pesaro; although amusing herself with parties and plays and trips into the country, she also took part in all the great religious

* Here Lascaris is making a play on the Italian word *devota* which can mean both pious and devoted; obviously he was chaffing Azzolino.

ceremonies and visited convents. Nevertheless from time to time an almost uncontrollable longing to go to Rome and see Azzolino evidently came over her. It was not so much the plague but the fact that she had no money which prevented her and, possibly, the fear that she might not be able to conceal her secret plans from this very able man who attracted her so strongly. In fact Christina was in a fever-heat of impatience to get on with the invasion of Naples. Ludovico Santinelli had been dispatched to Paris to back up Monaldeschi in impressing upon Mazarin the need for dispatch in carrying out the expedition. They returned in February, with a little money and promises, but, having signed a treaty with England, Mazarin was now planning an all-out attack on Flanders, and the Naples scheme was, for the moment at any rate, in abeyance.

It seems to have been in a moment of discouragement about this time—indeed only a few days after she had written to the Duke of Modena complaining that Mazarin did not even bother to answer her letters—that on 27th March Christina wrote to Belle. This is the last of her letters to the Countess Sparre of which we possess any record. In it the Queen appears to be more resigned and definitely to realize that she will probably never see her friend again, but she still wishes to assure her of her admiration and love.

It seems that in the isolation of Pesaro Christina was looking back on her life, particularly to 1645—that crucial year in which the emotional crisis that led to her abdication and conversion had its roots. For, in assuring Belle of her continued love, she recalls "A friendship which has been tried by three years' absence should not be suspect to you if you have not forgotten the rights which you have over me, and if you remember that it is already twelve years that you are in possession of my love." Twelve years ago Christina had been torn by her unreciprocated love for Magnus. Now she feared that the crown of Naples—which would solve all her problems—might be slipping through her fingers, and she could not even see or tell Azzolino of her worries, but pictured him surrounded by "the wiles of the Roman ladies." So in the midst of her troubles Christina writes to Belle, remembering the consolation she had afforded to her and recalling "the power that you have over me." But this letter does not ring with the same sense of loneliness and longing as the other two already quoted, and at the end Christina says "adieu, live happily and remember me," as if she realized that this chapter in her life was closed.

If Christina was to play her part as planned in the Naples expedition, she would have to start from Rome, but she would also need money to get there and establish her household, and Mazarin had sent her only 15,000 écus. However she dispatched Francesco Maria Santinelli to Rome to discover the situation there, estimate what the expense of the move would be and make discreet enquiries as to whether the Palazzo Farnese would again be loaned to her when she came back to Rome in the autumn. In the meantime the Queen wrote somewhat sarcastically to Mazarin about the money. According to her calculations France still owed Sweden 900,000 écus of subsidies from the Thirty Years War. But the weeks passed and, apart from keeping in contact with the Duke of Modena, who was party to the Neapolitan project, nothing happened. The flood of letters that Christina addressed to Mazarin, filled with grandiose schemes including marriage projects for Louis XIV, only produced a few discouraging replies telling her to wait and not to come to France.

At last Christina could stand it no more. Here she was wasting her time in Pesaro, whereas if she could only see Mazarin she might be able to galvanize him into definite action for the following autumn—at the very least she might be able to get some money. Without waiting for an invitation or even permission to come to France, Christina set out from Pesaro on 22nd June 1657. Before she left she had dispatched Francesco Maria Santinelli to Rome with 6,000 écus of Mazarin's money. With this Santinelli was to redeem four of her diamonds which had been left as security with the Marquis of Palombara for a loan of 2,000 scudi, and to deposit them with Azzolino. The rest of the money was to be spent in preparing the Palazzo Farnese to receive the Queen in the autumn, Santinelli having quite untruthfully told her that the Duke of Parma was again prepared to put it at her disposal. Though Christina did not know it, two letters from Mazarin crossed with her on her journey, in which the Cardinal warned her not to come to France. It was the first indication that this expedition was to end very differently from the last.

Lascaris was clearly uneasy about the Queen's journey. He seems to have had an instinct, rather than definite suspicions, that things were not altogether what they seemed. On 8th July he had already written to Christina asking her if his letters arrived with their three seals intact, and he took the precaution of binding a packet of Azzolino's with fine wire. Moreover a few days later he wrote a very cryptic letter to Azzolino saying that he would like to talk to him, and asking if it would not be possible for Azzolino to come to stay with him for a couple of days. Lascaris's letter must have been something of a shock to Christina, but probably it also confirmed already existing suspicions. On 15th October however, within a few days of her arrival at Fontainebleau she was evidently certain that her correspondence was being tampered with. She wrote to the Postmaster at Lyons, where she had stayed for some time, giving instructions that her letters were not to be locked in the postal valise in the normal way (the valises were opened at various places along the route), but given to the courier who could then deliver them to her personally. She also directed that her household's correspondence should come to her, so that it could be read before being handed on.

This time there had been no triumphal progress across France, not even an invitation to come to court or an interview with Mazarin. The Swedish Queen had simply been given a small apartment in the conciergerie of the Château of Fontainebleau which Louis XIII had used when he went there for small intimate hunting parties. The apartment comprised only four rooms—a bedroom, closet, ante-chamber and study, looking out on what is now a rather gloomy corner of the park. It was in fact a rather isolated lodging, connected to the main body of the palace only by the immensely long Galerie des Cerfs, so called because of the hunting trophies of deer's heads that are ranged along its walls, the walls themselves being decorated with frescoes of the French royal châteaux.

While waiting for the invitation to court, then in northern France, which never came, Christina kept herself furiously busy with administrative matters. This was in fact an excellent cover for her real reason for coming to France, as again she made use of her financial difficulties as an excuse for wishing to see Mazarin. Appelman, now the Intendant of her Pomeranian estates, was summoned and then dispatched on another mission to Charles Gustavus. This time he was to propose that the King of Sweden should take over Norrköping and the island of Öland and in exchange make Christina an allowance of 100,000 riksdaler a year out of the subsidies which he should receive from France. The Queen offered to undertake the French end of these negotiations herself.

Christina also wanted to effect another exchange with Charles Gustavus. She proposed to make over to him all her claims on the residue of the war indemnities from the Empire, in return for his agreeing to let her have the right to collect the 900,000 écus still said to be owing from French subsidies promised during the Thirty Years War. Apart from the hope of raising some money somewhere, these proposals had the double advantage of giving the Queen a good excuse for long-drawn-out negotiations with Mazarin in France. If they succeeded they would conveniently free her from any financial dealings with the Empire, which might become awkward to negotiate after Christina had seized Naples from the Emperor's cousin, the King of Spain. Silfvercrona, the Queen's agent in Holland, was also charged to make arrangements for redeeming her jewels pawned in Flanders, and dispatching her library and other valuables from Antwerp to Italy; no doubt with the idea of their being conveniently close at hand so that they could be installed in the palace at Naples when she got there.

Under cover of these open and legitimate arrangements, Christina was also feverishly planning even the smallest details of the Naples expedition. She was now in touch with quite a number of Neapolitan émigrés, one of them, the Duke of Castelnuovo, even having entered her service. New uniforms and liveries for the guards, pages and lackeys of her Neapolitan household were ordered in quantity from French tailors; they were to be of violet stuff trimmed with crimson and white braid. Helmets, trumpets and swords were also ordered, even complete new outfits for the maids, while for the Queen herself there was an entire trousseau including six masculine pourpoints, each with sword to match, and a pair of men's riding boots—evidently Christina meant to take her duties as Commander-in-Chief seriously.

Meanwhile Francesco Maria Santinelli was making hay while the sun shone in Rome. Although there was no question of Christina again being loaned the Palazzo Farnese, by some means Santinelli had managed to get himself a small apartment there—

Christina as she appeared on her triumphal entry into Rome in 1655, by J. Testan.

Pope Alexander VII by Bernini.

Cardinal Decio Azzolino by Besinini

The *Giostra delle Caroselle*, the most spectacular entertainment given by the Barberini family during the carnival of 1656 in honour of Christina, painted by F. Gagliardi and F. Lauri.

The Palazzo Riario in Rome, where Christina resided from 1659 for most of the rest of her life.
The sketches (top) were sent to her in Hamburg by Cardinal Azzolino to show the Queen the proposed arrangement of the famous Room of the Muses.

he was a plausible rogue. He did indeed redeem the Queen's diamonds from the Marquis of Palombara, but promptly proceeded to pledge them again for a higher sum, pocketing the money himself. Nor was this all. The trusting Queen had allowed him access to her remaining possessions in Rome, with the result that Santinelli helped himself to such of her plate as he wanted, having his own arms substituted for hers, and sold the rest. To northerners of any period it is difficult to imagine how Santinelli ever believed that he would not be found out. Possibly he hoped that in the general upheaval over Naples such small matters would be forgotten, but his type is still part of the Italian scene today—sheer stupidity often endows them with the belief that their most glaring peculations will somehow escape detection. However Santinelli had a peer, and by now a bitter rival, in Monaldeschi, who was being kept informed of what went on by a certain Peruzzi.

By using this information at the right moment, Monaldeschi evidently hoped to oust Francesco Maria Santinelli from his privileged position in Christina's entourage, but his own activities later inspired him with an idea which he believed to be an even more subtle and definitive means of disposing of Santinelli. As he travelled across France with the Queen, however, Monaldeschi noticed that the number of letters coming to him through the post was diminishing. During the stop at Lyons he tried to make other arrangements, but communications were slow and this was ineffectual. Finally, at Fontainebleau, he waited anxiously day after day for letters that never came. In his tortuous mind Monaldeschi must have wondered who was responsible, possibly the hated Francesco Maria's brother, Ludovico, possibly French spies, possibly the Queen herself. It is not difficult to imagine his state of mind during those autumn weeks at Fontainebleau.

By now, however, Christina was in no doubt. For more than a month she had managed to intercept both Monaldeschi's incoming and out-going mail. She knew that Louis XIV and Mazarin were due back in Paris at the beginning of November. They arrived on the fifth, and the Queen wrote immediately to ask for a conference. In spite of the months of delay caused by the campaign in Flanders, in the autumn preparations for the Naples expedition were really going ahead. With great secrecy a fleet was being concentrated in the Mediterranean and troops in Provence. Christina was aware of this but also, after the rumours of peace, that her last chance had probably come. Now more than ever secrecy and complete surprise were essential to success, so on 6th November she acted.

That morning Père Le Bel, Prior of the Monastery of the Trinity at Fontainebleau, was surprised to receive a summons to go to the Queen of Sweden who was staying at the château. He had already paid his respects when she arrived, and could not imagine why she wanted to see him now. The Prior was conducted to the Queen's ante-chamber, where she said she wished to speak to him undisturbed, and asked him to accompany her into the Galerie des Cerfs. Here Christina said that she knew that because of his cloth she could trust the priest, but nevertheless asked him if under the seal of confession he would keep secret what she was going to tell him. Père Le Bel assured the Queen of his absolute discretion, whereupon she handed him a small paper packet, sealed with three seals but with no superscription, and asked him to keep it until she asked for it, saying that then he could give it back to her even in the presence of others. Christina also asked the Prior to make a special mental note of the day, exact time and the place at which she had handed him the packet. He therefore recorded that on that day, 5th November 1657, he was back at his monastery by 10 a.m. This and the other events he later witnessed, the Prior afterwards set down in a statement, probably made for the Papal Nuncio in Paris (an early copy exists in the British Museum).

Four days later, at one p.m. on 10th November, the Prior was again summoned to the château by the Queen. Taking the packet with him, Père Le Bel was this time ushered straight into the Galerie des Cerfs. Here he saw the Queen standing talking to a man who was addressed as Marquis, another man was standing near her and two more a few paces away. The Prior saluted the Queen and she asked him for the packet, looked at it closely to see if the seals were intact, and then opened it. She handed the letters and documents it contained to the Marquis, asking him if he recognized them. He denied it, for they were copies in the Queen's handwriting, but the Prior noticed that his voice was shaking. The Queen now showed the Marquis the original papers, calling him a traitor, and finally he was forced to recognize his own writing and signature. The Queen then questioned the Marquis, who answered as best he could, trying to lay the blame on other people, finally he threw himself at the Queen's feet and asked for grace. This part of the Prior's relation concludes with the sinister words "the three men drew their swords and did not sheath them until the Marquis's execution was over."

According to Le Bel, Monaldeschi now rose to his feet and followed Christina from place to place in the gallery, begging, pleading and trying to excuse himself, while she listened apparently entirely unmoved by anger or pity. Finally she turned to Le Bel and said, "See, be my witness that I am not being rash or hasty to this man, that I am giving this traitor, this perfidious man, good time, more time than he can expect from one to whom he has done so much harm, so as to justify himself if he can." Finally Monaldeschi gave Christina some papers and some small keys out of his pocket, and Le Bel noted that "this trial had lasted at least two hours." At this point the Queen came towards the priest and said in a louder voice, "Honourable Father, I am going to retire and leave this man to you, prepare him for death, take care of his soul. If this verdict had been passed on myself I could not feel worse agony." Both Père Le Bel and Monaldeschi now threw themselves at the Queen's feet and begged for mercy. But she replied that it was impossible, saying the traitor was all the more guilty because, as he very well knew, that believing him to be a faithful subject, the Queen had told him her thoughts and secrets. She did not want to mention the kindness that she had heaped on him, she could not have done more for a beloved brother, and indeed this was how she had always regarded the Marquis. "His conscience alone should be his executioner for this ingratitude," and with these words the Queen left the gallery.

Monaldeschi now begged the priest on his knees to intercede with Christina, though Ludovico Santinelli and the two guards threatened him with their weapons to try to make him begin his confession. Finally even Santinelli was moved by the scene, and himself left the gallery to try to persuade Christina to mercy. After a while he returned looking very sad, and told Monaldeschi that the Queen had ordered him to proceed with the execution, and that he must die. Monaldeschi now became hysterical, then again he begged the priest to intercede for him. Père Le Bel went to see Christina, and found her sitting calmly waiting. In his relation the priest stresses the Queen's absolute calm throughout, but no appeals would move her. She said that in the past she had condemned many to be broken on the wheel who had not deserved it as much as this traitor. Le Bel then tried to point out to her that after all she was a guest in a castle of the King of France. But the Queen was adamant, replying that she was not moved by hatred, but was simply passing judgment on a crime of treachery "which had never had its like and concerned the whole world." Moreover, she added, she had the sovereign's right to do justice to her subjects and was answerable for her actions only to God, and what she had to do now was not unprecedented. However the Prior got the impression from the Queen's tone of voice that if she had felt that it was possible to retract, she would have done so, but that she knew things had gone too far, and that if he was not executed now Monaldeschi might escape.

Le Bel returned to the gallery, torn between his horror and his duty as a priest to this man who was undoubtedly about to die. Weeping, he told Monaldeschi he must make his confession, and the wretched man began, but was in such a state of terror that he could not find the words. The Queen's Italian chaplain now appeared and talked for a while with Monaldeschi. He went away, taking Santinelli with him, evidently to make a last attempt to save Monaldeschi. But they soon returned and told Monaldeschi that he must make his peace with God, as he must die without delay. After the confession an appalling scene followed; the three armed men drove Monaldeschi to the far end of the gallery and one of them lunged at him with his sword, trying to run him through. Monaldeschi parried the blow with his hand, losing three fingers and, to their horror, they discovered that under his clothes he was wearing a coat of mail, which meant that the deed could not be done quickly. There were more blows, and Monaldeschi cried out to the priest that he had a further confession to make. After he had received absolution the three men closed in on him where he lay on the floor. More blows rained down on Monaldeschi's head but still the unfortunate man lived. Finally he signed to his assailants to give him the *coup de grace* in his throat, but even this did not kill him. In spite of his horrible injuries Monaldeschi crawled to the feet of the Queen's chaplain, who at a sign from Le Bel also gave him absolution. At last, with a final stab in the throat, the deed was done, Monaldeschi collapsed and drew his last breath fifteen minutes later. Père Le Bel recorded that this was at some time between half past three and a quarter to four. The body was removed to the monastery church for burial and the Queen sent Père Le Bel money for masses to be said for the repose of Monaldeschi's soul.

Even in that day and age a cold shudder passed through Paris when tales of this mysterious slaughter began to leak out. At first very few knew exactly what had happened, as there were only four or five witnesses to the scene—the three guards and the two priests, one of whom was not present throughout. But it was not possible for a screaming man to be threatened and done to death by three swordsmen, in a long-drawn-out agony that seems to have lasted for the best part of an hour, without some people in the château having an inkling of what was going on. In all countries in the seventeenth century justice was rough, ready and cruel, in France itself a man could be consigned to a living tomb without a trial, simply by a *lettre de cachet*. But executions were carried out by the machinery of the law, or at least by the command of the King or ministers who were ruling the country. It was the idea of a woman giving orders to her servants to kill a man, and then sitting in the next room waiting for his end that horrified people, particularly because she had done this when a guest in a palace of the King of France. Inevitably these facts became known, and in their memoirs both the Grande Mademoiselle and Madame de Motteville record the horror of the King, the Queen Mother and the entire court.

At first everyone was so shocked that they do not seem even to have looked for a motive, regarding it as a senseless crime committed by a "barbarous princess." The tales that Christina had sat and laughed and chatted while the slaughter was going on, or even mocked the terrified Monaldeschi for his cowardice, gave colour to this picture of senseless savagery. But enraged and horrified as he was, Mazarin knew better. He must also have known from his intelligence service—what Christina did not—that even before she took the law into her own hands, thus desperately trying to prevent a leakage of the Naples plans, it was too late. The leak had already occurred. Today in the Vatican archive there lie dispatches from the papal nuncios in Paris and Naples, both written at the end of October and beginning of November, giving reports of information received of an impending French attack on Naples, those from Paris even mentioning Christina's involvement. The nuncios were mystified and not altogether convinced, there had in the past been so many rumours of attacks on the Italian coast, but the Naples Viceroy was also informed and evidently seriously alarmed, for he began strengthening the defences. Still, if no further sign had been forthcoming suspicions might have been lulled, and a surprise attack achieved later. Even Monaldeschi's death might have been hushed up or passed off as vendetta among Italians, leaving only those to whom he had sold his information wondering exactly what had happened.

This is precisely what Mazarin tried to achieve. He sent his confidant, Abbé Ondadei, and Christina's old friend Chanut to see her, to try to persuade her to agree that Monaldeschi's death should be attributed to a vendetta. Evidently he also instructed Chanut to do everything in his power to frighten the Queen into complying, even to threatening her with the fury of the Paris mob if her responsibility became known. Christina refused absolutely and indignantly to hear of such a thing. With a hand so shaking with rage that the letter is covered with blots, on 15th November she wrote to Mazarin. She assured the Cardinal that Chanut had carried out his instructions faithfully, and said "if he has not succeeded in filling my soul with panic fears, it is not for lack of having represented (these terrors) as awfully as he was able. But to tell the truth we northerners are fierce and not naturally given to fears . . . I ask you to believe that I would willingly do anything to please you, except be afraid . . . I find it a great deal easier to strangle people than to be afraid of them. As to what I have done about Monaldeschi, I can tell you that if I had not done it, I would not go to bed tonight without doing it, and I have no reason to repent it, but a hundred thousand ones to be delighted. These are my feelings in the matter, if they please you I am delighted, if not, I will not cease from having them, and will remain all my life your affectionate friend, Christina."

It took no little courage for a woman all alone thus to defy the real ruler of France, but Christina was not the daughter of the Lion of the North for nothing. Her action was brave but it was also singularly ill-advised. Monaldeschi's death could not be concealed, but the reason could. What Mazarin wished to do was to hush up the word treachery, but Christina clung to it resolutely as the justification of her act and for exercising her royal authority. She seems to have remained blind to the fact that to publish abroad the word treachery inevitably invited the question—what treachery? Mazarin saw this only too clearly, and although there could be no question now of Christina getting Naples, the project, or even the threat of it, could still be useful in the war against Spain, and no foolish woman was going to be allowed to wreck it.

Inevitably, with all the means of a powerful state at his disposal, Mazarin won. His agents acted swiftly. Even before Christina wrote her furious letter to him, stories that Monaldeschi had been slain in a vendetta were all over Paris, the foreign diplomats reporting them in their dispatches. Further to confuse the issue, Mazarin inspired a Neapolitan in Paris to write a pamphlet in which it was said that the Queen had sentenced Monaldeschi as a liar and a forger. The Neapolitan, who was an old contact of his and a member of one of the dissident groups, probably hoped like the cardinal that thus the secret of the expedition might be saved and at some time later his country liberated from Spain. Not long afterwards yet another Italian wrote a defence of Monaldeschi. In it he said that the Marquis had written an anonymous letter in a disguised hand, with the intention of turning the Queen against Santinelli. The letter contained a warning that the Queen should look after her good name and reputation, and in a fit of irresponsible rage she had had Monaldeschi killed.

The curious thing is that although the nuncio in Paris and the representatives of Sweden and the Italian princes had all received information which pointed to Monaldeschi's having contact with Spain, and to the famous letters having been concerned with Italy (the nuncio was even told that he had revealed information about Naples to Spain), none of them believed it. They thought that *this* was the lie put out to save Christina's reputation, but they swallowed the vendetta story.

The Queen, however, was determined that the truth should out—or at least part of it. She could not say what the treachery was, even from her own point of view, as Spain was the great power in Italy and it would have meant that she could never return there. At the same time as all these rumours were circulating, Christina herself prepared a relation and had it circulated round Europe. Factually it was the same as Père Le Bel's, though she traced the story of her suspicions of Monaldeschi back over two months. She also described an interview she had with him, in which she said that she knew that she was being betrayed by one of her household, but led Monaldeschi to believe that she thought it was by Francesco Maria Santinelli. Monaldeschi then asked her not to forgive the traitor, saying that he should die, adding "I offer myself to carry out the judgment, or to have it happen to me." Whereupon, grimly, Christina promised not to forget what he had said.

If what the Queen related was the truth, then Monaldeschi must have believed that his plans had succeeded completely, as apparently in his letters he had imitated Santinelli's writing, with the idea that if they were ever discovered it would be believed that Santinelli was the traitor who had tried to inculpate him, Monaldeschi, by writing the letters in his name. The Queen must have destroyed these letters herself, and the remains of burnt papers were also found in Monaldeschi's room at Fontainebleau after his death, so no evidence has ever emerged to show exactly how Monaldeschi had betrayed the Queen's plan, or to whom, though the obvious assumption is that he was in contact with Spanish agents, as is suggested by the leakage of the invasion plans to the Naples Viceroy.

The greatest mystery of the whole affair is really Christina's own conduct. The secrecy and surprise which would have gone far towards ensuring the success of the Naples expedition were as much in France's interest as her own. Why therefore did she not inform Mazarin as her suspicions mounted over a period of two months? He would have been well able to deal with the matter swiftly and secretly, Monaldeschi could have been the victim of an unfortunate accident, or simply disappeared. Secrecy was of the essence, and yet this brilliantly intelligent woman, who was capable of the utmost dissimulation and proud of it, chose the course that rendered secrecy impossible. To have a man killed in a palace of the King of France, and then to refuse to allow it to be passed off as a brawl or a vendetta, even in the seventeenth century meant courting the maximum publicity. But Christina was evidently as incapable of foreseeing the storm of fury that her act would arouse as she was unable to realize the horror with which she was regarded afterwards. Blindly, she was determined to vindicate her right of exercising her sovereign's prerogative of meting out justice to her subjects—in this case her own household. In fact this right had been reserved to her in her act of abdication, and in law she had good grounds for exercising it as she saw fit. This was the reason for Christina's fury against Mazarin and her determination to brandish the word treachery round Europe. What is incredible is that she was quite incapable of recognizing that by so doing, she was burying forever such chances of her getting Naples as had not died with Monaldeschi.

The tragedy was over and the rest of Christina's stay in France degenerated into a farce. Pamphlets appeared in Paris comparing her to Astarte and Semiramis—a woman who killed her lovers so that they should not tell. No doubt these appealed to the masses, for all the foreign diplomats reported that the "barbarous Gothic Queen" was universally loathed and despised, but it was in her summing up after Monaldeschi's death that Madame de Motteville said she had no doubts of Christina's chastity, nor evidently had anyone at court. Still the Queen was a terrible source of embarrassment to everyone, especially to Mazarin. Unbelievably she even wrote to him five weeks after Monaldeschi's death asking for a dukedom for Francesco Maria Santinelli—the brother of Monaldeschi's executioner. Worse still, Christina had even shown signs of wanting to come to Paris and to the court to see the King, but this was swiftly and efficiently dealt with by the King making a "casual and informal" afternoon call on her at Fontainebleau. The Queen met Louis and his brother at the foot of the grand staircase and accompanied them to her apartment. Amiably chatting they passed through the Galerie des Cerfs, a pleasant conversation ensued, then the King departed, leaving Christina to her own devices for three dreary months.

Isolation among the dripping trees of Fontainebleau, with the gallery and its grim memories at her very door, might have wrought a change or at least brought some realization of what they had done, to other women, but not to Christina. One of her rare visitors was Benserade, the ballet expert who had been in Stockholm. The Queen told him the story of Monaldeschi, and when at the end her guest could not repress a shudder, charmingly she smiled at him and said, "Are you afraid that I will do the same to you?" Christina's companion in disgrace, the Grande Mademoiselle, also came, and found the Queen looking very well, dressed in flame colour and black velvet. But even Mademoiselle, who during the Fronde had ordered the cannons of the Bastille to fire on the King's army under his very eyes, felt a frisson of fear. In her memoirs she wrote, "While I was talking to her [Christina], I thought of what she had done . . . ," and of the Galerie des Cerfs "although they had washed it well, the marks were still there." No wonder that at one moment the Queen meditated a journey to England. Cromwell after all had killed a king. However, he did not even reply to her letter.

Still, Christina was the cousin of the King of Sweden, France's most valuable ally. Also, she now knew an uncomfortable amount about some of France's plans in the Mediterranean, which could still interest Spain. Mazarin had to make the best of an exceedingly awkward situation. He had discussions with Christina in the country and, finally, she was invited to Paris for the carnival in February and given the cardinal's own suite in the Louvre. "It was done expressly, to make her understand that she could not stay long" noted Madame de Motteville. But the conversations with Mazarin continued, he leading Christina to believe that he was still perfectly prepared to carry out the Naples project and for her to lead it. There was after all no harm in the Spaniards getting to hear of this. If she ever passed the information on to them, all the better, it would cause them to pin down more of their troops in Naples, where the Cardinal no longer had the slightest intention of sending his own.

Christina again advanced her plan for taking over the payment of the French war subsidies still owing to Sweden, and the cardinal agreed to set up a commission to look into the matter. Finally he got rid of the unwelcome guest with a loan. Sardonically he wrote to the French Minister in Stockholm, "Tell the King of Sweden that I have applied myself with care and success to prevent this Queen from collapsing into his arms, but that it has cost the King [of France] 80,000 écus." He seems to have extracted some security out of Christina however, cases of her treasures from Antwerp had arrived in France and several of her most precious tapestries remained behind with the cardinal, who let her have them back bit by bit as the money was refunded.

The Queen at last went to court, where she saw the King dance in Benserade's ballet *Alcibiades*, to music by Lully, and she was received by the Académie. Apparently this was the only occasion although, according to Madame de Motteville, she tried hard for invitations to the carnival celebrations. But the Queen passed them alone, evidently defiantly flinging herself into a whirl of gaiety. From the same source we know that "she showed little wisdom, little idea of how to behave and a great desire for pleasure. She rushed, masked, to all the balls, she went all the time to the theatre all alone with men, in the first carriage she came across. No one ever seemed so far removed from philosophy as her. She left in the first days of Lent, having received some money from the King, and she went back to Rome, where the deed that she had done in France brought her little esteem."

No doubt in order to make quite sure of getting rid of her, Mazarin had agreed to lend Christina the Palazzo Mazarin to live in. It was the same palace that had been used as a French residence by Hugues de Lionne. So when she arrived there in May 1658, the Queen was really returning to the spot where her French adventure had begun, for her insistence on going there to see Molière's play at the end of carnival two years before had been the spark that had touched off the final blaze of the Spanish diplomats' enmity. At first the Queen had no idea that now for her the crown of Naples was a mere phantom, she surrounded herself with Neapolitan émigrés and even said that she was only awaiting the arrival of the French fleet to go there. The Pope was both alarmed and embarrassed, guards were put on the gates of Rome to make sure that large numbers of men could not come into the city to be recruited by the Queen of Sweden. The guard on the papal residence of the Quirinal Palace, most embarrassingly opposite the Palazzo Mazarin, was doubled: Alexander was not risking any trouble with Spain. He even sent a message to Christina to say that it would be much better if she did not live in Rome, and refused to receive her at his summer residence at Castel Gandolfo.

The Pope need not have worried; as usual lack of money was

bringing the truth home to Christina. All remittances from Sweden were going to Mazarin to pay off her debts, not another word was heard from him of the French fleet that was to take Naples. The Queen was reduced to dismissing her own guards, the gay Neapolitan uniforms were given to Francesco Maria Santinelli to sell, so were many of the Queen's treasures including her coronation mantle, to sell or pawn. They were of course, but not for their owner's benefit. Santinelli had finally got himself into real trouble; he was trying to marry the rich widow of the Duke of Ceri and it was generally believed that he had poisoned her husband. Even Christina's eyes were opened at last—by Azzolino. To the Queen it must have seemed that the life which she had dreamed of leading after her abdication was falling to pieces around her. The Crown of Naples had faded into thin air, the Pope regarded her with suspicion and apprehension, even Charles Gustavus was deaf to her appeals—he was too busy with his victories, and now the treachery of yet another member of her household was revealed to her. The only person that Christina had to turn to was Azzolino, and in this moment of despair he did not fail her. With infinite tact and diplomacy he helped her to pick up the pieces.

CHAPTER 9

The Phantom Crown II: 1658–1668

"A woman born a barbarian, barbarously brought up and living with barbarous thoughts" was Pope Alexander VII's description of Christina to the Venetian Ambassador in June 1658. It was not a very good omen for the Queen's future in Rome. The Pope's attitude is understandable. Monaldeschi had been one of his own subjects, and his executioner's brother, Francesco Maria Santinelli, also suspected of murder, was now trying to marry into one of the great papal families. His *innamorata*, the Duchess of Ceri, was born Donna Anna Maria Aldobrandini and was a great-niece of Clement VIII. No wonder the Aldobrandini were besieging Alexander with prayers and protests. But the talk of the Naples expedition was much more serious, with men like Santinelli in command of the Queen's guards and household anything could happen, and Spain would hold the Pope responsible for such plots being hatched in the Papal States. With considerable Spanish forces in Naples and Lombardy the situation was indeed uncomfortable, and Alexander knew from past experience that this Swedish Queen, with her "ferocious and almost intolerable pride," was not easily brought to heel.

This miracle was however accomplished by Azzolino. His first step was to turn Christina's thoughts from the Naples expedition and, her character being what it was, this could only be done by substituting for it some other scheme—a greater and grander one if possible. Azzolino knew Angelo Correr, the Venetian Ambassador in Rome, and coming as he did from an Adriatic province himself—his native town of Fermo is only seven miles from the narrow sea which then separated Christian Europe from the Turkish Empire—he was more alive to Venice's problems in this quarter and the Levant than the Romans or many other Italians. At first Christina was only concerned with the idea of rehabilitating Ludovico Santinelli in the eyes of the world and she proposed to Angelo Correr the raising of a regiment for him to serve under Venice, whose eastern possessions—notably Crete—were threatened by the Turks. The Queen had several conversations with Correr about this—she actually paid up 3,100 scudi towards raising the regiment—but her active mind soon passed from the personal aspect to the general one, of the Turkish menace to the whole of Europe. This was no figment of an overheated imagination, as the loss of Crete and the threat to Vienna were to show within the next twenty years, and Christina now became fired with the idea of forming a league of Christian princes to fight the infidel. Needless to say, Correr welcomed any means that would open the eyes of the rest of Europe to the Turkish danger, and he now became one of the Queen's supporters. Azzolino must have heaved a sigh of relief that Christina's energies were now directed to a thoroughly respectable cause, one moreover that had brought him a useful ally. Together, he and Correr approached the Pope's confidant, Monsignore Sforza Pallavicino, to further the good work.

The next step was to detach Francesco Maria Santinelli from the Duchess of Ceri and get him out of the country. The Pope had taken a firm hand in the matter by having the Duchess incarcerated in the Castel Sant' Angelo at the end of 1658. Azzolino persuaded Christina to write to the lady urging her to give up Santinelli and finally, to send Santinelli on a mission to Vienna. Thus early in the New Year a good deal had been achieved towards paving the way for the resumption of better relations between the Pope and the Queen. One thing however remained. Alexander had taken a violent objection to having Christina's unruly and troublesome household living almost literally on his own doorstep. But Christina was living there rent free, no small consideration in her present circumstances, and the problem of finding an alternative which would be both dignified and inexpensive was not easy.

At last, however, Azzolino found it. He must have made use of all his native acumen (Marchigiani, the people of his native province, are notoriously tightfisted) to get it for the rent he did. It was the Palazzo Riario, which was to be Christina's home for the rest of her life. The Palace had been built in the fifteenth century for relations of the great Julius II. Together with Agostino I Chigi's villa, which stands opposite, it was among the earliest Roman examples of the Renaissance suburban villa. The term then had a very different connotation from today, these palatial houses with large gardens on the outskirts of a city being regarded as the ideal retreat for cultivated men of letters. No doubt it was this aspect that appealed to Christina, for the palace had lost something of its former splendour, having been let to numerous tenants over a long period, but it had an extensive and really lovely garden. In the lease (of which a copy still exists) Azzolino had wisely concealed who the actual tenant was to be. It was drawn up for him as acting on behalf of "a person to be named"—and as a result the rent was only 1,125 scudi per annum.

The lease is dated March 1659, and in March the garden of the Palazzo Riario (now Palazzo Corsini) is still a place of beauty and romance. Although today there are no longer parterres filled with spring bulbs (in the lease it was specified that these must be maintained and replenished) nor pergolas of jasmin and secret gardens filled with orange and lemon trees (all carefully noted in the lease), groves of blossoming trees and ilex still stretch out from behind the palace to the summit of the Janiculum, the highest hill in Rome. Shady paths wind up the hill, passing by fountains Christina must have known, but the Casino on the hill-top, where the Queen lived at first until the palace was ready for her, unfortunately no longer exists. It had a marvellous view over all Rome and it is not difficult to imagine the enchantment that this garden house must have held for Christina, who really loved gardens and had been the first to introduce pleasure gardens to Sweden, summoning André Mollet, son of the King of France's gardener, to lay out one for her.

Here in the languorous heat of a Roman summer the Queen went to live in July 1659. The casino had only nine rooms but it also had its own enclosed gardens filled with the music of fountains and the scent of orange and lemon blossom. It was scarcely a royal residence, but Christina probably preferred this romantic little house, hidden away among the ilex groves, to the publicity of a palace, because she was now deeply in love. This was the reason why Azzolino had been able to perform the miracle of taming her. No one had ever before been able to bend Christina's will, nothing had ever made her give up one jot of her independence—she had boasted that she had been "born free" and would accept no man as husband and master—but at last she had found one to whom she wrote: "I want to live and die your slave."

Christina had been attracted to Azzolino from the moment she met him, she wept when she was forced to leave Rome and him. Even during the excitement of that first journey to France and the secret negotiations concerning the Naples expedition, she could not get him out of her mind, surprising and probably amusing the Venetian Ambassador in Paris by the enthusiasm with which she constantly talked of him. In Lascaris she found a more sympathetic listener, and an observant one, who noticed the joy and excitement with which she received Azzolino's letters. Then, after the tragedy of Monaldeschi, with her life falling in pieces around her, Azzolino had proved himself to be not only an attractive man but also a good and faithful friend. In view of the embarrassment which she had become to the Pope, who now only wanted to get rid of her, it took quite considerable courage and character on Azzolino's part, even though he was a cardinal, to stand by this woman in disgrace. He was an ambitious man, and he had no great family or vast wealth behind him to help him in his career. His family owned only a modest house and garden in Fermo, and he had made his way by his own intelligence and capacity. To be friends with the Queen of Sweden when she had just arrived in Rome in 1654 was one thing, to remain so in 1658 was something very different. Christina was then a liability to any ambitious man. But, in contrast to what many others would have done, Azzolino did not fade quietly out of the picture. In this heredity probably played a part: the Marchigiani are known to the rest of Italy as being dour and tough, but they are also known to be reliable. Theirs is a poor, remote province, with none of the splendid history and riches that Tuscany, Venice or the prosperous cities of the north have known—it was all the more so in the seventeenth century.

Coming out of such a background, Christina must to Azzolino

have seemed a figure from another world—the daughter of a great king who had herself been a Queen regnant. Even after years spent in the sophisticated Roman world, to be singled out by her would inevitably have flattered and pleased him. But his behaviour when she came back in disgrace showed that there was more to it than that. Was it loyalty or pity, or was it something more that made him behave as he did? No word, not a line of writing in his hand has survived to show that Azzolino ever felt anything more for Christina than friendship. He himself destroyed all her intimate papers in the few weeks that intervened between her death and his own—all but one packet of letters from her to him. These were weekly letters written while the Queen was separated from him, living in Hamburg during the years 1666–68.

On the surface most of these are the sort of letters that one old friend would write to another who shared common interests, but here and there appear short phrases written in a special cypher, to which only the Queen and Azzolino possessed the key. When deciphered, these passages reveal that Christina was even then passionately in love with Azzolino—she did not hesitate to use to him the word "lover," although now it was to lament that "piety does not allow you to be my lover." In fact in many of her letters at this time Christina reproached Azzolino for having changed, although her love remained the same—"all the changes that can happen in your heart will not change mine" or "all your coldness will not prevent me from adoring you to 'V'," or again: "I merit your friendship by the most tender passion and the most 'L' in the world. . . . I 'R' you till death." The passionate messages in cipher were not enough, the letters V, L and R and others had some secret meaning shared only by these two and they were always used by Christina in declaring her adoration. This and her constant references to Azzolino having changed, bring the inevitable conclusion that in the past he had responded to her passionate love.

From Christina's replies to his first letters written to her in Hamburg, it is evident that Azzolino then made use of their private cipher to express "tender sentiments." His cooling off, coupled with appeals to her piety, coincided with the news that the Pope was seriously ill (Alexander VII did in fact die in 1667 while the Queen was in Hamburg). Azzolino was ambitious, and although at the age of forty-five he was still too young to be *papabile* (a likely candidate for the papacy), from a new Pope he might expect advancement, and a marked association with the Queen could do nothing but harm to his immediate prospects and probably ruin all future hopes. So in 1667, with the prospect of a conclave not far ahead, Azzolino was anxious and, as Christina clearly perceived, not enthusiastic about her returning to Rome in the near future.

But in 1659 no such clouds obscured the horizon, Christina had even received Alexander VII's blessing before moving into her new home in July. Azzolino had indeed worked miracles, he had not only achieved this all-important reconciliation, but had at last succeeded in opening the Queen's eyes to the peculations of which Francesco Maria Santinelli had been guilty at her expense during the last four years. The ruffian had in fact also robbed the Duchess of Ceri, and in July Christina not only wrote to give him his *congé* but also denounced him to the Governor of Rome.

Azzolino now took over the whole of the Queen's administration. He was well qualified to do so and the care with which he chose her servants is evident from the fact that they remained with her for the duration of their respective lives. They were nearly all hard-working Marchigiani, the new Captain of the Guard, Lorenzo Adami, was in fact a relation of Azzolino; of the others, both the Italian secretary, Abbé Matteo Santini, and the major-domo, Canon Stefano de Marchis, were in Christina's service when she died, while the doctor, Cesare Macchiati, and Giovanni Francesco Pezza, librarian and accountant, died in harness.

Azzolino did not make a completely clean sweep; Davidsson remained as Swedish secretary, so did Landini as a member of the Queen's guards, and the Passaglia sisters, Ottavia, Francesca and Portia, who had been with her since Pesaro, continued as her maids. Clairet Poissonnet, who had left Bourdelot to enter the Queen's service as valet de chambre, had now for long been the only link with Stockholm days. The little household was completed by a general factotum, Count Galeazzo Gualdo Priorato, who although he was Italian, had been recruited in France, and had written a biography of Christina.

With these trusty servants around her, the Queen's household at last took on some character of dignity and order, and Christina could now write to Antwerp asking for her precious pictures, books and other possessions which she had not seen for so long. Some of these at least could be installed in the Casino, which from the first was arranged as a self-contained residence, even to containing a small presence-chamber or throne-room for audiences, furnished with a green brocade canopy and chair of state. Here there hung portraits of Charles Gustavus, Louis XIV and his brother and, curiously, savants such as Pico Della Mirandola and Vossius. In the Queen's bedroom hung three paintings by Rubens —a picture of Abraham, a bacchanale and a still life, also a Danae by Giulio Romano; her bed had a canopy and cover of green silk edged with gold. Evidently Christina continued to follow Bourdelot's prescription for taking warm baths, as in the corridor nearby there was a wooden bath lined with lead and copper water cans. According to the custom of the time, in the kitchen and storeroom there were dining tables of different sizes which could be set up in different rooms or in the loggia or surrounding gardens. Of these there were no less than four, described in one of the inventories as "the garden," "small garden," "theatre" and "secret garden." Probably they were walled or hedged enclosures like open-air rooms, which are one of the great charms of Italian gardens. The secret garden seems to have been particularly attractive, with a small grotto and orange and lemon trees in pots standing on stone pedestals.

But Christina was not destined to enjoy her small paradise for long. Charles Gustavus's victories were glorious, but wars cost money and disrupt a nation's economy. As a result his cousin found her revenues dwindling, so that even with the modest life she was now leading in Rome, and Azzolino keeping a shrewd eye on her administration, by the beginning of 1660 the Queen realized that she could not make ends meet. Knowing his cousin's predicament, Charles Gustavus, even though in 1659 he was fighting alone against the Empire, Poland, Denmark and Russia, allowed her an extra 20,000 riksdaler a year from the customs revenues, but this was not enough to bridge the gap left by the almost complete cessation of any revenues from war-torn Pomerania. Christina herself had done everything she could to raise more money, getting a further loan on her jewels pawned in Antwerp in 1654. She had even approached Mazarin, but to no avail. So now again she turned to the rival camp, treating even with the Emperor with whom her own country was at war, offering to get advantages for him and Catholics in Sweden in the ultimate peace treaty. But the Hapsburgs were now wary of Christina, and the secret emissary she had asked the Emperor to send to meet her in Hamburg never came.

Already in January 1660 the Queen was contemplating a journey to Sweden to try to settle her affairs, even before the news of Charles Gustavus's sudden death on 3rd February reached her at the beginning of April. This was a terrible blow and, of course, made such a journey absolutely necessary. As long as her cousin lived, Christina knew that she could count on his gratitude and generosity, but now that he was succeeded by a rather sickly child of five her position was serious indeed, bad enough if the little Charles XI lived, but really desperate if he did not and another, possibly hostile, dynasty ruled Sweden. In any case she must be present in the country to ensure that her appanage, even for the little it now seemed to be worth, was confirmed to her at the first diet of the Riksdag after the new King's accession.

In the seventeenth century things moved slowly and even in this very serious situation Christina did not leave Rome till July, arriving in Hamburg on 18th August, and in Stockholm finally only on 12th October. The Regency Council, and particularly the widowed Queen Hedvig Eleanora who was only twenty-five, must have viewed this visit with considerable apprehension, but it was not possible to refuse the ex-Queen, and above all Gustavus Adolphus's daughter, permission to return to Stockholm after her cousin's death. Putting a good face on it, they received Christina with royal honours, and at first all went well. By the beginning of November, the Queen Mother, the Regency, Senate and Estates had confirmed the ex-Queen's privileges with the exception of ecclesiastical jurisdiction over her lands, also the financial provisions of her appanage. A few days later, however, the declaration which Christina sent to the diet, stating that in the event of the little King's death and his line becoming extinct she reserved her own right to the succession, was immediately returned to her without an answer. Furthermore she was now forced to sign a confirmation of her abdication.

As usual Christina could not avoid asking for trouble. She was ostentatious in parading her Catholicism, attending the services in her private chapel with a frequency and publicity which she did not normally practise in Rome. This provoked remonstrations and finally a furious attack upon the Queen by the Lutheran clergy. During this onslaught Christina is said to have wept and humbly begged for her Mass, but her chaplain, Santini, was forced to leave Sweden and Christina herself retired in dudgeon to her own city of Norrköping early in January 1661. The French Ambassador, the Chevalier de Terlon, sent his own priest to her, and the Mass was now celebrated in private but, evidently realizing that here they possessed a powerful weapon against Christina, the Regency insisted that he also should be sent away. It was an astute move. After hurriedly setting her financial affairs to rights and again dispatching Gualdo Priorato to France to try to raise funds on the grounds that Mazarin, who had died recently, had been in possession of money that was rightly hers, in May the Queen bade farewell to Sweden, probably with no regrets save one. Owing to the vindictiveness of her brother-in-law Magnus, who was now Chancellor and was determined to make use of his powers to revenge his disgrace of eight years before, Christina had never seen Belle. Magnus's action was all the more cruel because Belle was already in bad health, and although Christina at one time hoped that she might come to Hamburg, they never saw each other again, Belle dying in 1662.

The Queen returned to Hamburg and stayed there for a year. During this time it looked as if at last she had really set her affairs in order. In July she signed an agreement with Manoel Texeira, who had evidently taken over his father's business. As a result of her visit to Sweden Christina evidently considered that she could now count on an assured income of 107,000 riksdaler a year, a little over half of what she had originally expected. On this basis arrangements were made for her to pay back the 19,154 riksdaler that she owed Texeira, and afterwards that Texeira should pay her 8,000 Riksdaler a month. The balance of the Queen's income was to go to paying the interest on the money advanced on her jewels in Antwerp and finally towards redeeming them. There were, of course, also administrative and banking expenses and Texeira's own emolument of 1,000 riksdaler a year. But it now looked as if, although the Queen's income was halved, she could count on receiving it regularly, more particularly because Sweden was at last at peace with all the world. Peace treaties had been rapidly concluded after Charles Gustavus's death and it was unlikely that there would be fresh warlike ventures while the King was still a child.

Even during the troubled months in Sweden Christina had not been entirely occupied by her own mundane affairs. With Gualdo Priorato she had discussed the most magnificent and far-reaching projects. Evidently her confidant did not possess the robust good sense of his compatriot Montecuccoli (also he was probably anxious to keep his salary of 200 scudi a month). At any rate Gualdo Priorato did nothing to discourage the Queen's idea that she might yet become governor of the Spanish Netherlands, despite the Naples débâcle and Monaldeschi's death. They even solemnly discussed arrangements for her court in Flanders. There were also such questions as the league of Christian princes against the Turks and liberty for Catholics in the Protestant countries of the north. This last Christina again took up in Hamburg during the summer of 1661, writing to the Emperor, the King of Spain and Louis XIV and King John Casimir of Poland, also to the nuncios in the various capitals. Louis XIV was the only sovereign to display, not exactly enthusiasm, but at least courtesy, in the form of a letter written in his own hand. But in the end the project fell flat, as so many of Christina's other schemes were to do in the years to come.

The Queen left Hamburg on 20th May 1662. She and several members of her household had been in constant correspondence with Azzolino during her absence and, apparently thinking the Queen would travel at her usual speed, the cardinal waited more than two weeks for her arrival at Terni, a staging post about two days' journey north of Rome. An affectionate welcome also greeted the Queen on her arrival in the Eternal City on 20th June. Several cardinals had ridden out to meet her and members of the Pope's family were waiting at the gate of the Borgo. With them Christina was received immediately by the Pope, all dusty as she was, with masculine breeches clearly visible under a thin skirt. If Alexander noticed this, he gave no sign, but greeted the Queen in the friendliest fashion. It was a very different homecoming from the last, and like a good omen it ushered in what was to be one of the happiest periods of Christina's life.

For the first seven months after her return, the Queen continued to live in the garden Casino, as the Palazzo Riario was not quite ready for her, but during this time there was all the excitement of unpacking and arranging the treasures from Prague and Stockholm most of which she had hardly seen for nearly ten years. Collecting pictures, sculptures, books and works of art generally, was the one passion in Christina's life (other than her love for Azzolino) to which she remained faithful always—that and the pursuit of learning. Although it is true that, in common with other crowned heads and rich nobles, the Queen also regarded her collections as status symbols—the necessary adjuncts of an exalted station in life—when money was short she might sell or pawn her jewels and even her coronation robe, but she never parted with a picture and she somehow always managed to go on collecting. The surviving inventories of the Palazzo Riario date from a later period—about 1677—so that we do not know how the ground-floor rooms of the palace were arranged when the Queen first moved in. But afterwards they were filled with the classical sculptures that she subsequently bought or herself had excavated in Rome.

As time went on this collection became vast, and the whole of this floor of the palace was filled with statues, busts, columns and reliefs. The two "show" rooms were those of the Muses and of Clytia. These were most carefully arranged; Azzolino even sent designs for the decoration of the Muses room to the Queen during her second stay in Hamburg. The goddesses, who were represented seated, were ranged round the walls, alternating with a succession of gilded columns.* To complete the group, Francesco Maria Noccheri made a statue of Apollo, and in summer—using it as her throne room—Christina herself appeared seated opposite the god on her throne. Like many of her contemporaries Christina adopted the sun as a device, and she was evidently also attached to the legend of the nymph Clytia, who was changed into a sunflower while adoring the sun. The Queen had this mythological scene reproduced on one of the ground-floor rooms of the Palazzo Riario. Using a fragment of an original hellenistic statue of the nymph as a basis, the Queen commissioned the sculptor Giulio

* The statues are fine classical Greek copies of hellenic originals and are now one of the treasures of the Prado.

Cartari to add the upper part of the torso, head and limbs, the latter merging into stalks and leaves. This reclining figure was placed in the centre of the room, looking upwards to the ceiling upon which a sun was painted. At the far end of the ground floor, near a small staircase leading to the Queen's bedroom, a most luxurious bathroom was installed. This had two marble baths, with taps for hot and cold water and a boiler; above the baths there were statues in niches of Venus and Cupid or Narcissus. The bathroom even had a small ante-room, in which stood a bust of Christina.

The first floor of the palace was given over to a series of reception rooms, culminating in a throne room, and the Queen's own private suite. On this floor hung the finest pictures of Christina's collection. In the main gallery, or *stanza dei quadri*, the walls were covered from floor to ceiling with pictures, after the fashion of the time. Here hung the masterpieces of the Venetian school, which scholars and travellers were allowed to come and see. Legend has it that the Queen would watch them through a secret peep-hole. Christina had also brought with her from Sweden the best of her family tapestries, including the sets woven with gold and silver thread representing the stories of Scipio Africanus, Antony and Cleopatra and Julius Caesar, which had belonged to her father, as well as some antique ones of the triumphs of Petrarch (similar to those now at Hampton Court) and the familiar "Alexander" set which had decorated her own rooms in Stockholm Castle when she was a child.

Judging from the inventories, most of the other hangings and curtains in the palace were crimson or green, though whether this was due to Christina's personal taste or simply to fashion it is difficult to say. There seem to have been innumerable canopies, one of them made of Indian brocade. There were also white silk embroidered bed-covers and a notable number of "Indian" furniture and objects, some of them lacquered, anything that came from East of Suez, or for that matter from across the Atlantic, being referred to at this time as "Indian." Some of the most prized pieces of furniture were made of the wood called *fico d'India*. What this really was is difficult to determine, as the wood of the Banyan (*ficus indicus* today) is porous, and neither it nor cactus (*fico d'India* in modern Italy) seem suitable for furniture making. Nevertheless Christina's own bed was made of this wood, it had a crimson brocade canopy, and was evidently of considerable value, for it was specifically mentioned with two other of her favourite possessions on a separate sheet in the inventory prepared for the sale of the contents of Palazzo Riario after her and Azzolino's deaths. Pathetically, the other two items were Bourdon's equestrian portrait of the Queen with her dogs, and her spinet with gold strings, this latter covered with red cordovan leather stamped with gold. Blue and gold cages for a parrot, a sparrow and nightingales listed in the inventory of 1677, give another touching insight into Christina's domestic life and tastes.

The Queen's love of music of all kinds is attested by the number of instruments noted in the various inventories. These include two organs—one belonging to Azzolino—two harpsichords, two more spinets and numerous string instruments. One particularly splendid harpsichord decorated with gilded putti and foliage is listed as belonging to the Accademia, probably indicating that it stood in the great hall, used for concerts, academic gatherings and as a theatre, on the top floor of the palace. The famous library was installed on the same floor, when Christina went to live in the palace in January 1663. The manuscripts and books had already been examined by her friend the Vatican librarian, Lucas Holstenius. After his death most of the cataloguing was done by the archaeologist Benedetto Mellini, but the well-known connoisseur Giovanni Pietro Bellori was in charge of all the collections and in the 1680s was awarded the title of royal antiquarian.

Curiously, the Queen seems to have preferred fine carved wooden furniture of chestnut or walnut to the customary gilded consoles and cabinets then most fashionable in Rome. Possibly she felt more at home with this type of furniture, reminiscent of Sweden, for she also displayed a typically Swedish taste for cabinets of rich inlaid woods and ivory. It is amusing to note that stools and tabourets outnumber to a disproportionate degree armchairs or even ordinary chairs in the inventories; rare and few indeed were the guests at Palazzo Riario to whom the Queen would have accorded the distinction of such seats. Still, reading through the inventories, the northern preference for some comfort as well as show in a palace is evident. The fireplaces were really put to the use for which they were intended (unlike most

Roman palaces even in the nineteenth century), as firescreens of all kinds are mentioned, also a number of braziers, several of them silver, while there is a long list of carpets from Cairo and Smyrna which in all likelihood were really Persian.

Nor was Christina content with simply setting her house to rights. The garden also claimed her attention, and in the early spring of 1663 no less than 275 orange and lemon trees and 200 jasmin plants were cleared on her behalf at the Roman customs house. At this time it did not, of course, mean that these came from outside Italy, but simply from outside Rome, possibly from Naples, which was then famous for its gardens. No mention is made of more exotic plants, but this does not exclude the possibility that the Queen received them from friends, as the Pope's nephew Cardinal Flavio Chigi did, from as far afield as Constantinople, for his flower garden at Formello.

Evidently Palazzo Riario was well in order by 19th March for on that day the Queen received the signal honour of a visit from the Pope. This illustrious example was naturally followed by the whole of Roman society, even though the ladies complained of the scant ceremony with which the Queen received them. Christina's metamorphosis into a more tranquil and respectable member of society had not however rid her of impatience with bores. To one unfortunately very dull grandee, who lamented his solitary life, she replied: "Better three days alone than half an hour with you."

All Azzolino's efforts and Christina's devotion to him, did not entirely eliminate the Queen's penchant for amusing rascals. Two of them somehow managed to insinuate themselves into the little court of respectable marquesses and counts that Azzolino had so carefully selected for her. Possibly the Queen managed to smuggle them in because of their resounding names. But the Duke of Northumberland (of Imperial creation and *not* by the King of England) was the scapegrace son of Sir Robert Dudley, the naval engineer who had taken service with the Duke of Tuscany. Another, of apparently even more illustrious birth, was the Marquis Horazio Bourbon Del Monte, whose claim to descent from the same family as Louis XIV did not however prevent him from turning more than a dishonest penny out of the extraterritoriality accorded to the streets near the Queen's palace. This gentleman cheerfully accepted bribes from smugglers and prostitutes to allow them to live in this privileged area, where they were exempt from arrest by the papal police. Possibly Del Monte had some fellow-feeling for the miscreants as he himself had been exiled from the Papal States, and it says a good deal for his wit and capacity to please that in spite of this awkward situation Christina brought him back with her to Rome in 1662.

Still, the fact that Alexander VII came to visit her shows that the Queen was now regarded as eminently respectable, though again there was a certain amount of *quid pro quo* in their relationship. For the visit took place when, after a struggle of months, Christina had finally sided with the Pope against Louis XIV in the notorious affair of the Corsican Guard. On the same day in May 1662 that Christina had returned to Rome, the Pope had received in audience the Duc de Crequi, the first French Ambassador (as opposed to minister or chargé d'affaires) to be accredited to the Holy See since 1653. However, this effort on the part of France to improve relations seemed destined to fail from the first. Conscious of his exalted diplomatic rank, Crequi created difficulties about making the first call on the Pope's relations. He also let it be known that as Ambassador of the King of France he expected always to be accorded an armchair when he paid his respects to the Queen, and not only when he did so in the company of cardinals, as was her usual custom with diplomatic representatives. Christina handled the matter well, following up Azzolino's letter to Louis XIV and memoir to Lionne, by a clever letter of her own. Louis, who was tired of protocolaire delays and wanted his ambassador to get on with serious negotiations, now ordered Crequi to make the first call on the Chigis and to do what the Queen wanted. The Duke perforce gave way, but this preliminary brush probably rankled in the French Embassy (then as now installed in the Palazzo Farnese) and the feeling evidently spread even to the guards and lower orders. In any event, on 20th August 1662, a brawl developed between the French Embassy guards and the papal Corsican guards, whose ultimate commander was unfortunately the Pope's brother, Prince Mario Chigi. In the midst of the mêlée the Duc de Crequi came out on to the balcony of the palace to see what was happening, and at that crucial moment someone discharged an arquebus and the shot rattled against the palace walls, narrowly missing the sacred person of the Ambassador. But worse was to follow. The carriage in which the Ambassadress was returning to the Embassy was attacked, one of her pages was killed and from a mere brawl the affair had now developed into a diplomatic incident of extreme gravity.

This Christina, with her knowledge of the outside world and particularly of the character of Louis XIV, perceived a great deal more rapidly than the dilatory officials of the Roman Curia. Immediately she sent her condolences to the Ambassador, she also wrote to Louis XIV and Brienne, while in a letter to Azzolino she pointed out the danger of the whole affair. She asked him to do his utmost to see that full satisfaction was at once rendered to the French, saying, characteristically, that if the real culprits could not be discovered scapegoats must be found and adding: "What I say will appear terrible to you, but in situations of extreme gravity the same remedies must be applied." The Pope himself was evidently aware that the Queen was sincerely anxious that the affair should be settled as soon as possible, and asked her to mediate. But his offer that his nephew, Cardinal Chigi, should call on the Ambassador to convey His Holiness's apologies, was scarcely enough. After all, the lives of the Ambassador and Ambassadress had been endangered and a member of the Embassy killed.

Having got no better offer of redress than this, the Duc de Crequi left Rome on 1st September, taking up temporary residence at San Quirico in Tuscany, where he awaited further developments and instructions from France. In the interval, however, Christina's attitude had changed, probably because a friend of Azzolino, Cardinal Imperiali who was also a member of the flying squadron, had become involved in the recriminations because he was Governor of Rome. Her letters to Louis XIV and Lionne about the affair now took on a different tone. She urged the King to "draw a sponge over this disagreeable picture, to wipe it out," and for the first time placed a certain amount of responsibility upon the servants of the Embassy. Finally she blamed the Ambassador himself for leaving Rome.

Louis XIV was furious; in one letter he even made an oblique reference to Monaldeschi's death, remarking caustically that Christina herself was unlikely "to forgive bad treatment received in the person of one of the least of her domestics." As the Queen had seen so clearly from the start, the quarrel was destined to drag on for years, and in the end France was to exact the most humiliating conditions from the Holy See before the King would agree to consider the matter closed. By the terms of the Treaty of Pisa 1664, Cardinal Chigi was obliged to go all the way to Paris personally to tender the Pope's apologies to the King, who stipulated that the Corsican Guard should be disbanded for ever, also that a monument with an inscription recording the circumstances of its inglorious end should be erected in Rome.

It was another year before Christina herself was forgiven for having changed camps. The King of France only unfroze towards her when Alexander VII's failing health made it evident that the support of Azzolino and the flying squadron might be useful at a conclave that could not be too far ahead. It says a good deal for Louis XIV's magnanimity that although at one time his indignation against the Queen caused him to make representations about her behaviour to the Swedish government, and even to hint that a reduction of her income might have a salutary effect, he rapidly repented of this. Further instructions were hurriedly sent to the Chevalier de Terlon, who was now the French diplomatic representative in Sweden, telling him not to proceed further with the matter. This provoked a revealing comment upon Christina from Terlon. Although he had been on personally friendly terms with Christina for over twenty years, he wrote to Louis: "Your Majesty should know that she is the most timid and at the same time most blustering Princess in the world, and that it is necessary to speak to her boldly in order to be esteemed and feared. I know this, having seen her here in the midst of the most malicious affair in the world, when only Your Majesty's authority saved her through my offices." Terlon was evidently referring to the scenes which followed Christina's ostentatious parade of her Catholicism in Sweden in 1660 and her final withdrawal to Norrköping.

The Queen herself, after some reflection, had been very much afraid that Louis XIV might take some action of this kind, knowing as she did only too well how readily the Regency would comply with it. Moreover she had been informed by friends in Sweden that since her last visit the Regents, obviously with the intention of preventing another one, had decreed that if she returned she would not be allowed to practise her religion (which was illegal for Swedes) or to bring a priest with her.

By these somewhat unprincipled means the Regency was able to avoid the return of the unwelcome guest for some years. But by 1665 Christina's financial affairs had again reached such a state of crisis that something had to be done. For the moment, however, upon Azzolino's advice, it was decided to send Lorenzo Adami on an exploratory mission because both the Queen and the Cardinal had begun to have grave doubts about the efficiency of Appelman and the other administrators. The choice seemed a strange one: Count Lorenzo Adami was only Captain of the Guard, a country gentleman from the remote province of the Marche, with no experience whatsoever of foreign countries and administration on a large scale, but his portrait, painted by Wuchters with Dutch realism, shows the pleasing and highly intelligent face of a man who was evidently both clear-sighted and honest. Adami left Rome in June 1665, stayed some days at Hamburg to go through Texeira's accounting of the Queen's affairs, and arrived in Stockholm in August. His entire staff consisted of an interpreter hired in Hamburg for six écus a month, yet in the space of seven months Adami examined in detail the administration, or rather maladministration, of Christina's estates, visited many of them and collected considerable financial arrears. By March 1666 he was ready to dispatch a secretary to Rome with a résumé of his activities and the account books balanced at last. At the same time he had succeeded in making friendly contact with important personalities in Sweden and was thus able to inform the Queen of the political situation there.

Briefly, Adami had found that although the Governor General of the Queen's Swedish estates, Seved Bååt, claimed that the muddle and delay in payments arose from the fact that Texeira had now taken on the collection of rents and other income from all the Swedish estates except the town of Norrköping, much of the trouble really derived from his own carelessness. Since the Queen's visit in 1661–62 the accounts had never been properly kept, and in making over to farmers general the collection of her revenues, Bååt had neglected to get the customary deposit as security from them, or even to make sure that the money from the rents was collected on Christina's behalf.* He had also allowed the Swedish government to expropriate some of the Queen's lands for the payment of her outstanding debts, but had never claimed back from the Government sums that were due to her. Finally, he had allowed his brother-in-law to keep one of Christina's estates for several years without paying a sou for it. Texeira, too, had not carried out his charge with complete honesty, but worst of all was the situation in Pomerania. Here Appelman lived like a lord, fought with everyone, and was generally believed to have enriched himself to the tune of 150,000 écus at Christina's expense.

With no one but the interpreter to help him, Adami visited even the outlying islands of Ösel, Öland and Gotland, inspected the accounts, reorganized the whole system. He found honest farmers general with whom he prepared an agreement for the payment of an income of 20,000 riksdaler a year from the rents of Ösel, 17,000 from Öland and 21,000 for Gotland, thus ensuring for the Queen an income of 58,000 riksdaler from the islands alone. The word must now have got around, even to Pomerania, that this simple gentleman from the Marche was a person to be reckoned with—no doubt Adami's country upbringing had helped him in his investigations of what was after all mostly farming property—that he was absolutely honest and somehow had a knack of making friends in high places. As a result Appelman came to heel, even without Adami's setting foot in Pomerania, promising a regular income of 30,000 riksdaler from the Pomeranian estates, while Båât also undertook to send 20,000 from Norrköping. Thus, when in March 1666 Adami dispatched the secretary Stropp to Rome with the account books and documents for the Queen's approval, he had succeeded in putting her finances in order, and it looked as if the income from her estates, stipulated under her agreement with Texeira in 1662, would now really be forthcoming.

But this was not all that Adami had achieved. He had made friends, first with the French Ambassador Terlon, then with his successor Pomponne and also with Wrangel and Tott; these

* The practice of farming out tax or rent collection had existed in Europe since Roman times: the abuses of the notorious tax-collecting office of the Farmer General in France was one of the contributory causes of the French Revolution. The system is still used in Italy.

were all, of course, people who would in any case have been well disposed towards Christina. But, with remarkable ability, Adami also succeeded in penetrating what Whitelocke, for one, had found to be a very difficult milieu—that of the Swedish nobles who were members of the Råd. Given such a different background and upbringing—he was also after all a Catholic—and the language difficulty, it says much for Adami's personal character and charm that he was on excellent terms with Biörenklou, who was in charge of the Ministry of Foreign Affairs, and with the brothers Knut and Gustav Kurck, also senators.

Apart from his purely administrative duties, Adami had received instructions from the Queen to take as many soundings as possible to find out if the Regency really intended to apply the religious ban if she came back to Sweden on a visit. Understandably, Adami does not seem to have been at all sure about this. But in March 1666 he was able to report to Christina that she still had many friends in Sweden who would welcome her return, and that the Estates were to be summoned in June. The reason for this special diet was that relations with Holland and Denmark had so far deteriorated as to make a new war seem possible. This would of course affect the whole fabric of the Queen's financial stability, so recently regained by Adami's months of effort. War in the Baltic would threaten not only the security of the Islands of Ösel, Öland and Gotland, from which more than half her income was derived, but was also likely to reduce the revenues from her other lands. The only way to avert such a threat was to try to obtain from the belligerents some form of neutrality for Christina's possessions, possibly with the aid of Louis XIV.

As soon as the Queen became aware of the situation and the extraordinary meeting of the Estates, she felt that she must at all costs be present at the diet. Azzolino agreed with her, possibly as we have seen, in view of the Pope's health, not entirely disinterestedly. There was also the fact that although she was only forty, in appearance at least Christina herself was ageing visibly. She was now definitely portly, possessed a marked double chin, and persisted in dressing her hair as unbecomingly as possible—parting it in the middle and pulling it down severely flat on either side to her ears, from where it sprouted in two bunches of untidy

The banquet given in the Quirinal Palace in Rome by Pope Clement IX on 9th December 1668, from a drawing by P. Sevin.

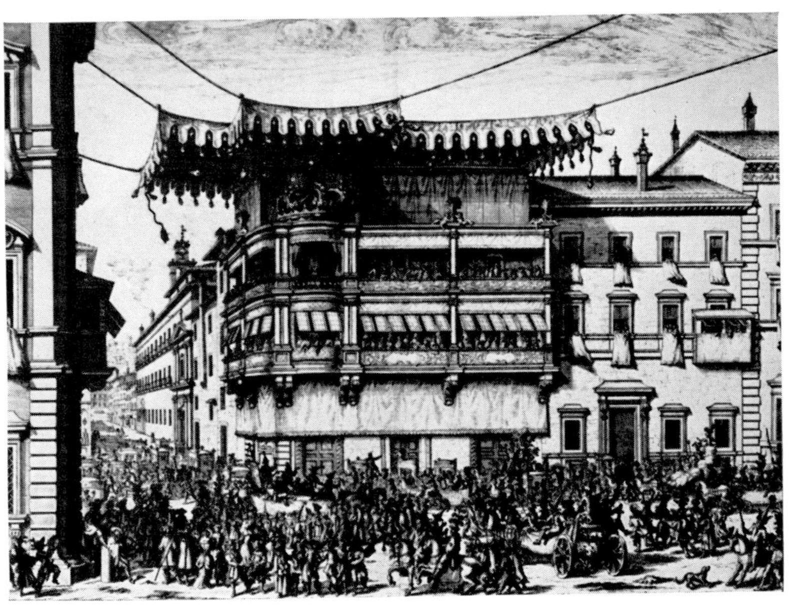

Christina's box erected for the carnival of 1666 in what is now the Piazza Venezia in Rome, from an engraving by G. B. Falda.

Christina at the age of thirty-five, painted by A. Wauchters in Norrköping in 1661, where the Queen stayed shortly after the death of Charles X.

Christina at the age of forty-one, attributed to W. Heimbach.

Christina lying in state on 23rd April 1689, in the Church of S. Maria in Vallicella in Rome, from an engraving by N. Dorigny.

ringlets or plaits, sometimes secured by bows. The eccentricity of her dress had also increased with the years: in privacy or for travel she favoured a man's coat reaching nearly to her knees, buttoned down the front and worn with a jabot; her skirts were not much longer. Even for state portraits, painted with the emblems of royalty, the Queen's dress was basically the same although her skirts reached to her feet.

Whatever, in fact, their relations may have been in the past, it is doubtful if now on Azzolino's part there was more than the warmth of an old and well-tried friendship, a sympathy and kindliness for this strange and really pathetic woman whom he knew depended upon him for all her happiness in life, as well as wise counsel and support. As the years went by, Christina's adoration must have become a trifle embarrassing, not to say wearing—for her letters during the next two years show that she could be jealous of young and pretty women. So, although Azzolino's first letters after the Queen left Rome on 22nd May evidently included carefully cyphered tender messages, these were probably not dictated by his own unmixed sorrow at her departure.

Christina spent the night after the first stage of her journey sleepless and in tears. Afterwards, apparently making up her mind that the sooner she got to Sweden the better, she tore post-haste across Europe to Hamburg, arriving there on 22nd June. Even so, Clairet Poissonet had been sent on ahead to get the letters awaiting her there, with instructions to return immediately. He lost his way, but Christina gave no peace to anyone until he was found asleep in an inn at one in the morning and Azzolino's letter, which was in the packet, was brought to her. Although in her reply, written next day, Christina thanked Azzolino a million times for his "tender sentiments" she was clearly already worried by a chance phrase referring to her not wishing to stay in Rome, but to go to Sweden and perhaps stay there. Probably Azzolino was joking, but he received the emphatic retort: "Believe me, I would rather live in Rome on bread and water, with only a maid of all work to serve me, than possess elsewhere all the kingdoms and treasures in the world . . . also let me assure you that I merit your friendship by the *most tender passion and the most* 'L' in the world. I do not know if I will ever be happy again, but I know well that *I* 'R' *you until death*. Adieu." (The words in italics were written in cipher.)

Three weeks before she left Rome the Queen had written to Seved Bååt and Adami to tell them that she was coming to Sweden, instructing them to inform the Regents, telling them frankly that she wished to be present at the diet. Christina was not so frank about the religious restrictions which she well knew had been placed on any future visit she might make to her native country. These had never actually been conveyed to her officially, so she decided to ignore them completely.

The news of the Queen's impending arrival must have come as a most unpleasant shock to the members of the Regency Council. Adami's successful mission had probably raised false hopes that now that Christina's financial affairs were practically settled, she was not likely to trouble them in the near future. Inevitably, they would also have been much better informed than Adami about the current of feeling in Christina's favour now existing in Sweden. Knowing only too well her capacity for stirring up trouble, they feared more than ever her presence at what promised to be a difficult diet.

The Regency of Charles XI was a less united and powerful body than that of Christina's own minority. The Queen Mother, Hedwig Eleonora, was but a figure-head, and there was no dominant personality such as Axel Oxenstierna. Magnus De la Gardie had stepped into the great man's shoes, primarily for lack of a better candidate. Per Brahe was still High Steward, Charles-Gustav Wrangel, Grand Constable; Stenbock, Grand Admiral; and Bonde, Grand Treasurer. But Per Brahe was now too old to have much influence in affairs and Stenbock and Bonde were nonentities, while Wrangel, who was a fighting soldier and bored with administrative work, was still a good friend of Christina. As Chancellor, Magnus of course held the dominant place, but he was not altogether beloved—for instance by Adami's friend Biörenklou, who was his deputy at the Foreign Ministry. Vacillating as he undoubtedly was, Magnus was not such a fool as to have illusions about Christina's capacity for making trouble at the diet, or his colleagues' ability to quell it. Characteristically, he evidently decided that the best way to prevent Christina's inopportune arrival was by honours and flattery—he had always been at great pains to present himself as her devoted friend.

Needless to say the Queen at once saw through this ruse. On

23rd June she wrote to Azzolino: "The Grand Constable Wrangel has been ordered to come and visit me here on behalf of the King and, from what he says, he will obey with great joy. I think their intention is to try and persuade me not to go to Sweden, but nothing in the world is going to stop me if the diet takes place, if it doesn't I won't go." These words put the situation in a nutshell—Christina's only reason, as the Regency well knew, for going to Sweden was to be present at the diet, and it was the one thing that Magnus, naturally the Queen Mother, and probably Stenbock and Bonde, who were at all costs anxious to avoid trouble, were determined to forestall.

Shortly after her arrival at Hamburg, Christina received the unwelcome news that the diet might not take place. It was obvious that the Regents hoped that if it was delayed the Queen might have come and gone before it was actually held. So that there should be no mistake about her intentions, however, she actually wrote to Bååt to say that she was even meditating taking up permanent residence in Sweden—an idea that she knew very well would fill the Regents with horror. Although this must have afforded Christina some malicious pleasure, the suggestion was a tactical error because, faced with such an appalling prospect, the Regents were even less likely to be accommodating about the religious question. Nevertheless, in her letters to Azzolino, Christina presented the situation in an unjustifiably rosy light, saying that she had some hopes that this would be settled, in which case she would go and stay in Sweden until the diet took place. Possibly this idea was influenced by the fact that Wrangel, who was in command of the Swedish army stationed at Stade, not far from Hamburg and preparing for an attack on Bremen, had indeed come to see her with all his family in the most friendly fashion, and had given free rein to his discontent with the present government in Sweden.

In July Christina finally made up her mind to tackle the religious question openly. Stropp was dispatched to Stockholm with a formal letter to the child King, asking for freedom of worship and that she might bring her Italian entourage with her. A few days later, however, Christina was depressed to get confirmation that it was unlikely that the diet would be held at all. Nevertheless, in August she wrote to Azzolino: "When I am sure that it [the diet] will take place, I will go, whether they accord me it [freedom of worship] or not. I will go in person to ask it from the Estates, who will not refuse it to me." In this the Queen was probably right, as the Regency had encountered considerable difficulty in obtaining the Estates' approval of the religious ban. During the whole of her stay in Hamburg Christina had kept in close contact with the French court, writing constantly to Louis XIV and Brienne, giving them among other things accounts of the present political situation in Rome. From this she obviously hoped to receive in return French support when she was in Sweden, and had instructed Stropp to make contact with the French ambassador, Pomponne; that he did not do so was probably because he was aware that the Regents feared Christina's relations with France. Finally at the end of August the Queen received definite news from Stropp that the Regents had told him formally that in Sweden she would not be allowed freedom of worship.

The autumn brought further troubles. Stropp was called before the Råd and commanded to show them Christina's letters. He only had a few but these contained instructions to take counsel with Pomponne and to noise abroad the Queen's complaints against the Regency—evidence that the Queen was prepared to ally herself with foreign powers and trouble the internal peace of Sweden. Nor were the Regents at all happy about Adami's plans for Christina's revenue to be collected by farmers general. The upshot of all this was an offer to pay the Queen a fixed income of 100,000 riksdaler if she would make over her lands to the government. On the face of it, this appeared to be an advantageous proposal, but Christina now had some experience of the difficulty of getting money out of Sweden. Moreover the offer would place her entirely in the power of the government. Both Gustav Kurck and her old protégé John Holm, now Leijoncrona, advised against it, so in his own day had poor Charles Gustavus; wisely, the Queen refused the offer.

Adami was now dispatched to Stockholm. Poor man, he had lately returned from weeks of travel as far as Pomerania, but his final settlement of the rent collection at Ösel had been received with reproaches for not having got more. Moreover he now received some very devious instructions regarding his mission to Sweden—namely that he was to assure Magnus and his supporters that the Queen had no intention of taking up residence in Sweden, but to tell her friends the exact opposite. Fortunately Adami had too much good sense and honesty to put these into effect and finally, after negotiations which lasted throughout the month of December, he was able to report that the Queen and her Italian household would be welcome in Sweden provided there was no priest. However he added a note to the effect that he believed that if Christina brought one with her—obviously in secular dress—no attention would be paid. Magnus had even gone so far as to offer the Queen the loan of his own house. However the Regents were still firm in their resolution that Christina should not come to Sweden while the diet (expected for the month of May) was in session. Needless to say this was the one condition that she would not accept, so Adami was instructed to tell the authorities that his mistress intended to come to Sweden immediately, but to inform her friends that she had not the slightest intention of doing so. To Azzolino the Queen wrote to say that she would delay her departure till the following autumn if need be, in order to be in Sweden for the diet.

In fact, if she had wished to use it, Christina had a very good reason for delaying her journey to Sweden. Since early December she had been far from well, and the New Year brought no change for the better. Her old symptoms returned with increased gravity, the pain in the left intercostal region was agonizing, the sleeplessness, headaches and sickness were worse, particularly at certain periods in the month. But to them were now added a continual thirst and loss of weight. The last two symptoms may well have been premonitory signs of the appearance of diabetes, to which modern medical opinion attributes the Queen's death twenty years later. But her Italian doctor, Macchiati, was not far wrong in his diagnosis of the cause of the old familiar complaints when he wrote to Azzolino saying "it all comes from the mind." Also, as long ago in Sweden, Christina was imposing upon herself an impossible life in impossible conditions. She shut herself up in her bedroom, where she worked far too much, slept badly, ate worse, gave audiences and even had Mass celebrated, taking no air or exercise in the frigid cold of Hamburg in winter. The Queen had indeed many anxieties, deriving both from the situation in Sweden and her own finances, but what was probably at the root of the trouble was the increasing coldness of Azzolino's attitude. Already in September Christina had felt ill when she had received a letter from the Cardinal telling her of Alexander VII's illness and, significantly, in her answer she ends by saying: "I am not replying to the ciphered part of your letter, because I do not know what to say, if it is not to confirm to you all that I have said in my other letters. I can only assure you that *all the changes* which may occur *in your heart will not change mine, and that I will remain faithful to you until death.*" Again in November she wrote: "I have nothing more to say to you. Only I must assure you that *all your coldness* will not prevent *me from adoring you to the 'V'.*"*

In December it is evident that Christina was well aware of the fact that Azzolino was not anxious for her to return to Rome. Her health was worse and she refused to reply to the ciphered passages in Azzolino's letters, simply reiterating that she did not change. In January there was no improvement in her condition and her replies to Azzolino continued in the same strain, until finally, evidently hurt beyond endurance, Christina lashes out: "*If Hamburg is not far enough away from Rome to satisfy your cruelty, I will go to the end of the world and never come back.*" What with worry, ill health and Azzolino's increasing coldness, which he tried to disguise with pious injunctions, Christina was by now at the end of her tether. For in her last letter, written in January, she breaks out in a passionate protest: "I think that I gave sufficient reply to the ciphered passages in your letters by the last I wrote. But all the same I will add that I never *wish to offend God,* by His Grace, or ever *give you* reason to be *offended*, but this resolution *will not prevent me from loving you until death,* and as *piety* does not allow you to be *my lover*, I will dispense with your being *my* servitor, because I wish *to live and die your slave.*"*

The pros and cons of the history of Christina's relationship with Azzolino have been argued by many people, but the fairest judgment of them all was written by Baron Bildt, the Swedish Ambassador in Rome at the end of the last century, who discovered these letters written in the Queen's own hand lying unknown in a remote villa in Tuscany (he also found the key to her and Azzolino's private cipher). Bildt wrote: "What were the

* The words in italics were written in cipher.

personal relations between the Queen and Azzolino, and what was their nature? After having read the letters which follow, the reader will know as much as I. Certainly love speaks in these letters . . . it does not matter much, in my opinion, whether Azzolino did, or did not, share the Queen's bed. In any case he, and he alone, played the role of master in the Queen's life." This was Christina's tragedy, the love that had come at last could never know true fulfilment or even be acknowledged. Revealingly she once wrote: "True love asks for nothing but to love."

However, tragedy was never very far removed from comedy or even farce in Christina's life. By the middle of January she was writing to Azzolino about alchemy, of which they were both passionate devotees. A week later, on Shrove Tuesday, she was actually entertaining all her friends to a ballet in which she took the part of a slave heavily laden with chains—the scene was set in the Holy Land at the time of the Crusades. Thirteen years before, the Queen's dancing had been much admired; that the years and her own silhouette might make some difference apparently never occurred to her. As long ago as 1658 the Comtesse de Brégy had experienced some difficulty in preventing Christina from making herself an object of ridicule by dancing at the court in Paris. But now, at the age of forty-one—especially in view of her appearance in her portraits—imagination boggles at the idea of such a spectacle. Nevertheless one of the Queen's household, the priest Santini, wrote to Azzolino to say that the spectators thought she looked "like a goddess descended from the sky." Obviously he knew that Christina read her household's letters, but equally that she never applied to her own case the maxims which she wrote, such as: "It is in vain that Princes hope to learn the truth from others, if they do not admit it to themselves all the time."

Nevertheless it is just possible that Christina was beginning to realize that her dancing days were over, for not long afterwards she lashed out, as only a jealous woman can, at Azzolino. He must have been so unwise as to mention the attractions of two young women appearing in a comedy at the French Embassy in the same letter as he read the Queen a moral lecture. In her reply Christina's rage was such that she did not even trouble to cipher such passages as, "But without doubt you went there (to the comedy) following the Lord's example, to convert them. Otherwise virtue as scrupulous as yours would not have profaned its eyes with such a spectacle for any reason. I imagine that they will soon confide themselves to the hands of Cardinal Barberini to be put in the *Convertite* (a home for fallen women in Rome) after they have left yours."

Meanwhile, on the strength of the Queen's assurances that she would shortly be coming to Sweden, the Regents had felt bound to prepare a suitable reception for her. At the end of February Magnus's brother, Pontus De la Gardie, and poor Belle's brother, Per Sparre, had set out from Stockholm for Hälsingborg to meet the Queen when she arrived in Swedish soil.* Accommodation for travellers in the Swedish countryside had not improved much since Whitelocke had complained so bitterly about it in 1653, so, as well as a numerous retinue of gentlemen and their servants, the deputation of welcome was accompanied by a caravan of sledges filled with tapestries, furniture and other household goods, intended to render Her Majesty's journey more comfortable in the winter cold.

In fact they need not have worried about the cold; knowing that the diet was not to take place till May, Christina did not stir from Hamburg until 28th April. By 9th May she had arrived at Korsör on the Danish island of Zeeland, where the Chevalier de Terlon was waiting for her and, if we are to believe her own account of her journey, she was lucky to get further than her next stopping place.

The Queen had experienced a violent attack of her old symptoms just before leaving Hamburg, caused no doubt by the nervous tension aroused by the prospect of the journey to Sweden, and what might await her there. What with fever, palpitations, violent pains and vomiting, following upon a bout of insomnia, Christina was obviously in no fit state to start on the journey at all, and although she improved during the first few days, the fever returned. The news of the Pope's death, soon proved false or at least premature, with which Terlon met the Queen at Korsör, must have increased her nervous excitement, for she collapsed completely the next day in the little village of Sorö. Here Christina had to be put to bed on a few planks in a cottage "which deserved

* Since Charles Gustavus's victories of 1658 the whole of the southern part of the Scandinavian peninsula now belonged to Sweden.

rather the name of cavern." Her doctor, Macchiati, had run out of medicines and was at his wits' end, when the situation was saved by Terlon sending for his French surgeon from Copenhagen, but probably even more by his French cook, who produced what the distracted Macchiati later described in a letter to Azzolino as "a very gallant soup in the French style." Rested and for once decently nourished, Christina felt fit enough to take the road again the next day, but she had had a serious fright. To Azzolino she wrote: "I can assure you that I found myself within a hair's breadth of death, and I had prepared myself as does anyone who believes he has reached the end." A further shock was in store for the unfortunate Queen when she was met by John Holm-Leijoncrona just before she crossed the Sound. The Regency had just passed an edict against Catholics and had forbidden Swedes to attend Mass at the French Embassy. It was their reply to the Queen for having delayed her arrival in Sweden in order to be there for the diet.

The welcome at Hälsingborg was, however, as triumphant as the Queen's subsequent progress through the south of Sweden. Not very surprisingly, since there had been a delay of over two months in which to make the arrangements, every detail of the reception and journey worked according to a plan. Three luxurious meals a day were served to the travellers en route, and at each stopping place the Queen's room was hung with tapestries and provided with a canopy, under which she sat to receive her loyal ex-subjects. In fact Christina received an enthusiastic welcome wherever she went, particularly from the people. There were good reasons for this. Since Charles Gustavus's death there had been no royal progresses through the countryside and, Catholic or not, Christina still carried with her the glamour of being the great and beloved Gustavus Adolphus's daughter. True, there had been discontent at the end of her own reign, but her successor's great victories had not made the lot of the people at home any happier, and now they looked back to the past—as people always do—as a golden age when compared with the present.

This popular acclaim would certainly have been reported to the Regency and increased their apprehensions at the thought of Christina's being present at the diet. The risk of war breaking out in the Baltic—Christina's original pretext for attending the diet—

had died down. None the less in Hamburg she had continued in her intention to be present at it. It must have been obvious to the Regency that she wished to reassert her influence in Sweden with an eye to future advantage. Her reception after she had landed would have confirmed them in their suspicions. They acted swiftly to put an end to Christina's hopes. A letter from the Regency to Pontus De la Gardie, which arrived at Jönköping, stated that the Regents could not tolerate the presence of a Catholic priest in the Queen's retinue. Although Santini (the same priest as had accompanied her to Sweden before) was ostensibly and in actual fact also her secretary, everyone was well aware that he was a priest and that Mass was celebrated by him in Christina's presence every day, though behind closed doors. Naturally, and very understandably in view of her recent collapse which she apparently believed had endangered her life, the Queen refused to part with him. It was finally decided that both she and Pontus should write to Stockholm—Pontus sent a cautious letter asking for instructions, Christina a haughty one addressed to the little King, which ended with the words: "I ask you to believe that you were not born to give orders to people of my kind. I am, in spite of your strange conduct, Monsieur my brother and nephew, your good sister and aunt, Christina Alexandra."

For a short time the party waited at Jönköping, but the Queen was anxious to reach her own domain of Norrköping in order finally to settle the arrangements with the farmers general for the collection of her revenues. So after a day or two they continued, arriving at Norrköping at the end of May. Whether it was due to Christina's letter to the King, which had of course been aimed at Magnus, or increasing fears of trouble, in the meantime the Regents' attitude had hardened. At Norrköping Pontus received instructions telling him that not only must the priest be sent away immediately, but that the Queen herself would not be allowed to go openly to Mass at the French Embassy in Stockholm, but would have to use the pretext that she was calling upon the French Ambassador.

Whether the provocation was deliberate or not, nothing could have been better calculated to raise Christina's fury to white heat —and to make her leave the country. "What! I, I call on Pomponne! If he suggested it to me I would have him beaten, and that in the presence of his own King!", she raged. It was indeed an insult, but it was also the type of insult that Magnus knew better than anyone would rouse the Queen's fury. He was correct in his calculations. In her rage Christina refused to stay another instant on Swedish soil, or to accept any further hospitality from the Swedish government. Pontus De la Gardie and all the Swedes received their *congé* from Christina and she ordered post horses for her departure at dawn the next day. It was only by pointing out to Her outraged Majesty that in all likelihood the commanders of the fortresses en route would not let her pass without him, that Pontus succeeded in obtaining the Queen's assent to his accompanying her to the frontier. They got there in four days, exhausted and dishevelled. As they galloped along, fears of arrest and hopes of recall seem to have alternated in Christina's mind, for she kept on asking Pontus if he was not expecting a courier. Apparently she was unable to believe that the Regents would simply be thankful that she had gone. But the anti-climax was complete. At 9 a.m. on 5th June, accompanied by Pontus and all the officers of the garrison at Hälsingborg, the Queen was accorded a ceremonious farewell to her own country, which she never saw again.

No one was allowed to draw breath until they were back in Hamburg. Five days later they arrived, filthy, worn out, "looking like gypsies"—all but the Queen, who was as fresh as if she had never been away and in fact, extraordinary woman that she was, completely restored to health. Naturally Christina wrote to Azzolino saying that she was sure that the Regents were "as much worried by the resolution she had shown in leaving, as they had been by her presence, because they are blamed for it by the whole of Sweden and all the world, and the results could be very disagreeable for them." But, after a conversation with Magnus, Pomponne was convinced that the Regency had really been prepared to treat with Christina. In fact if she had been willing to stay in Stockholm only for a short time, and leave before the diet (at which her presence would now have been illegal), she would probably have been allowed to keep the priest. However, the Ambassador was sure that although the Regents would have preferred not to have used such rough methods, their "joy at seeing her leave the realm outweighed such delicate considerations as what world opinion might be." Magnus had also told Pomponne, that everywhere she went Christina had talked to the Swedes who came to see her about the poor state of the King's health, saying that there was little hope that he would live, and asking them if after his death they would not like to have her as Queen. However, as these allegations were coupled with others suggesting that the Queen had also tried to stir up trouble for France and Pomponne himself, the Ambassador had not paid much attention to them. Pomponne took Adami into his confidence over some of this, with the result that the Ambassador later received a letter from Christina, in which she assured him that Magnus was simply trying to stir up trouble between her and France. Adami was also convinced that for purely selfish reasons the priest Santini had been largely responsible for the Queen's precipitate departure, and he wrote to tell Azzolino of the suspicions.

The practical result of the whole affair was that Christina had sacrificed everything to her obsession of being present at the diet, even after the need for it had vanished, and that none of the business connected with the administration of her estates had been completed. If only she had gone to Stockholm when she said she would, genuinely to settle her affairs, it was more than likely that in their anxiety to get rid of her, the Regents would have agreed to any provision she wished to make for the collection of her rents. As it was, the agreements with the farmers general had not all been sanctioned, and Adami's months of patient negotiation bore little fruit. In fact Christina's financial situation had advanced little since she had left Rome more than a year before. As usual the Queen had sacrificed basic necessities to chimerical dreams of glory.

The first news that greeted Christina on her return to Hamburg was that of Alexander VII's death. Azzolino had written to tell her that the conclave was to be held in the Vatican and not, as often at that time, at the Quirinal. Christina was well aware that private correspondence with the Cardinal in conclave would now be much more difficult and, cautiously, she does not even refer to the word cipher in her reply to Azzolino, simply saying: "I have not replied to the last paragraph in your letter of the 28th." Characteristically, however, she reassured him of her feelings with the high-flown phrase: "No change in my fortune will alter my sentiments, whether I am on a throne or in irons."

Poor Adami, for whom the *débâcle* in Sweden must have looked like the ruin of months of painful endeavour, was now so misguided as to say in a letter to the Queen that in Stockholm they were blaming his advice for her sudden departure. Even more unwisely he tried to advise her to be moderate and conciliatory. Worst of all, Adami had mentioned Her Sacred Majesty in a letter to Macchiati (which she naturally read), saying that in Stockholm they feared that she might marry King John Casimir Wasa of Poland now that he was a widower. Christina who would have read with complacency Santini's description of herself dancing "like a goddess descended from the sky," was moved to fury when she found that these underlings dared to discuss HER. It required two letters to bring home to Adami the enormity of his act. The second letter contained an interesting phrase, the Queen informing Adami that he could reply to people in Sweden that: "It is not impossible that I might succeed the *King* of Poland, but I will certainly never succeed the Queen."

In June 1667, however, the main focus of the Queen's attention was naturally the Conclave then in progress in Rome, in which Azzolino was bound to play a leading part. In fact he played a decisive role in Giulio Rospigliosi's accession to the papacy on 20th June and, although both he and the Queen were intimate friends of the newly acclaimed Clement IX, this reflects nothing but credit on both of them. For Clement is universally acknowledged to have been a good, modest and kindly man, as well as a hard worker and skilful diplomat. Prior to his election he had been Secretary of State—an office to which he now appointed Azzolino—and in spite of this his election was, almost unbelievably, welcomed both by France and Spain. The Pope's character is perhaps best illustrated by the fact that he really broke with the iniquitous tradition of nepotism—members of his family were not enriched at the state's expense, receiving only small salaries from the offices granted to them. At the same time the Pope, who himself heard confessions in St Peter's, limited the daily expenses for his own table to fifteen baiocchi (or less than sixpence of the currency of the time). No wonder that such a man was universally beloved, or that for the first time in history the newly-elected

Pope was greeted with a panegyric ode, instead of the usual pungent epigrams, by the omniscient Pasquino.*

Needless to say, when the news of Clement IX's election reached Christina in Hamburg, her joy knew no bounds. When a courier from the nuncio at Vienna arrived bearing a personal letter from the Pope, announcing his own election and Azzolino's appointment as his Secretary of State, the Queen was determined that such an event must be celebrated in royal style. Accordingly, some days later a solemn Mass was celebrated and the Te Deum sung in the main hall of the Queen's house, followed by a salute fired by her cannon. While she and her friends partook of a banquet, wine flowed free for the benefit of the populace from a fountain erected in the street outside. At the same time an enormous painted inscription with an illuminated papal tiara and the words "CLEMENS IX PONT. MAX. VIVAT." was hoisted up on the façade of the house.

This was scarcely a tactful action in a Protestant city such as Hamburg, where Christina's Catholicism and her residence in a house owned by Jews had already attracted the hostility of the Lutheran pastors and anti-semites alike. All went well, however, as long as the crowd, which had been surging around the area all day, could drink at the Queen's expense. But the end of this junket coincided with the firing of more cannon and the illumination of the inscription at nightfall, and the existing hostility, latent until then, began to rise. Finally, at midnight, just as the Queen was going to bed, a shower of stones rattled against the house, breaking some of the windows, and the infuriated crowd started to try to force the door. Christina had been well aware that her action could provoke trouble, for she had laid in an extra store of powder and shot for her guards, and she had cannon. At the outbreak of trouble one of the Queen's guests set out to ask help from the Commandant of Hamburg, but had returned with the answer that the Commandant had received orders not to interfere. It is possible that some shots were fired from among the crowd at the Queen's house. In any event, Christina ordered her

* The name of Pasquino had been given by the Roman populace to a classical statue standing near the Piazza Navona, to which lampoons attacking the popes and their government were frequently attached, hence the word pasquinade.

guards to open fire, which they did—not over the heads of the crowd as a warning—but aiming a volley right into the tightly-packed mass of people, with the result that eight were killed and twenty wounded. After having received urgent entreaties from yet another of the Queen's guests, the Commandant now arrived with troops and restored order. But her house had been so much damaged that Christina had to take refuge for a few days with the Swedish Resident.

Although the whole affair was due to her own provocation, the Queen wasted no sympathy on the dead and wounded; instead she tried to revenge herself upon Hamburg by placing an embargo on trade between the city and any of her lands, and ordering the seizure of any Hamburg ships that might be in her island ports. Fortunately there was neither trade nor ships, but the Swedish government would not countenance a friendly city thus being gratuitously insulted, and in the end Christina was obliged to rescind her orders.

Naturally, as with the *débâcle* in Sweden, Christina attempted to present the Hamburg incident as proof once again of her own sang-froid and wisdom in the face of grave provocation. But she had in fact experienced two serious blows within a few weeks of each other, galling reminders that hers was no longer the power to command. Another prick to her self-esteem came in the autumn. Adami, who had been suffering for months from the Swedish government's determination to make matters as difficult as possible for Christina's administration, as well as the Queen's own ingratitude and impatience and the jealousies of her household, asked to leave her service. Realizing too late his ability, Christina tried to persuade Adami to remain in Sweden, but he had had enough. To the Queen's gracious farewell and expression of the hope of seeing him again if she went to Loreto (at no great distance from his native town), Adami made the curt reply: "Yes, if I am at Fermo," leaving her with the strong impression that she had made yet another enemy.

So the Queen's business affairs dragged on without reaching any definite conclusion—there was even the humiliating prospect of the Swedish government's sending a commission to enquire into the administration of her Pomeranian estates. Miserably, Christina realized that she must reconcile herself to spending yet another winter in Hamburg. She found distractions where she could, Borri the alchemist for one, a dubious character but clever enough to convince the Marquis Del Monte that he had cured him of a serious illness. But the hope of playing some grand role in politics was what sustained her most. A brilliant new idea now occurred to the Queen, which would at one and the same time solve all her troublesome financial problems and give her a basis of personal power upon which to base her future operations. This was a proposal that Sweden should take over all her lands for the sum of a million and a half Riksdaler, but that pending the payment of this vast amount in full, Christina should receive as security the Duchy of Bremen (awarded to Sweden under the terms of the Treaty of Westphalia). Realizing that such an important project would require her return to Sweden for negotiations, Christina now appointed—not as her agent but as her "envoy"—a Pomeranian gentleman called Bernard von Rosenbach to represent her at the Swedish court, for even she realized that a good deal of pacification would have to take place before the Regents were likely to agree to her again setting foot on Swedish soil.

For his mission Rosenbach received a secret memorandum of instructions, which was more revealing of the mind that dictated it than of the actual conditions prevailing in Sweden. New as he was to his job, even Rosenbach would have taken with a grain of salt phrases such as "Her Majesty loves her native country, and will love it until death. It is this love that has made her suffer everything with a patience which is even more admirable because she is in possession of a hundred means of revenging herself, but her love for her country will always triumph. . . ." While in following Her Majesty's instructions to cultivate her friends, Rosenbach must have found it a trifle misleading to be told that they were as numerous as the inhabitants of Sweden, even including the Lutheran clergy. Christina did admit that there were a few exceptions, whose names she had communicated to her envoy by word of mouth, but from the tone of the rest of his instructions it is evident that these enemies were the powers who ruled Sweden. The main object of Rosenbach's instructions was to convince the Swedish authorities that the Queen would be prepared to return without a priest to carry out negotiations—though in actual fact, she was not.

Christina reiterated her belief that all Sweden was for her, except the government, in a letter written to Azzolino about this time. She said: "All who command in Sweden fear and hate me, and all who obey, love and desire me . . . you can please yourself by believing the reports of others whom you consider to be better informed. I assure you however that I do not love life enough not to be willing to expose it to some risk on this occasion. . . . I have lost all that makes it agreeable to me. . . . For your consolation I will tell you only that my return to Rome is not as close as you fear. Your happiness will not be troubled for long by my presence, and if I can, as I hope, overcome the strength of the fatality that links me to Rome, I will go in search of some corner of the world where poverty is not an ignominy as it is in Rome, and where I will have the consolation that mine will not be eternally cast at me as a reproach by you."

Having certainly received reports from Adami of what had actually occurred during the Queen's last journey to Sweden, Azzolino was justifiably worried about her proposed return. Clearly he was also trying to instil a little common sense into her projects by pointing out that the settlement of her financial affairs was more important than any grandiose gestures that she might be meditating. But, reading between the lines of Christina's letter, it seems that relations between them had degenerated—as Secretary of State Azzolino would have to be doubly careful of his reputation—and the Bremen plan was an alternative to the Queen's returning to Rome without the money which was essential to her leading there a life on the lordly scale that suited her.

Rosenbach arrived in Stockholm at the end of June 1668. The diet was in session and he thought it an opportune moment to tackle the Råd on the question of the Queen's return to Sweden, but immediately realized that the religious question constituted an insurmountable obstacle. He need not have worried, however, as shortly afterwards he received instructions from Christina to concentrate all his energies on the question of the Duchy of Bremen. Hoping, no doubt, that agreement to this proposition might distract the Queen from other issues, the Regency were surprisingly willing to lend an ear to this project, interpreting it to mean that Christina would be willing to exchange the revenues from her other estates for those of Bremen. Nothing could have been further from Her Majesty's mind: full sovereign rights were what she demanded, including a vote in the councils of the Empire, the right to coin money and, of course, to practise the Catholic religion in a Protestant duchy. Rosenbach's failure to negotiate an agreement along these lines was a foregone conclusion. But well before his efforts had reached their predestined dismal end, his royal mistress was hot in pursuit of much bigger game.

A year had passed since June 1667 when the Queen had let fall in her letter to Adami the significant comment that she "might succeed the King of Poland." Events were now to show that this was no chance phrase penned in a moment of anger. The death, on 10th May, 1667, of Queen Maria Luisa (Gonzaga) of Poland, had indeed precipitated a crisis in that country. Her widower, King John Casimir, the last male representative of the Wasas, had twenty years before renounced his religious vows and cardinal's hat under pressure from the Pope and Mazarin, to take up the burden of his dead brother's crown—also marrying the now dead Maria Luisa. What with wars and insurrections the King's reign had not been a happy one, and now he was determined to lay down the burden. He had come to a convenient arrangement with Louis XIV that he would receive some comfortable benefices and an annuity of 20,000 écus if he abdicated before 20th September 1668. The King of France already had two candidates ready for the electors of the Polish throne to choose from—the Duke of Neuburg and the Prince de Condé. In spite of pressure from Rome—Clement IX feared the chances of a schismatic candidate, the Tzar's son, and even more the threat of insecurity in Poland at a time when the Turkish menace to Crete was increasing daily—John Casimir remained firm in his resolve and abdicated on 16th September 1668.

The idea that benefits might be obtained from her relationship to the Polish Wasas had been in Christina's mind for several years. In 1661 Azzolino had written to enquire from the nuncio in Poland about the provisions of John Casimir's will. For, by the marriage to a Sforza of one of his predecessors, the King still owned estates in Italy and Christina evidently had hopes of inheriting these (in fact she later contested the provisions of his will for years, because he had made the Princess Palatine, born

Anna Gonzaga, his heir). It is also probable that, long before, Azzolino and Christina had discussed the possibility of her becoming Queen of Poland after John Casimir's death, for she now acted with remarkable promptitude in putting forward her candidature.

In fact there were no less than four candidates for the throne of Poland. Apart from those already mentioned, there was Prince Charles of Lorraine, who had the backing of the Emperor, but so did the Duke of Neuburg, who was also supported by Sweden and Brandenburg. It is doubtful, however, if any of them held much appeal for the Poles, with the possible exception of Condé, who was supported by the great John Sobieski. It is understandable therefore that Christina should feel that as the last available Wasa, she would have a good chance of success.

Even without consulting Azzolino, early in August 1668 Christina dispatched a messenger to the nuncio in Poland, Monsignore Marescotti, bearing a letter of credence and a request for assistance in presenting her claims to the Polish electors. The messenger was Father Hacki, a Polish monk of the Order of Citeaux, who had for a while been the Queen's chaplain in Hamburg. Naturally Christina based her claims upon being a Wasa—a member of the House that had ruled both Sweden and Poland—and stated that she would never have abdicated if she had reigned over a Catholic country. She went on to say that as she neither desired to marry, nor was of an age to do so (and therefore would have no heirs), the Poles need not fear for their liberty, for after her death they would be free to elect a representative of another House as their king. For the rest she confided her case to the nuncio, asking for his prudent counsel. However the Queen lost no time in writing also to the Pope, to request his support.

Although Clement IX had already promised this both to the Duke of Neuburg and the Prince of Lorraine, who had also asked for it, his nephew Cardinal Rospigliosi was now instructed to write to the nuncio in Poland, telling him to add the Queen's name to the list of the Pope's favoured candidates. There was a rider, however, that this was to be kept secret until a favourable opportunity presented itself. Still, Monsignore Marescotti was assured that His Holiness was much interested in the matter and wished to do everything to bring it to a successful conclusion. A few days later Cardinal Rospigliosi wrote again, to say that the Pope's support of the Queen's candidature should be made known to the electors, but again there was the saving clause that this should only be done "when you see an opportunity for probable success or a well-founded hope for the Queen." Azzolino wrote by the same post, admitting the difficulty raised by Christina's sex, but discounting this on the grounds that all the world considered her to be superior to a mere man, and promising on the Queen's behalf that the nuncio would get a cardinal's hat if she was elected.

This was not the first offer of its kind. The Duke of Neuburg had been first in the field, and Marescotti had a firm belief in his chances which, knowing the Poles, he certainly had not in Christina's case. However, with so much pressure from Rome the good nuncio felt that it was at least his duty to point out to them and to the Queen that her sex and her well-known desire for celibacy were serious obstacles to her election. Having done this, he asked for a papal brief to support the cause, but from the first he did not conceal from Azzolino that there was little hope of the Queen's success. The brief was duly dispatched early in September and, always in secret, the negotiations ran on for months. At first the Queen kept her secretaries furiously busy copying out declarations for the Poles, but after the first rush of enthusiasm it is evident that in her own mind Christina was not at all sure whether she really wished for the success of her venture.

This fact emerges very clearly in the Queen's letters to Azzolino. Although she thanked him effusively for all his efforts on her behalf, sent him copies of all her communications with Poland, and declared that she would abide by his judgment in everything, she still held back. The reason was, of course, her fear of separation from him. For now with a project on hand in which they both worked in unison, their relations were restored to normal, though Christina accused Azzolino outright of working so hard for her in order to get rid of her. Fears of living in a barbarous country of which she knew neither the language nor the customs, she told him, appalled her, and the only means to make such a life bearable would be for Azzolino to become Polish too. Otherwise she would not accept the crown of Poland "even if it was offered to me with that of the Universe."

If Christina's attitude is not difficult to understand, the same cannot be said of the Pope and Azzolino. How two men so well informed about the political world could ever have believed that a warlike people like the Poles would accept a woman of forty-two as their sovereign, is a mystery. In addition to this, good and kindly as he was, Clement IX could hardly have ignored the fact that the Queen's reputation in Europe was not exactly spotless. The reasons for his sanctioning her candidature must surely be found in his personal friendship for Christina and Azzolino's influence.

Azzolino's motives are very much more difficult to assess. The Queen's election would, of course, have solved her financial problems, and governing the ungovernable Poles would have absorbed even her restless energy, which at present was driving her to pursue one wild plan after another. But at this juncture in history, with the Turkish threat to Christian Europe growing daily, might Christina on the Polish throne not prove to be more of a liability than an asset? Here we have to consider Azzolino's personal situation. He was an ambitious man who had come a long way, like everyone else in Rome he knew that Clement IX was delicate and unlikely to live for more than a few years. Given some time as Secretary of State, he himself might stand a chance of achieving his ultimate ambition of being elected Pope, an opportunity that would probably never return. If Clement died early this was highly improbable and a new Pope would want one of his own relatives as secretary of state. In either event it seems likely that Azzolino thought that Christina's presence in Rome would not help his chances and, possibly, he calculated that if she was Queen of Poland he could rule there as Mazarin had done in France, if his hopes of achieving the papacy seemed impossible. Whatever his reasons, the cardinal now exerted himself to his utmost to get Christina elected Queen of Poland.

From the first the nuncio and Hacki had warned everyone that, apart from her sex, the biggest obstacle to Christina's being elected would be her refusal to marry and, even if she did so, at her age the unlikelihood of her producing heirs. In private Christina was perfectly honest about the fact that nothing would induce her to marry. But she agreed to connive at allowing the Polish electors to believe that she would in fact do so, though she never personally committed herself further than to say that she would not marry without the electors' consent.

Azzolino tried by every means—except the expenditure of money, which was the only one likely to work with the electors—to convince the somewhat harassed nuncio that Christina was the ideal candidate. He held up dazzling visions not only of the return of Livonia to Poland but of union with Sweden if little Charles XI died, and that country's ultimate conversion to the true faith. He also suggested that the Queen would surely make a brilliant marriage, and there was every likelihood of her producing children. In his concern to reassure the nuncio on this important point, Azzolino for once forgot the extraordinary discretion that usually characterized his every action. In cipher he informed Monsignore Marescotti that the Queen's "temperament is still so flourishing, that now one could certainly hope that her fertility would continue for another ten years (until Christina was fifty-two), whereas before her excessive ardour might possibly have prevented it." This apparently frank statement has been interpreted to mean that Azzolino himself believed that Christina had led an immoral life, but as he was lying unblushingly about the Queen's willingness to marry in order to secure her election, the same motive could well have induced him to lie about the rest. For he evidently knew full well that despite Christina's reputation in Europe, in spite of all the lovers who were attributed to her, there had never been a rumour of her having had a child and that this, coupled with the stories of her being a hermaphrodite, would make the Poles believe that she was barren. Hence Azzolino's "admission" of the Queen's former "excessive ardour," which coincided with the belief, still current in Europe at the end of the eighteenth century, that a woman given to over-indulgence in sex was unlikely to conceive.*

* According to H. Acton, *The Bourbons of Naples* (London 1956, p. 294 ff.), in the last quarter of the eighteenth century the Austrian-born Queen Maria Carolina of Naples was pre-occupied by her daughter-in-law's failure to conceive, and attributed it to the fact that "her husband is her husband two or three times in 24 hours, a matter which interests her" and was of the opinion that until the young couple settled down to a "more moderate" existence, they would be unlikely to have children. The theory has also been advanced that in referring to Queen Christina's "excessive ardour"—in the

However, Azzolino had not penned this final effort at persuasion until April 1669, long after the Queen had left Hamburg. Indeed, "filled with joy that souls feel on leaving purgatory" she had taken her departure on 20th October 1668. In her heart of hearts Christina knew very well that her two and a half years of exile had accomplished nothing, except to increase the suspicion and hatred with which she was regarded by the government in Sweden. None the less, she announced to Azzolino that she was returning "glorious, having arranged everything in a way that will please you" and that "all my affairs in Sweden are settled and signed. The diet has given me liberty to practise religion and ordered that all my pretensions should be satisfied. . . . The same diet has furiously cut the talons of the Regency. I will give you an exact description of everything and you will be pleased."

The truth was very different. The Regents had made able use of Christina's embargo on trade between Hamburg and her own estates to point out that this was an insult to a power which had always been friendly with Sweden, thus illustrating the dangers involved in the return of such a woman to the kingdom. As a result the Queen had now been formally forbidden to return to her native land during the young King's minority (this news had actually reached her the day before she wrote her glowing letter to Azzolino). The vaunted freedom of religion therefore did not apply to Sweden at all, but simply to one or two towns in the Duchies of Bremen and Verden. It was true that the appointment of the farmers general had been completed, and that they were proving to be much more efficient than the former governors whom the Queen had dismissed. But as the latter had included

original Italian *soverchio calore*—Azzolino was using these words in the contemporary medical sense, because the Queen had been diagnosed as a "hot dry woman." But even this interpretation does not cast a more favourable light on the Cardinal's veracity, because a description of the Queen written about this time (actually it is believed in connection with the Polish election campaign), begins with the words "Queen Christina's temperament is hot and dry to a supreme degree, dominated by bile . . . She possesses to the utmost degree all the defects and all the virtues which are to be found in so hot and dry a temperament, she is choleric, proud . . ." Evidently at the age of forty-two, Queen Christina was just as "hot and dry" as she had been at twenty-six, when Bourdelot examined her and confirmed this diagnosis, therefore presumably she was now even less likely to bear children.

influential members of the Swedish aristocracy, upon whom the government had felt it was able to rely to respect the interests of the central power, the Regents were now so incensed against the Queen that she was in danger of losing the right to administer her own lands. All in all it was a disastrous balance sheet.

But Christina did not care, she was on her way back to Azzolino and Rome, where with Clement IX reigning, she was sure of a warm welcome. It was in fact almost as triumphant as that of 1654. Azzolino was waiting to meet her at Terni, the Pope's own nephew outside the city, and in a papal carriage she drove through the Porta del Popolo to be greeted by prelates and nobles. To the booming salute of the cannons of Sant' Angelo the Queen then drove to the Quirinal to be received by His Holiness himself. Christina had returned to the city that was to be her true realm. What did it matter that now for her the phantom crown of Poland was rapidly vanishing into its northern mists?

The final curtain came down on Christina's search for a crown in the spring of 1669. Then at last Monsignore Marescotti plucked up enough courage to tell the Bishop of Poznan (one of the most influential electors) the secret that the Queen was Clement IX's favoured candidate. The pious Bishop crossed himself several times before replying, and then he earnestly begged the nuncio never to let this name pass his lips again for fear of general derision.

CHAPTER 10

Her True Realm: 1668–1689

"Whoever has nothing else in life should come and live in Rome." The words were written by Chateaubriand nearly two centuries after Christina returned there in 1668 for the remainder of her life, but possibly they applied even more to her than to him. During fourteen years lack of money and her own insatiable spirit had driven the Queen in pursuit of a mirage—of the crown, the power and the money that were never again to be hers and, like phantoms, her hopes of Naples, of Poland, even of Sweden perhaps, had vanished. But now in Rome she found at last the realm that she had dreamed of nearly twenty years ago—the realm of the spirit and of the arts with the leisure in which to enjoy them. Surely her old friend Giulio Rospigliosi, that good and kindly man who shared the Queen's love of pictures, of music and the theatre, had realized all this. For now benevolently, as Clement IX, he used his influence to make Christina feel that, whatever tribulations she might have passed through, here in Rome she was welcome and at home, and to his kindliness and understanding she owed one of the happiest years of her life.

Even before the Queen set foot in the capital, the Pope had prepared a welcome for her at Castelnuovo di Farfa, her last stopping place before reaching Rome. For ten days beforehand preparations had been going on in this remote castle in the Sabine hills, so that when Christina arrived there on 21st November she found the whole castle decorated with flowers and garlands of bay leaves and the suite of rooms she was to occupy scented with rose and myrtle water and warmed by log fires fragrant with the perfume of "Portugal pastilles" (probably scented with essences of sweet oranges and lemons). A splendid banquet followed, complete with gilded *trionfi* of sugar and marzipan made in the form of a swan, a phoenix, fountains, fruit trees and flowers; a musical accompaniment was provided by a harpischord specially brought from Rome. This banquet and *alloggio*, as it was called, was the official welcome of the *Camera Apostolica*, the government of the Papal States and, appropriately, twenty-four cardinals met Christina at Castelnuovo to accompany her back to Rome.

Clement IX was, however, determined to demonstrate in person his pleasure at the Queen's return. Early in December he visited her at Palazzo Riario, making a tour of her pictures and shortly afterwards gave a public banquet for her, as Alexander VII had done on her arrival thirteen years before. Rather amusingly, Christina had in fact been invited privately to a meal by the Pope the day before, and also to hear a sermon. Both Clement and Christina were very abstemious in matters of food and drink, and although on that occasion there was a splendid collation served on silver dishes, the Queen only drank a cup of chocolate. This abstemiousness was not, of course, permissible on the tremendous occasion of the public banquet on 9th December, when Don Giambattista Rospigliosi came with a troop of Swiss Guards to accompany Christina from Palazzo Riario to the Quirinal. The tables were laid in the huge saloon which is now the ballroom of the palace, and which on this occasion was hung with strips of red brocade bordered with gold. The seating arrangements seem to have been the same as on the occasion of Alexander VII's banquet, with the Pope's larger table raised on a dais under the canopy and the Queen's placed on his right and standing on the carpet on the floor. This time her chair had arms, but these were neither gilded nor upholstered. On the wall beneath the canopy hung a magnificent tapestry, portraying the Virgin seated on an orb, flanked by Justice and Charity and guarded by lions holding banners; it was in fact the same that is still hung behind the papal throne for public consistories in St Peter's.

A few minutes after the Queen's arrival at the Quirinal Clement came into the banqueting hall and they exchanged greetings; as a graceful compliment Christina herself insisted on handing the Pope his table napkin when he sat down. After this their conversation was limited, owing to the distance between their seats and the musical accompaniment provided by a full orchestra with organ and a choir. But Monsignore Febei acted as messenger between the Pope and his guest, passing from one to the other with reciprocal compliments as the splendid meal progressed. An assembly of distinguished churchmen and gentlemen were honoured by being allowed to watch the proceedings.

Even in the midst of all this grandeur there were some homely touches. Etiquette did not allow even the ladies of the Rospigliosi family to be present, but so great was their desire to witness this magnificent spectacle that they were permitted to stand hidden behind the brocade wall-hangings. Thus the French artist Sevin portrayed them peeping out between the panels in the sketch he made of this august occasion. Clement did not even now drink wine but toasted his guest with a cordial of strawberry, cherry and lemon juice, specially concocted to look like wine, while she stood to receive the compliment and the onlookers knelt. When the table cloths were removed after the dessert, a chair was actually placed for the Queen at the Pope's table, thus offering her a greater honour than any woman had received within living memory. It was Clement's acknowledgment of the friendship and esteem that he felt for Christina, and of her good offices in having from the first assured the all-powerful Louis XIV that he was the most worthy candidate at the Conclave of 1667. As further earnest of his goodwill, in the New Year the Pope awarded Christina a pension of 12,000 scudi a year.

The reign of a liberal Pope, combined with Christina's return and the residence in Rome of another carnival enthusiast, Marie Mancini, now Princess Colonna, combined to make the carnival of 1669 the most brilliant that Rome was to see for many a long year. Since the days of Paul II at the end of the fifteenth century, the carnival celebrations had usually been held in the Corso and Piazza Venezia (then called Piazza di S. Marco). Entertainment was provided by races of all kinds, in earlier days these had included races by prostitutes and Jews—the latter had only been finally suppressed by Clement IX in 1668—by men, boys and horses of all kinds, culminating in the grand finale of the wild career of the riderless Barberi or Arab Barbs. These were constant features, but there were also the spectacular processions of carnival cars, which varied from year to year according to the attitude of the reigning pontiff to such diversions and the whims and fancies of the Roman nobility. For, surprising as it may seem, such august persons themselves paraded, clad in gorgeous robes and jewels, upon the allegorical cars that processed down the Corso. The previous year Clement IX's young Rospigliosi nephews had staged a spectacular hunting procession, while the beautiful Marie Mancini had ridden on a car representing the personification of the planets.

In 1669, to celebrate her return, Christina had erected in front of one of the houses in the Piazza Venezia what really amounted to a grandstand from which to view the carnival, outmatching even her previous one of 1666 which had cost 3,000 scudi. Although outwardly they were on the best of terms, in fact there seems to have been a certain amount of subterranean rivalry between the Queen, who had been dubbed *Padrona di Roma*, and the ravishing twenty-five-year-old Marie Mancini, whose husband was the head of one of the oldest and most powerful Roman families and fabulously rich as well.

For the carnival of 1669 Marie arranged not one, but two processions, of which she was the cynosure, first as the sorceress Armida, riding with a train of gallants dressed as Turks, then as Circe, triumphantly seated on top of a car filled with wild animals (safely "cabined, cribbed and confined" in a very restricted cage). Evidently even Christina realized that she could not compete with the glowing beauty of youth. So, taking her stand firmly on her royal dignity, she watched the displays from beneath the enormous crown which surmounted the central box of her grandstand, surrounded by a court of twenty-four cardinals, unfortunately exactly the same number as Marie's Turks—there was some argument among the Romans as to which lady had come off best. However, there was a special display in the piazza in front of the Queen's grandstand, staged as a tournament in mediaeval style with mounted cavaliers riding at the ring (a contemporary form of tent-pegging) and tilting at the Saracen's head, which like the English quintain swung round and gave the unsuccessful marksman a buffet.

These were popular entertainments. For the *cognoscenti*, however, this year's carnival was chiefly memorable for the theatrical season sponsored by the Queen in the Palazzo Colonna in the Borgo, usually known as the Palazzo Inglese because it had been the English Embassy in the days of Henry VIII (it is now Palazzo Torlonia). Christina had taken a lease of the palace early in December 1668 just after her return to Rome, its great attraction being the theatre, which did not exist in Palazzo Riario. It also seems that the Queen and Azzolino were prudently preparing against the day when he might no longer be Secretary of State, and would therefore lose his official lodging.

Christina took advantage of the presence in Italy of Tiberio Fiorilli, the famous Scaramuccia, with his troupe (on a year's holiday granted him by Louis XIV), to engage him to play two comedies a week for her—Italian on Fridays, Spanish on Sundays. The series began on 18th January with Scaramuccia's *Gelosia*. But the great event of the season was the first performance of Filippo Acciajoli's comedy *L'Empio punito*. The author was a melodramatic poet of some renown (his burlesque melodrama *Il Girello* had been the sensation of the previous carnival) and was descended from the dukes of Athens (his brother Niccolò Acciajoli was soon to be created cardinal). It is not surprising therefore that the practically all-male audience assembled for the first performance included twenty-six cardinals and, discreetly hidden away incognito in a box, Princess Marie Colonna.

Acciajoli was not only an author but also producer, he had travelled a great deal and made a serious study of stage machinery and techniques, and his production on this occasion was welcomed as a triumph. There were ten, some say twelve, changes of scene, involving both the wings and the flies—indicating an advanced technique hitherto unknown in Rome. The sets were universally admired as being of remarkable ingenuity; they varied from halls, galleries and ante-chambers to woods and gardens. However, in spite of his ancient lineage and priestly brother, Acciajoli's comedies were acknowledged to be extremely salty, which was possibly the reason for the absence of the six cardinal bishops—apparently the only members of the Sacred College then in Rome who did not attend the performance. Not that this saltiness would have troubled Christina, for according to the Genoese diplomatic representative the comedies given by her in Palazzo Riario in 1666 had been *sporchissime* (very dirty).

Happily settled in Rome, Christina now turned to a new venture, that of archaeologist. She obtained the Pope's permission to excavate the ruins of Decius's palace near the Church of S. Lorenzo in Panisperna on the Viminal Hill. Excavation at that time was, of course, far from scientific, in fact rather in the nature of a treasure hunt for marbles and mosaics. On this occasion the Queen was rewarded by the discovery of a remarkably beautiful Venus with a dolphin, dating from the first century A.D. and resembling that of the Capitol.

While she was still in Sweden Christina had collected classical sculptures, but these she was forced to leave behind and nearly all of them were lost in the disastrous fire which destroyed Stockholm Castle in 1697. It is not certain exactly when the Queen began to collect in Rome, but it was probably as soon as she was established in the Palazzo Riario. She continued doing so right through the years, so that at the time of her death she possessed more than 160 sculptures, apart from columns, urns and decorative adjuncts. For her early purchases whilst still in Sweden Christina had naturally been obliged to rely upon the taste and knowledge of scholars and travellers whom she had commissioned to buy for her. But once she was settled in Rome her collection was a matter of personal choice, much more so in fact than her famous gallery of pictures, the cream of which had been provided ready-made, as it were, by the Italian schools represented in the Emperor Rudolf II's collection. The only addition of major importance made by the Queen herself to this nucleus had been twenty paintings from the Imperiali collection bought en bloc for her in Genoa by Azzolino while she was in Hamburg in 1667, which included a Titian and a Rubens and some smaller works by Raphael.

Christina's sculpture collection is therefore of great interest as revealing her own personal taste and knowledge, more particularly because it was built up over a long period of time, when rarely if ever did she have much money at her disposal. Each item must therefore have been the result of a definite personal preference, gratified only at the expense of something else (or of incurring further debts and Azzolino's disapproval) and probably as the result of careful negotiation because there were many other richer buyers in the field.

An outstanding example of an acquisition made in the latter

circumstances is the famous group originally thought to represent Castor and Pollux, now called after the King of Spain's gardens of S. Ildenfonso, where it stood for many years.* The Queen first heard of this group from Carlo Maratta, who wanted to buy it himself and present it to the Capitoline Museum. Evidently the price was too high for Maratta, as Christina persuaded him to act as her agent and buy it for her, thus securing one of the most admired classical sculptural groups of her time. Infinitely more prized today, however, is the bronze head of a Greek athlete, dating from about 300 B.C. which was also evidently one of the Queen's greatest treasures. This stood among her most prized possessions, on a table in the *Sala dei Quadri* in front of the famous mirror that Bernini designed specially for her, framed with figures representing Truth being unveiled by Time. It is true that Christina believed the head to be a portrait of her hero Alexander the Great, and would have valued it particularly for this association, but it is also a consummate work of art, evoking the life and beauty of the Hellenistic age.

Although, in accordance with the custom of her time, Christina employed sculptors to restore her classical statues by replacing broken and missing limbs (and even in the case of Clytia using the fragment of a torso to create an entirely new composition), it is notable that the most important works in her collection were classical Greek or early Roman copies of Greek originals of about the third century B.C., indicating a classical taste of considerable perception. This is all the more remarkable because it must be borne in mind that until the nineteenth century, with very rare exceptions, Greek sculpture was only known to the Western world through Roman copies. Canova's exclamation: "If only I could begin again," on seeing the Elgin marbles for the first time as an old man, indicates the impact of that revelation. Nevertheless, in the baroque age of the seventeenth century, Christina was evidently endowed with the eye to see and appreciate the beauty of sculpture that did not correspond to the taste of her time, but

* The large majority of Christina's sculptures are now in Spain in the Prado, having been bought by Philip V from the Odescalchi family in Rome who had bought them, together with most of Christina's treasures, from Azzolino's nephew, who had inherited them from the Cardinal to whom Christina left everything.

approached more closely "the glory that was Greece." In fact her friend the French scholar Gilles Menage said of her: "The Queen of Sweden would not have been one of those who today advocate the new before the old. She preferred the old."

By the spring of 1669 the halcyon months of Clement IX's reign were drawing to a close. Everything was overshadowed by fears for the fate of Crete, the last bulwark of Christianity in the eastern Mediterranean to survive from the days of the Crusades. For long the Pope and Christina had shared an awareness of the Turkish menace to Christian Europe and, friendship apart, this had probably been one of the underlying reasons for his having sponsored her candidature as Queen of Poland. So able a man as Clement could not have shared the Queen's illusions about her military capacities, but with Christina as a figurehead Poland could have been strengthened as the eastern bastion of Christianity, and indeed in the end salvation was to come from there in 1683 in the person of the great John Sobieski. But now for months Clement had been striving to awaken the sovereigns of western Europe to the peril, and to galvanize them into action to save Crete. His diplomatic action in hastening the Peace of Aix-la-Chapelle, which finally brought an end to the Franco-Spanish war in May 1668, had also been undertaken with this aim in mind. Clement had his reward, for at last in July of the same year Louis XIV agreed that a body of volunteers should be recruited under the command of the Duc de La Feuillade and should sail for the relief of the Venetian garrison besieged in the fortress of Candia under the banner of the Knights of Malta. Help was indeed forthcoming from many European states, but internecine jealousies among the various forces had a negative effect. In order to try and counteract this, in March 1669 the Pope named his own nephew, Vincenzo Rospigliosi, as Commander-in-Chief of all Forces, creating the Duc de Beaufort and the Comte de Vivonne, the commanders of a further French expedition, papal admirals, because Louis XIV still refused to declare war on the Sublime Porte.

Thus united under the Papal banner, a mixed force of Papal, French, Venetian and Order of Malta galleys and transports made a rendezvous near the island of Cerigo, and on 20th June at dead of night the troops disembarked in the harbour of Candia. They were confronted by a scene of destruction and horror, everywhere there was the smell of corpses, and the garrison was practically reduced to wounded and crippled men. In a desperate effort to redeem the situation, the Duc de Beaufort led a sortie on 25th June, but he was killed and the action was a failure. So too were all subsequent ventures of the kind. Further reinforcements from Bavaria, Italy and Malta, which arrived during July and August, were decimated by sickness as much as attacks and enemy bombardment. On 20th August, owing to disagreement among the commanders, nearly all the French troops re-embarked and left, followed not long afterwards by Rospigliosi, the Maltese and the Savoyards. With the fortress reduced to ruins by a siege of two years, at last on 28th August the gallant Venetian commander, Francesco Morosini, opened negotiations for surrender. On 6th September the capitulation was actually signed, but in recognition of Morosini's glorious defence, as a peace treaty.

Definite news of the fall of Crete did not reach Rome until 25th October. For months the bells of all the city churches had rung every night calling for prayers to save the island. Now they were silent and the Romans knew that all hope had gone. What they did not know was what had happened to the Pope after he had made a pilgrimage to the seven churches.* When he heard the news of Crete, during the night of 25th October Clement IX had a stroke. It was officially announced that the Pope, who had rallied afterwards, was suffering from severe catarrah in the head, but he himself was well aware that he had not long to live. Although again on 1st November Clement visited the seven churches, during the whole of the rest of the month he was ill. Evidently he hoped that a slight change for the better might enable him to hold a public consistory, for he wished to create seven new cardinals and so strengthen the Sacred College before his death. But a relapse on the 29th made him realize that this hope was to be denied to him. So on the same evening in his bedroom in the Quirinal, the Consistory took place. Among those created cardinal was Clement's *Maestro di Camera,* the seventy-nine-year-old Emilio Altieri. After receiving Extreme Unction on 2nd December, the Pope said goodbye to his closest friends. Christina was

* The seven great basilicas of Rome: St Peter's, St Paul's-Without-The-Walls, St John Lateran, S. Croce, S. Sebastiano, S. Maria Maggiore and St Lawrence-Without-The-Walls, normally visited by pilgrims in Holy Year.

present and was so touched by the tenderness of Clement's farewell that she burst into tears.

At dawn on 9th December Clement died. That night his body was carried in an open litter through the darkening streets of Rome to the Vatican. The sorrowing crowds realized that the loss of Crete had also brought about the death of one of the most beloved popes who ever reigned. For Christina the day had an added poignancy: exactly a year earlier, well and cheerful, Clement had honoured her by his banquet.

The Queen's and Azzolino's mourning for Clement IX, as pope, friend and benefactor was no less sincere because they knew that his death would bring with it a crisis in their own lives, and particularly in that of Azzolino. Their joy at Clement's election and the popularity of his reign must always have been tempered by the knowledge that, given his delicate health, his pontificate was not likely to be a long one. Equally they were both aware that the coming Conclave would be a crucial one in Azzolino's career. Although at the age of forty-eight there could be no question of his being numbered among the *papabili*, the prolonged reign of a hostile pope could result in the Cardinal being relegated to the background, perhaps for ever. Azzolino was admittedly ambitious, but his ambition was by no means entirely personal. His membership of the flying squadron, that small independent group which in many ways represented the best in the Sacred College shows this. For the squadron's avowed intent was to fight old abuses such as nepotism, and above all, by its non-alignment with any particular country, to assure the freedom of the Church from the political interference of the great powers. In the seventeenth century this was indeed a courageous and forward-thinking attitude, for the emperors and kings of France and Spain possessed the right of exclusion, which meant that during a Conclave they could place a veto on any particular cardinal whom they did not wish to see elected, thus excluding him absolutely from the papacy.*

When the Conclave opened in the Vatican on 20th December, 1669, several of the cardinals had not yet arrived in Rome, and in

* This right was still exercised as late as 1903 by the Emperor Franz-Joseph who excluded Cardinal Rampolla at the Conclave of that year. It was however finally repudiated for ever by Pius X immediately after his election.

fact only sixty-five out of the total of seventy finally took part in it. From the first most people realized that this was likely to be a long and difficult Conclave, for there were no really outstanding figures and the number of *papabili* was reckoned as high as twenty-one. In preparation for the event Christina moved into the Palazzo Colonna in the Borgo, because it was within the Leonine City, and her messengers to Azzolino would not be required to show a pass to the guards at the gates, as they would have done if they were coming from Palazzo Riario, thus drawing attention to the closeness of their relationship.

At this time Conclave security regulations were such that even the windows of Azzolino's cell in the sealed-off area in the Vatican were walled up, though Christina could see the bricks and mortar which blocked his window from the garden of the Palazzo Colonna in the Borgo. Nevertheless they were in constant communication, for the Queen had taken it upon herself to provide Azzolino with a very effective intelligence service. She wrote to him constantly, sometimes as many as three long letters a day, keeping him minutely informed about Roman and European politics, the gossip of the salons and the piazzas. The aim and object of so much effort was to get Cardinal Vidoni elected. Indeed he seemed a very likely candidate, for Vidoni was one of the most talked-of among the *papabili*—able, energetic, neither too young nor too old and acceptable to both France and Spain. But there is an old Roman proverb which says: "Who goes into a Conclave a pope comes out a cardinal."

The first few weeks of the Conclave were really spent in marking time, because under Louis XIV French power had become so preponderant in Europe that no decisive action could be taken before the arrival of the French cardinals, Retz and Bouillon, and the Ambassador, the Duc de Chaulnes, bearing the King's secret instructions. Nevertheless, from the very first moment, even before the sealing-off of the Conclave area, Azzolino and Christina were acting their parts. Their opening gambit was to show a complete disregard for Vidoni, for Azzolino believed in operating in secret and only revealing his real aims at the eleventh hour. In fact, he wrote a number of political aphorisms on this very subject. Thus, when the Queen and other privileged persons made a tour of the Conclave area before it was sealed off, Christina, while standing in front of Vidoni's cell, was heard to exclaim "not *papabile*." As a finesse this was not really of a very high order. The whole of Rome knew very well that Vidoni had been one of the most discussed candidates, and by denying it Christina did not make people believe either in her ignorance or her lack of interest, but instead indicated clearly to the intricate though not very subtle Roman mind that there was *qualche cosa di sotto* (more than meets the eye) in her apparent indifference.

Through one of the coldest winters within memory, Azzolino and the Queen were there at their posts of duty, bravely fighting their devious battle for Cardinal Vidoni. Like many other members of the Sacred College, Azzolino succumbed to the freezing draughts and mediaeval lack of comfort of the Vatican, and caught a violent cold. Being younger and of a stouter spirit than the others he did not escape to the comfort of his own home, but remained confined to his bed in his icy cell. However, on 6th January he wrote a note to Christina to tell her that he was recovering rapidly and, whether by accident or design, began the missive with the letters "S.M." In Italian these would represent an abbreviation of the correct form of address to a Queen—Sua Maestà—but in times gone by these letters had evidently had another esoteric meaning for Decio Azzolino and Christina. For in her reply the Queen was so overjoyed that she wrote: "Am I mistaken, or do the letters S.M. no longer signify what they used to do? If you could imagine the joy that the sight of them has given me, you would believe me really worthy of this title which I prefer to that of Queen of the Universe. But I cannot be worthy of it because you have taken it from me. Do what you like, I am yours to such a degree that only by terrible injustice and cruelty can you doubt that I am worthy of 'S.M.'" Poor Christina, she was so carried away by the joy that the secret meaning of these letters afforded her that she neglected to write this highly personal note on a separate piece of paper from her long and detailed account of her first political discussion with Monsignore Zetina. This earned a stiff rebuke from Azzolino (with whom, one suspects, business nearly always came first). Drily he suggested to the Queen that in future she should separate personal from political affairs, because he had been unable to show her interesting letter to his colleagues.

At last on 16th January the all-important French contingent arrived, and their activities seemed to favour Vidoni's prospects. After some weeks of ostensible neutrality, which had led Cardinals Medici and Chigi who were working together, supported by the Spanish faction, to propose the candidature of Cardinal d'Elce, the Duc de Chaulnes, acting on the instructions of his master, declared D'Elce excluded by France. This was doubly reassuring for Azzolino, as the French were now evidently supporting Vidoni, while Cardinal Chigi had suffered a setback, all the more gratifying because he had become Azzolino's personal opponent, and was determined to block Vidoni's candidature at any cost.

For another two months the struggle in the Conclave continued, the candidate of one faction being ruthlessly turned down by the others. The long duration of the Conclave was arousing unfavourable comment among its members, in Rome, and in the world at large. This was variously expressed by Cardinal Hesse justifiably writing to the Emperor to complain of the interference of the secular powers, and the gardner of the Villa Medici naming two new anemones *sede vacante* and *conclave arrabbiato* ("See vacant" and "conclave enraged"). Finally, seeing that the situation could continue indefinitely, Cardinal Chigi broke with the Spanish faction. In transferring his allegiance to France however, he succeeded, with the help of the Venetian Ambassador, in getting the principle accepted by the French and the Spaniards that a cardinal created by Clement IX would be acceptable to them both. The only question that now remained to be solved was which. Finally the choice fell on the devout, kindly but aged Emilio Altieri (he was seventy-nine). Thus on 29th April Azzolino and the flying squadron were taken completely by surprise. Vainly Azzolino tried to delay the final vote, but now practically his only supporter was Cardinal Altieri himself, who with tears in his eyes protested his own unworthiness and age.

Aged though he was, Clement X (as Altieri styled himself in gratitude to his predecessor) reigned six years and proved to be a devout and kindly pope. But his accession was a triumph for Azzolino's enemy Chigi, who inevitably now attained considerable power. The result of the Conclave was a heavy blow to Christina and the Cardinal, who for months had strained every nerve to get Vidoni elected, and for the most honourable reasons. However estimable a man and pope Clement X might be, the forces of foreign political influence which had ultimately brought about his election were exactly those from which Azzolino and the flying squadron were trying to free the Church. They failed, as perhaps they were bound to do in the seventeenth century, but their action pointed the way for the future.

It is possible that this failure was partly due to the fact that Christina and Azzolino were themselves typical representatives of their age. The Queen was not the only one who could congratulate herself upon her "profound dissimulation." Azzolino also seems to have preferred the twisted to the simpler course, even when striving for the most admirable ends. With what appears to us today to be a childish belief in his own powers of deception, Azzolino was capable in the Conclave of stooping to so trivial a device as letting fall a misleading note, ostensibly intended for the Queen, but written with the intention of leading the rival faction to believe that he was now prepared to desert Vidoni. Possibly a little less subtlety might have won the day (for he deceived no one but himself), but that was something that neither the Cardinal nor Christina would ever have believed—very humanly, they were united in their failings no less than in their advanced ideas of freeing the Church from secular power-politics.

The Queen's reaction on hearing the news of Clement X's election was characteristic. She swore, and then promptly ordered her carriage so as to be among the first to show her obedience to the new Pontiff. Christina was now forty-six and, had she but known it, the part that she had just played in helping Azzolino in the Conclave was the last really significant political role of her life. Judging from comments in her letters right up to the time of her death, she was rarely if ever aware of this, but in fact the years were now having a mellowing effect upon the Queen, who was beginning to take life more slowly and philosophically.

Something of this had already become evident by inference in her letters written towards the end of her stay in Hamburg. Though the caustic wit was still there—in a letter to Vossius, asking for his edition of Ptolemy, Christina wrote: "You are aware that I am at present in a country where the conversation of the dead (the ancient writers) must console one for that of the living." Nevertheless it was plain that her chief consolation in her present boredom and unhappiness were the comfortable ones of age—books and letters from her friends. Christina's epistolary output was in fact tremendous, and from these letters it is evident that she really did value her old friends, keeping in touch with them even after she had not seen them for years. So, from Hamburg we find her writing a letter of condolence to Countess von Dohna, now the widow of that once gay young blade Christopher Delphicus, who had died a Field Marshal, but had lived in Christina's memory as the companion of her flight from Sweden fourteen years before. In her letter she recalled "the friendship and affection he always showed me."

But the recurrent theme in the Queen's letters from Hamburg had been requests for all the Roman gossip: "Were the French Ambassador and Ambassadress sincerely pleased with my apartment, furniture and pictures? What is the gossip of Casa Rospigliosi (of the Rospigliosi family)? Of the Borghese's hunt? I want to hear the story of the balcony and all the intrigues of the women in Rome," are fair samples of Christina's requests for news. She had in fact so taken her second country to heart that the *pettegolezzi* (an Italian term for gossip and rumour) were as much the breath of life to her as to any Roman born. There were, of course, to be many more serious pursuits in the Queen's life in the Eternal City, but it is against this comfortable gossipy background, so strangely at variance with the drama of her earlier years, that the remainder of it was to be spent.

It is significant that many of the Queen's requests for Roman gossip had been addressed to the Comte Jacques d'Alibert, a young man of parts who had entered her service as her French secretary, after he had succeeded in attracting the Queen's attention by designing a remarkable carnival car upon which Apollo and the Muses were represented. It is doubtful if an impresario's gifts would have been considered suitable qualifications for the post of secretary at most royal courts, even in the seventeenth century. But Christina had always expected members of her household to be versatile, as indeed she was herself, and Alibert seems to have given satisfaction in both capacities, as he remained with the Queen until her death. In 1670 in fact he was engaged on a project which interested Christina greatly. This was the founding of a new theatre that was being built on the site of the dreaded

Tor di Nona prison and was to be run under the Queen's patronage. Unlike such great Roman families as the Barberini and Colonna, whose means enabled them to support private theatres in their own palaces, Christina had to content herself with contributing to the Tor di Nona theatre's maintenance by taking a lease on five boxes, as Venetain patricians had long been doing in the public theatres of their city.

The value of Christina's patronage was somewhat lessened by her lack of tact. For example she tried to get Clement X's permission for comedies to be staged all the year round in the theatre, and not just in the carnival season, but the way in which she made her request so annoyed the Pope that he refused, and in fact saw to it that the theatre was licensed in Acciajoli's name and not that of Alibert. However these two entered into a not very easy partnership, the first acting as impresario and the second as manager. In spite of this the theatre was a great success. It opened in January 1671 with *Scipio Africano*, an opera dedicated to the Queen. Several of the performers were singers in her service, including two beautiful and gifted women—Angelica Quadrelli and Antonia Coresi. Antonia's gifts were so much admired by her patroness that she was rewarded with the present of Maratta's copy of one of the most famous pictures in the Queen's collection, Correggio's Leda. Indeed Antonia's fame was such that the Duke of Mantova sent specially to Rome to ask Christina if she could come to Mantova to perform for him.

There was in fact considerable rivalry between the princely courts of Europe for the services of such singers. On the whole there was a good deal of give and take over the men. Christina actually got the loan of the numerous codices of Peruzzi's notes and drawings of ancient monuments from the court of Savoy, in exchange for allowing one of her singers to overstay his allotted time there—the singer returned but not all the codices. At a later date however the Duke of Savoy's enticement of one of her stars, Antonio Rivani or Cicciolino, away from her, aroused the Queen to fury. Characteristically she wrote to Alibert: "I want it to be known that he [Cicciolino] is in this world only for me, and that if he does not sing for me he won't sing long for anyone else, no matter who they may be. Although he has left my service I want him back, get him back at any price. People are trying to make me believe that he has lost his voice, it doesn't matter, such as he is he shall live and die in my service, or ill will befall him!" Cicciolino was one of the best singers in Europe and much sought-after outside Italy as well. He did in fact return to Christina and die in her service in 1686. There was even greater jealousy over the women singers, many of whom were beautiful.

During her years of exile in Hamburg Christina had found relief from her boredom in the experiments of Borri, an Italian alchemist who had been forced to flee his native country because he had been condemned by the Inquisition. Azzolino had warned the Queen about him, and indeed Borri ended his days in imprisonment in the Castel Sant' Angelo, but he was apparently really a clever doctor and, thanks to the representations of Christina and other influential people, he was from time to time allowed out to attend illustrious sufferers in his capacity of physician. In spite of his warnings about Borri, Azzolino shared the Queen's passion for alchemy; they were both devout believers in the philosopher's stone, so was the Marquis of Palombara, a gentleman of Christina's court. As soon as the Queen had established herself at Palazzo Riario she had it equipped with an astronomical observatory, and herself received instruction from Cassini, a serious astronomer who had discovered the four moons of Saturn.

Although Christina corresponded with Glauber, the inventor of the famous salts, and was the patron of scientists such as Borelli, author of *De motu animalium* (who incidentally believed "that it is not impossible that men will one day fly"), and Marsigli, the first oceanographer, it is to be feared that the Queen's own scientific interests were much more closely related to alchemy. From 1670 until her death, Christina's household included a court alchemist, Pietro Antonio Bandiera, who carried out experiments in her "distillery" which were followed with eager interest by herself, Azzolino and the Marquis of Palombara. But in spite of a salary of sixty scudi a month and a liberal expense account Bandiera never discovered the philosopher's stone. The Palazzo Riario did also, however, afford hospitality to the *Accademia di Esperienza* founded in 1677 by Giovanni Giustino Campini, who constructed a new telescope and conducted serious astronomical observations.

In the meantime, however, in 1674 the Queen had founded an

Academy of her own—the third and last of the series, and by far the most important. It was called the *Accademia Reale*, and evidence of the serious thought which its foundation had cost the Queen is to be found in no less than eighteen extant drafts of its statutes written in her own hand. The Academy does indeed seem to have been well organized. There was a regular secretary—Francesco Camelli, keeper of the Queen's coins—and secret meetings were held once a month at which the agenda for the public meetings was decided upon. These followed a regular programme, beginning with a lecture, continuing with two short papers being read, and concluding with a discussion on their contents. Many of the members were serious scholars and intellectual priests, such as Cardinal Albani who later became Pope Clement XI. For us today the main interest of the *Accademia Reale* lies in the fact that it was the precursor of the famous *Arcadia*, the great Academy of eighteenth-century Italy, whose founder members originally met in the gardens of Palazzo Riario after Christina's death.

The Queen was, of course, invited to be a member of many Italian academies, including the *Accademia dei Misti* of Orvieto. An interesting light is cast upon the way of life in seventeenth-century Italy by the fact that the letter of invitation was actually written in 1680 by Count Paolo Monaldeschi, a relative of the Marquis murdered at Fontainebleau. In fact good relations between the Queen and the Monaldeschi family were so far restored for it to be possible for her to arrange a marriage between one of them and the daughter of the Marquis Del Monte.

The even tenor of the Queen's life in Rome was broken in the summer of 1676 by the death of Clement X. Although his election had been such a disappointment to Christina, and the Pontiff's relations with the Queen had not been on the intimate footing of the previous reign, they had nevertheless been friendly and placid, very different in fact from what they were to be with his successor. After a Conclave lasting under two months, on 21st September Cardinal Benedetto Odescalchi was proclaimed Pope Innocent XI. Possibly more than anything else, the weeks of negotiation preceding Innocent's accession had served to illustrate the power that Louis XIV now wielded in Europe. Owing to the King's hostility it was known from the start that neither the late Pope's nephew, Cardinal Altieri, nor any of his supporters had any chance of being elected, and the same applied to the Chigi faction. In fact Cardinal Odescalchi was only finally elected after the French Ambassador the Duc d'Estrées had written to ask the King's approval, and two cardinals had also written giving the impression that Odescalchi's accession would be a bitter blow to Altieri. On 13th September Louis's sanction arrived and, with the pretext of reading the King's letter to the Sacred College acknowledging theirs announcing Clement X's death, the French Ambassador made a speech at the Conclave in which, without mentioning Odescalchi's name, he indicated clearly that this candidate would have the all-powerful King's support.

Although the manœuvring preceding Innocent XI's accession had nothing to commend it, the Pope himself was a man of the highest character, who only accepted his own elevation with reluctance after fourteen articles of reform, adumbrated at the previous Conclave, had been agreed to by all the cardinals. The Odescalchi were a rich merchant family of Como and, traditionally, northern Italians have little sympathy for the ease and laxity of life in Rome, or for the Romans. Rapidly the new Pope's reforming zeal and the determined negative which he opposed to gaieties and requests for favours alike—he said that the chief duty of princes was the administration of justice not the granting of favours—earned for him among the Roman populace the nickname of *Papa minga* or *mingone* ("Papa No," *minga* being the word for "no" in his native Milanese dialect). Carnival celebrations were reduced to a minimum, two comedies only were permitted to be staged in a small theatre and women were barred from the stage. Even the breast of Guido Reni's famous Madonna was painted over because the Pope considered that it was too exposed.

No doubt there was room for reform in Rome, and Innocent himself eschewed all forms of nepotism, living the life of a threadbare hermit—if Clement IX had reduced the expenses of his table to a few *baiocchi*, Innocent limited his to even less *giuli*, the smallest copper coin. The new Pope's capacity for economy and administration soon made itself felt, the finances of the Papal States emerged from their usual indebtedness, while Innocent's organization of the Secretariat of State prevailed until modern times. Like Clement IX the Pope perceived the great danger of Turkish expansion and strained every effort to bring peace to Europe to confront this menace. But in foreign affairs Innocent was handicapped by never having been a nuncio and possessing little idea of the world outside Italy or of how to handle men, while his lack of sophistication and of general and even theological knowledge laid him open to deception.

Although Christina was at one with the Pope about the Turkish menace, the evils of nepotism and safeguarding the independence of the Church—Innocent once told his confessor that he would rather be flayed alive than allow the rights of the Church to be curtailed—it is not difficult to imagine how little they had in common on other subjects. The first blow—and bone of contention—was the closing of public theatres. It sounded the death-knell for the Queen's own particular theatre, the Tor di Nona, which was converted into a granary for the duration of Innocent's reign. Further causes of friction were to follow.

On other and more serious counts the Queen's situation in life, however, improved greatly towards the close of the 1670s. Young Charles XI of Sweden's sound conduct of financial policy after his majority in 1672, and his ultimately successful conclusion of the Danish war which resulted in the Peace of Nimwegen, led to the Queen receiving regular monthly payments in cash of 5,000 riksdaler from her appanage. This sum increased as the years went on, as at last Christina had found an able and honest administrator in the person of John Paulinus Olivecrantz.

The new tranquillity brought by this unaccustomed financial security is reflected in the letters which the Queen wrote to Bourdelot about this time. Bourdelot, the gay and frivolous Bourdelot, was now eighty. Although he and Christina had not seen each other for twenty years, they evidently both enjoyed the comfortable relaxed relationship of old friends. The doctor does not seem to have changed much with the years, he was still writing verses, playing the violin and looking for yet another benefice to add to his comforts. Bourdelot was evidently piqued because he did not think that the Queen took his poetry seriously enough and assured her that it was much appreciated by the French court. On her side Christina was indulgent, affectionate and chaffing, asking him: "How does it feel to be eighty?" But her faith in Bourdelot as a doctor, whom she verily believed had saved her life, was obviously unshaken, for she gave him a detailed account of her state of health and way of life. This makes it clear that Christina was still following the régime he had prescribed for her, maintaining a simple light diet, with plenty of vegetables and fruit, "very refreshing" she called it, no wine, no spices and regular blood-lettings. However she still slept for only five hours a night. "This was more than I used to," she wrote, "but, more than before with all this leisure, I am almost always mistress of my time, and I give myself a little more rest to refresh my temperament, which is but fire and flame."

With such a "temperament" and "all this leisure" on her hands, Christina in her fifties turned her superabundant energy to writing. It is true that she had already made an effort in this direction during her last stay in Hamburg, when in 1666 Azzolino had suggested to her that she should write her autobiography. No doubt this had been a kindly idea for finding some means to distract Christina from her present troubles and exile in a country which she heartily disliked. In any event the Queen seems to have made one or two efforts to begin this serious undertaking, as she mentioned it in letters to Azzolino and another unidentified prelate, possibly Sforza Pallavicino who had himself written a biography of the Queen. But, not very surprisingly in view of her troubled situation and nervous state, Christina was so discouraged with her first efforts that she destroyed some of them, and told Azzolino that her handwriting was so bad that the others were unreadable.

Somewhere about 1680, however, the Queen seems to have returned to the idea in all seriousness. One result was a synopsis of the events of her reign until her abdication, entitled "*Mémoire de ce qui s'est passé durant le règne de la reine, avec notes ajoutées par elle-même*", of which a copy in a secretary's hand still exists, with comments added by the Queen herself. Another was an autobiography written in the first person entitled "*Histoire de la Reine Christine faite par elle-même. Rome, 11 Juin 1681, dediée au Dieu*". The latter text covers events in Christina's life between 1626 and 1632 and was never finished. There are several copies and variations in existence. But the Queen must have been either dissatisfied with her work or, as seems more probable, her nervous flighty temperament rendered her incapable of the prolonged effort that the writing of a book entails.

However Christina found another literary form which was more suited to her character. This was the then highly fashionable one of maxims of the kind made famous by La Rochefoucauld's *Reflexions ou sentences et maximes morales*, published in 1655. If she was incapable of supporting the discipline required to write a full-length book, Christina's letters, annotations and reported sayings show that she possessed an incisive mind and pithy wit. Thus the formulation of opinions expressed in short phrases was a medium eminently well suited to her, but unfortunately her natural spontaneity seems to have deserted her when it came to conscious literary composition. From the manuscripts that have survived it is evident that Christina laboured long and earnestly in trying to produce sayings worthy of herself, and the maxims were altered and rewritten countless times before the Queen was satisfied with them—if she ever was. In this fact Christina showed judgment, for even those maxims evidently not intended to be markedly profound, often lack originality. For instance Molière had anticipated Christina by at least ten years in *L'Avare* with "One must eat to live, not live to eat."

The more serious maxims included in the collection entitled *Les Sentiments Héroiques* are, however, of very considerable interest for the light they shed upon Christina's own life and aspirations. More particularly because these maxims reveal the gap which existed between these two things. The sentiment that "The good faith and word of a Prince should be inviolate" is unexceptional, but it comes strangely from the pen of a woman who prided herself on her dissimulation and was capable of revealing her country's secrets for personal gain. So does the maxim "One never repents of pardoning offences, but almost always of having punished them" from the pitiless judge of Monaldeschi; while "A Prince must consider himself the crowned slave of the public" is an ideal which the imperious and extravagent Christina scarcely fulfilled. It is even more doubtful if the very true words "It is easier to deceive others than ourselves on the subject of self" could ever have been applied by the Queen personally.

Nevertheless here and there among these elevated thoughts, so often so far removed from Christina's actual self, it seems that the truth is sometimes revealed. This is particularly so when she is writing on her religious beliefs and on love, and the tragedy of the latter in her own case seems unmistakably to have deepened her feelings in respect to the former. "True love asks for nothing but to love" and "Love exists always, be it happy or unhappy," are surely sayings drawn from the depths of Christina's own bitter experience. But "Love effaces and consumes all faults and all crimes, once one loves God one is innocent," clearly reveals the trend that the Queen's own life was taking. So too does "When one examines one's heart one finds that nothing can fill it or console it but God alone." Even more so does the final resignation expressed in "All abandon us sooner or later. One must foresee this abandonment and resolve to quit all voluntarily. We must remain alone with God from now on, as he alone suffices for us to live and die happy."

This sense of solitary abandonment consorts ill with our picture of the forceful Queen, who was so much attached to the political world that she wished to send her personal representative to the peace negotiations at Nimwegen, who cherished and added to her vast collections and did battle with Innocent XI for her rights of diplomatic immunity and the pleasures of the theatre. But this inner life of spiritual travail was nothing new in Christina, Chanut had sensed it long ago. Undoubtedly it predisposed her to fall under the influence of the Spanish priest Migual Molinos, the proponent of Quietism.

Molinos was two years younger than the Queen. He was already forty-five and a Doctor of Theology when he left Spain to come to Rome in 1663, to urge the cause of beatification of the founder of the college in which he had studied at Valencia. Molinos was dark, with a fresh-coloured complexion and a goatee beard and he evidently possessed a persuasive personality and could write, for his *Spiritual Guide*, published in 1675, had an enormous success. By then, however, the author was already a figure in Rome, the spiritual director of monks, nuns, priests, prelates, princesses and cardinals, who esteemed him highly, as did Azzolino and even the austere Innocent XI.

Molinos can scarcely, therefore, be dismissed as yet another example of that recurrent phenomenon, the fashionable preacher or drawing-room priest. He was both more able and more dangerous than this. Molinos's early history in Rome really provides the clue to his character. He migrated from church to church for celebrating his Mass. The reason for this was that instead of occupying himself with personal devotions either before or after his celebration of the Mass, he soon acquired the habits of giving spiritual conferences which attracted a number of women. These conferences became more and more prolonged, so that the sacristans complained that it was difficult to close the church. There was trouble with the authorities and Molinos moved to another church, but did not change his habits. He was also assiduous in the pursuit of well-known persons. These he would approach boldly, then appear to retire modestly; if they accepted the bait and asked for advice, Molinos would require a week's delay for prayer in order to know God's will. It was noticeable that this was nearly always in the affirmative in the case of the influential seeker after truth; God's will was nearly always what they wanted to hear.

In common with providing other popular religious writings of this period, which aimed at a new and easy approach to prayer, Molinos's *Spiritual Guide* might in modern parlance be colloquially described as a beginner's guide to contemplation. François Malaval's *Pratique Façile*, published in 1664 (of which the Italian translation had been dedicated to Christina) had been something of the same kind. But the danger of Molinos's teaching (which was not apparent at first except to some very wide-awake Jesuits) was that in urging upon his followers the value of contemplation and the total absorption of the soul in the love and contemplation of God, the Spanish priest went much further. According to his preaching, all personal effort, prayers, penance and the normal spiritual exercises were to be regarded as superfluous, and even acts that would normally be deemed wicked would not be considered as such because, although they might be the work of the devil, they were made without the devotees' consent.

Naturally this last part of Molinos's teaching did not appear in his printed works, though there was ample documentation of it in letters later discovered by the Inquisition. But it is easy to understand how this urge to contemplation, to the mystic life imbued with thoughts devoted only to the love of God, and aimed at reaching personal contact with Him, had a great attraction for many pious but unhappy people. Its appeal to Christina was even more compelling. Not only had Molinos acquired the approbation of Azzolino (though it might have been supposed that his native Marchigiano good sense would have given him reason to pause), but her dislike of outward show and false piety in religion would have led the Queen instantly to appreciate Molinos's esoteric and personal approach. But the chief reason why Molinos's teachings appealed to Christina was that they coincided with her lifelong conviction that she was responsible only to God for her actions. This had actually been written into her act of abdication, thus releasing her from obedience to the tribunals of other secular powers. At the time most people must have imagined that this was done in order to free the Queen from obedience to her successor. But to Christina the interpretation of the phrase was evidently of far wider significance. At Fontainebleau she had made use of it to Père Le Bel as justification for her passing sentence on Monaldeschi, independently of the justice of the King of France. It was also the basis of her public justification of this deed. Even now in Rome Christina was to make use of the same phrase, when, replying to remonstrations sent to her by the Sacred College for flouting the Pope's authority by allowing comedies with actresses to be played in her palace, she mocked at Innocent XI's disapproval.

Nowhere does this idea of Christina's find more clear expression than in her autobiography dedicated to God. Hers was not the only example of such a dedication. She had precursors as she was to have successors. But even when allowing for the high-flown style of the period and attempts at would-be humility, the reader cannot fail to be struck by the boundless self-satisfaction that informs the colloquies with God, which the author introduces into her narrative. Some of these do afford flashes of self-revelation, as in the preamble where Christina wrote: "Because you know Lord that you gave me a heart that nothing will satisfy. . . . Nothing can fill me, nothing can satisfy me but you. You have made me so great that if you could give me the Empire of the entire world, I would not be satisfied. I would count for nothing that which was not you. After the grace that you have afforded me by introducing me into this admirable and mysterious solitude, where one searches and finds only you, I must regard as of no account all the rest of the world."

This conviction of having been singled out for this "admirable and mysterious solitude" does seem to be the negation of the humanity and humility of Christ, whose name is never mentioned in the autobiography or in the maxims. Both these works of Christina's were in fact written at a time when Molinos's ascendancy over her was at its height, and Quietism as interpreted by him considered that "Christ's sacred Humanity was a material object, so that love for it was not a purely spiritual love," and though there is no evidence to show that Christina ever subscribed to, or was even aware of, this terrifying aberration in Molinos's form of Quietism, the passages just quoted from the Queen's autobiography serve to illustrate, perhaps better than anything else, the inordinate self-esteem that is generally conceded to have been Christina's greatest failing. Nor could anyone who has studied her life believe otherwise than that this aggressiveness, this overwhelming preoccupation with self, with her own interests, her glory, her virtue, and the impression she would make on the world and posterity (as Chanut clearly saw) was the flaw that brought nemesis down upon her head. Running parallel to this is Christina's insistence, from childhood until well into middle age, upon her virile character, her physical endurance and her dreams of leading an army; to say nothing of her predilection for men's clothes and wearing arms. Philip of Macedon had been great but he was entirely eclipsed by his son Alexander. In her essay on Alexander, Christina obviously identified herself with her hero, and it is tempting to assume that this, combined with her passion for glory (noted by Chanut as her dominant characteristic) indicates her desire to outshine her own father.

But if Christina really felt that she had inherited Gustavus Adolphus's great qualities, would she have experienced the need to assert herself in this manner? True, she was a woman, but Elizabeth of England (whom Christina always so studiously ignored when insisting upon women's unfitness to rule) never seems to have been impelled to insist upon her authority, her glory or even her learning with such emphasis. Did Christina in her heart of hearts fear that she had inherited much, perhaps even more, from her despised mother than from the great Gustavus? In justice to the unfortunate Maria Eleonora and Christina herself, it must be admitted that the blots on her pedigree came from both sides. In fact an abnormal ancestry must be taken into account in forming any estimate of Christina's character.

The Queen's precocious intelligence enabled her very early in life to take stock of her surroundings. Here the absence of normal family affection (except that supplied for a short while by her aunt), evidently sharpened her already shrewd estimate of the failings of those around her. For in recalling these years in her autobiography, Christina said that "those who believe that the only time when truth approaches princes is in their childhood deceive themselves. Because they are feared and flattered from their cradles . . . they handle them like little lions who can always maul." Recalling these early memories seems to have brought back to Christina the sense of importance possessed by that childish Queen regnant of long ago. Understandably perhaps, because at the time of writing fifty years later, this importance had vanished. But not even that would make a normal woman of over fifty maintain that the sight of herself aged six and seated on the throne, had inspired men with awe. The explanation of this twice-repeated figment of Christina's imagination may perhaps be traced to an unconscious desire to compensate for the childish fears of darkened rooms filled with repulsive dwarfs, and awareness of her own deformity.

How much the effects of this grisly background and inherited Wasa suspicion might have been dispelled if only Christina had been permitted to grow up in the company of her Palatine cousins, it is difficult to estimate. But at least it seems that the gay and humorous side of the Queen's character, that as a child caused her to twit her counsellors about their long beards and in later life inspired uproarious practical jokes and her love of dancing and the theatre, might have developed in a more normal and balanced fashion. But instead political reasons, arising from the fear of Palatine schemes, resulted in a nervous, difficult adolescent being thrust back upon herself to spend her life in loneliness, alternating her days between exhausting physical exercise and even more exhausting hours of feverish study.

No wonder that a very strange suspicious young woman, who prided herself upon her powers of dissimulation, emerged at the age of eighteen to rule Sweden. This first exercise of power made Christina realize that she had outgrown her boy-and-girl romance with Charles Gustavus, and from the adult passion for Magnus which succeeded it arose the crisis that altered her entire life. Certainly inherited tendencies and early environment contributed to this, for if she had been a different woman, Christina would have perceived that in the contrast between these two men the balance was heavily inclined in favour of her cousin. But then and for the rest of her life Christina was deluded by externals. Thus in her thirst for glory and fame she confused the outward show with the reality. The power of inward strength that brings them unsought had been denied to her—unlike her father. But some realization of this in her heart of hearts drove her to search for them even more avidly.

With all her brilliant intellectual facility, her political dexterity and her sharp incisive mind, Christina was easily deceived by appearances. The procession of specious rascals to whom she gave her favour or confidence—from Duncan de Cerisantes to Molinos—shows this clearly. Azzolino was the exception: able and attractive, he seems also to have been a man of ideals and certainly he did not desert Christina in her hour of need. But Azzolino was not outstanding, in no way to be compared with Oxenstierna who was one of the greatest statesmen of the age, though poor Christina in her passionate devotion did so to Oxenstierna's detriment. Nevertheless the Queen recognized the exceptional when she came in contact with it. She was fully aware, for example, of the greatness of Descartes, but she was instinctively hostile because she sensed something for which she was no match. This explains her later dislike for Oxenstierna, and is revealed by the comment in her autobiography on the Russian Ambassadors "who felt what all men feel when they approach anything that is greater." It is doubtful if the Russians felt it on the occasion she mentions, but the Queen herself had evidently experienced the sensation.

The shock with which Christina perceived that her rising passion for Magnus was unrequited was the catalytic moment in her life, for then to her inferiority complex about her father was added the consciousness that even a crown could not compensate for the lack of feminine attraction which she affected to despise. This brought in its train psychosomatic illness and the relationship with Belle, and from this period, too, undoubtedly date the origins of the aversion to marriage and first thoughts of abdication. It cannot be wondered at that such a crisis also led Christina to examine her religious beliefs, and to doubt and question the faith in which she had been brought up. It would not be the first or last time that the shock of personal tragedy, of ill health and the feeling of a burden too great to be borne, produced such a reaction. Understandably its effects were increased later in Christina's case when she came to feel out of tune with her own country, its people and its beliefs, and was reaching out to a wider and richer world outside.

The excitement of the political game of chess and all the complicated moves that led up to her abdication, and the secret negotiations which surrounded her conversion, carried the Queen through the stress of this period of her life. But it was not long before disillusionment set in. Although financial stringency had already become an incentive in Antwerp, it does not seem to have been the only one that led Christina tentatively to sound out the ground with Montecuccoli about the possibility of her becoming the ruler of the Netherlands or Naples. Again, the lack of money need not necessarily have driven the Queen into the Naples venture. Alexander VII would have been the first to approve, and undoubtedly would have come to the financial aid of, a Queen who had given up her throne for her faith, and was prepared to live a life of quiet dignity in a convent, though not necessarily one of secluded religious retirement, as many royal ladies had done in the past. But no, in spite of her early admiration for stoic philosophy and her later pursuit of the mysteries of Quietism, Christina could not bring herself to forgo the trappings of royalty. The insistence upon her royal state and its protocol (though it cost her the friendship of Condé), the passion for extravagance and display, even the art collections, and above all the desire to have a finger in any and every political pie, are signs of the inner unrest that drove Christina for fifteen years in search of a crown, until in the end the mirage collapsed in ridicule.

In her later years, when her continued attempts to assert herself in European politics received at best polite and evasive replies, it must have seemed unbelievable to the younger generation of her day that the Queen of Sweden had once been a great political power. But the truth was that when Christina's undoubted capacities and extraordinary energy had been harnessed to ruling a state, they had been contained within the bounds of the practical possibilities of power, and while subject to these and the constitutional checks imposed by Swedish custom she was an able and effective sovereign. When these limitations were removed by abdication, her innate lack of balance became increasingly evident, especially with the passage of the years.

Abdication had been the fatal step. Not only in itself, but because Christina had envisaged it as a grand gesture—a claim to universal fame that would single her out among a few exceptional beings in history—and not as a real resignation of power in favour of the religion which to her was the true one. She had made the great gesture, but for the wrong reasons. Thus the years that followed instead of being ones of fulfilment, inspired by the religion she had chosen and enriched by the arts she really loved, became a tragic pursuit of the very thing she had abandoned. Christina's one genuine chance of regaining a crown failed owing to her own inherent weaknesses. These prevented her from recognizing a ruffian for what he was, and caused her to confuse a brutal and ill-considered act with a triumphant assertion of her own glorious independence of everything but God.

However, very genuine courage underlay the rather sententious phrases of her letter to Mazarin after the Monaldeschi tragedy. If Christina did not understand the horror aroused by her action, she could not have failed to be aware that it placed her in a dangerous situation. In spite of Terlon's description of her on one occasion as boastful but timid, the Queen had certainly inherited her father's physical courage, as witness her behaviour on the two occasions in 1648 when her life was endangered by an assassin and when she almost drowned. Her father had been no bigot, but Christina went further and seems genuinely to have believed in religious freedom. Naturally her own conversion inclined her to proselytizing, but she had the courage publicly to condemn Louis XIV's brutal methods of dragooning French Protestants in an attempt to make them forsake their faith.

The Queen's complete lack of racial prejudice also singles her out in her century. Not only did she treat Jews on complete equality with Gentiles, but she went out of her way to be courteous to them and show them favour. There still exists among her papers a proclamation declaring that the Queen had taken the Jews of Rome under her protection; it is dated 15th August 1686, but there is no record of its having been made public. In spite of her extreme consciousness of her own royal rank, Christina's recognition of talent as a claim for consideration superior to high birth also singles her out from among the majority of her contemporaries. The Queen who denied the Prince de Condé an armchair would stop her carriage in the street to greet Pasquini, whom she called "the Prince of Musicians." It is on record that she fingered with reverence the rough working clothes that Bernini wore in his studio, and when he died and Christina heard that he had left the modest fortune of 40,000 scudi, she exclaimed: "Had he died in my service I would have been ashamed that he had so little to leave." Meanness was indeed a vice entirely foreign to the Queen. The one maxim she really lived up to was: "The greatest pleasure that money gives is to spend it."

Thus Christina's courage, her belief in rights and liberties, rare in her day, her recognition of religious and spiritual values and her generosity, went far to mitigate her glaring faults, which she paid for with a life of great unhappiness. The blame for many of them can be laid upon her heredity and early life: the first might not have mattered so much and the second would have been entirely different if only Gustavus Adolphus had lived. That is the great "if" in the history of Christina's life. It was only much later in her career that she found in Azzolino the wise counsel and steady guiding hand allied to warmth of affection, which earlier might have made so much difference.

During the 1680s the Queen certainly stood in need of good counsel. For most of that time she was on the worst of terms with both the Pope and Louis XIV. Nevertheless 1683 brought a crisis which it might have been supposed would for once unite at least Innocent XI and Christina. In that year the long truce between the Sublime Porte and the Christian West was broken by Kara Mustapha, who reached the gates of Vienna in June. This was the peril to which both Pope and Queen (and she for a great deal longer than he) had tried to awaken the European powers. The time for a *rapprochement* between Innocent and Christina did at last seem to be at hand, but in his zeal to raise funds with which to combat the infidel the Pope revoked the Queen's pension of 12,000 scudi granted by Clement IX, and instead sent the money to swell the coffers of the Holy League formed to fight the Turks. Years of encouraging others to confront the Turkish menace had not prepared the Queen for the effect on her own pocket, and her fury knew no bounds. Apparently, on the Pope's instructions, the news had been conveyed to Christina in a letter by Azzolino. Her reply is one of the most notable, if perhaps not the most praiseworthy of her epistolatory efforts, for on her own admission Christina was now enjoying a total annual revenue of 100,000 scudi. However she wrote: "The 12,000 scudi that the Pope gave me were the one blot on my life, and I suffered it from the hand of God as the greatest mortification that could humiliate my pride. I see that I am in His grace because he has done me this great favour of taking it away from me so gloriously. . . . This grace is worth a thousand realms. . . . The only regret I feel is that it has not been possible to take away the 100,000 scudi which I still have. . . ." Pope and Queen were not to be reconciled until her death-bed.

For some time Christina had also evidently been aware that hostility to Molinos was mounting, for already at the end of 1681 she had written to his friend the Archbishop of Palermo about it. Molinos figured officially as her theologian, and regularly every Monday morning he spent three hours with the Queen. If the often, but not invariably, tendentious author of the *Intrigues and Gallantries of Christina, Queen of Sweden* is to be believed—and he does appear to be well-informed about the domestic details of Christina's life in Rome—these weekly meetings had a notably calming effect upon her and "certainly helped her household as Molinos moderated her violent transports (of temper) which would become so excessive that no one durst come near her."

Although a book attacking Quietism, written by the most distinguished Italian Jesuit missionary preacher, was put on the Index in 1681, in 1682 and again in 1684 Christina's letters to her and Molinos's archbishop friend continue to mention the "persecution" of the Quietist. In fact during these years reports had been coming in from various parts of Italy of the extraordinary effects that Quietism had upon people. The nuns in a convent in Naples, for instance, never said the Rosary or prayed aloud, and if they believed that they had committed a sin, simply ascribed it to the Devil and regarded themselves as innocent. In 1685 such grave accusations against Molinos had for some months been received by the Inquisition that in spite of hesitation the Pope eventually gave his consent to Molinos's arrest, which took place on 18th July. Quietist supporters were shocked but not convinced, Christina sent messages asking after Molinos's welfare every day, and even the discreet Azzolino would not at first admit that he might have been mistaken in the matter. Innocent XI himself seems to have been far from sure, for in September he created Petrucci, who was a noted Quietist, a cardinal.

However, no less than 20,000 of Molinos's letters were collected, in which he had asserted that the Devil could gain control of a man and force him to acts apparently sinful for which he himself was not responsible. How much Molinos himself practised his own preaching emerged from the subsequent questioning of his women devotees, who revealed that he had apparently for a long time been subject to sexual aberration. Nevertheless, and in spite of the damning evidence, the fact that a man who was now a Cardinal of the Church would necessarily be involved in Molinos's downfall meant that the investigations which preceded it, and his trial itself, would be a long drawn-out affair. In fact Molinos was only finally condemned in September 1687.

One of the main targets of Innocent XI's reforming zeal in Rome were the diplomatic quarters. Understandably so, because large areas round the various embassies and the Palazzo Riario, for which diplomatic immunity was claimed, had become the refuge of the criminal elements of the city. It might have been imagined that this abuse of privilege had its inconvenient side for the diplomats themselves; for instance, in the case of the French Embassy the courtyard of the Palazzo Farnese itself had become a dormitory for thieves and vagabonds. But in the seventeenth century any privilege was defended tooth and nail by the holder. However by the beginning of 1687 the Pope had succeeded in suppressing this abuse except in the case of the French Embassy and the Palazzo Riario, when in January of that year the French Ambassador, the Duc D'Estrées, died very suddenly. Innocent XI immediately informed the French government that he would not receive another ambassador until France had also relinquished her quarter. Relations between Innocent XI and Louis XIV were already strained by the struggle over the *régale*.*

* This was a very old custom by which since the Middle Ages the kings of France claimed the right to appropriate the revenues of a number of dioceses

Cardinal d'Estrées, a relative of the dead Ambassador, was in Rome at this time and also living in the Palazzo Farnese, on a confidential mission from Louis XIV to examine this question. Determined to create a *fait accompli* before another French Ambassador could arrive, Innocent XI gave instructions for the French quarter to be cleared. In order not to embitter the struggle further, Cardinal d'Estrées, who did not believe that the French right of the quarter could be maintained, arranged with Cardinal Spinola, the Governor of Rome, that on the grounds of health he would leave Palazzo Farnese and take up residence in the more salubrious quarter of the Villa Pamphilj on the Janiculum. After the Cardinal left, the French quarter was occupied by the papal police, thus leaving Christina as the sole defender of the right of quarter in Rome. It was a situation which could not last for long and, probably on Azzolino's advice, in February 1687 the Queen made the wise gesture of announcing that she had spontaneously renounced the rights to her quarter. From what we know of her character it is not difficult to imagine the effort that this must have cost her. In fact Christina's loathing of the Pope and the restrictions which his reforming attitude placed upon her life in Rome, had already inspired in her the idea of leaving the Eternal City. In May of the previous year she had written to Olivecrantz to tell him so, saying that the thought of it "is like a dagger in my heart . . . but I owe it to God, to my glory and the present situation." She instructed her administrator to return to the project of ten years ago, of exchanging her Pomeranian estates for the Duchy of Bremen adding "if you can arrange it, my place of retreat is found."

The blow of giving up her quarter even made the Queen reconsider her attitude to Louis XIV. They had been on bad terms for a long time, but the nadir of their relationship had been reached in 1686, with the publication of Christina's letter to Terlon (now French Ambassador at The Hague) condemning Louis XIV's

on the death of the bishop, also certain benefices. In 1608 the Parliament of Paris had sanctioned the extension of the *régale* to the whole of France, and in 1673 Louis XIV confirmed this by decree. The money was in fact most carefully administered for the benefit of the Church and by the Revocation of the Edict of Nantes in 1685 Louis hoped to mollify Innocent XI, but with a Pope so jealous of the Church's rights a long drawn-out struggle was inevitable and the question of the quarter now seemed destined to prolong the battle of wills between the unyielding Pope and King indefinitely.

persecution of the Huguenots in France. To her just indignation at the infamous *dragonnades*, which consisted of quartering dragoons on Huguenot families and by sheer brutality forcing them to abjure their faith, Christina added a shrewd observation: "I foresee on the contrary the irreparable misfortune that will result from this unheard of proceeding everywhere. Do you in good faith really believe in the sincerity of these new converts?" As history was to show, the Revocation of the Edict of Nantes and these persecutions of honest, industrious people, resulted in the emigration of thousands and a disastrous blow to the French economy.

In this letter of 2nd February 1680 to Terlon, the Queen wrote with withering scorn: "Soldiers are strange apostles" and "As our Lord did not make use of these methods they cannot be the best." Somehow it leaked out and the letter was printed as a pamphlet and circulated widely in Paris. In May, Bayle published it in Amsterdam in the *Nouvelles de la République des Lettres*, without apparently being certain that Christina was really the author. Nevertheless he attributed her protest to the "remains of Protestantism." Although she was not at all averse to her letter receiving publicity, the comment about her Protestantism annoyed the Queen and she told her secretary to write Bayle an anonymous letter that would make him uneasy. This letter still exists with corrections written in the third person in Christina's own hand, one of which on her own religious evolution is interesting. It reads: "If by misfortune she had not chosen to be a Catholic, she would have remained completely neutral in matters of religion, in which she had formed a simple one for herself, but very different from that of Luther or Calvin." The Queen evidently protested to Bayle for having published her letter without her permission, and remonstrated with him about mentioning her Protestantism, but admitted that she was glad that the letter had been published.

The letter was also published in the much less reputable *Mercure Galant*. This produced some characteristically sharp and amusing comments from the Queen in her correspondence with Brémond, which also indicated clearly that righteous indignation had not alone inspired her protest. In July Christina wrote: "I have been punished enough by the cruel vengeance meted out to me, by appearing for the first time in the *Mercure Galant* . . . in that book in which appear pell-mell all the heroes and bourgeois of France, with their names, surnames, arms, devices and colours. Truly a terrible vengeance. But I will find a way of showing people that I am incorrigible, and that I still dare to amuse myself at the expense of those who imagine mistakenly that they make the whole of Europe tremble." It was, of course, Louis XIV she was aiming at, and again in December Christina wrote to Brémond: "I am the only person in Europe who has not bent the knee before the golden calf of our day." But this was before the affair of the right of the quarter, and when it came to a choice between the Pope and Louis XIV, Christina now preferred the King. He was further away and, if indeed she did decide to leave Rome, probably the more useful of the two. Within a month of giving up her quarter the Queen mentioned to Olivecrantz Louis's desire for a *rapprochement* with her, which in reality meant her desire for peace with him.

Innocent XI, who was ill and besieged on all sides by political problems, displayed a saintly patience in the face of the Queen's provocations, the worst he ever said of her and them was "*è donna*" (women!). Although on one occasion the provocation did not originally come from the Queen herself, she soon made it her own. In the summer of 1687 one of the servants of the French Embassy was arrested for having defrauded the customs. He escaped and sought sanctuary in the Church of Regina Coeli, close to the Palazzo Riario. The papal police tried to arrest the man on the steps of the high altar during Mass, but some of Christina's guards rescued him and got him away. The Frenchman and his rescuers were tried *in absentia* and condemned to death. The Queen then wrote to the magistrate a letter which began: "You dishonour yourself and your master" and ended with the threat: "I give you my word that those condemned to death will live, if it please God, for some time, and if by chance they do not die a natural death, they will not be the only ones to die."

Her famous phrase: "I love the storm and fear the calm" should really have been the Queen's motto. But like many unquiet spirits, throughout her life she had found solace in music, of all the arts possibly the one she loved and appreciated best. In contrasting music with painting and sculpture in her maxims Christina wrote some lines which are strangely revealing: "Music is something more touching [than painting and sculpture]. It seems that it is made specially for the soul, harmony bringing with it a kind of sympathy which charms; but it is dangerous for an upright man, above all a Prince, to know too much about it." The key to this extraordinary statement is supplied by something Scarlatti once said. When praising the Grand Duke of Tuscany for his perception in appreciating Gesualdo di Venosa's music, Scarlatti added: "such speculative compositions pleased the late lamented Queen of Sweden, my former mistress, more than anything else."

Don Carlo Gesualdo, Prince of Venosa, had lived in the last half of the sixteenth century and, music apart, is known to history for having had his unfaithful wife, her lover and their child, murdered. He has been characterized as a "brilliant psychopath" and modern critics describe his music as "impressionistic" and as an "antithesis of voluptuous eroticism and self-tormenting longing for death." The madrigals for which Gesualdo also wrote the musical setting, do indeed harp on death, and his music was very far in advance of his time. Her preference therefore shows Christina's fastidious and informed taste, and also that she "understood his morbid style as human passions dressed up as chamber music."* Thus, strange unhappy creature that she was, Christina realized that Gesualdo's *fin de siècle* brilliance revealed his inner disharmony, as indeed her appreciation of his works revealed her own.

The Queen has been criticized for "preferring the old," in other words for the fact that her collections of pictures, sculpture and drawings were almost exclusively devoted to the works of dead masters and that she did not encourage contemporary talent. This is true to a certain extent, but there is also the fact that Christina had not enough money to patronize the great of her day. Although Bernini was her friend and she admired him enormously the Queen never possessed a major work of his, only a few paintings and drawings and the famous mirror, of which the decorative figures were made of gilded clay.

This criticism, however, cannot be extended to her patronage of music. The genius of the two outstanding composers Corelli and Scarlatti, who came to Rome after Christina was established there, was instantly recognized by her. Her appreciation and

* Carl-Allen Moburg on "Christina and Music" in the Catalogue of the exhibition "Christina Queen of Sweden," Stockholm, 1966.

encouragement of Corelli when he first arrived as a very young man was acknowledged by the composer, who dedicated his first work to her in 1681. The Queen also recognized Scarlatti's genius from the first. He was only twenty when Christina heard that this unknown young Sicilian's pastoral comedy *Gli equivoci nel sembiante* was being given in a private house, and insisted that it should be transferred to the Collegio Clementino where she could hear it. An amusing incident occurred because Scarlatti did not dare to appear to play the harpsichord; he was under a cloud with the ecclesiastical authorities owing to his sister's runaway match with a young seminarian. The Queen was not going to be put off by such a trifle, her carriage was sent to fetch Scarlatti, and play he did to the Cardinal Vicar as well, who was seated in Christina's box. The following year Scarlatti became the Queen's *Maestro di Cappella* (leader of her musicians, literally of her chapel music), and dedicated his next work, *Honestà negli Amori*, to her. He remained five years in Christina's service before going to the court of Naples.

Some of the most remarkable musical performances given in Rome during the seventeenth century did in fact take place in the Palazzo Riario. The most notable among them were undoubtedly the three musical evenings given by the Queen to celebrate the arrival in Rome of James II of England's Ambassador, Lord Castlemaine, and her hopes of the ultimate return of England to the Catholic faith. How formal and outstanding the occasion was, is shown by the fact that no less than 200 ladies were present (a rare event at any of Christina's entertainments) and their dresses and jewels were of such splendour that a contemporary chronicler described them as looking like "200 suns." Their glamour was, however, definitely eclipsed by the music, a cantata was performed by a choir of 100 singers, accompanied by a string orchestra of 150 under Corelli's direction, one of the largest orchestras to have been heard in Rome at that time.

Castlemaine was not the only new ambassador to make his appearance in Rome in 1687. In November the new French Ambassador arrived, the Marquis de Lavardin, with a train of 300 and a caravan of baggage wagons. The 300 included a large percentage of well-armed soldiers, and the baggage was largely victuals with which to stand a siege, Louis XIV not being the man to renounce the right of quarter easily. The Pope held to his resolution, however, and refused to receive the Ambassador accredited to him by the Most Christian King unless the right of quarter was formally renounced, with the result that no one else in Rome could receive the unfortunate Marquis and his family. No one that is except the Queen of Sweden, who accorded the French Ambassador a solemn audience with every mark of cordiality and wrote exultingly to Brémond over the sensation that this had caused.

Lavardin in fact became very much *persona grata* with Christina, and was present in 1688 at one of the Queen's musical entertainments at the Palazzo Riario given on a hot summer evening. In view of the papal ban this could not have been a formal affair, but from an eye-witness description it was evidently a gay one. For the last time we see Christina, at the age of sixty-two, still enjoying herself with almost the same spirit and abandon as when she was a girl. The concert was given in the garden, probably in one of the hedged garden rooms filled with the heady scent of jasmine, which seems to have been one of Christina's favourite flowers. Her protégée, Angelica, the beautiful girl who was the most admired woman singer in Rome, had sung with her sister Barbara. Afterwards the company was strolling around in the garden or sitting drinking wine in the arbours, when on the hillside Lavardin's trumpeters struck up the air of Flon Flon, the popular song of the day, which was taken up by the whole company including Christina herself, and they all sang till the garden rang with the melody. Perhaps in return for this hospitality, on 20th September, the Marquis Del Monte organized a musical entertainment in the jasmine garden of his lodging across the road from the Palazzo Riario. Angelica, Mariuccia (Del Monte's illegitimate daughter by Christina's maid Landini) and other members of the household sang, and the entertainment lasted late into the night while the Queen sat chatting with the Marquis. Possibly the excitement and exertion had been too much for the old man, for the next day he died of a stroke, and rascal though he undoubtedly was, he had evidently been an amusing one, for he was sincerely mourned by his old friend the Queen.

Del Monte's death must have cast a shadow over the little household in the Palazzo Riario, which with the passage of the years had now come to be composed mainly of women. Of the

Passaglia sisters two survived and had been promoted ladies-in-waiting. Ottavia had actually married the Marquis Capponi. Of the younger generation there was Del Monte's daughter Clarissa and Mariuccia Landini (his illegitimate daughter) and the sisters Angelica and Barbara Giorgini, whom the Queen had taken under her protection to save them from being placed in a convent. The Capponis had two children, a boy and a girl, who also apparently lived in the palace. Christina was evidently very much attached to the little boy, as she played with him, spoiling him and giving him presents of fruit and sweets; in her will she left him an annuity of 200 scudi a year until he grew up—more than she left to any of the other children of her household.

So far as her domestic life was concerned, the Queen had also mellowed with the years. Long ago Madame de Motteville had been shocked at the scant ceremony of Christina's private life and at the intimacy she shared with her maids the Passaglia sisters. Now they were old old friends, and with them and the children, the haughty Queen of Sweden would often sit down in the kitchen to eat large quantities of peasant food like boiled chestnuts and cauliflower. Indeed, except for her strange clothes and coiffure and that still commanding eye, Christina in her domesticity must have looked very much like an old peasant woman herself. For the last description of her appearance, written in April 1688 by the French traveller François-Maximilian Misson, could well be that of an old Swedish countrywoman. "She is more than sixty years old," Misson wrote, "very small of stature, exceedingly fat and corpulent. Her complexion, voice and face are those of a man; but she has a big nose, large blue eyes, blonde eyebrows and a double chin, from which sprout a number of isolated tufts of beard. The upper lip a trifle prominent, the hair light chestnut, a palmsbreadth in length, powdered and standing on end uncombed over her forehead. A smiling expression and a very obliging manner. Imagine as regards her costume, a man's knee-length *justaucorps* (a skirted coat) of black satin, buttoned all the way down. A very short black skirt revealing a pair of men's shoes. A very large bow of black ribbons instead of a cravat. A belt drawn tightly round the coat over the lower part of the stomach, most clearly revealing the rotundity of this."

Misson, like other travellers, had been permitted to visit the fabulous collections of the Palazzo Riario, but he was one of the few who were allowed to see their owner as well, though laughingly in her old age Christina herself admitted that, on a par with the ancient monuments, she was now one of the sights of Rome. During the autumn of 1688, however, she held to her determination to leave the city. The Marquis Del Monte's son had been dispatched to Stockholm as her Ambassador to the Swedish court, to reinforce Olivecrantz' representations about the Duchy of Bremen. In her instructions to her Ambassador something of the old Christina appears. She wrote to tell him not to show that she was really interested in Bremen. In fact of course she was, because she considered it to be the only place other than Rome where she could decently reside, and she wanted full sovereign rights.

Despite these activities, some presentiment that she really had not long to live seems to have come to Christina at the end of 1688. She ordered what was for her an extraordinary dress, of white silk embroidered with flowers and trimmed with golden fringe. On Christmas Eve the Queen tried the dress on, studying its effect in two mirrors, watched by the Passaglia sisters. As they all stood admiring the dress a wise-woman called Giulia arrived, a story-teller, clever at concocting draughts of simples and something of an alchemist. The Queen said: "Looking at this dress makes me think of important things, I will soon wear it," and turning to Giulia, she asked: "Sibyl, do you divine in what ceremony?" The old woman replied: "Your pardon, Madam, but your Majesty will be buried in that dress not long from now." The others protested, but Christina said: "The Sibyl has told the truth, that was what I was thinking."

In the New Year, however, such gloomy thoughts seemed to have been banished from the Queen's mind, for she set out on a journey to southern Italy, from which she returned safe and sound in February. Shortly afterwards, she had a fainting fit and fell ill, seriously this time, with what was diagnosed as erysipelas, probably owing to the swelling of her legs from which she had suffered in the spring during the two previous years. However this time the Queen had a high fever, and three days later another fainting fit occurred. It was so serious and followed by such weakness that everyone believed that she would not recover. But by the middle of March Christina was much better and prayers of thanksgiving were said in the Roman churches, especially at S. Salvatore in Lauro, the national church of the Marchigiani, which was decorated for the occasion, while the nearby Via dei Coronari was illuminated. Although she had made her will, the Queen herself was evidently optimistic about her recovery, for on 2nd April she wrote to Olivecrantz, whom she was expecting in Rome, to say that she hoped he would find her "plump and happy."

It seems likely that the Queen might indeed have recovered had her convalescence not been interrupted by a severe shock. During her illness a horrifying incident had occurred in the palace, which on Azzolino's orders had been kept from Christina because it involved her favourite Angelica. This beautiful and gifted girl was the daughter of Caterina Voglia, who had married an honest tradesman called Giorgini, but her real father was a Knight of the Order of Melchisedek. The fame of Angelica's beauty and voice was such that she was constantly pursued by men of all ranks, including apparently a cardinal. It was believed to be because of her that Innocent XI gave orders that in future no woman was to be taught to sing; he also ordered Angelica's incarceration in a convent. But the girl escaped and came to Christina for protection.

Angelica had lived for some time in Palazzo Riario in safety, but during the Queen's illness a notorious libertine, the Abbé Vanini, succeeded in bribing her mother with 1,000 scudi to let him have Angelica. It was difficult to entice the girl away, so her worthless mother introduced Vanini into the palace, and one evening when Angelica went to her room she found her mother there with Vanini and two Neapolitans of the Queen's household. Reassured by the presence of the others, Angelica agreed to take part in the supper party, although she knew Vanini and disliked him, being in fact in love with a young French sculptor. On some excuse or another, the three slipped quickly out of the room, leaving the unfortunate girl alone with the Abbé. She rushed to the door screaming, Vanini caught her, and a terrible struggle ensued. Some other members of the household heard the noise and Angelica was saved. Vanini escaped and fled from the Papal States, not daring to return until after the death of Innocent XI.

While Christina was convalescent she had asked continually for Angelica, but was told that the girl was ill. Finally, however, probably out of dislike of Angelica's mother, old Giulia told the

Queen that the girl was perfectly well. She had in fact recovered from the shock, but some sense of false modesty evidently made her frightened of going to see Christina. Angelica was summoned and the whole story came out. The Queen's fury at such an outrage having been perpetrated on a girl living under her protection in her own palace can be imagined. She called for the Captain of her Guard, berated him for not having done his duty and, summoning one of her bravos, told him to pursue Vanini and bring her his head. Then in a paroxysm she fell fainting to the ground.

Christina lingered on for a few days, but for most of the time she seems to have been unconscious, though she confessed and was able to respond to the prayers in the office for the dying. Their differences forgotten, Innocent XI sent the Queen his blessing, but he was ill himself and not destined to live for long. At six o'clock in the morning of 19th April 1689, Christina breathed her last. Azzolino was with her at the end and he survived her only for a few weeks, dying on the 8th of June.

In her will Christina had said: "It is our wish that our dead body be shrouded in white and buried in the church of the Rotonda, or in some other that our heirs may decide; without exhibition of the corpse and forbidding any funeral pomp and all other such vanity." The Church of the Rotonda is the Pantheon, the only building of classical Rome which has survived the centuries intact, and in it still lives the calm and majestic spirit of the ancient world, its architecture having the classic purity that Christina loved so well. There lie also the bones of Raphael, the genius for one of whose works the dead Queen said she would have given all the paintings of the northern schools that came to her from Prague. Thus, after half a lifetime spent in Rome, and the inevitable disillusionment it brought, Christina at the end wished to be laid to rest in the building that more than any other linked her world with that of classical Rome.

Her wish was to be denied to her, although Azzolino fought for it. After her death, the Queen's body lay exposed for four days in the Palazzo Riario, then, in an open carriage accompanied by a vast procession, it was taken to be exposed again in the Church of S. Maria in Vallicella. This is still called the Chiesa Nuova, or New Church of the Oratorians, as it had been when

Christina was young and had written all those years ago from Sweden to Paolo Giordano Orsini to ask about the frescoes that Pietro da Cortona painted there. While she lived, the Queen had admired them greatly; the fact that they now provided the setting for her lying-in-state would possibly have consoled Christina for the violation of her last wishes. But one small detail of this ceremony would probably also have appealed to her grim humour—the crown suspended above her bier was the self-same one that had hung above her box in the Piazza di S. Marco, from which she had witnessed so many gay carnivals.

Relentlessly, the splendour of the funeral that Christina had wished would be without "pomp and other vanity" moved on to St Peter's. Here at last the Queen was laid to rest in the crypt. Since the Empress Maria, the wife of Honorius, had been buried nearby in the fourth century, the bones of only three other women had during the ages been laid to rest in St Peter's. Azzolino, who was the Queen's sole heir, would have been expected to raise a monument to her memory, but his death occurred so soon after her own that nothing was done. Innocent XI too died in the summer of 1689, and the generation that had known the Queen was fast following her to the grave.

For a while it seemed as if the last resting place of the daughter of Gustavus Adolphus in the greatest shrine of the Catholic world would remain unrecorded. Then in 1696 Innocent XII commissioned Carlo Fontana to design a monument, but the Pope died and funds were lacking to complete it. At last the situation was remedied in 1701 by Christina's old friend Cardinal Albani, now Clement XI, who decreed that for the first and last time in history the Fabbrica of St Peter's (the administrative body of the Basilica) should bear the cost of the monument—thus the Queen's last debt was discharged.

But to those who look for Christina's resting place in the vast echoing spaces of St Peter's, Fontana's monument comes as something of a disappointment. Although admirably designed, it might record the memory of many exemplary queens, but somehow it does not seem appropriate for that strange but fascinating being it commemorates. The cold marble warms to life a little when we realize that the medallion with the Queen's head was modelled by Jean Théodon, the French sculptor who was loved by the beautiful Angelica, but the spirit of the Queen herself escapes us.

There is only one place in Rome where something of Christina's enigmatic being seems to dwell. That is among the ilex groves, now wild and overgrown, that clothe the slopes of the Janiculum behind what was once the Palazzo Riario. There one can tread the same paths that Christina herself once knew, though her palace has practically disappeared beneath the eighteenth-century Palazzo Corsini. One room alone remains, her bedroom. Painted, gilded and ornate, it recalls vividly the splendour which surrounded that plump, shabby, but indomitable figure dressed in rusty black. It was a strange setting for a strange woman, but as one of her contemporaries said of the Queen: "She freely followed her own genius in all things and car'd not what anybody said." That is perhaps her best epitaph and the one which would have pleased Christina most.

Acknowledgments

Few woman have created such a sensation in their lifetime and been the subject of such conflicting opinions then and after her death, as Queen Christina of Sweden. Any attempt at presenting an unbiased account of the life of this strange, complex and in many ways pathetic woman, must take into consideration not only the times in which she lived, but also her own antecedents; Christina's heritage was a tainted one, there was insanity on both sides of her family; even without this, her upbringing was such as might have marred a very much better balanced constitution. To whatever causes it was due (and in this connection lesbian tendencies cannot be entirely excluded), it was Christina's antipathy to marriage that first pointed the way to abdication. This salient fact, and indeed the entire background of the Queen's abdication and conversion, are admirably documented in Sven Ingmar Olofsson's *Drottning Christinas Tronavsägelse och Trosförändring* to which I am much indebted, as I am also to Curt Weibull's *Drottning Christina och Monaldesco*, in which the mystery of this unfortunate man's death is unravelled with masterly skill. Even after more than two centuries J. Arckenholtz's *Mémoires concernant Christine reine de Suède* remains a basic source, so too are John Ekeblad's letters for court life in Stockholm, while the journals of the French, English and Imperial Ambassadors—Chanut, Whitelocke and Montecuccoli, particularly the latter—combine to present a vivid picture of life in Sweden, the European political background and the Queen's personality. For Christina's life in Europe after her abdication many sources are available, but for the crucial question of her relationship with Azzolino, her letters to the Cardinal, discovered by Baron Bildt at the end of the last century, constitute the only documentary evidence. Sven Stolpe's *Drottning Kristina Maximer, Les Sentiments Héroiques* and *Från Stoicism Till Mystik* have cast considerable light on the Queen's thought and literary activities and the contemporary currents that influenced them. Finally, any student of Queen Christina's life owes a debt of gratitude to the authors who contributed to the catalogue of the "Christina Queen of Sweden" Exhibition of 1966 and the three volumes of the *Analecta Reginensia*, and I am particularly indebted to Per Bjerstrom's *Feast and Theatre in Queen Christina's Rome*.

My gratitude is specially due to Professor Carl Nordenfalk, Director of the National Museum, for having invited me to Stockholm for the second meeting of the European Organization Committee of the Exhibition. I would like particularly to thank Monsieur Emmanuel d'Harcourt, Minister of the French Embassy in Rome, and Monsieur M. Blachant, Conservateur en Chef of the archives of the Ministère des Affaires Etrangères, for their kindness in having some of Chanut's dispatches copied for me, also Madame Portemer and Madame Pamphilova for similar assistance in the Bibliothèque Nationale. I am also most grateful to the Librarians of the Kungliga Biblioteket in Stockholm and the Kungl Biblioteket in Copenhagen for having books and articles photographed for me, also to Miss von Platen of the Nationalmuseum in Stockholm for her help with the illustrations of this book. My researches in the Vatican Library were greatly assisted by the late Father Guy Ferrari O.B., and in the Secret Archive by Father Charles Burns. I must also acknowledge the kindness of Swedish and Italian friends—Mrs Scharf for her patience in translating Swedish texts for me, Miss Thalberg for her prompt help on many occasions and Torgil Magnuson for keeping an eye on my Swedish spelling, also Nietty Forneris for doing the same with my Italian. Finally, as ever, I must thank Julian Vranek for assistance in proof reading and Vicky Stordy for her capacity to read my writing and turn it into orderly typewritten form.

Bibliography

Among the works consulted, the following are suggested as of special interest for the study of Christina, her character and period.

GENERAL HISTORICAL BACKGROUND

L. Von Pastor *History of the Popes*, Vols XXX, XXXI and XXXII, London, 1940.
L. Ranke *History of the Popes of Rome*, London, 1840.
M. Roberts *Gustavus Adolphus*, London, 1953–58.
F. Steegmuller, *La Grande Mademoiselle*, London, 1959.
Ed. A. W. Ward, G. W. Prothero, S. Leathers *Cambridge Modern History*, Vols IV and V, Cambridge, 1934.
C. V. Wedgewood *The Thirty Years War*, London, 1944.

BIOGRAPHICAL

C. D. N. Bildt *Christine de Suède et le Cardinal Azzolino*, Paris, 1899.
J. P. Catteau-Calleville *Histoire de Christine Reine de Suède*, Paris, 1815.
G. Claretta *La Regina Cristina di Svezia in Italia 1655–1689*, Turin, 1892.
F. Gribble *The Court of Christina of Sweden and the Later Adventures of the Queen in Exile*, London, 1913.

P. de Luz *Christine de Suède*, Paris, 1951.

Galeazzo Gualdo Priorato *Historia della Sacra Real Maestà di Christina Alessandra Regina di Svetia*, Venice, 1656.

M. Goldsmith *Christina of Sweden; A Psychological Biography*, New York 1933.

S. Stolpe *Christina of Sweden*, London, 1966.

Ida A. Taylor *Christina of Sweden*, London, 1909.

C. Weibull *Christina of Sweden*, Göteborg, 1966.

M. Weibull *Drottning Christina och Monaldescho*, Stockholm, 1936.

CONTEMPORARY SOURCES AND DOCUMENTS

E. Alberi *Relazioni degli Ambasciatori Veneti*, Florence, 1838.

C. Arckenholtz *Mémoires pour Servir à l'Histoire de Christine de Suède*, Amsterdam and Leipzig, 1751.

Mémoires de Chanut, Paris, 1675.

L. H. de Lomenie, Comte de Brienne, *Mémoires*, Paris, 1916–19.

J. Ekeblad *Johan Ekeblads Brev Till Brodern Claes Ekeblad*, Göteborg, 1965.

M. L. *Lettres Choisies de Christine Reine de Suède*, Villefranche, 1760.

R. Montecuccoli *I Viaggi*, Modena, 1924.

F. de Motteville *Mémoires pour Servir à l'Histoire d'Anne d'Autriche*, Paris, 1869.

Thurloe State Papers, Vol. 2, 1653–54, London, 1742.

B. Whitelocke *Journal of the Swedish Embassy*, London, 1855.

CONVERSION AND RELIGION

P. Bayle *Dictionnaire Historique et Critique III Macedo*, Amsterdam, 1740.

G. Boero *Conversione alla Fede Cattolica di Christina Regina di Svezia*, Modena, 1874.

P. Dudon *Le Quiétiste Espagnol Michel Molinos*, Paris, 1921.

P. Negri *Lettera Inedita del Padre Malines sulla conversione di Christina di Svezia*, Archivio della Reale Società Romana di Storia Patria XXXIII, Rome, 1910.

S. I. Olofsson *Drottning Christinas tronavsägelse och trosförändåring*, Uppsala, 1953.

S. Stolpe *Från Stoicism Till Mystik*, Stockholm, 1959

LIFE IN ITALY

C. D. N. Bildt *Un Banchetto al Quirinale nel' 600*, Rome, 1901.

C. D. N. Bildt *Christina di Svezia e Paolo Giordano Orsini*, Archivio della Reale Società Romana di Storia Patria, Rome, 1906.

C. D. N. Bildt *Christine de Suède, et le Conclave de Clement X*, Paris, 1906.

C. Campori *Raimondo Montecuccoli, la sua Famiglia e i suoi Tempi*, Florence, 1896.

C. Festini *I Trionfi della Magnificenza Pontificia*, Rome, 1656.

G. Gigli *Diario Romano 1608–1670*, Rome, 1958.

L. Grottanelli *La Regina Christina di Svezia in Roma*, Florence, 1889.

P. Hollingworth *History of the Intrigues and Gallantries of Christina Queen of Sweden*, London, 1927.

Bartolomeo Lupardi *Vera e distinta relazione della solenne cavalcata*, Roma, 1655.

Ferdinand de Navenne *Rome et le Palais Farnèse*, Paris, 1923.

Sforza Pallavicino *Descrizione del primo viaggio fatto a Roma dalla Regina di Svezia Christina*, Rome, 1838.

L. Sebastiani *Discrizione e Relazione Istorica del Palazzo di Caprarola*, Caprarola, 1741.

THE ARTS

A. Ademollo *I Teatri di Roma nel Secolo Decimosettimo*, Rome, 1888.

C. D. N. Bildt *Queen Christina's Pictures in the XX Century*, London, 1904.

C. D. N. Bildt *Les médailles romaines de Christine de Suède*, p. 38–42 and p. 19 note 1, Rome, 1908.

P. Bjurström *Theaterdekoration*, Stockholm, 1964.

P. Bjurström *Feast and Theatre in Queen Christina's Rome*, Stockholm, 1966.

A. Cammetti *Christina di Svezia, l'Arte Musicale e gli Spettacoli Teatrali in Roma,* Rome, 1911.

G. Canevazzi *Papa Clemente IX Poeta,* Modena, 1900.

Christina Queen of Sweden, Catalogue of Exhibition, National Museum, Stockholm, 1966.

F. J. Fielden *Court Masquerades in the Seventeenth Century*, Modern Language Review XVI, Cambridge, 1921.

F. Haskell *Patrons and Painters*, London, 1963.

O. Granberg *La Galerie de Tableaux de Christine de Suède*, Stockholm, 1897.

M. Misson *Nouveau Voyage en Italie Faite l'Année 1688*, Paris, 1717.

R. Pintard *Le Libertinage Erudit dans la Première Moitié du XVII Siècle,* Paris, 1943.

Ed. M. von Platen *Queen Christina of Sweden, Documents and Studies*, Stockholm, 1966.

J. Q. van Regteren Altena *Les Dessins Italiens de la Reine Christine de Suède*, Stockholm, 1966.

P. Skippon *An Account of a Journey Through the Low Countries, Germany, Italy and France*, London, 1752.

S. Stolpe *Drottning Kristinas Maximer, Les Sentiments*, Stockholm, 1959.

SPECIAL ASPECTS

B. Andersen *Dronning Christina,* Dansk Historisk Tidskrift, Khun, 1932.

H. Ellis *Studies in the Psychology of Sex*, London, 1948.

E. Essen-Möller *La Reine Christine, Etude Médicale et Biologique, Hippocrate II*, Paris, 1937.

D. J. West *Homosexuality*, London, 1962.

N.B. Unpublished documents consulted among the following sources have not been cited:
Archivio Segreto, Vatican; Archivio di Stato, Rome; Biblioteca Barberini and Biblioteca Chigi, Vatican Library; Bibliothèque Nationale, Paris; Riksarkivet, Stockholm.

Index